D1583302

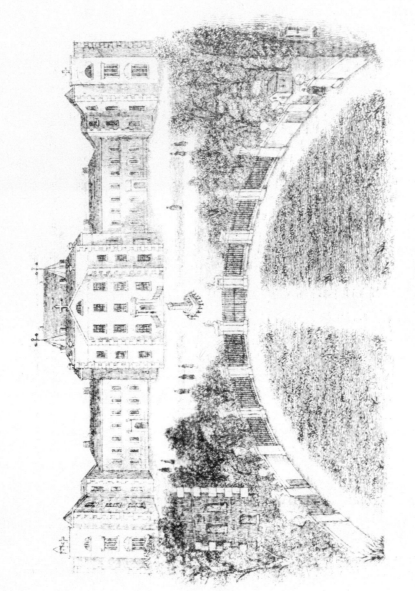

Maynooth College.

Maynooth And Victorian Ireland

By
Jeremiah Newman

1983

First published 1983
Kenny's Bookshops and Art Galleries Ltd.,
Galway, Ireland.

Cloth   —ISBN 0 906312 25 6
Limited
Edition —ISBN 0 906312 26 4

Binding: Kenny Galway Fine Binding Ltd.,
Printed by: Emerald Printers Ltd., Prospect Hill, Galway.

Contents

Illustrations

Preface

In the mid-nineteen fifties, as a young member of the staff, I was inspired by Estella Canziani's *Oxford in Brush and Pen* (London, 1949) to put together a collection of extracts from publications about Maynooth College together with a number of illustrations. It was the late Robert I. Simington of the Public Records Office, Dublin, who persuaded me to knit these pieces together into my own biography of Maynooth. As the years passed, the material grew. Some of it has already appeared in *Maynooth and Georgian Ireland;* much of the rest is now produced here.

I wish to thank various people who have provided me with considerable help in the editing of it. Mr. Liam Irwin, Lecturer in History, Mary Immaculate College of Education, Limerick, made some very important corrections. Monsignor Liam Boyle and Father John Fleming also read the manuscript and made a number of valuable suggestions. My most profound thanks go to Mr. Desmond Kenny of Kenny, Galway, the publishers, for his painstaking work in ensuring that the book be as free as possible from historical and literary defects.

Very sincere thanks are also due to Mr. Eric Patton, R.H.A. who designed the dust jacket and Mr. Thomas Ryan, R.H.A. for the fascinating drawings which carry his initials. The other cartoons are the work of the late Monsignor Martin Drea of the Diocese of Ossory, whose relatives I thank for permission to reproduce them. I thank also the National Library of Ireland for permission to reproduce the Lawrence photographs, Mr. Alf McLochlainn, Librarian, University College Galway, for the reproduction of *The Maynooth Act, 1845,* and Mr. Derek Biddulph for the drawing of the Pugin Quadrangle. A special word of thanks is owed to Miss Mary Spain who prepared the typescript for the printers and to Canon John Corkery who read the proofs so efficiently.

I do hope that *Maynooth and Victorian Ireland* will be enjoyed by all those who read it and, in particular, by those who, like myself, love the great College of Maynooth.

JEREMIAH NEWMAN

Kilmoyle,
September, 1983.

i

Introduction

This book is a sequel to *Maynooth and Georgian Ireland* which was first published in 1979. And just as did the latter, the present volume seeks to provide not a formal history of Maynooth College during Victorian times but rather to tell its story in an entertaining way. For that reason, like its predecessor, it tends to highlight the more colourful episodes in the life of the College during the period which it covers. It tries to look at Victorian Ireland through the eyes of the College.

The Victorian period was one in which the foundations of Irish nationhood as we know it today were laid. It was also the period during which Maynooth grew to maturity and contributed greatly to those foundations. It swiftly emerged as the foremost seminary in the world, sending out a stream of clergy not only for the home mission but for missions abroad, in the wake of Victorian expansion. But its influence did not stop at that. In the domain of scholarship, the College made important contributions in the fields of literature and science, and played a leading part in the development of 19th century theological thought. Despite the efforts of many enemies, Maynooth went from strength to strength, becoming independent of the English government and surviving investigations by Rome into the orthodoxy of its teaching. It became an integral part of Irish life, and its story mirrors the story of Ireland itself and its struggle for national identity.

Many of the glimpses of Victorian Ireland that are caught here in looking into life at Maynooth during those years are new and should help towards a better understanding of the Ireland of that time. Intended as it is to be a story rather than a history, the book is not furnished with footnotes. At the same time, the major archival sources of the material which it uses can be found referred to in the text. In so far as possible, these and other published sources are allowed to speak for themselves; hence the long extracts that are a feature of the book. In this connection, it may be well to note (as this was sometimes missed in the case of *Maynooth and Georgian Ireland*) that some unusual spelling and inaccurate geographical or historical attributions which can be found here and there in its pages are directly traceable to the sources that are being used. They have been allowed to remain as part of the *reportage* which they constitute and are not likely to mislead the erudite.

At the beginning of the book I have endeavoured to provide a link between the Georgian and Victorian periods of the College. This has made it possible to include some material relative to the earlier volume which I have since discovered and also to correct some errors, unrelated to source quotation, which were contained in it.

Chapter 1

Great Expectations

It was at twelve minutes past two on the morning of 20 June, 1837, when King William IV of England died. Even though his name was William, he is regarded as marking the end of the Georgian era.

William was succeeded by Victoria. The night that he died, messengers were dispatched immediately to Kensington Palace, where the young Princess was sleeping in her mother's bedroom. The latter — the Duchess of Kent — was inclined to refuse them admission, until Lord Conygnham, the Lord Chamberlain, peremptorily demanded to see "the Queen". Victoria received them in dressing gown and slippers.

It was the beginning of a new and long era. On 21 June, Victoria was proclaimed Queen to the sound of trumpets from an open window in St. James's Palace, and a year later on 28 June, 1838, was crowned at Westminster Abbey. She was then only nineteen years old.

When Queen Victoria came to the throne of Great Britain and Ireland, her Irish subjects were enjoying a period of quiet. The Rebellions of 1798 and 1803, although far from forgotten, had receded into the past. True, the legislative union of the two parts of the kingdom that had been effected in 1800 had failed to achieve the incorporation of both in a genuine copartnership. Irish questions continued to be treated as distinct, even though now they were thrashed out in the imperial parliament.

There they often occupied more than their due share of time and sometimes secured quite favourable treatment. An example was the attainment of Catholic Emancipation in 1829. By and large, however, the Victorian age was to be one in which Irish issues had to strive hard to be treated fairly.

LOOK BACK WITH PRIDE

By all accounts, the Queen's subjects in Ireland were generally speaking not averse to her succession. She was young and at that time reasonably pretty, which was scarcely likely to have been lost on them. Despite the harsh memories of the '98 and Emmet's rebellions, they were not entirely anti-English. After all, Emancipation had recently been achieved and the future held out high hopes.

This seems to have been particularly true in the Queen's own College of Maynooth, of which an ex-student — one Denis Murphy, formerly of the Lay. College — composed an ode to Her Majesty on her accession to the throne.

One wonders whether at this stage Her Majesty herself had ever heard of the Royal Catholic College ? In all probability — no, even though many travellers from England had visited it since its foundation and had written copiously about it.

In Ireland, the College had long made its mark, so much so, that everything associated with it and with its neighbourhood had become a matter of country-wide interest. In March, 1833, a writer in *The Dublin Penny Journal* gave the following account of the origin of the place-name under the heading 'Magh Nuadhat, now Anglicized Maynooth, where Garrett, Earl of Kildare, founded a college in the beginning of the 16th century':

"I have given the original Irish name of Maynooth here, for the satisfaction of Irish scholars, because I have heard many disputes about the origin and signification of the name. O' Reilly called it Magh an Fhuaith, and the Translator of the little book called 'Think well on it', makes it Magh na n-Ogh Dubh, i.e. the plain of the black virgins or nuns; but all this is etymological delirium. Duald McFirbis calls it Magh Nuadhat, i.e. the plain of Nuadhat; Nuadhat was a man's name, formerly very common in Ireland; and we state it as a historic fact, that this Nuadhat, from whom Magh-Nuadhat (pronounced Maw-Noo-Ath) received its name, was the maternal grandfather of Fionn Mac Cumhail, so celebrated by Macpherson under the name Fingal, whose patrimony was Magh-Nuadhat (Maynooth) and Almhain (Allen) in the now Co. Kildare."

2

Whatever about the 'historic fact' of being linked with Fionn Mac Cumhail, Maynooth was by now quite famous by reason of the presence there of St. Patrick's College. It is true that Caesar Otway (1780 - 1842), son of Loftus Otway of Co. Tipperary, Church of Ireland minister, miscellaneous writer and co-operator with George Petrie in the production of the *Penny Journal,* had visited the College during the 1830's and contrasted it unflatteringly with Oxford and Cambridge, but this was not the case with all visitors.

One of the most extensive of these accounts is contained in Thomas Cromwell's *Excursions Through Ireland,* dating from 1820. Cromwell (1792-1870) was a respectable antiquary and a man of much literary information. At the time of his visit to Ireland he was connected with the Church of England but was later to join the Unitarian Church, of which he became a Minister. His book on Ireland summarises the state of the College before Victoria:

> "Crossing the Royal Canal, we arrive, at the distance of two miles from Leixlip, at the town of Maynooth, chiefly remarkable on account of the Royal College of St. Patrick, for the education of the Roman-catholic clergy, there situated. This establishment, founded, in pursuance of an act passed in 1795, by the Irish Parliament, stands at the south western termination of the principal street; which, being very wide, forms a spacious vista to the front of the building, while it extends from it to a noble avenue leading to Cartown, the princely and picturesque country residence of his Grace the Duke of Leinster. The edifice of which the centre is formed, was originally a handsome private house, built by a steward of the late Duke of Leinster, from whom it was purchased by the trustees of the institution. To this, extensive wings, of the same elevation, were added; so that the whole front now presents a grand and ornamented facade, 400 feet in length, and consisting of three stories; the pile, or original building, standing forward 50 feet, and the extremities of the wings, which are similar in form, having a corresponding projection. In this front, besides the spacious lecture-rooms, etc., are the chapel and refectory, both neat and commodious: the latter is of considerable dimensions, and judiciously divided into different compartments by handsome Ionic columns and arcades, which support the ceiling."

Behind this central building at the north-west was a wing that was only half completed at the time of Cromwell's visit. He continues:

> "The latter is principally laid out in dormitories, opening

3

from galleries, each about 300 feet in length, and which serve as ambulatories for the students in wet weather: the whole on a plan, not only judicious in arrangement, but, neat, simple, and inexpensive. The kitchen is lofty and spacious: over the principal fire-place, the stranger notices the following admonition, in large letters, to the cook:

> 'Be always cleanly, show your taste,
> Do not want, and do not waste !'

— a piece of grave advice, which obtains as we have chanced to see, and as it deserves, an equally conspicuous situation, in the kitchens of many mansions, hotels, etc. in England."

Then he speaks about the library, which he describes as being yet in its infancy, even though an important part of the seminary. And he goes on:

"Attached to the College are about 50 acres of land. In front is a lawn of nearly two acres, laid out in gravelled walks, and separated from the street by a handsome semicircular iron railing, on a dwarf wall, erected by the original proprietor of the building: but, either because it was supposed to be an insufficient barrier on the side of the town, and a greater degree of seclusion considered more favourable to study and to the maintenance of internal discipline, or from what other motive — of any of which the visitor must lament the necessity — a wall of coarse masonry and mean appearance has been built in front of this fine railing, and completely conceals it from public view. In the centre, the piers of the principal gate of entrance are ornamented with sphinxes, while others gracefully break the railing into parts, and are decorated with lions couchant and sculptured urns. The piers, dwarf walls, and decorations, are of the finest Portland stone, and the workmanship in the best style."

The unsightly wall to which Cromwell refers had been erected by order of the Trustees in 1807, possibly because of the student unrest and political ferment that marked that time. It may or may not have been removed by the beginning of Victoria's reign. It certainly was gone shortly afterwards. By Victoria's time too, the wing behind the front building on the north-west side had been replaced by what was known just as 'New House'. But let us continue with Cromwell's narrative:

"The lawn is terminated on the right hand by the tower of

4

Maynooth Church, beautifully mantled with ivy, and on the left by the stately ruins of a Castle, the ancient residence of the Fitzgeralds, ancestors of the Duke of Leinster; features which, as they appear to greater advantage in perspective, as the traveller approaches, render the whole scene extremely interesting.

The rear of the building, is an extensive tract of level ground, part of which forms a garden, and part is laid out in spacious retired gravelled walks, for the recreation of the students: the latter well planted, and there is in particular a fine avenue of majestic elms."

An account of the students, their way of life and courses of study, follows. It would hold broadly also for 1837, although by then their number was some 460 whereas it was 250 in 1820. In the latter year the student body was composed as follows:

"The proportion to be sent from each district of the island was prescribed by the statutes: — the ecclesiastical provinces of Armagh and Cashel to furnish 60 each, those of Dublin and Tuam 40 each; but, in consequence of an additional grant from Government, 50 more have been added to the establishment, who are sent in the same proportions. The whole are provided with lodging, commons, and instructions from the funds; but each student pays the sum of £10, as entrance money; and his personal expenses for a year are estimated at about £20. They have a recess during the months of July and August; and another, for a few days only, at the festivals of Christmas, Easter and Pentecost. As it is requisite, even during these vacations, for students, who may wish to absent themselves, to obtain permission from their respective prelates, they, for the most part, remain in College during the whole year, employing themselves, in the intervals, in preparations for the ensuing course. During term, the obligation to residence, imposed by the statutes, is strictly enforced. For the admission of a student, besides other things specified, the recommendation of his prelate is required: the usual as to which is, to select a certain number from the candidates in each diocese, as recommended by their respective parish priests; but as, in the diocese of Cashel, a severe examination is previously held, and those only who appear best qualified permitted to be sent hither, the students from that district are, in consequence, said to maintain a decided superiority in the course..."

Cromwell's description of the courses of study pursued in the College is rather fascinating. We are not surprised, of course, to find the usual Greek and Latin texts used in the course in Humanity and Belles Lettres, but it is somewhat surprising to find Locke studied in the course in Philosophy. In Theology the ideas of Hooke, Bailly and Tournely, among others, were followed. English and Irish were also taught, as well as an extensive course in Natural and Experimental Philosophy, dealing with Mathematics, Algebra, Geometry, Conic Sections, Astronomy, Mechanics, Optics, Hydraulics and Chemistry.

> "The following is the general order of each day: — The students are summoned by a bell: at half-past five, they meet for public prayer; from six, they study in the public halls; at half-past seven, Mass is performed; at eight, they breakfast; at nine, study in public halls; at ten, attend class; at half-past eleven, recreation; at twelve, study in public halls; at half-past one, attend class; at three, dinner; at five, class for modern languages; at six, study in public halls; at eight, supper; at nine, common prayer; and, at half-past nine, all retire in silence to their chambers."

There were, we are told, two public examinations held each year, at Christmas and Midsummer. At them, premiums were distributed "proportioned to the merits of those who pass these ordeals." The period of study was usually five years, two in Humanity and Philosophy and three in Divinity. Besides the President, Vice-President, Dean, Bursar and Sub-Dean (actually a second full Dean was appointed in 1837), there were eleven Professors and two Lecturers. Under the leadership of the French *emigré* Delahogue, they had laid the foundations of Maynooth's reputation for scholarship.

Cromwell was very appreciative of the beneficent influence of Maynooth. He wrote: " The establishment at home of a seminary for the Catholic priesthood, and for giving a munificent education, in their own country, to those, who are with reason supposed to exercise a strong, and, under all the circumstances, very natural controul, over the principles and opinions of the larger mass of the community, was no less an act of strict justice, than of sound and enlightened policy."

In spite of this beneficence and enlightenment on the part of the Government, the Royal Catholic College at Maynooth had had a turbulent history before Victoria. In truth, it had survived only with difficulty. Indeed, one branch of it, the Lay College, which the Trustees seem to have decided to establish as early as their inaugural meeting held in the Lord Chancellor's chamber on 24 June, 1795, had been terminated in 1817 — as a result of Government opposition, the extent of which is still undetermined. At the time of Cromwell's visit, its ultimate fate seems to have been still in the balance for he does not speak of it as something that had been irrevocably abandoned.

The ups and downs of the College during its early years of existence have been dealt with in *Maynooth and Georgian Ireland*. It is a story of much intrigue within the ranks of the establishment, with Fitzgibbon, the then Chancellor, pitting his wits against Lords Cornwallis and Castlereagh, and with the Protestant Bishop of Meath trying to play the role of honest broker. The College had survived and had produced a couple of hundred priests by the time of Cromwell's visit.

However, when Victoria ascended the throne, there were many people who had reservations about the quality of the Maynooth-educated clergy. It is true that they might follow the exhortation which Cromwell had found inscribed over the College kitchen fireplace, endorsing the Victorian penchant for shibboleths. Lord Melbourne had taught the young Victoria herself four maxims: "Fear God. Honour the King. Obey your parents. Brush your teeth."

Victoria-like though they might be in some respects, the Maynooth products of the first third of the 19th century gave much cause for concern to loyalists, whether Protestant or Catholic. Angus MacIntyre, the author of a 1965 biography of Daniel O'Connell, continues to trade the old story that the Maynooth priests, who replaced their Continental predecessors, were widely regarded as having changed the general character of the priesthood in Ireland. Compared with a lot of priests of the old school, the Maynooth product is said to have been "generally more insular and more nationalist", a view that is shared by a contemporary memorandum in the State Paper Office, which contrasts the Maynooth priest with the "quiet, easy Priest of the old school."

That the Maynooth priests were certainly inclined to nationalist sympathies is attested to by another biographer of O'Connell – C. M. O'Keeffe – who tells us that, during O'Connell's early period, the Bishop of Kildare and Leighlin, Dr. Doyle (J.K.L.), drew attention to the fact that, in the event of a French invasion, the Government need not look to the help of those clergy who were ex-students of Maynooth. They had come, he said, from a people who had been ill-treated, and had themselves imbibed the doctrines of Locke and Paley more deeply than those of Bellarmine. He said too that the "Maynooth Manifesto" of 1826, which expressed the loyalty of a number of the Professors to the Crown, had been drawn up at the request of Lord Wellesley and did not have the support of the then President, Dr. Crotty, nor of the student body in general. It is interesting to note that O'Keeffe regarded this 'disloyalty' as having created an obstacle to O'Connell's politics.

Nevertheless, following the passing of the Emancipation Act in 1829 – the Catholic Relief Bill – which received Royal Assent in the April of that year, both students and staff at Maynooth had joined in a 'Gaudeamus'. We are told about it in the evidence of the Commission of

Inquiry of 1853, by the Reverend Mr. Burke: "I was much shocked at what I witnessed that night. The students invited the authorities to join them on the occasion of the celebration, and they did so; it was celebrated with music and singing. The best singers were selected to sing on this occasion, and amongst the songs sung that night was one said to be composed by Dr. England — he was Bishop of Charleston, in America." Part of the song ran:

> "The toast we'll give is Albion's fall,
> And Erin's pride on Patrick's Day."

Mr. Burke went on: "At this last sentiment being uttered, the authorities and students were instantly on their legs, and cheered the sentiment; they encored the song over and over again; and, as well as I recollect, it was the only one they encored that night." Furthermore, to Mr. Burke's indignation, instead of the prayer "Domine, salvum fac regem" in chapel, they were in the habit of saying "Domine, salvum whack regem" !

All in all, the College in 1837 had good reason to look back with pride on the first forty years or so of its life. Not only had it expanded in student numbers, erected new and impressive buildings, created an enviable reputation for learning and priestly dedication — it had also launched missions overseas.

Its greatest achievement in this last respect was its giving birth, in the early 1830's, through a handful of staff members and students, to the Irish Province of the Vincentians from which the missionary college of All Hallows was to spring in 1842. The leader of this group had been Dr. Philip Dowley, Dean in the College since 1816. In 1832 he was approached by five or six students who wished to devote themselves to missionary work.

An interesting document in the *Archives of the Irish College, Paris,* tells us that, as these students still had one year to finish their studies at Maynooth, they banded together there and met regularly as a kind of identifiable entity. Hence it was that the President, Dr. Crotty (1813 - 1833), came to propose, with the consent of the Archbishop of Dublin, that the nascent society should establish itself in Maynooth itself, offering them the dwelling formerly used for the Lay College. This project was opposed by Dr. Anglade, the second senior of the original French Professors. He felt that such a move would be fatal to the venture, for the members would not be free if they remained in Maynooth and their independence was absolutely necessary. At Pentecost, 1833, they were ordained.

Dr. Dowley still had hopes of joining them, but did not feel free to do so. On the Tuesday of the fourth week of June, 1834, he wrote to them to say that, as he had not received a reply from his Bishop giving him permission to resign, he could not do so. So worried was the little group by this, that they wrote at once themselves to Dr. Dowley's Bishop, Dr. Barron of Waterford, asking him for a reply by return of post. In the meantime one of their number, Father John McCann, had hastened down to Maynooth.

In truth, it would seem that the powers of this world had intentions for Dr. Dowley other than the missions, for at a meeting of the Trustees of Maynooth held on 25 June, 1834, the Reverend Michael Montague was appointed President of the College and the Reverend Philip Dowley, Vice-President. To the amazement of the group's emissary:

> "On entering the gate he was surprized to see the College illuminated, and on asking the reason was told that it was for the new nominations, that Dr. Montague had been appointed President and Fr. Dowley Vice-President. This was a new difficulty. He visited Fr. Dowley but the latter could only repeat what he had already written, that he could not resign without permission. If the answer, however, arrived in time, he promised to be with them immediately. Thursday was spent in great anxiety for Friday was the last day for the sitting of the Board. On the close of the sessions on that day, the Bishops and lay gentlemen who form this 'Council' would return to their respective homes, not to meet again for another year. On Friday the answer was expected but the ordinary delivery of the post would be too late. Fr. McCann therefore called early at the General Post Office and fortunately found the desired letter. Immediately he rode down to Maynooth in all haste and found Mr. Dowley and the Archbishop, Dr. Murray, walking in the grounds. Fr. McCann approached and presented the letter. Fr. Dowley read it and handing it to Dr. Murray said 'Here, my Lord, is the permission, you will do the rest'. The Archbishop took the letter and graciously promised to arrange all with the Board."

So Dr. Dowley resigned from the Vice-Presidency. It was a dramatic conclusion to a dramatic series of events and the beginning of a new enterprise of which Maynooth could be justly proud.

DICKENSIAN OVERTONES

In spite of the justifiable pride which the College might feel at many of its achievements since its foundation, the atmosphere there in the 1830's had a distinctly Dickensian flavour. Dickens had begun to make a name for himself in 1836-37 with the serialisation of *The Pickwick Papers*, shortly to be followed by *Nicholas Nickelby* and *The Old Curiosity Shop*.

Maynooth in its own way was curious. At this time it took particular pride in its pulpit orators, one of the most famous of whom — the Reverend Tom Maguire from Leitrim — had made quite a name for himself debating with Protestant adversaries. In 1827 he had debated for no less than six days with the famous Reverend Richard Pope, O'Connell acting as one of the chairmen. We are told that, on Maguire's being declared the winner, O'Connell presented him with a silver plate worth no less than £1,000 !

Maguire, in fact, was not the greatest of orators. Later, in 1840-41, *The Catholic Luminary* in a series on 'Orators of the Pulpit' declared that he was "not graceful — No. Rusticity found him before the narrow paradromes of Maynooth hemmed him in from the sight and sound of larch trees, songs of birds, and all the joyousness of rural life which surrounded his father's dwelling." None the less, those who wished to claim his prowess for the College were not to be put off:

> "When young Maguire left home for college
> To improve his knowledge in famed Maynooth
> A rich fair lady who lived near Kildare
> Tried for to ensnare this religious youth.
> She brought a clear resate of a large estate
> To the College gate and this did say
> 'Come marry me and you will see
> That a lord you'll be on your wedding day.'
>
> Maguire blushed and he wept in silence
> Saying: 'noble lady you must forbear
> For I have vowed to the Queen of Angels
> No earthly lady would me ensnare.'
> The Church of Rome is my chosen consort
> And from its standard I'll never stray
> Like Martin Luther or cursed John Calvin
> Or Harry Tudor as I hear them say'."

13 October, 1830, saw a visit to Maynooth by the more famous Montalembert, then still a young man. He was met by the Duke of Leinster at Carton and Archbishop Murray at the College. The visitor's account of his experience is typically French, torn as he was between examining the seminary and being entertained by the ladies at Carton. "*Je ne savais pas lequel préférer, du séminaire où se trouvait l'archevêque, où du château où se trouvait la belle duchesse de Leinster avec sa nièce. Enfin je me suis arrangé de manière à passer l'après-midi et la soirée au château et à diner avec l'archevêque*". He was quite impressed by the Archbishop. Of his dinner with him in the College, he observes that, without any affectation of sanctity, he can truthfully say that he found the session better than

10

the evening ball. His humility had obviously been strained, because the President of the College had asked the Archbishop and all present to drink his health. Indeed he confesses to have been moved to tears.

During these years there was a quick turn over of Presidents. In 1830 the President was Dr. Bartholomew Crotty, who in 1833 went on to become Bishop of Cloyne. He was succeeded for one year by Dr. Michael Slattery, who in 1834 went on to become Archbishop of Cashel. Dr. Foran of Waterford appears to have been elected immediately in Dr. Slattery's place and the Secretary asked to inform him. After accepting, or so it seems, he changed his mind and resigned and Dr. Michael Montague was appointed President. That was in June, 1834.

The College which Montague inherited was difficult enough to handle. Even though on 27 April, 1834, Pope Gregory XVI accorded an indulgence to them on the performance of stated religious devotions, the students were to a considerable extent an unruly lot, whose loyalty, beneath the surface, to the Government was never entirely certain.

During 1835, the brothers, Michael and William Crotty, who had been educated at Maynooth, wrote a series of letters to the papers, published the following year under the title *The Catholic Not the Roman Catholic Church*. Michael Crotty said he believed Maynooth to be a "hot-bed of bigotry, intolerance and superstition", which had "never yet produced a gentleman or a scholar." The letter continued in the same strong language. Its "four hundred bigots" were, he said, "the busy and active agents of Mr. O'Connell". Shortly afterwards he became a parson.

The truth really was that gentlemen and scholars were indeed to be found at Maynooth. This was evidenced by the presence there of men such as Dr. C. W. Russell, editor in all but name of the distinguished *Dublin Review*. Russell, in fact, was also its chief contributor for a number of years, penning more than one hundred and forty articles for it between 1836 and 1877, most of them anonymously as was then the custom. At the same time, he was busy producing more than six hundred articles on all the Catholic and Irish subjects that appeared in *Chamber's Encyclopaedia*. To be fair to the encyclopaedia, it should be noted that this commission had resulted from his having exposed the anti-Catholic and anti-Irish bias of some of its early volumes.

That scholarship should have flourished at Maynooth was only to be expected, given the rigour of the concursus which preceded appointments to professorships. In a letter of 28 April, 1838, the Archbishop of Dublin described to Dr. Cullen, Rector of the Irish College, Rome, the method of determining their occurrence. Three days after the death or resignation of a professor, the President would announce that in sixty days a concursus would be held prior to filling the post. Some of the most famous of these concursuses occurred in the years 1838 and 1841.

In 1838, on 3 September and following days, a concursus for the Chair of Dogmatic and Moral Theology was held, between Robert F. Whitehead, John Gunn and Edmund O'Reilly, the latter just back from Rome. Cullen, already interesting himself in ecclesiastical appointments in Ireland, had written from there to the Archbishop of Cashel, recommending Dr. O'Reilly for that Chair, and for any philosophical chair that might be vacant the Rev. Michael O'Connor of Cloyne, who was "very profound in metaphysical and mathematical speculations." If only he had known it, Dr. Cullen would have realised that it would be hard for him to influence the appointment. This was because Lord Ffrench, a member of the Trustee Body itself, had already intimated his desire that his kinsman, Reverend Robert Ffrench Whitehead, be appointed to the Chair of Theology, without concursus. At that time he was Professor of Logic. Awareness of this was conveyed to Cullen by at least two Irish Bishops, one of whom added that such interference by the noble Lord was without Whitehead's knowledge. *He* was a learned and respectable man. The concursus, however, did take place and was nothing if not elaborate. The *College Records* for 1838 give an account of the proceedings:

> "The Council resolved that, out of three propositions taken by lot from each treatise of Theology, one should be taken also by lot, on which each candidate for the Theology Chair should deliver a premeditated dissertation for twenty-five minutes, and answer the objections which each of his competitors should in the same space of time propose against it. That ten questions from Moral Theology should be proposed to each on the second day. That on the third day each candidate should interrogate and object to each of his competitors in Logic, Metaphysics, and Ethics for half an hour, and answer the questions and objections, and that each should demonstrate four Propositions or Problems proposed them from Algebra, Geometry, Mechanics, and Astronomy. That on the fourth day two hours at least would be allowed them to write on a question of Theology, selected by lot in the same manner as the dissertation of the first day."

It is no wonder that Dr. Whitehead began to feel ill, which he did, for the *College Records* tell us that, in consequence of his being suddenly indisposed, in order to give him an opportunity to recover, the Trustees deferred the concursus in Theology until 6 September.

In the meantime, another concursus, for the Chair of English Elocution, was held, the contestants being the said Reverend John Gunn (who was pitching his cap at both posts), the Reverend Richard O'Brien and the Reverend Patrick Murray. It is worth noting that two of the participants in this double concursus, O'Brien and O'Reilly, were of the Diocese of Limerick. O'Reilly was later to become a famous Jesuit while O'Brien became a well-known author and founder of the Catholic Young Men's Society. He, even though not yet ordained, had been urged by his Bishop, Most Reverend Dr. Ryan, to compete.

The concursus for the Chair of Elocution was as demanding as that for Theology. Out of it emerged as Professor the Reverend Patrick Murray, of whom there is much to follow. As far as the Chair of Theology was concerned, "the Rev. Mr. Whitehead not being yet sufficiently recovered, the concursus for Theology was commenced on 6th September between Rev. Mr. Gunn and Dr. O'Reilly". Out of this O'Reilly emerged victorious. John Gunn, without prejudice to his merits vis-a-vis his competitors for the Chair, was appointed Junior Dean in succession to the Reverend Mr. Cussen — also of Limerick Diocese — who had conveniently resigned.

By all accounts, O'Reilly had put up a magnificent display at the concursus and afterwards proved himself to be a fine teacher. At the end of his first year as Professor, he was presented with a gold snuff box by his students. Dr. Cullen's sister so informs her brother in a letter of 7 July, 1839. As for O'Reilly himself, in a letter to Kirby, Vice Rector, Rome, of 23 of that month he volunteered some notes on Maynooth. He is not displeased with the College. The professors are amiable and the students work hard although they have not enough opportunity for literary exercises. "They take copious class-notes and tend to repeat them verbatim." (That practice was not unknown amongst them long afterwards and expected by some professors.) He has better to say on other topics: "The papal infallibility is not looked on in any odious light ... Of course the temporal power is not dreamt of and why should it ?"

Poor Whitehead was singularly unfortunate in his concursus engagement. In August, 1841, he tried again for another Chair of Theology. His opponent was the Professor of Elocution, Dr. Murray. Their dissertation was on the infallibility of the Church, a theme about which the Murray of the future was to write much and make his mark. The first day of the concursus — 25 August — went reasonably well for Whitehead. He conducted himself with distinction, as did Murray, from ten to twelve o'clock that day. The next day was to bring him problems. The *Records* tell us:

"In consequence of Mr. Whitehead's delicacy of health, and his hesitation about attempting the other remaining labours of the concursus, the exercises of this day did not commence till two o'clock in the evening. At that hour Mr. Murray proceeded to answer the ten questions proposed from Moral Theology. Mr. Whitehead ascended the pulpit at three o'clock to give his answer to the same; but after saying a few words, in answer to the first question, he became too weak to persevere, and retired. Thus the public exercises of this concursus terminated; and after the Board had awaited the recovery of Mr. Whitehead and spent some days in deliberation, the Rev. P. A. Murray was

13

appointed Professor of First Year's Divinity."

The students probably enjoyed all this. As far as one can gather, at the time life in College would seem to have been more attractive to many of them than life outside. We find the *Trustees* resolving on 26 June, 1839, "that in future any student not in holy orders shall not be permitted, without the express approbation of the President, to remain in the College after having finished the usual course of three years Theology." Strangely enough, at the same time, there seems to have been a certain paucity of students in some of the theology classes, for in that same June the Trustees decided to empower the President to send students into any of the theology classes as he so decided if the number for any of them were small. In this way, or so it may have been thought, competition between the professors would be averted !

Meanwhile, Victorian Ireland was getting underway. Even though the people as a whole were poor, impressive strides were being made in some spheres. Road building was proceeding rapidly and was followed by the development of trade. Coach services were quickly provided on them, the most famous being that of the Italian immigrant, Bianconi, which had begun in 1815. In 1832, his cars covered 1,800 miles and 23 centres. The railway system too was introduced. In 1842 there were twenty-two services, covering some 2,000 miles per day. All this encouraged a growing tourist traffic, many of whose visitors have left us written accounts of their journeys. Most of the people still lived in the countryside. The 1841 Census reports that at that time there were only eighteen towns with a population above ten thousand. Dublin over-shadowed all the rest — the second city of the Empire, with forty peers of the ruling class living in or around it. It is true that it no longer enjoyed the glory that it had known in Georgian times. But it was still a superb city by any standard of those times. And both in Dublin and outside it, schools and hospitals were being set up and the general lines of political and administrative institutions laid down. The big problem was the poverty of the masses, whether rural or urban, and which was bound to come to a head. This was the Ireland that Victoria inherited.

The Queen herself was in quite "bad temper" during the second half of 1838. In early May, 1839, her form can scarcely have been improved by the resignation of her good friend Lord Melbourne, over the Jamaica Bill. Peel became the new Prime Minister. At the beginning he did not get on with Victoria, notably because of his efforts to get her to give up some of her ladies in waiting — which she interpreted as all of them — an episode which came to be known as 'The Bedchamber Plot' ! She won out in the end, for on 10 May,1839, at a quarter to two in the morning, word came that, after a debate in the Commons lasting three and a half hours, Peel had failed. That evening she gave a ball at Buckingham Palace, in honour of the Grand Duke of Russia, but inevitably it came to be

14

called 'The Bedchamber Ball' !

For a while it looked as if 1839 was not going to be the Queen's best year. As late as 10 October, an intruder had broken some of her windows at Windsor. But then everything changed utterly. That very evening Albert of Saxe-Coburg arrived at the Palace, sick sure enough from the Channel crossing and without baggage, but the Queen had found him "beautiful". She proposed on 15 October and was accepted, it is said, passionately. It was not long until 10 February, 1840, when she was able to enter into her Diary: "Monday, February 10 — the last time I slept alone". The tenth of the month did seem to be a red-letter day for her. On the following 10 June an attempt was made on her life, by a lunatic named Edward Oxford. But it passed over her head without trauma as she was happy with her Albert. After the attempt, the Board of Maynooth — on 29 June 1840 — sent an address of congratulations to Her Majesty on her escape, and another to Prince Albert. It was signed by the Trustees, the President, the Masters and the Scholars, and dispatched through none other than Lord Fingall to be presented to the Queen.

Against this backdrop of expressed loyalty to the British monarch, it is intriguing to read a letter from the Senior Dean in the College, the Reverend Myles Gaffney (appointed in 1834), to Dr. Cullen in Rome (dated 7 March, 1840), commissioning a painting of St. Patrick — wanted for Maynooth — 3'9" in length, 3' 3" in width. He would prefer a standing figure, with mitre and crozier, and "it would be well to have a serpent at the feet under the end of the crozier."He also commissioned a painting of St. Joseph for the small chapel of the Infirmary, adding that "no College can be more attached to the Holy See than St. Patrick's College of May-nooth." One wonders what Cullen was thinking then, in view of his later thoughts on that subject.

In the College, domestic life continued. Not, however, without some problems. On 29 January, 1838, Mr. Cavanagh, of Clogher had been apprehended entertaining Mr. Canning of Down (both students) in his room — with wine which he, Mr. Cavanagh, had introduced — at 1 a.m., as a result of which he had become intoxicated *(Liber Poenarum)*. Mr. Cavanagh was duly expelled, on March 27 following. Justice was absolute in those days.

It is not surprising, therefore, to find the great apostle of temperance, Fr. Theobald Mathew, (who himself had earlier felt it necessary to leave the College before the posse because of indulgence *in vino)*, visiting Maynooth in June, 1840, at the invitation of the President. His visit covered the Maynooth area generally. His biographer, John Francis Maguire, tells us that "of those outside the college walls, no less than 35,000 were computed to have taken the pledge." Of Fr. Mathew's visit to the College proper, Maguire speaks about the "extraordinary enthusiasm which the presence and preaching of Father Mathew excited in

15

the minds of hundreds of educated young men, whose days were divided between severe study and the practices of piety. If such were the effect produced by the Apostle in the halls of an ecclesiastical college, what must it not have been in the market-place, or on the hill-side, with working people and peasants for his auditors ?"

In the College, eight professors and two hundred and fifty students enrolled for the pledge of total abstinence. The good father was also received at Carton where the housekeeper "stated she never received any order as to the preparations which she should make for the reception of the most distinguished nobleman, even for the Lord Lieutenant; but when Father Mathew was expected, the Duke requested that she would take 'particular care' in the arrangements for his reception." It is not too difficult to understand what the Duke had in mind.

At this time relations between the Duke and the College were good. It is true that, now and then since the inauguration of the College, there had been some friction between them. It is doubtful whether the Duke would have been too pleased about a lease effected in 1826, between the Trustees and the Royal Canal Company, to the benefit of the College, in respect of a piece of ground on the canal bank, for he was generally jealous of any dealings in land to which he might conceivably have any kind of rights. In 1829, we find the Secretary to the Trustees ordering the College Solicitors to prepare a lease to the Duke of a plot of ground in front of the College adjoining the Protestant church and "already enclosed by His Grace", at the annual rent of fifteen shillings. That difficulties arose as regards the transaction is clear from the fact that the deal was not completed before 1834. When Fr. Mathew came in 1840, Duke and College were on the friendliest terms.

It was on that same day — Sunday, 14 June 1840 — that the new Parish Church of Maynooth village was dedicated by Archbishop Murray. The sermon was preached by Fr. Mathew. Over £200 was collected for the project, Dr. O'Kelly, Senior, Physician to the College, and his son, Dr. O' Kelly, Junior, acting as collectors. The Vice-President of the College, Dr. Renehan, was present, together with Drs. Callan, Furlong, O'Reilly, Russell, Lee, O'Hanlon and others, as well as the "High Priest" *(Freeman's Journal)* Dr. Gaffney, who was the Senior Dean, together with deacons, sub-deacons and chanters from the collegiate body. "The choir under the direction of Mr. Hayden Corri, was very effective. The *Laudate Pueri,* by Mrs. Corri....Mozart's Mass No. 12, Rossini, Ricci, Corri, etc. by Mrs. Corri, Masters H. and P. Corri, and Mrs. Morrison, were all calcul-ated to excite the most lively and striking emotions in all present."

Father Mathew had arrived at about twelve noon and was shouldered to the church. It was afterwards that he was guest at Carton.

The beginning of the Victorian period saw many other visitors to Maynooth, some Irish, some from across the water. While the accounts of the College which they have left us are somewhat repetitive, nearly all of them have something new to recount in some domain or other and their Dickensian flavour lends atmosphere to the place.

Henry Inglis published his *Journey Throughout Ireland* in 1834. H. D. Inglis (1795 - 1835) was a traveller and a writer on miscellaneous topics. He was of Scottish descent. His book about Ireland in 1834 attracted considerable attention and was quoted as authoritative by speakers in Parliament in 1835. It reached a fifth edition in 1838. In it Inglis had the following to say about Maynooth and his journey to it:

"The road from Dublin to Maynooth is an extremely interesting one; but there are two roads; I speak, however, of the low road, which skirts the left bank of the Liffey. All the way to Leixlip, the softest and richest scenery lies along both banks of the river, which glides, a clear and rapid stream, even at a very short distance from the metropolis. Here are the strawberry banks, and here, the tea-drinking cottages, that attract the citizens of Dublin during the strawberry season; and I know few cities, whose environs offer greater inducements for recreation, than the Irish capital. The people of Dublin, however, are a pleasure seeking people; and need few inducements to force them from the desk and the counter. The situation of Leixlip is very attractive; and I venture to predict that whoever halts to break-fast at Mrs. Collings' Inn, a quarter of a mile beyond Leixlip, will certainly order dinner to await his return, unless he has predetermined to accept the hospitalities of the college."

Inglis's account of the order of the day in the College was similar to that already given by Cromwell, but he does add a colourful passage about the students' retiral to bed at ten p.m.:

"At that hour an individual goes round the college, and visits every dormitory: *Benedicamus Domine*, he says, and all must then be quiet. No conversation is allowed during breakfast and dinner. Some individual is appointed to read aloud; sometimes it is history that is read; sometimes the lives of the saints; but I have reason to think that the latter is the usual kind of reading. From the moment of meeting at supper, until meeting again at breakfast, there is total silence; in order, as I was told, that meditation might have its due effect. By study is meant preparation for lectures; and students may either study in their own rooms, or in the library; but they are not permitted, as at Carlow, to study in the open air."

In 1840 came another visitor, who, later in the Autumn of that year,

17

wrote anonymously in *The Catholic Luminary and Ecclesiastical Repertory:*

> "The ride from Leixlip to Maynooth presents a view of land and water agreeably diversified. Beneath the bridge, that here carries the road over the Royal Canal, is one of the most beautiful spring-wells, perhaps, in the country. It is observed, that, if their majesties of the Royal Canal Company, instead of gratifying the idle taste or foolish desires of a certain nobleman, had turned off the bed of this canal to the north, through the plains of Meath, rather than to the southern direction, it would.....have contributed to the health and increased comfort of those in the Royal College."

The reference here is to the suggestion that, when the canal was being constructed, it had been brought through Maynooth to satisfy the whim of the Duke of Leinster. It had long been looked upon as a cause of the dampness which, in later days, was thought to bring sickness to the College. Of this the visitor of 1840 says:

> "We think, because of the contiguity of the College to the canal and not from its low situation, that it must be naturally damp. The construction of dykes outside the canal might diminish, in a great degree, this dampness. Stoves or ventilating grates have been erected in the library and halls; but they should be constructed on a more improved principle, so as to remove a bad smell, and to convey warm air or heat to the students' rooms, particularly during the severity of winter.....Notwithstanding the damp referred to, owing, we suppose, to proper exercise, regularity of living, and order in the discipline, there is, in general, far less disease than in any other place where there is not half the number."

The writer gives us a detailed account of the discipline and spiritual life of the students :

> "The students are required to maintain silence during the hours of study, of lecture, and of meals, and, also, from the time of night prayer, when they retire to their rooms, until after morning prayer the ensuing day. The hours of recreation, rather less than four in each day, are those only in which they are at full liberty to speak to each other during five days of the week. On Wednesdays and Saturdays, and other occasional vacant days, the liberty of speaking is less restricted. During the 'Spiritual Retreat', which takes place twice in the year, an

18

unbroken silence is rigidly preserved for five days. At these periods the time is generally spent in prayer, spiritual reading, in exercises of piety, and in attending to spiritual instructions, which are given to the students in the Chapel. A portion of the day is allowed for exercise, during which the students walk in solitary contemplation. A subject for meditation is given out each day, and is explained generally by the conductor of the retreat on the day following. The subjects are such as relate to the duties of clergymen, piety and moral duties, the observance of order and the preparation for administering the rites and Sacraments of the Roman Catholic Church."

The Catholic Luminary, from which this account is taken, also contains a vignette of the College. It is the same as that which was first used by H. Fitzpatrick in 1814 to adorn the title page of his quarto *Menochius,* printed for the use of the Maynooth students. It presents a view of the front of the early College similar to a larger one published in 1817 by T. Cadell and W. Davies of London, which is unsigned but may have been by one of the Brocas family. The vignette, tiny though it is, shows the small lodge at the entrance referred to by some visitors. This does not appear in a larger print, which shows a great expanse of lawn, with a fountain, in front of the College.

In 1842, no less a personage than William Makepeace Thackeray visited Maynooth. Thackeray (1811-1863) had been born in India but educated in England. The year 1842 was actually the first year of his literary career for it was during it that he began to contribute to *Punch* and published *Vanity Fair.* He was friendly with Charles Lever, the well-known Anglo-Irish writer of novels about life in Ireland, including *Harry Lorrequer,* with its tales of Maynooth during the Rebellion of 1798. At the time of Thackeray's visit, Lever was living near Dublin. Fitzpatrick in his life of Lever tells us that Thackeray had come to Ireland that June for the purpose of collecting material for his *Irish Sketch Book.* He stayed, says Fitzpatrick, at the "Shelburn" hotel.

"Some evenings later at Lever's, Thackeray said 'Can you go with me to Maynooth one of these days? I have seen Trinity College, and now wish to have a look at the Roman Catholic establishment.' On the day appointed we started from the Broadstone, by canal passenger-boat, for our destination. It was one of those 'chill Summer days' peculiar to Ireland; the country through which we journeyed presented no feature of interest; the sky was dull with leaden-coloured clouds, and as we sat cooped up in the long narrow boat, the outlook was dull enough. What the French call 'un morne silence' was spread around us, as we glided noiselessly along the surface of the

19

canal, and we were only too happy when the steward informed us that we had reached the point of debarkation. I had never before seen the village of Maynooth, it appeared to both of us to be dirty and dismal, the colour all grey in grey, the houses half-ruinous, whilst the surrounding country seemed quite in harmony, being flat, dreary and bleak. On asking the way to the College, a woman pointed to a mass of grey buildings, that looked like a sadly neglected military barrack. This was previous to the erection of the new College. Thackeray was, as I saw, busily engaged in noting down all the 'features' of the place, a sardonic smile of utter derision and contempt overspreading his own. I confess to have felt dismayed at the withering expression, part of which was very like satisfaction at having found out something very positive to fasten on. 'What a shameful mistake', he said, 'to plant down an educational establishment of so much importance in such a miserable locality, where there is absolutely nothing to enliven existence.' One of the professors soon appeared, and very courteously offered to conduct us over the establishment. Thackeray said in a few words that he was a literary man, and asked what was to be seen ? The professor replied with some hesitation, 'perhaps the library and (as well as I can remember) a small collection of mathematical instruments', adding that not very much could be expected as the funds at their disposal were very limited. I think we did go into the library, but Thackeray, after asking a few questions as to the number of students and professors, looked at his watch, and said, that, as we were to return to Lever's to dinner by the next boat, we must away.

Thackeray expressed great disgust at the filth and discomfort he had seen. I could not help saying that Maynooth certainly was most desolate-looking; but Thackeray shut me up, by replying that Trinity College was not a whit better in respect of cleanliness; he was evidently in a censorious and perhaps combative humour; I felt pained and disappointed; he had shown himself in a new, and, unexpected light: he had hitherto seemed so genial and amicable that I began to doubt his identity; but I saw more of the same thing subsequently......."

The picture painted here is not very pleasant, either of the College or of its distinguished English visitor. The professor acted as would be normal in the presence of a journalist. Actually, the library was one of the best things that could be shown. The writer in the *Luminary* of 1840 had noted that it then contained about ten thousand volumes, although "owing to the wretched means of its support, we did not see a perfect set of the Fathers, or many ancient and modern works, nearly indispensable in such a place."

Of course, Thackeray does seem to have been a throughly unpleasant individual, one of those pompous and insufferably articulate people who so frequently grease the literary scene. Hopefully, on the evening of his first visit to Maynooth, he may have mellowed a little, for Fitzpatrick says that "there was a friend of his, a Captain S——, employed on the staff in Dublin, who lived in a pretty villa on the canal banks. We got the boatmen to put us ashore near this place, and went to make a call........We walked through the Park into Dublin."

Over a hundred years later, L.T.C. Rolt in his *Green and Silver* was to give a very full description of the Royal Canal, devoting eight pages to Maynooth. He informs us that the passenger boat services that operated between Dublin, Mullingar and Longford, during the hey-day of the canal era, were neither as grandiose nor as profitable as those of the Grand Canal and were particularly lacking in hotel accommodation along the route. Rolt himself went "by yacht" to "Maynooth Harbour". His comments on the College are unusual. "Maynooth College is the twentieth century equivalent of Clonmacnoise or Clonfert, and in the influence which it exercises over Irish life and thought, I would say that while it is one of the least publicized of Irish institutions, it is the most important. ......Within the tomes at Maynooth there lies the germ of truth, however sorely it may be misapplied........Maynooth is still a pool of dogma, deep it is true, but dead, and the minds that come to her are so many empty buckets to be dipped and filled. Seldom or never do they spill over."

But to come back to Thackeray. Funnily enough, what he did eventually write about Maynooth in *The Irish Sketch Book* was gleaned in the course of a coach journey — by Bianconi car in all probability — between Athlone and Dublin.

> "I have seldom seen a more dismal and uninteresting road than that which we now took, and which brought us through the old, inconvenient, ill-built, and ugly town of Athlone....At the Quaker town of Moate, the butcher and the farmer dropped off, the clergy-man went inside, and their places were filled by four Maynoothians, whose vacation was just at an end. One of them, a freshman, was inside the coach with the clergyman, and told him, with rather a long face, of the dismal discipline of his college. They are not allowed to quit the gates (except on general walks); they are expelled if they read a newspaper; and they begin term with "a retreat" of a week, which time they are made to devote to silence, and, as it is supposed, to devotion and meditation.
>
> I must say the young fellows drank plenty of whiskey on the road to prepare them for their year's abstinence; and, when at

21

length arrived in the miserable village of Maynooth, determined not to go into college that night, but to devote the evening to 'a lark'. They were simple kind-hearted young men, sons of farmers or tradesmen seemingly; and, as is always the case here, except among some of the gentry, very gentlemanlike and pleasing in manners. Their talk was of this companion and that, how one was in rhetoric and another in logic, and a third had got his curacy. Wait for a while; and with the happy system pursued within the walls of their college, these smiling good-humoured faces will come out with a scowl, and downcast eyes that seem too afraid to look the world in the face. When the time comes for them to take leave of yonder dismal looking barracks, they will be men no longer, but bound over to the church, body and soul; their free thoughts chained down and kept in darkness, their honest affections mutilated. Well, I hope they will be happy tonight at any rate, and talk and laugh to their hearts' content. The poor freshman, whose big chest is carried off by the porter yonder to the inn, has but twelve hours more of hearty, natural human life. Tomorrow, they will begin their work upon him, cramping his mind, and bitting his tongue, and firing and cutting at his heart, breaking him to pull the Church chariot. Ah! why didn't he stop at home, and dig potatoes and get children ?"

We get no description of the College itself from Thackeray, "for the reason that an accurate description of that establishment would be of necessity so disagreeable, that it is best to pass over it in a few words." The words he used about it are "ruin" and "filth", "a look of lazy squalour", "scores of shoulders of mutton lying on the filthy floor" of the dining hall. He recommended that the next Maynooth grant should include a few shillings worth of whitewash, hundred weights of soap and drill sergeants !

He was much more fascinated with Naas and its agricultural show and a dinner which he had at "Macavoy's Hotel", with toasts of the Queen and Prince Albert, to "great cheering", although one of the Lord Lieutenant was "received rather coolly". The Sallymount Beagles and the Kildare Foxhounds were, however, toasted warmly.

In 1842, Mr. and Mrs. Hall brought out the second volume of their *Ireland: Its Scenery, Character, etc.* As a writer, the wife, Anna Maria (1800 - 1881), was the dominant partner. Born in Dublin, she had married Samuel Carter Hall in London, 1824. Her first literary contribution appeared in 1829, after which she became an author by profession, writing much about the character of the Irish. While containing fine rural descriptions of their travels around the country, the 1842 account of the couple's visit to Ireland was not generally appreciated there, as it had failed to please either the Orangemen or the Catholics. It was a joint effort by them both. In it they indicated that they were not at all convinced that Maynooth College had lived up to the purpose for which it had been founded, namely, to produce a loyal Catholic clergy. "On the contrary, the race of young men who leave Maynooth to discharge their parochial duties throughout Ireland are more hostile to the British Government than were the priests of the old school who received their education in France, Italy, and Spain."

Still, on the occasion of the triennial visitation, held on 17 April, 1843, the Lord Chancellor, Sir Edward Sugden, found no complaints in the Royal College and had no complaints about it himself. He expressed himself as being most impressed and commented most favourably on the college. We can take it that Victoria was not overconcerned about it. She had had her first child in November, 1840, and was fully taken up with home life. Public affairs and appearances she did have to attend to and not always without distress. On 30 May, 1842, a further attempt was made on her life by a man called John Francis. The pistol misfired and he slipped away in the crowd only to repeat the attempt the very next day. At that time Ireland and Maynooth were unlikely to have much occupied the Queen's thoughts.

THE CROSS BEHIND THE FLAG

On 3 September, 1838, Dr. Patrick Carew, former Professor in the College, now a Bishop, left Maynooth for London to arrange for the voyage to Madras where he was to begin his work as Vicar Apostolic. Five priests were to follow him within a matter of days. A pattern had begun to unfold which was to make Maynooth and Victorian Ireland noted for the spreading of Christianity in the colonies.

The Victorian Empire grew quickly. Canada was amongst the first of the overseas possessions to be secured within the fold. While there had indeed been rebellions there in 1837, on the part of both the English and French speaking peoples, they had not been militarily significant. By 1840, Canada was firmly linked to Britain – the eldest daughter of the Empire, to become the First Dominion in 1867. In 1836, New Zealand had been extolled by Edward Gibbon Wakefield before a Select Committee of the House of Commons as eminently suitable for settlement, in fact, "the fittest country in the world for colonization." In 1839, he founded the New Zealand Company which, between 1840 and 1850, had established six colonies that quickly flourished after a number of gold strikes. The year 1837 also saw British rule consolidated at the Cape of Good Hope, although it too was the year of The Great Trek, when large numbers of Afrikaaners crossed the Orange River to settle north of it in Natal. Britain was to annexe Natal in 1843.

In 1839, she invaded Afghanistan, in the hope of stemming Russian and Persian ambitions. That April Kandahar was occupied. The escapade was not entirely unlike that of Russia there in more recent times. The war went on for three years and ultimately went against the British. By January, 1842, the retreat from Afghanistan had begun. But success attended the Empire elsewhere. In the 1840's, emigration from Britain to Australia was running at the rate of 15,000 per annum; in 1841 it reached a level of 33,000. As a result, the population of New South Wales was 160,000 in 1842. It was to be further boosted by the great Australian gold rush of the early 1850's.

The great days of Victoria had come. In 1843 the Gold Coast was taken and in 1844 Prince Alfred was born. In the Autumn of 1845, the Queen and Prince Albert went on a trip abroad — to "dear little Germany", as she put it. In 1845 too the first Sikh War erupted, with four battles between then and February, 1846. The British gained control of Kashmir. Then, in 1848, came the second Sikh War, while in 1852 Burma was invaded, ostensibly because of deteriorating relations between British merchants and the Burmese authorities, but in reality for colonial expansion.

These very same years were notable for a burst of missionary activity at Maynooth. In February, 1838, seven students left for Australia, to evangelize in New South Wales. One of the most colourful of them was a Limerickman named Slattery, who had been ordained at Maynooth in 1837. In Australia he was to work in many places — in Bathurst for a start, then in Western Victoria. Of him the *Warrnambool Standard* was to say later: "At that time his mission extended from Colac to the South Australian Border, and from the Ocean to the Dividing Range. With no roads, and settlements miles apart, his duties must have been of the most arduous nature, but his indomitable courage and untiring zeal overcame all difficulties. Old residents can tell of his braving the storms of winter, often swimming his horse in the darkness of the night across flooded rivers, and cheerfully undergoing the many other hardships incidental to an unsettled district when on his way to celebrate Mass or to bring consolation to a departing soul."

In May, 1838, three more Limerickmen went off from Maynooth to work in Scotland, hoping perhaps to undo some of the damage that had been done there by Michael Crotty, referred to earlier, who, after ministering for a while in that region as a priest, had conformed to Protestantism and turned to attacking all things Catholic.

Finally, in the fall of the year, the Limerick brothers, John and George Butler, had left for Trinidad and Dr. Carew and his companions for Madras. It was a veritable case of the cross following the flag, blazing the trail of an Irish Catholic Empire in the wake of Victoriam arms. The

Archbishop of Dublin, Dr. Murray, took a lively interest in promoting this missionary enthusiasm. Writing to Cullen, then Rector of the Irish College, Rome, in early 1838, he reveals that it was he who, in obedience to the Sacred Congregation of Propaganda, had proposed "Mr. Carew" as coadjutor for Madras, indicating that, if Carew were appointed to this, two colleagues, Messrs. J. Fennelly (Bursar) and W. Kelly (English and French), would in all likelihood accompany him.

This they duly did. Carew himself wrote to Cullen in March informing him that two staff and four servants from the College were to go. In point of fact, quite large numbers of Maynooth men seem to have joined in the Indian and Australian 'expeditions'. A letter from Madras around the middle of the century says that "the number of clergy in this part of the vicariate is twenty-six, and six more in Hyderabad. All Hallows counts nine of her children amongst the number; and, with the exception of one native priest and two Portuguese or Goa clergymen, Ireland claims them all." What accounts we have of their experiences are all too brief but reflective of their age. There is a letter in the *Archives of the Irish College, Rome,* written to Cullen in March, 1838, by Thomas Olliffe from Calcutta, which gives an account of his journey to India. On the way there he had passed through Egypt and visited the pyramids, having mounted the highest of them. He had entered into them also. He criticizes the French for having destroyed a portion of them to provide stones for a bridge across the Nile. And he gives measurements, as would all good Victorian travellers — assiduously calculating that even one of the pyramids could contain as many as 3,700 rooms ! Olliffe was a secular priest — a native of Cork — who was eventually to become Bishop of Calcutta, succeeding Dr. Carew.

The Indian Missions were colourful places. Madras, in particular, was interesting. It was the oldest city of the British Raj, built with an exotic exuberance, and is accepted as being the best skyline that the British erected in India. It had large and elegant buildings, widely separated and in different styles, "portly for Victoria and domed for the East," as James Morris, historian of the Empire, says of them. Calcutta was older and more Indian in tone, but made up for its lesser elegance by having a more developed Christian mission. Catholicism had been brought to Bengal by the Portuguese during the last decade of the sixteenth century, and by the 1830's had some 25,000 members, of whom nearly eight thousand were to be found in Calcutta. The city had four churches. Yet, although it was still only a tiny fraction of the population, the Catholic community was torn by dissension; and the missionaries had to bend all their efforts to an uphill task. They were glad of continuous help from Ireland and that they got in abundance.

In April, 1841, Mr. Fennelly terminated his position as Bursar at Maynooth and prepared himself to leave for the foreign missions. He was still in the College in May, when he presented an address on behalf of the students to Father Theobald Mathew on the occasion of the latter's second visit to the College in the course of his apostolate for temperance. Then, at the end of June, 1841, Dr. Fennelly was consecrated Bishop in the College Chapel — Dr. England of Charleston again turning up, at least in time for dinner.

The Freeman's Journal of Monday, 28 June, carried a lengthy report of the proceedings: "The church was filled with a most respectable congregation, who all seemed deeply interested in the solemnities." About two hundred students had remained back for the occasion and, as well as by many Irish bishops, it was attended by Dr. Polding, described as "Bishop of Australia and New Holland." In the evening "a splendid dinner" had as special guests Dr. England and Dr. Yore, Vicar General of Dublin.

The whole thing made a big impression and not least in Maynooth itself. For when Dr. Fennelly left for India that September, to replace Dr. Carew, who had by then been translated to Calcutta, he was accompanied by three students, while contemporaneously there was an affiliation with Madras by the Presentation Convent in Maynooth village. Three professed nuns and one lay sister sailed with them. So also did three Presentation brothers and three young candidates for the priesthood. They left from Kingstown for Liverpool on the first leg of their long voyage.

In Fennelly's place as Bursar, the Reverend Laurence Renehan, at that time also Vice-President, was appointed by the Trustees. The appointment was supposed to be for a year but seems to have lasted until 1845. One can imagine his reaction when the following epistle arrived from Liverpool in October, 1841, from a Mr. Thorn, a Protestant minister, who was hopeful that Maynooth might extend its missions as far afield as China: "The Revd. the President, the Revd. the Vice-President, and the other authorities of the Royal College of St. Patrick, Maynooth, are requested by the Reverend David Thorn to accept a copy of Aesop's fables translated into the Chinese language and published by the writer's brother Robert Thorn Esq., at present one of Her Majesty's interpreters in China, under the pseudonyme of Gloth". He "considered that, as it is possible that some of the young gentlemen at Maynooth may be destined for a Missionary career in the East, and particularly in China," such a work could help them with the language.

One would love to know whether the Reverend Mr. Thorn had made the acquaintance of Fennelly and Co. during their passage via Liverpool. In any case, destiny was to reserve the Maynooth Mission to China for other men in another century. Thorn, though, was not to be put off too easily. On 9 November he wrote again, forwarding another little book by his brother entitled *The Lasting Resentment of Miss Keaon Loan Wang*. He does seem to have done some business with the College, if not of the kind he had expected. On 11 November he sent on some books for Maynooth itself, for Cardinal Mezzofanti and for the Rector of Propaganda, asking Renehan to forward those intended for the last named distinguished personages. These too may well have been about the Chinese language in view of the said Cardinal's well-known interest in philology and the world-wide interests of the Rector. Thorn had just received news, in a letter dated Macao, August 16 - 17, from his brother, who was on the eve of departing on a military mission to China, as interpreter on the staff of General Sir Hugh Gough, the British Commander in Chief.

The Maynooth connection with Calcutta did not last very long. At the start, it seemed set for greater things. In 1841, Bishop Carew had arrived there amid scenes of great pomp. He was ably assisted by Dr. Kelly, whom he named Vicar General of Eastern Bengal. For a while, he toyed with the idea of the establishment of a hierarchy in British India, with himself as Metropolitan. But it was not to work out as he had hoped. Dr. Kelly died on 21 March, 1842, to be succeeded by Dr. Olliffe, who became Coadjutor to Bishop Carew in 1843. Carew himself had been nominated Archbishop some months earlier. For years they toiled on in the face of many difficulties, helped considerably, it should be said, by the Irish Catholics in the British army out there. They certainly left their mark. Archbishop Carew died on 2 November, 1855. Dr. Fennelly worked in Madras until 1868, when he was succeeded by his brother. Between them they kept the flag of Maynooth flying until well-nigh the end of the century.

Between 1838 and 1880, Maynooth produced no less than twelve Bishops in far flung parts of the Empire, including India, Australia, Canada and South Africa. America also got its quota, in places like St. Louis, Grass Valley in California, and Chicago. Eugene O'Connell, later to be Bishop of Grass Valley, was ordained in 1842. Following a short spell on the staff of All Hallows, which had just been founded, he worked as a missionary in California from 1851 to 1854, under the famous Bishop Alemany, who, after his consecration in the Summer of 1850, had visited Maynooth and All Hallows in quest of students on his way home as Bishop of Monterey. At that time his diocese covered the whole State of California. Presumably he had captivated the young O'Connell. The latter, after being Vicar Apostolic of Marysville from 1861 to 1868, became Bishop of Grass Valley in 1868 and died in 1885. With him in California was Fr. Daniel Slattery, a former Kerry student at Maynooth, who had been taken on by Bishop Alemany in September, 1854, and ordained by him that November. He ministered in Gold Rush Country, in conditions common to all his companions — harsh going, by horse and boat and stage, dealing with a rough people.

These Maynooth men were put off by nothing and accomplished much. In 1847, the matriculation class in the College included one James Richards from Ferns, who later became Bishop of Grahamstown in the eastern district of the Cape of Good Hope. Maynooth must have been proud to hear that, in addition to his missionary labours, he gave a series of lectures on electricity before a critical non-Catholic audience down there. As was only to be expected, there were demands for such men from all over the world. In 1850, Dr. Cantwell, Bishop of Meath, wrote to the College President asking him to present for orders a student who had completed his studies a few years back as he had "got a place for him in Buenos Ayros." On the other hand, there is evidence too of a surplus of priests at home at this time owing probably to a loss of population caused by the famine. In 1851, Dr. Derry, Bishop of Clonfert, wrote to the President: "I wish I may have it in my power to procure places in England or elsewhere for those in Maynooth that are approaching the term of the usual Collegiate course. Perhaps you may assist me kindly in doing so."

THE OXFORD CONNECTION

In those stirring days there was another side to Maynooth that could have been obscured amidst the excitement of practical doings. This is its role as a haven for scholars. In the 1840's a bright star had appeared in its galaxy in the person of Charles William Russell. A member of the staff, as Professor of Humanity since 1835, he had, as already noted, been editing and writing for *The Dublin Review* since 1836, taking a special interest in church history, particularly in Anglicanism and the then burgeoning Tractarian Movement. Not that he confined himself to this. Indeed during the entire history of Maynooth to date, nobody ever cast his net wider.

In 1841, Russell finished a translation of Leibnitz's *System of Theology*, although it was not to be published until 1850. In the meantime, much was to happen. Russell, who was never known to have shied away from correspondence with important people, had already, even though only twenty-nine years of age at that time, engaged in an exchange of letters with Dr. Wiseman. Ensuing from this, some time before Easter 1841, Wiseman had written to him concerning the movement of the Tractarians from Anglicanism towards Catholicism. He announced that it was prog-ressing every day and had good hopes that it would have a happy outcome. He quoted to Russell from a letter from one of them: "I will extract a few sentences, for *yourself and Dr. Murray only*, unless you think the

Archbishop would be glad to see what I write, from whom I have no secrets — *but no further*". Wiseman urged Russell to do what he could to push the Oxford Anglicans into the Roman Communion.

Before long, Russell was writing to John Henry Newman, endeavouring to explain how the latter in his Tract 90 had misunderstood the Catholic doctrine of Transubstantiation. Newman (1801 - 1890) had been born into Protestantism. Originally inclined towards Calvinism, he had become an ardent Anglican at a young age and vicar of St. Mary's in Oxford. An illness during a Mediterranean cruise in 1832 had caused him to visit Catholic shrines and churches in Europe and gradually he had been drawn towards Roman Catholicism. After his return (July, 1833) he had embarked on the publication of *Tracts for the Times,* the first of which appeared in December of that year. What came to be called the Tractarian movement quickly developed. Many of its publications were Romanizing in tendency, notably Tract 90, which was an attempt to interpret the Thirty-nine Articles of the Church of England in a Catholic sense.

It was against this background that Russell wrote to Newman. He wrote his letter on 8 April. It was the beginning of a correspondence that was to continue over the next four years as Newman struggled with his religious problems. And it is a tribute to Newman that, even though this letter was headed "Wellington Place, Dundalk" (Russell's homeland) and signed simply "C. W. Russell", whom Newman took to be an ordinary Irish priest, it still drew a considered reply from him. Russell wrote on Maundy Thursday. As he was to explain on 20 April to Wiseman: "I was just after celebrating the public services of the day; the thought came upon me that perhaps I might do some good by writing in a friendly spirit on that portion of his (Newman's) Tract which regarded the mystery of the day — Transubstantiation. I yielded to the impulse and showed him how far on this point he had misconceived us; how Bishop Taylor, whom he quotes, misstated Bellarmine; and, above all, how literally the very strongest phrases employed in the retraction of Berengarius, which he also brings forward, are copied from the Fathers, especially St. John Chrysostom. I referred him to Veron and to Bossuet to see how far, provided the 'really truly substantially' be secured, we may go in speaking of 'sacramental' and 'spiritual' presence as opposed to 'carnal' and natural', and I further took the liberty of requesting permission, if he had not Veron, to send him a copy."

Newman in Tract 90 had indeed gone rather far in interpreting Transubstantiation as involving "a shocking doctrine" that the body of Christ "is carnally pressed with teeth". In his letter to Newman, Russell had concentrated on this. For a young man, writing to one such as Newman, his expostulation had been vigorous: "Reverend Sir, It grieves me to observe, that, amid the varied and informed erudition in all that concerns your church, which your works display, there is to be met much apprehension of many doctrines and practices which I have been taught, since childhood, to venerate and which, were they, indeed, as you represent them, I should abhor as fervently as you yourself can do .....I trust that the date of this letter will sufficiently explain why I take the liberty of calling your attention to one precious doctrine in particular — that of the Blessed Sacrament. Your whole exposition......proceeds on the supposition that our conception of 'Transubstantiation' is of the most gross and repulsive nature........ Far from entering in any way into our belief of the Eucharist, the gross imaginations ascribed to us are rejected with horror by every Catholic."

In his letter to Wiseman, Russell enclosed the reply which Newman had sent to him, noting that it had justified Wiseman's confidence that Newman was indeed moving towards Rome: "You have the result enclosed; and it is a complete confirmation of all your Lordship's information. There is a frankness and cordiality in the tone of the letter which augurs happily....If the time were come, ... a single conference might arrange the differences now existing, if, indeed, even these shall not ere long be removed."

Newman had certainly been generous and forthcoming in his reply, dated Easter Tuesday, 1841, from Oriel College, Oxford. He wrote: "Dear Sir, — Nothing can be kinder or more considerate than the tone of your letter, for which I sincerely thank you. It will relieve you to know that I do *not* accuse your communion of holding Transubstantiation in the shocking sense which we both repudiate, but I impute the idea to our Articles which, I conceive, condemn a certain extreme view of it which some persons or many have put forward in your Church against the sense of the sounder portion of it .... I heartily wish that I could extend to all your *received* doctrines the admission I make concerning this ...... O that you would reform your worship, that you would disown the extreme honours paid to St. Mary and the Saints, your traditionary view of Indulgences, and the veneration paid in foreign countries to Images. And as to our own country, O that, abandoning your connection with a political party, you would as a body, lead quiet and peacable lives ....I will thankfully accept Veron's book at your hands, if there is any easy mode of conveyance of it." In this letter Newman put his finger on the central point that was for so long to prove an obstacle to his embracing Catholicism — what he called the 'traditionary' or secondary teaching of the Church, more especially concerning the veneration of the Blessed Virgin Mary and the saints.

Wiseman replied at once, congratulating Russell on what had occurred: "I see no insurmountable difficulties in Oxford against the return of Unity", and then in a postscript, dated 28 April: "I have the good news to communicate to you that the *real* Oxford men have resolved to attack O'Connell no more, and are quite altering their views of Ireland. An extract from Dr. Murray's letter to me, forwarded to them, has done wonders." There is no doubt but that Russell's own letter had done wonders, suffused as it was with love for Christ in the Eucharist and the assumption that Newman felt the same. As Meriol Trevor puts it in *Newman: The Pillar of the Cloud* (London, 1962): "In this way he at once reached Newman's heart."

Wiseman had been right in thinking that, before Russell had written at all, Newman had been hankering after Catholicism. On the very 8 April that Russell had written to him, Newman had penned an Easter message to Ambrose Phillipps: "You do me justice when you imply that the unity of the Church Catholic is near my heart. Only, I do not see any prospect of it in our time and I despair of its being effected without great sacrifices on all hands. Were the Roman Church in Ireland different from what it is, one immense stumbling block would be removed." With hindsight it is now evident that Russell was to contribute to its removal in a big way.

He wrote his second letter to Newman on 21 April. It was a long letter, like the first, explaining how he had to leave Dundalk to go to Maynooth "where I hold the Chair of Humanity" before receiving Newman's reply. He is most grateful for it as he had written in the first instance from impulse and "your kind letter completely reassures me". "Believe me, my dear Sir, our other doctrines and the practices which flow from them will bear the same rigid examination." He refers to Leibnitz's study of them and recommends his *Systema Theologicum* to Newman. Only examine our devotions, he says, and you will cease to fear them. "Every day, every new event, increases the confidence with which I put my humble prayer, that I may be permitted to see your Church once again in her ancient and natural position, to have the happiness of knowing that your devoted friends are ministering at the same altar to which my own life is vowed. I have long regarded you all as brethren in spirit, separated from us only because we did not know each other." But there were some points that he could not gloss over: "Our political position is, indeed, an unhappy one, but it is the result of circumstances which, as they created, may, and I trust will, amend it. We have suffered much and however it is to be deplored, one can hardly wonder at the violence of the reaction which long maintained oppression has produced. Would that I could see my Catholic countrymen in happier position ! and that, above all, I could see them freed from a political connexion with those with whom they have not and cannot have any community of religious interests and religious feelings." The young Russell certainly was a patriot.

Newman's reply, of 26 April, was defensive. "I do not look so despairingly at our Church as you do. While I think (of course) that she is a branch of the Church Catholic, I also have lately had my hopes increased as to the prospect of her improvement in doctrinal exactness by the very events which seem to you to show that Catholic truth is but barely tolerated within her pale." Russell seems to have realised his advantage and decided not to press the matter, at least for the time being. Hence, on 1 May, he signed off in a further long letter in which he apologizes for trespassing on Newman's time but says that it is only through "humility and singlemindedness, to be obtained by prayer alone, that we can hope for a great movement to which many human obstacles pose themselves." Many of his friends feel the same as he does and 'have long made this the subject of earnest prayer especially at the Holy Altar". He himself prays daily "that you and your friends may be strengthened to dismiss all fears of that secondary and traditionary system among us, which seems to haunt you." During the coming Summer he proposes to visit France, Rome, Austria and Bavaria, and hopes that in those places too he will find the same feeling as he and his friends have about the possibility of a movement back to the Church in England, and he asks God to hasten that day. Protestantism may once have had a function, by way of reforming abuses, but it has outlived its usefulness in not heeding the voice of Trent, through prejudice and misrepresentations, human pride and other human failings.

It was a hard-hitting letter and one to which Newman felt compelled to reply in an equally hard-hitting vein. "My Dear Sir — I have to acknowledge your kind letter, received during my absence from this place (Oriel College). I have only to observe upon it that, while I most sincerely hold that there is in the Roman Church a traditionary system which is not necessarily connected with her essential formularies, yet, were I even so much to change my mind on this point, this would not tend to bring me from my present position, providentially appointed, in the English Church. That your communion was unassailable would not prove that mine was indefensible. Nor would it at all affect the sense in which I receive our articles — they would still speak against certain definite errors, though you had reformed them. I say this lest any lurking suspicion should be left in the mind of your friends that persons who think with me are likely by the growth of their present views to find it imperative on them to pass over to your communion. Allow me to state strongly that if you have any such thoughts and proceed to act upon them, your friends will be committing a fatal mistake. We have (I trust) the principles and temper of obedience too intimately wrought into us, to allow of our separating ourselves from our ecclesiastical superiors because in many points we may sympathise with others. We have too great a horror of the principle of private judgement to trust it in so immense a matter as that of changing from one communion to another. We may be cast out of our communion, or it may decree heresy to be truth, you shall say whether such contingencies are likely; but I do not see other conceivable causes of our leaving the Church. For myself, persons must be well acquainted with what I have written before they venture to say whether I have much changed my opinions and cardinal views in the course of the last eight years. That *my sympathies* have grown

32

towards the religion of Rome I do not deny; that my *reasons for shunning* her communion have lessened or altered, it will be difficult perhaps to prove. And I wish to go by reason not by feeling. Pray excuse a note hastily written, though it expresses no hasty opinions." He will send on a volume of his sermons to Russell.

On 8 May, Russell simply acknowledged this letter. He will be glad to get the volume of sermons. But he does permit himself to comment that he will not willingly give up his hopes for Newman's joining the Church of Rome. Indeed he is looking forward not to individual movements towards Rome, but rather for a Catholic movement within the English Church itself, of a kind that would put no strain on the loyalty of the individual. A spirit to that effect is already in motion and must, in all likelihood, extend itself.

In the *Apologia* Newman speaks of Russell as having visited him twice in Oxford, once during the Summer of 1841, but it does not seem that he did. The only sure occasion is 1 August, 1843, when Newman "walked into Oxford from Littlemore to lionize Mr. Russell of Maynooth; walked back to 3 o'clock service." In 1875, writing to Russell's nephew, Matthew, Newman says that, whereas he always thought that Russell had called on him twice in Oxford, the latter had always insisted that it was but once. Possibly, in the *Apologia*, Newman had got his references about it mixed up. Between May and October, 1841, silence reigned between the two protagonists. Newman had gone to Littlemore to think in solitude, while Russell, as intended although not as extensively as he had hoped, was engaged in a journey on the Continent. On his return to Maynooth from Rome, he found the volume of Newman's sermons awaiting him. It had apparently been lying there for some months. Scholar to scholar, he informs Newman that while in Rome he had worked on the *Systema Theologicum* of Leibnitz, the text of which, with an English translation, he hopes to publish. He is full of praise for Leibnitz. "It is one of the most remarkable works I have ever read .... I know no work more calculated than it, coming from such a man as Leibnitz, to remove the difficulties which the pride of nature opposes to authority and none better fitted to smooth away the prejudices with which but too many regard the doctrines of the Catholic Church. He, at least, is an impartial judge." Russell feels that Newman would be interested in Leibnitz and will send him a copy when his publication appears.

This eulogy of Leibnitz is rather extraordinary, or at least Russell's view of him as promoting Catholic belief, but the exchange of books was entirely characteristic of the relationship between Russell and Newman. Veron's *Regula Fidei* and Newman's *Sermons* had already exchanged hands. They were not to be the last. Russell was always either looking for or presenting books. In December, 1841, we find him writing to Cullen seeking some other volume. He had just heard of the death of the Pope on the tenth of the month from a report which appeared in the *Gazette du Dauphine.* By 2 June, 1842, he was on his way to Rome again. He informed Newman of this, writing from Leicester Square on Whit Wednesday. He hoped to get to Rome for the feast of the Holy Apostles.

On his return, he forwarded in November a volume of *the Sermons of St. Alphonsus Liguori,* "translated by a very dear friend". This was undoubtedly Dr. Callan of Maynooth, who did quite a lot of work of this kind. Russell felt that the book might be of help in showing Newman "how far we are from suffering the subordinate and secondary devotion to the Blessed Virgin and the saints to trench upon the primary duty of loving God." This even in Italy, where a fair specimen of Catholic popular devotion might be expected to be found . Once again he reminds Newman that he never offers Mass "without remembering (shall I say affectionately ?) you and your friends in my unworthy prayer, without praying that, having, as I believe, brought you to be one with us in faith, he may also deign to give that faith the real and practical character of Catholicity, external membership of the true fold. Forgive me for the freedom with which I write, but my heart is full and I will speak."

Later, in the *Apologia,* Newman was to record gratefully that the book by St. Alphonsus was important to him in helping him to understand that Catholic devotion to Our Blessed Lady was not 'Mariolatry'. In fact, by 5 December, Russell is promising to send him another volume by the same author at present being prepared by the same translator. He wishes that Newman "could assist at the sacred exercises at St. Eusebius or at the retreats for the soldiers, etc. at the Ponte Rotto in Rome. I know no means more calculated to display the true character of our devotional practices than these and similar missions (as we call them)". He hopes to visit Newman some day; as a matter of fact in his letter of thanks for the first Liguori volume, Newman had invited Russell to visit him at Oriel. He doubts whether this will be possible now because "I was appointed, about two months since, bishop of the Island of Ceylon. A settled conviction of my unfitness from youth and inexperience (not to speak of graver wants) for a charge so difficult and important, as well as throwing the person entirely upon his own resources, determined me at once to decline it. But I have just had a letter from the Propaganda to say that his Holiness has refused to admit my resignation. I believe I shall be obliged to go at once to Rome, to solicit in person and through the influences of friends there, what my letters have failed to obtain. I cannot be canonically compelled, but it is a grievous thing to withstand even a wish, not to say injunction, of the highest ecclesiastical authority upon earth. If I fail of success, my career in life will be widely different from yours, and from what I had imagined for myself." But if he is ever passing through Oxford, he will be very pleased to call. Many of these letters are to be found in the *Archives of the Birmingham Oratory.*

Russell did manage to get out of the Ceylon appointment, although it does look as if he had to go to Rome in order to do so. In any case, he is to be found on 29 April, 1843, writing to Cullen from Naples, telling him about a trip there in the company of two fellow-travellers, called Norris and Farrell. One fears that the snob element in Russell had got the better of the day. He retails stories about his travelling companions, sometimes rather sarcastically. Norris had been relieved of a crown piece by a Neopolitan *gentilhomme* who was lecturing him on coins, and he had been pitched on his head from a donkey while riding up the sides of Monte Cassino. When asked by Norris, Russell had pretended that a mountain forty miles away was Vesuvius. Norris had immediately seen the smoke and Farrell the lava. Russell was clearly enjoying a respite from the many serious matters that had been bothering him.

Back in London at the end of July, he at once contacted Newman. His absence in Rome has been longer than he had anticipated and he is hurrying home quickly, but he would like to call at Oxford and visit Newman in his rooms. He hopes to reach Oxford by the early train on Tuesday, 1 August, and to wait on Newman at 11 a.m. The two met and the Maynooth professor was shown over some of the buildings of the University. From the *Apologia* we gather that they got on well, for Newman describes Russell as "gentle, mild, unobtrusive, uncontroversial. He let me alone." They did not speak about religion on that occasion. Still, in the *Apologia* Newman is definite that "my dear friend, Dr. Russell of Maynooth had perhaps more to do with my conversion than anyone else", and later still he was to dedicate *Loss and Gain* to Russell, because of "the warm and sympathetic interest which you took in Oxford matters thirty years ago."

Newman in 1843 had yet a bit to go before converting to the Catholic Church. But he was gradually coming nearer that decision. Russell continued to be of help. In February, 1844, he sent on a packet of little books which were intended to illustrate the nature of the popular devotional literature in use in Italy. He had collected them during his recent sojourn there and would have sent them on earlier but his books, trunks, etc., having been sent by sea from Leghorn, were very late in reaching him. He requested Newman to check a passage in a Bodleian MS. which he had been asked to look after by Cardinal Mai. Newman did so at once. He had good reason to be thankful to Russell for having sent him the collection of Italian popular literature. It was to prove most useful. He referred to it afterwards as follows: "Dr. Russell sent me a large bundle of penny or

35

half-penny books of devotion, of all sorts, as they are found in the book-sellers' shops at Rome; and, on looking them over, I was quite astonished to find how different they were from what I had fancied, how little there was in them to which I could really object." It may well have been that amongst them was *The Imitation of Christ, The Introduction to the Devout Life,* and *The Spiritual Combat,* for we do know that Newman examined these.

By the fall of 1844, it seemed to many that Newman's days with Anglic-anism were numbered. It was rumoured in some places that he had already taken the steps, but he had not. On 9 November, Wiseman wrote to Russell from Oscott; "I am very sorry all the reports about Newman should have turned out false; but no doubt the waters are being moved, and a commotion ending in a crisis may, I think, be expected." He was right. Within a year, on 8 October, 1845, Newman was writing to Russell to announce that he was about to be received into the Catholic Church. That same year, Russell himself had been appointed to the new Chair of Ecclesiastical History that had been established at Maynooth.

MITRES OR MORTAR BOARDS ?

It is quite possible that one of the friends in Rome to whom Russell had recourse in his effort to decline Ceylon was Dr. Cullen. This was the Rector of the Irish College, Rome, to whom reference has been made earlier. Paul Cullen was born in 1813 of substantial Co. Kildare farming stock. Educated for the priesthood in Rome, he was ordained in 1830. Following a short time as Professor at the College of Propaganda, he became Rector of the Irish College in 1832. In this capacity he also acted as the Roman agent of the Irish Bishops and came to wield considerable power. He was appointed Archbishop of Armagh in 1849 and was trans-lated to Dublin in 1852. Both as Rector of the Irish College and Arch-bishop in Ireland, he exerted an extraordinary influence — indeed domin-ated the Irish Church — despite having bad relations with such a doughty figure as Archbishop McHale of Tuam. While not generally regarded as a friend of Maynooth, he did much that was of importance for the College.

Cullen and Russell seem to have been somewhat close in the early 1840's. In August, 1842, Russell had written to Cullen inviting him to Maynooth and in October had told him about his disinterest in the espiscopacy in "India", owing to "a resolution to remain as I am, a simple priest." In spite of all this, the Archbishop of Dublin was able to write to Cullen on 25 April, 1843, to say that there was still no news about Dr. Russell's "release" from Ceylon; he would be a loss to the College, but is also needed outside. The Archbishop's information was dated, for a letter to Cullen from the Professor of Irish at Maynooth, James Tully, of 21 April, tells that Russell had "escaped" Ceylon. It was at the very time that Russell was touring in the Naples area, most likely celebrating his escape.

There were others on the Maynooth staff that were more concerned about exchanging their mortar boards for mitres. One such was Charles McNally, of the Diocese of Clogher, in whose favour a memorandum to Propaganda had been prepared on 8 December, 1842, signed by the Vicar General and quite a number of the priests of the diocese. This had been occasioned by a rumour that McNally's advancement to Clogher as Coadjutor was being opposed by the Metropolitan. It begged Cardinal Fransoni, the Prefect of Propaganda, to inquire about McNally from the Archbishop of Dublin and Dr. McHale of Tuam who knew him well. "No one in all the kingdom of Ireland has, for many years, so won the love and reverence of the clergy and laity as Dr. McNally has", but the Archbishop of Armagh "has an exceeding dislike for McNally." In the event, and possibly in the realization that the wording was somewhat intemperate, this remonstrance was not sent; but another along similar lines apparently was dispatched.

The clergy were divided on the issue. There was one Clogher priest who was particularly displeased at the idea. This was Dr. Patrick Murray, then Professor of Theology at Maynooth. From what has come down to us about him we can gather than he was a learned and holy priest. The *Journal of the Presentation Convent, Maynooth,* records that, during 1841-42, he gave substantial spiritual help to the convent, frequently coming in the evening to give an exhortation to the sisters, his favourite theme being the Blessed Sacrament. At the same time, he was involved in the copious writing which has made his name famous in College history. Some of it was combative and courageous, such as an article in the twenty-sixth number of *The Dublin Review,* in November, 1842, defending the scriptural argument for the doctrine of Satisfaction against the objections of Mr. Palmer, of Worcester College, Oxford. Murray was quite unhappy at the prospect of McNally being promoted to his native diocese and on 20 January, 1843, wrote to Cullen in Rome seeking his backing in petitioning for an *exeat* from Clogher. Murray declares himself "nervous" to get it. He has, he says, good personal reasons for asking for it and has been urged by everyone in Maynooth who is interested in him to seek it. He intends to keep the *exeat* private if he gets it !

Whoever was responsible for the move, the following month Propaganda did seek further views concerning the Primate's opposition to McNally, a man who, it said, had been strongly recommended by the clergy of Clogher, and was first among the professors of Maynooth in learning, indeed outstanding in all Ireland. A copy of this inquiry is to be found in the *Clogher Diocesan Archives.* Murray was inclined to take no chances and wrote to Cullen again in March bent on getting his *exeat.* He will not get on with McNally if the latter is Bishop of Clogher and he wants too to be "free of the factions and feuds" of the diocese. By April no coadjutor had been appointed to Clogher. At this stage, Murray, not yet having heard about Russell's eluding Ceylon, suggests that the Pope should appoint him to Clogher and so finish the whole business both as regards Ceylon and the dispute over that Diocese.

The matter was finally solved by McNally's appointment in August. Murray was on vacation at Glandore in Co. Cork, a place he loved dearly. He was agitated enough by the news and wrote straightaway to Cullen. McNally himself wrote from Maynooth on 8 September to a Reverend J. Duffy informing him that the Letters of the Holy Father had just arrived, one appointing him Bishop of Triconium *in partibus* and the other Coadjutor of Clogher *cum jure successionis*. At the moment, however, he is engaged in duties with the students' retreat. Shortly afterwards, he was to receive a letter from the Primate, Archbishop Crolly of Armagh, saying how glad he would be to perform the consecration ceremony, either in Maynooth or in Monaghan.

In the meantime, Dr. Russell was interested in the news from the West that Dr. Browne of Galway was to succeed Dr. Burke of Elphin, coupled with the gossip that Dr. Whitehead of Maynooth might succeed Dr. Browne. He was wondering and wrote to Cullen about it in September. It is hard to know what Cullen's thoughts really were. The Archbishop of Cashel, Dr. Slattery, was more outspoken. Writing to Renehan he says: "As to Galway, I make no doubt that *all* parties within College would agree to the translation of Mr. Whitehead but will the Galway Priests concur with them ? ......The Connaught folk are a very peculiar kind of People and that spirit of independence, which the Wardenship engendered amongst the Clergy, is yet alive, so that they may not be easily managed by the Archbishop if he wishes to have Lord Ffrench's Cousin appointed." As things turned out, he need not have worried; Dr. Whitehead remained at Maynooth.

One of the most acrimonious struggles about an episcopal appointment was to take place in 1849 when Dr. John O'Hanlon, Professor of Theology in the College, was being proposed for Armagh. O'Hanlon was a strong supporter of Archbishop McHale of Tuam and together with Dr. Whitehead and Dr. McNally (before he went to Clogher) constituted a kind of faction for his "party" at Maynooth. So Dr. Edmund O'Reilly had written to Cullen in December, 1844: "These men did their best to put persons of their side into the situations that became vacant. They machinated at the *concorsi* for professorships. Dr. McHale's party *as operating in this house* is mischievous ..... I do not look upon them as the friends of order. Dr. MacHale himself has given occasional signs of being a *turbulent* man, and his party seems to partake more or less of that character. Hence, I think, that party, *quatenus party*, as evil ...". O'Hanlon himself, in 1845, had made a similar denunciation to McNally of Dr. Patrick Murray, Dr. George Crolly and others of the staff, for "making to sink O'Connell ..... in the estimation of the students." He was critical too of O'Reilly, Renehan, Callan and even Russell. From all this it is clear that O'Hanlon could not count on too many friends in the College when the question came up of his possible appointment as Primate.

His colleague, Dr. Murray, found himself involved in the matter, for on 6 June of that year, the Bishop of Kilmore, in his own presence and that of the Bishops of Raphoe and Down and Connor, got him to make a sworn and signed statement about O'Hanlon for transmission to the Congregation of Propaganda. Murray's testimony is anything but flattering. The document can be found in the *Archives of Propaganda*. He speaks of O'Hanlon's proneness to anger, of how he often 'let go' at the authorities of the College, in the Aula Maxima and at Disputationes, and even before juniors and lay people. He, Murray, has consulted four prudent colleagues about this (under secrecy) and all are in agreement. While giving his views thus frankly, he is very concerned that they should not fall into the hands of O'Hanlon or of his episcopal patrons, for this would do himself no good. It was not the only time that Murray worried about a letter of his miscarrying.

Dr. O'Hanlon did have powerful friends. Dr. Browne of Elphin wrote to Rome in his favour in July, as also did Dr. Cantwell of Meath. Cantwell is emphatic that O'Hanlon is hoped for by every friend of ecclesiastical liberty in Ireland. The Government and some ecclesiastics are against him, but he would be a good choice. The candidates were Drs. Dixon of Maynooth and Kieran of Dundalk, as well as Dr. O'Hanlon. Around the same time, the Reverend Michael Lennon, a Parish Priest of Armagh, wrote saying that O'Hanlon was a stranger and Dixon timid; he would prefer Kieran.

Then in September, came a cannonade from Dr. Cantwell, at that time in the Irish College, Paris. He had just got a letter from a priest in Ireland telling him what the three Northern Bishops had done concerning

O'Hanlon in getting Murray to testify against him. He does not refer to Murray directly but to a professor of Maynooth "who is notorious for his calumny against every good and virtuous" man. It was remarkably strong language. Dr. Cantwell simply could not contain his indignation: *"Buon Dio ! chi potrebbe essere sicuro del suo bon nome con tāli testimoni, avanti un tal tribunale".* In his estimation, the former Deans and his former colleagues in Maynooth are for O'Hanlon, although Cantwell admits that those presently in Maynooth are not very favourable. But the Irish Bishops should not take this seriously if they are to be really interested in the good of the Church in Ireland.

Almost simultaneously with Dr. Cantwell's letter, the Archbishop of Tuam sent another, in favour of O'Hanlon. And like Cantwell, he insisted that the opinions of the professor who testified against him (Dr. Murray is not actually named) are nothing other than "atrocious calumnies." McHale was also in Paris just then. To back up their efforts, the next day (12 September, 1849), Drs Cantwell and McHale got two members of the staff of the Irish College, Paris, (O'Rourke of Achonry and Price of Cloyne) to sign a counterdeclaration in favour of O'Hanlon and dispatched it to the Congregation.

In the heel of the hunt, Dr. Dixon was appointed Primate and, although it was not to make for the best of relations with the Lion of the West, many people were in agreement. Fr. James Healy of Little Bray, who had entered Maynooth in 1843 and knew both Dixon and O'Hanlon, had this to say: Dr. O'Hanlon was "the ablest canonist of his day," but "was a destructive, not a constructive, theologian. He loved to demolish orally the arguments of all his ecclesiastical contemporaries, and to scatter to the four winds of heaven the dust of some of the most treasured authorities in the past. He left not one line of writing behind him. It was his custom to trace on a slate his most carefully digested views, and, when the class was over for the day, to erase all with a sponge or the sleeve of his coat."

Healy, as was his wont with the characters of whom he treated, trades yarns about Dr. O'Hanlon. Once, he tells us, O'Hanlon put a pinch of snuff into his own eye. "Again, intending to throw two letters into the fire, he consigned to the flames a valuable snuff-box and the key to his room." Healy also says, however, that O'Hanlon was consulted on knotty cases of conscience by bishops all over the world and his fund of wit and drollery made him welcome at the professors' table. Then comes the barb. "But for this reputation, he would probably have been raised by Rome to the Primacy" !

THE MAYNOOTH BATTERY

All sorts of things were happening in that then as now unique place that is Maynooth College. Under the able direction — indeed direction is too grand a term because he did nearly everything himself — of Professor Callan, Professor of Natural Philosophy, experiments were conducted there during the early Victorian period which were to create a name for the College for Experimental Physics. Under the heading 'Forgotten Genius', the Irish Electricity Supply Board's Magazine for December — January, 1977 - '78, goes so far as to say that it is now clear "that Callan by the 1830's had become Ireland's outstanding figure in the field of electromagnetics."

As early as 1832, Callan had penned a statement which meant that he was the discoverer of the principle of the self-induced dynamo, something that is usually attributed to Werner Siemens in a communication to the Berlin Academy of Science in 1867. In an article in the *Encyclopaedia Britannica* (1910), Dr. J. A. Fleming gives credit to Callan for the invention of the induction coil, previously attributed to Faraday (1831). In 1837, we find Callan sending a copy of this coil (the world's first) to Sturgeon in England, who exhibited it at the Electrical Exhibition in London that year, to the shrieks of the young bloods about town and their ladies. The copy was afterwards presented to Downside College. A year before, in 1836, Callan had constructed an electro-magnetic engine (he had begun it in 1834) and in 1837 he wrote: "I propose to construct an electro-magnetic machine that will do the work of one or two horses... From my experiments to date I conclude that with a battery of six square feet of zinc, my engine containing 40 electro-magnets will propel at the rate of 7 or 8 miles per hour a 13 cwt. carriage. An engine as powerful as the steam engine on the Kingstown Railway could be constructed for £250. It would weigh less than two tons and the annual expenditure would not exceed £300."

By 1839, Callan was in a better position to carry on his work. That year he had taken out probate on his father's will and was now endowed with private means, which enabled him to buy ample material for his researches and to employ the help of the local blacksmith at Maynooth. With that, by 1848, he was ready to test the largest primary battery ever made. Housed in cast iron, it electrocuted a large turkey and produced a dazzling arc light. *The Philosophical Magazine and Journal of Science*, published in London that year, contains Callan's own account of the invention:

> "I shall now describe a few of the experiments which were made with our large cast-iron battery on the 7th of last month. The first experiment consisted in passing the voltaic current through a very large turkey, which was instantly killed by the shock. The craw of the turkey was burst, and the hay and oats contained within it fell to the ground. In order to give the shock, a piece of tin-foil, about four inches square, was placed under each wing along the sides of the turkey, which were

previously stripped of their feathers, and moistened with dilute acid. The tinfoil was kept in close contact with the skin by pressing the wings against the sides. The person who held the turkey had a very thick cloth between each hand and the wing, in order to save him from the shock. As soon as the wire from the zinc end of the battery was put in contact with the tin-foil under one wing, sparks were given by the tin-foil, the shocks received by the turkey, before the connection was made between the negative end of the battery and the tin-foil under the other wing, although the negative and positive ends of the battery were on tables nearly 3 feet high, and 3 feet asunder.

"When a copper wire in connection with the negative end was put in contact with a brass ring connected with the zinc end of the battery, a brilliant light was instantly produced. The copper wire was gradually separated from the brass ring until the arc of light was broken. The greatest length of the arc was about 5 inches. As soon as the connexion was made between the opposite ends of the battery by the copper wire, which was ¼ of an inch thick, and about 5 feet long, a loud noise was produced by the combustion of the solder which fastened some of the copper slips to the zinc plates. I immediately went to the part of the battery from which the noise proceeded, in in order to try whether the connexion between the case-iron cells and zinc plates was broken; I found one slip of copper detached from the zinc plates to which it had been soldered. There were probably others disconnected with their zinc plates, but I did not find them. The result of this experiment showed that the turkey conducted only a part of the current circulated by the battery, for the current which killed the turkey produced no combustion of the solder by which the copper slips were attached to the zinc plates".

THE MAYNOOTH BATTERY

One wonders what would have been the reaction of such as the Animal Rights Movement or Animal Liberation Front of 1983,if they had existed in Callan's time. Yet without men like Callan, today's electrical amenities would not have developed. Even the Trustees of the Royal College were impressed. Otherwise they would not have agreed, as they did in October, 1854, that funds — some £19 — should be allowed for an electrical instrument for him and for the cast-iron cells of his new battery. By now the local blacksmith had become inadequate as helper. The new castings for the battery would appear to have been made in Belfast, for on 7 December, 1854, the Bishop of Down and Connor, Dr. Denvir, wrote to the President of Maynooth to tell him that Dr. Callan's castings would be finished "on Saturday evening next." He wished to know whether they should be sent to Dublin by railway or by steamboat. Callan was mightily pleased with his battery, and well he might be. Sometime in 1855, after closing the shutters of the Science Hall, he found that the arc-light was sufficiently intense to enable a person to read the smallest print at the most distant part of the room. The cost, by the way, was only 9 pence or 10 pence an hour — not enormous for such a luxury in those days. As a result, he was prompted to expound 'On a New Single Field Cell more powerful and less expensive in construction and use than any nitric acid cell.'

That same year, the 'Maynooth Battery', designed by Callan — a plate of zinc in an iron tank of acid — began to be commercially produced. It was a coincidence but an enthralling one that, in November of 1855, Newman, over in Dublin in connection with the Catholic University, prepared a lecture on Christianity and Physical Science for the School of Medicine. In it he advocated freedom of investigation. His approach was approved of by Dr. O'Reilly, whom he once described as "the best theologian he had ever known" (Ward), also by Dr. Russell, but deemed by most to be inexpedient in view of the prevailing temper on matters theological and the views of Dr. Cullen. The lecture was never delivered but was later published under the title 'Christianity and Scientific Investigation'. It was to be one of Newman's most famous papers.

By the late 1850's, Callan himself was to be rather famous. In 1855, according to one of the students: "Dr. Callan is still experimenting night and day with gases and metals. In fact there is no knowing where he will stop if his health does not fail. In the Physic Hall today before the whole class he had his Box hopping by itself all over the floor. But he is a very holy priest!". On Tuesday, 1 September, 1857, he read a paper in Dublin to a learned society. The following day, *The Freeman's Journal* reported: "The Rev. Prof. Callan (Maynooth College) communicated some exceedingly interesting discoveries, the result of experiments made by him on the electro-dynamic induction apparatus. The president, in introducing Professor Callan, referred to the great service which the reverend gentleman confirmed on science by his valuable discoveries." Callan's paper on that occasion, 'On the Induction Apparatus', was printed in full in *The Freeman's Journal* for Friday, 4 September. Actually, the decade 1853-64 was Callan's most prolific. During it he was to invent galvanized iron and patent it, also, as already mentioned, methods for using electricity for lighting, even though they were not actually employed until the 1880's in Liverpool. His coils he produced on request for scientists in many countries.

Chapter II

Imperial Largesse

At the beginning of Victoria's reign the Royal Catholic College found itself in straitened financial circumstances. By the standards of the time, it would not appear to have been too badly off, at least in its provision for the staff. In 1838, the President commanded a salary of £326 per annum, the Vice-President £150, the Senior Dean, Bursar and three Professors of Theology £122 each, the Prefect of the Dunboyne Establishment £142, the Junior and Second Junior Dean, the Professors of Scripture, Mathematics and Elocution, Natural Philosophy, Logic, Metaphysics and Ethics, Humanity, English Elocution and the Irish Language £112 each, and the Secretary to the Trustees £73. But the provision for the students was not at all adequate and the buildings had gone into disrepair. Thackeray's impressions were not altogether without foundation.

THE ROYAL COFFERS

In September, 1838, a committee was appointed to draw up a memorial to the Lord Lieutenant on the subject of an increased Parliamentary Grant. It was raised again in 1839. But the tide was not running favourably for the College just then. On the contrary, due to resentment against Catholic Emancipation and the Repeal Agitation, there were many voices ready to criticise Maynooth. In June and July, 1835, The Times of London had carried four articles, and in July no less than eight articles, critical of Dens's Theology, which was said to be followed in the College. In 1839, the beginnings of a full attack on the existing grant were evident in a number of publications by the Protestant Association, issued in London. One of these was The Popish College of Maynooth, by 'the author of The Progress of Popery'. Another was The Speech of J. C. Colquhoun Esq. M.P. upon The Maynooth Grant.

These wanted the withdrawal of the grant altogether. In the same vein was *Twenty Letters on Popery*, by 'a Layman', commenced in 1839 and published as a unity in 1842. It was very critical of the textbooks used at Maynooth, notably those by "Messrs. Delahogue and Bailly." *The Times* too kept up its campaign, reporting periodically during 1839 and 1840 about attacks on Maynooth made at Conservative Association banquets and meetings in places like Blackburn, Pudsey, Bolton and Barnsley. In 1840 the third edition of Delahogue's *Tractatus de Mysterio S.S. Trinitatis* had been published, of all places in Belfast, as the attribution has it "Belfastiae, ex typis Josephi Smith". Across in Colchester, at a dinner of the Essex Conservative Association on 17 November, another Smyth, Sir G. H. Smyth, had castigated the classbooks of Maynooth as containing what could only be described as "beastly doctrines". *The Essex Standard* faithfully reported him.

Whether the signs augured well or not, the Trustees had to do something about the College finances. True, a bequest had been received following the death of one of the original French professors, Dr. Anglade. In January, 1840, Dr. McNally sent £150 from this to Rome to Cullen for the purchase of books for the Library. McNally was Anglade's executor. Anglade had been generous also to the poor of the Maynooth neighbourhood, having left £200 towards creating a fund to give breakfast to poor children attending the convent schools. *Notes* by Mrs McKeever, the first Reverend Mother, which are kept in Maynooth Presentation Convent, declare that "he was one of the best friends and benefactors of this community." He had left a further £400 for the general benefit of the convent.

The College, however, was in dire need. In June, the Trustees decided that, owing to the insufficiency of funds to meet the current expenses of the College, twenty-seven free places, i.e., one for each diocese, should be suppressed and notice given that the Trustees at their next meeting should consider the expediency of applying to Parliament for an increase of the Annual Grant. Expediency was the order of the day. It was only natural that the Trustees should have added a "dutiful address" of congratulation to the Queen and the Prince Consort following the escape of Her Majesty from the attempt that had just been made on her life.

The situation had not improved by April, 1841, when Mr. Fennelly resigned as Bursar and left for India. At the very meeting which received his resignation, the Trustees found it necessary to agree to seek a loan of £1,500 from the Bank of Ireland on the joint and individual security of the four Archbishops, Drs. Crolly, Murray, Slattery and McHale. The following November, a general meeting of the Bishops was held, caused by the "embarrassed state of Maynooth College — £4,500 in debt". A petition to Parliament for an increased grant was the result.

At the time, nothing was forthcoming, and 1842 passed without any increase in funds. So did 1843, despite renewed soundings by the College during the previous Winter to ascertain whether an increase might be possible. In a way, Maynooth was being lucky to retain even what it had, for in March, 1841, Mr. Colquhoun was again attacking it in Parliament, supported by Sir Robert Inglis, member of Oxford University.

As far as can be ascertained, this Inglis was not related to the traveller, H. D. Inglis, already referred to. Born in 1786, he was an old-fashioned Tory, a strong churchman too, with many prejudices and no great ability. But he accurately represented the opinions of the country gentlemen of his time and his genial manner and high character are said to have enabled him to exercise considerable influence over the House of Commons, where he was very popular. In Robert Inglis, Maynooth had a redoubtable opponent.

Colquhoun's motion — for the repeal of the statutes by which Maynooth had been established — was welcomed by the *Dublin University Magazine* for April. It hoped that the raising of the issue would lead to a full thrashing out of the Maynooth question. It would be good if Maynooth could be got rid of, because its work had arrested the dissolution of Popery in Ireland. It is obvious that at that time Maynooth and Trinity were far from being friends. But on this occasion O'Connell defended Maynooth effectively in Parliament, one of the few times that he did so.

Nonetheless, the gates had been opened and Maynooth came in for an attack that it could well have done without. That Spring, the *Quarterly Review* made the suggestion that it was high time for a full investigation of the extent of the Romish intrigues for which it had been responsible: "The Jesuits, through the first Principal, Dr. Hussey, Dr. Tray *(sic)*, Father Betagh, Dr. Murray, and Mr. Kenny *(sic)*, soon procured access to Maynooth, and that it by degrees passed into their hands, or under their influence, can no longer be doubted. What connection exists between Maynooth and Clongowes will be well worth the attention of the Legislature". Sir G. H. Smyth was also back in the fray, with the publication of his *Maynooth College: Justification of the term 'beastly' as applied to the Instruction at Maynooth College:* (Colchester, 1841). Having been challenged by Rev. J. E. North, R. C. priest of Stoke, near Colchester, to justify this application, he had entered the fray on Tuesday, 13 April, before "a numerous assemblage of the gentry, clergy and others of Colchester and its vicinity", in the library of Colchester Castle. Mr. North, he says, declined to be present, because he had wanted the discussion to be restricted to six on each side. When it took place, the public were admitted by ticket, without restriction of creed, but persons of immature age were excluded. Fair enough, since Bailly's *Treatise on Matrimony* was amongst the texts examined, and "involuntary exclamations of horror and disgust frequently burst forth from the auditory". It is hard to know who was the most affronted, the audience or Bailly, who had written and was lampooned for having done so: *"Debitum nec reddi potest, nec pati in loco publico, nec coram liberis, aut domesticis; nec eo modo qui sit contra naturam. Proh. pudor !!!"*. The Chairman had declared that Smyth was fully justified in what he had said about such textbooks ....

In the College things were in such short supply that the Summer vacations for 1841, which would normally have been from 1 July to 25 August, were prolonged to 1 September, and no student was permitted to remain in College during that period. The reason was the increased price of provisions and the accumulated debt. In a later letter, the Reverend Matthew Flanagan, Secretary to the Trustees, made the point that the latter "reluctantly had recourse, amongst other retrenchments, to a prolonged and compulsory Vacation as a means of diminishing the expenditure of the College". *The Parliamentary Papers: Accounts and Papers* (col. XXVIII, 1845) contain the relevant data. From correspondence in the *President's Archives* at Maynooth there is plenty of evidence that the students were not enamoured of some of the "retrenchments" that the College had seen fit to make. In 1842 Mr. Flanagan sent Renehan a copy of a reply which he had just been directed by the Trustees to forward to certain student petitioners: "1. To the Theologians: — — Gentlemen, I lost no time in laying your Petition before the Trustees who desired me to inform you that after the most attentive consideration of it, they find it to contain no permanent cause of just complaint and they have such entire reliance on your superiors that they are sure if any casual cause of complaint shall at any time occur it will be immediately removed on a respectful application being made to them. 2. In Answer to the Members of the Choir: — Gentlemen, I read your Petition for the Trustees and am directed to inform you that they are of the opinion, and have given directions accordingly, that you shall be allowed tea and cakes without wine, on Easter Sunday Evenings and at breakfast the following morning."

On 17 April, 1843, Easter Monday, the Triennial Visitation took place. It is a measure of the docility of the place in those days that when those assembled were asked as to whether they had any questions about the running of the College, a "profound silence" reigned. That is when the Lord Chancellor, Sir Edward Sugden, "highly eulogised the College" *(College Records)*. By June, the pictures of St. Patrick and St. Joseph that had been commissioned earlier had arrived and sixteen pounds was voted to the Bursar to cover their cost, together with the expense of carriage, duty and frames !

In England, Sir Robert Peel was beginning to interest himself in Maynooth. That very year he was the recipient of an expostulation from Lord Stanley to the effect that the Maynooth Grant was unjustified: "And though the withdrawal of the grant would engender very bitter feelings, its continuance on its present scale, and subject to the present conditions, does not effect the object which I conceive to have been originally contemplated, of giving the State at once a control over the education and a hold upon the affection or the interests of the Roman Catholic priesthood." In Stanley's opinion, "an inquiry conducted with temper (if such a thing can be on Irish subjects) into the character of the institution" might be thought about.

On the other end of the scale, *The Dublin Review*, under Russell's able leadership, defended Maynooth's claim to increased revenue in a review of Thackeray's *Irish Sketch Book*, which had just appeared: "Mr. Thackeray, perhaps, did not know that the income is not equal to the essential charges laid upon it; that every gain which economy the most rigid, by self-denying rules, can effect, goes to further the real purposes of the establishment — the furnishing of as many clergy as possible to the people; and that had a choice to be made between mere outward show, and more numerous pupils, zeal, and a sense of duty, would infallibly plead in favour of the latter. But, at least, the pains which he took to enquire into the whole system of ... comparatively paltry institutions .... might have been not unworthily bestowed upon making himself acquainted with something more at Maynooth, than ..... the roasting of the mutton". The wheel had come full circle and Maynooth had dealt with Thackeray.

THE RIGHT HON. MR. PEEL

It was in February, 1844, that Sir Robert Peel first came to prominence in relation to Maynooth. McDowell, in his *Public Office in Ireland, 1801-46*, sets out the background as Peel saw it: "The existing grant to Maynooth was insufficient and the State gained no credit 'for indulgence or liberality'. The standard of living and the habits engendered at the college produced every year 'fifty spiritual firebrands', sour malignant demagogues, instinctively by their low birth hostile to the law, living by agitation, and fitted to it, 'by our elementary but penurious system of education' ".

As early as 6 February, 1844, a letter against increasing the Maynooth Grant had appeared in *The Standard*. In face of this, it was not only enlightened but courageous of Peel, on Sunday, 11 February, to have penned a memorandum for the Cabinet on two subjects, one of which was about Maynooth. The fact that the memorandum was 'secret' does not matter. It ran: "First, the state of Maynooth, and the education provided at Maynooth for those who are hereafter to be the parochial clergy of Ireland. Each year we grant a sum of money for the education of the priesthood. It is insufficient for its purpose, and the practical result seems anything but favourable. The State gets no credit for indulgence or liberality. The style of living, the habits engendered at the College, the requirements probably of the tutors and professors, bearing a relation to the stipends provided for them, all combine to send forth a priesthood embittered rather than conciliated by the aid granted by the State for their education, and connected by family ties, from the character of the institution, with the lower classes of society rather than with the arist-ocracy or gentry of the country ..... Can we undertake to appoint a Select Committee for the investigation of the state of Maynooth College, avowedly for the purpose of improving the character of the education there given, elevating the condition of the persons admitted within its walls, and this with the certain prospect before us of an increase to the vote for Maynooth as the result of the inquiry ?" Peel sent a copy of this to the royal couple.

The Cabinet did nothing. Still, he must have been greatly encouraged when, on the 16th of the month, Prince Albert wrote to him saying: "I return the *private* memorandum respecting Maynooth, and repeat to you my regret, that you were *not* enabled to carry out your wise intentions. The Queen joins with me in hoping that you may in no distant time overcome the difficulties which now stand in your way." February 18th brought further encouragement, this time from Lord Stanley. It concerned Gladstone: "From a few words which I have had with Glad-stone, I think he might be brought to assent to a remodelling of May-nooth and its establishment as one of three or more provincial colleges... I should like to see three colleges established; one in the north, if necessary, at which Presbyterians might receive education, one in Munster and one in Connaught, which would be principally but not exclusively Catholic; in which young men destined for the priesthood might receive *a liberal* ecclesiastical education, in connection with a general education which they would share with others not so destined; and the conversion of Maynooth into a similar establishment, unless it were possible to engraft a Roman Catholic religious education, as a separate branch, on Trinity Coll-ege, Dublin — and this last, I fear, would be found impracticable".

William Ewart Gladstone was then, at thirty-three, a very young member of the Cabinet. He had been President of the Board of Trade since May, 1843. He was interested in Peel's proposition about the Maynooth Grant as part of a policy of conciliation in Ireland. Either do it right or don't do it at all was Peel's message. For one such as Gladstone this had merits. Yet, despite Stanley's impressions, it quickly became evident to Peel that things were complicated. On 12 July, Gladstone wrote to him indicating that he would be happy to be appointed envoy in Florence or Naples, and by Autumn it was clear to him that, if he went ahead with the idea of increasing the Maynooth Grant, he would lose Gladstone.

At Maynooth itself things were tranquil. Early in March, the Vice-Pres-ident, Dr. Renehan, brought out a *Choir Manual* and received a letter of thanks from Dr. Murphy of Cork (whose manuscripts he was to inherit), who noted that his views on Plain Chant "are very conformable to those of the Pope's Cardinal Vicar at Rome." He did complain though that nobody knew the price of the book and hoped that it would be saleable to the public at large and not just to the students.

A recent past student, the Rev. Denis Brasbie of Kerry, was on that 30 May sent by his Bishop, Cornelius Egan, to minister in Kilmalkedar. He did not like his posting, quarrelled with the Bishop, and on 21 July renounced the Church of Rome in Dingle Church of Ireland. He was later to describe the young priests of his day "as issuing from Maynooth with ardent and blind zeal; filled with the sincere belief of the Romish tenets" and, like himself, unfitted to decide things for themselves: "I have read no history since I left Maynooth and there we read only 'one-sided histories' where Protestantism is represented as the persecutor, and Romanism the victim". Dr. Renehan of Maynooth was to hear about Brasbie again.

Life in the College went on. Russell was writing to Cullen to tell him that Mr. Ruskin had been to Ireland and was to go to Rome, also seeking a Roman MS. for a book which he was writing. Dr. Montague, the aged President of the College, had an ulcer in the mouth and was quite out of sorts. Later in the year he resigned.

Given the precarious financial position in which the College found itself at this time, it is hard to understand how Maynooth could have harboured ideas about development. That it did emerges from a memorandum prepared for Archbishop Murray which is to be found amongst Dr. Renehan's papers. It is hard to know whether it was ever posted, as the Maynooth document is folded and addressed. In it Renehan reports that, in compliance with Murray's desire, he has conferred with his confreres "on the expediency of having a Brief obtained to authorise the collation of Academical Degrees in this College" and on the qualifications which candidates should possess.

All, he says, agree on the first point. There is no need to labour the reasons for it. Renehan points to the large number of universities in many continental countries — in some one to a million inhabitants, in some even one to half a million. Degrees in the Faculty of Theology are conferred in all of these. The undoubted learning of the Irish Catholic Clergy should, as elsewhere, be recognized by appropriate degrees.

He adds that Ireland has always been in the forefront in this respect. Within a century after the institution of academical degrees, and before Germany, Holland and several other countries had instituted a university, and while there was as yet scarcely a dozen such schools in the universe, "Dr. Leke", a predecessor of Dr. Murray's, had applied to Pope Clement V and in 1311 had obtained a Brief for erecting one in Dublin. This was confirmed under Dr. Bicknor by Pope John XXII in 1320 "and there were accordingly created at that time some Doctors in Theology and others in Canon Law".

He continues that on the petition of the Regular Orders, on 27 April, 1475, Pope Sixtus IV had issued a Bull granting their request to erect a new university in Dublin. The Catholic College founded in 1628-9 at Dublin has also been styled a university, although Renehan cannot say whether any new faculties were ever received by it. Maynooth has the requisite qualifications. In respect of these, there is a strong feeling at Maynooth that more talent, a more searching examination and altogether a higher standard should be demanded than is at Rome, especially because "everything Irish is undervalued at home".

He emphasises that in Rome no extra studies are required for the Doctorate and the lower degrees demand no more than what competency for orders does at Maynooth. In truth, the doctorate student in Rome is no more than the first-class ordinary student at Maynooth. Paris, Salamanca and Louvain demand more than does Rome. Oxford and Cambridge require much standing (years of study) rather than much talent.

Renehan then goes on to suggest his own ideas for qualifications for the Bachelor of Arts., M.A., Bachelor of Divinity, Licentiate of Divinity and Doctor of Divinity. At Maynooth, he says, out of every twelve students in a class of average ability, six would have talent enough for the degree of AB, four for AM, three for B, two for L and one for the Doctorate in Divinity.

It was a remarkable statement and very likely true, whatever about Renehan's lack of diplomacy. He was never noted for that. Indeed the lack of it shows through also in a long letter of 7 November, 1844, on the reasons for an increased grant to Maynooth. They included: "the insufficiency of the Masters' salaries which .... were better suited to the condition of menial servants than that of Scholars and Professors ... the plain style of our buildings ... inferior to the ordinary style of a Poor House or barrack ..... the want of suitable furniture in our halls, refectory and apartments, the want of suitable accommodation and comfort for the students". The estimate allows only £23 per head for each of only 250 students − to cover "subsistence, including coals, commons, candles, furniture, repairs, etc." An increase is needed for all such items. A proper library is also badly needed. The place presently used for such "is on a third storey and exposed to considerable peril from 14 fires burning day and night directly under it in the rooms of so many Dunboyne students" !

This letter was addressed to "My Lord". Whether it was a civil or ecclesiastical person that was involved, we do not know; the copy is even incomplete. Indeed, like the document about the university, we don't even know whether it was ever sent. Most likely, it was a draft of a document to the Lord Lieutenant, which Renehan knew would shortly be asked for. That was on 7 November, 1844. On 9 November, Russell was writing to Cullen informing him that the President is to resign and that Dr. Renehan is expected to be appointed in his place. That was not to come until June, 1845.

On 14 November, 1844, the Maynooth Trustees ordered the Secretary and the President of the College to draw up an address to the Lord Lieutenant, "soliciting his Excellency's kind interposition with the Government in favour of the intended application to Parliament for an increased grant" on the same terms on which the former grants were made. The Archbishop of Cashel felt that it might be necessary to get the power of attorney for Renehan to follow this up, in place of Montague whose health was declining rapidly. He was optimistic for the future: "I am delighted to find that everything goes on well in the College and sincerely hope matters may so continue".

The memorial to the Lord Lieutenant was duly presented at the turn of the year. It was long and compelling in nature, complaining about many things — the mere fifteen foot high ceiling to the chapel, the entire lack of "architectural ornament or academical character", the abridgement of courses and the condition of the library — and here we can see Renehan's hand — "exposed to peril from fourteen fires burning night and day directly under it". Peel was in a quandary. Gladstone especially worried him; he was clearly opposed to increasing the Maynooth Grant. As Sir James Graham wrote to Peel, on 4 January, 1845, referring back to the letter of the previous July about an envoyship, "though Gladstone's letter is obscure, the resolution, I fear, is taken; and you must consider his note as an announcement that, if we proceed with our Maynooth measure, he will retire before the meeting of Parliament". On 21 January, a 'secret' letter from Gladstone confirmed this.

Around the same time, the Chief Secretary, Henry Goulburn, declared to Peel that the Master of Trinity, Cambridge, liberal though he was, was fearful of the measure. Goulburn himself regarded it as "putting arms into the hands of the enemy". The climate in the College at this time is well conveyed in a letter from Edmund O'Reilly to Cullen (21 January, 1845). Religion and politics, he says, is the big issue right now. There has been unrest about the Church Bequests Bill. Maynooth is in an awkward position as the Government is asked to increase the grant to it. "Some of us in the College have said in joke that if the Government require *an additional candle* to be put on the parlour table after dinner, the innovation would be deemed insufferable. I fear such would in matters of not much importance be the case. I have been told some of the Bishops are quite ready *at the least provocation* to withdraw their subjects and set up another college to be maintained by voluntary contributions of the people. *The Maynoothians* would then be looked on as *an odious governmental pack*". It was not the last time that the Irish Bishops threatened to abandon Maynooth.

On Tuesday, 4 February, 1845, Peel announced the introduction of two new measures, one the 'Maynooth Bill', the second relating to other university provisions in Ireland, the 'Colleges Bill'. He was ably helped by some of his Ministers, such as Sir James Graham, also by the Lord Lieut-

enant, Baron Heytesbury, and by Anthony Blake, the lay Catholic comm-
issioner on the Board of National Education. It was proposed to provide
for an increase in the annual grant to Maynooth from £9,000 to £26,000,
so as to allow 500 students to be accommodated. In his *A History of
Ireland under the Union* (London, 1952), P.S. O'Hegarty says that "the
object of the educational concessions was to outflank and weaken Repeal;
to draw the Church from it by increasing materially the endowment of
Maynooth, and to draw the middle classes from it by giving them facilities for university education".

Gladstone, true to predictions, was against the Maynooth proposal. He
immediately announced his resignation from the Board of Trade and
tendered his decision to the Queen. In some ways, it is hard to understand
his motives, he who had published a stout defence of the establishment
of the Church of England *(The State in its Relations to the Church,*
London, 1838). On the other hand, it could be argued that his book was
against any Church establishment *except* that of the Church of England.
At any rate, Gladstone resigned from the Board of Trade, thereby losing
his seat in the Cabinet.

Peel's proposal went ahead. There were many speeches for and against
it. Lord Sandon, while not aware of the peculiarities of the position in
Maynooth, considered it an inheritance from the past and as such they
had a duty "to carry out the spirit of the engagement entered into with
the Irish parliament". Others had different views. Peel, however, was not
to be put off. As he saw things, the grant was inadequate, professors'
salaries being "below the allowance for reputable clerks" and the President being compelled frequently to save on catering by sending students
home for a couple of months. He had a long, hard haul before him.

ENEMIES IN WAIT

Peel had no sooner indicated that he proposed to proceed with the
increased grant than the enemies of Maynooth began to clamour. Within
a week, Lord Ashley noted in his diary: "The country is becoming
furious, the Free Church of Scotland, the 'religious public' of England,
Wesleyans, dissenters, all alike are protesting and petitioning". And so
indeed they were. One clergyman from Liverpool said that those who
supported the grant "might as well found a college for the promotion of
theft and adultery, and the difference between the Maynooth priest and
the polished Jesuit is that between the highwayman and the pickpocket".

Naturally, Maynooth had defenders who were in favour of the increase
being granted. *The Freeman's Journal* ran an article on 7 February,
entitled 'Educational Facilities in Maynooth and Trinity', which demanded that "the honours, emoluments and advantages of Trinity College
shall not be the exclusive property of one-tenth portion of the people of

this country". The near neighbour of the College, the Duke of Leinster, wrote from Carton to Eneas MacDonnell, Esq. on the 13th of the month saying that he was in favour of the measure: "As a Magistrate, residing near the College of Maynooth, I can bear testimony to the general good and peaceful conduct of its inmates, and I think they fully deserve the proposed increase of the Parliamentary Grant". Before the end of the year, MacDonnell was to publish his own *Letter to the Rt. Hon. W. E. Gladstone respecting the Maynooth Grant* (London, 1845).

The signs of opposition, however, were ominous. On 24 February, *The Freeman's Journal* was reporting on a meeting of the previous Friday held in the New Infant School, Southwark, J. D. Plumptre presiding, to oppose the grant, while, between 8 February and 13 March, Dudley M. Perceval, Esq. wrote three letters to *The Morning Herald* to the same end. The College itself seemed to be hopeful about the outcome. We find the Bishop of Ferns writing to Renehan that March conveying his pleasure at hearing that Dr. Montague was recovering, and his hope "that the present prospects of the College will add years to his life". Dr. Russell spent Shrove Tuesday with some friends near Maynooth and was shocked at having stayed on too late. He published some verses about the incident in *Dolman's Magazine*, entitled 'Shrovetide Festivities Prolonged':

> "What! feasting still, though long ago
> Midnight hath chimed on high
> And the waning stars more faintly glow
> Along the eastern sky,
> Depart, thou thoughtless one, depart !
> Or stay — to pray and mourn,
> To mourn and think that 'Dust thou art',
> To dust thou shalt return".

Early in March, the Vice-President, Dr. Renehan, wrote to Rome to Cullen giving him details about Peel's proposition. He is hopeful that it will go through and that the College will soon have more students and buildings, including a new chapel and library, without likelihood of Government interference. But there is always reason for a *'timeo Danaos'*. He himself would prefer no increase if the people's respect for the clergy were to be endangered. "Dan's thunder and the Queen's intended visit to Ireland may help to protect us".

Every protection possible would be needed: the Protestants were sharpening their knives. On 12 March, the Committee of the Congregational Union of England and Wales passed resolutions against the Maynooth Grant. Then, with the holding of a public meeting in Exeter Hall, London, on 18 March, what came to be known as the Anti-Maynooth Committee got off the ground. It is not surprising that one of its moving forces was the Reverend Baptist Wriothesley Noel. He had visited Maynooth in 1836 and had in no way been impressed. And so on 18 March, 1845, a Central Committee was set up to fight the increased grant by pamphlets, meetings, the use of the press and petitions to Parliament, deputations to M.P's and a national day of prayer. In Dublin *The Freeman's Journal* noted these preparations by "the organs of effoete fanaticism" to stimulate opposition to Maynooth, but noted too that information had just been received through one of the London evening papers *(The Sun)* that Peel had announced his intention to see his measure through.

On 24 March, Parliament went into recession and the big wait for the Maynooth Bill began. Its opponents did not let grass grow under their feet. What *The Freeman's Journal* called symptoms of bigotry and organized agitation became plainly evident. March 26 saw resolutions against the grant passed by the British Anti-State-Church Association. This at least was logical for, as *The Freeman's Journal* noted , resistance to all establishments was the only honest way of opposing the grant. On that issue the Non-Conformists had no problem. Hence 26 March also saw anti-grant resolutions passed by the Committee of the Baptist Union of Great Britain, and 1 April resolutions by the Deputies of Protestant Dissenters of three denominations in and within twelve miles of London. The latter were to follow this up on 9 April by resolutions on the part of the General Body of Dissenting Ministers in the same area.

In an effort to press home the point that the grant was incompatible with separation of Church and State, on 31 March, Sir Culling Eardley Smith, Bart., Chairman of the Central Anti-Maynooth Committee, wrote *Maynooth: A Letter to Daniel O'Connell, Esq. M.P.* (London, 1845). If O'Connell is for religious liberty, urges Smith, how could he favour a grant which is an endowment of religion ?

There was no shortage of anti-grant protesters in Ireland among defenders of the religious establishment there. Prominent members of the Church of Ireland and of Trinity College had no qualms about ranging themselves against Maynooth. A meeting was held in the Rotunda on 31 March at which an effort to marshall public opinion on it — 'orchestrate' is the word that would be used today — was made. *The Freeman's Journal* reported that it was a "so-so affair" and that, as the meeting dispersed, there were scuffles following 'No Popery' cries and the police had to intervene.

The same day, that newspaper carried another piece, entitled 'Trinity College v the College of Maynooth', which dealt with a Petition from the Trinity electors to the Representatives of the University of Dublin. In respect of Maynooth, the petitioners had claimed that it was "inconsistent with the duty which a Christian people owe to God to endorse an institution for the education of the ministers of a church whose principles are directly opposed to His revealed will and the true religion established amongst us, but likewise to convey to your honourable house their sincere conviction, that if parliament were really aware of the course of inst-ruction pursued in that college, and its necessary influence on the morals and social order of the country, they would feel it inconsistent with right principle and sound policy to give such system endowment and perpetuity".

The Freeman's Journal certainly played a creditable role in its defence of Maynooth in 1845. It kept a weather-eye on its opposite numbers across the Irish Sea. Thus on Wednesday, 2 April, as the day for the prop-osal of the Bill in Parliament (3 April) approached, it noted that *The Standard, The Herald, The Globe* and *The Morning Post* were busy grumb-ling about lack of State control in compensation for an increased grant, and added: "Once, for all, we tell the *Globe* there shall be no State control permitted". Fighting words indeed.

The Times, for some strange reason, did not begin to exercise itself about the matter until 2 April, when it ran its first article opposing the grant, which it made out to be the first step towards the endowment of the Roman Catholic religion in Ireland. This was reproduced by *The Freeman's Journal* for 3 April, which also had a leading article 'Endow-ment of Maynooth — Difficulties of the Premier'. What, it asked, would happen if Peel should fall by reason of his proposal to endow Maynooth adequately? *The Times* has been dumb up to now but now it has spoken and it is obvious that the endowment is to be opposed by it. "The Coming Debate" is scheduled for "this night".

THE GREAT DEBATE

On Thursday, 3 April, Peel moved for leave to bring in the Maynooth Bill. A more liberal salary should, he said, be paid to the staff, £260 and £270 for professors of theology, and £600 or £700 for the President. There should be 500 free places for students, the three senior classes receiving a stipend of £20 each for expenses and the Dunboyne students £40. He was supported by Lord John Russell, leader of the Whigs. Late that night, the motion was carried by a majority of 102, with 216 for it and 114 against. *The Greville Memoirs* call this majority "a queer one, for above 100 of his own people voted against him, and above 100 of the Whigs with him .... The Carlton Club was in a state of insurrection afterward and full of sound and fury .... It is a very odd state of things and may be productive of great events before long".

The Freeman's Journal of 7 April carried a full account of the debate of the previous Thursday and was gratified at what it saw as Peel's triumph. It went to pains to make sure that he was not misreported or Maynooth portrayed in a bad light: "We have authority to correct a mistake in which the London reporters or printers have fallen at that part of Sir Robert Peel's speech where the right hon. baronet is made to say — 'It is impossible to assign to each of those students a room for his accommodation; in many cases several of them are placed in one room —

and even in some instances in one bed'. The latter words were not used on the occasion, nor had such at any time ever been the case; the words of Sir Robert Peel were 'several in one garret' "!

There was a long way to go yet and indignation against the Maynooth Bill mounted. *The Greville Memoirs* for 6 April had it that "everybody is talking about the great stir that is making in the country against the Maynooth grant", and *The Mail* for 7 April maintained that the Tory minority was in high spirits, calculating on the defeat of the grant on the second reading of the Bill. On 8 April, *The Freeman's Journal* paid tribute to Peel and, incidentally, printed the text of the Bill.

Those in favour of it were not taking any chances. O'Connell had received letters from Pierce Mahony, Anthony Blake and a number of others, urging him to come to London or the cause would be lost. He did so and its propsects brightened. Henry Warburton, however, urged him not to endanger the Bill by injudicious words. Writing from the Reform Club at two o'clock in the morning of 8 April, he had the temerity to say to O'Connell: "If you can come into the House on Friday, and there meet with perfect calmness and indifference those noisy expressions of dislike which are sure to come from some quarters, and to speak in commendation of the measure, I think your presence will do good; and though you are excitable, I think you have that command over yourself not to lose your temper under any provocation, when by remaining calm you can effect a great good".

O'Connell's interventions on behalf of Maynooth had always been sparse. He does not seem to have liked the place very much, or at least not what it had come to be towards the second quarter of the century. He is said to have expressed a preference for the kind of place it had been earlier. In any case, he was a liberal at heart, of the kind that did not approve of the endowment of church institutions. When he was persuaded to speak in its favour, he was usually brief and not to the point, as when he called its opponents, Colonels Verner, Sibthorpe and Perceval, "the Church militant of the House" and raised peals of laughter by concluding with a parody on Dryden, which commemorated that two of them looked as if they had never need to shave, whereas the third was all beard:

> "Three colonels in three different counties born
> Did Lincoln, Sligo and Armagh adorn;
> The first in gravity of face surpassed,
> The next in bigotry — in both the last.
> The force of Nature could not further go;
> To beard the third she shaved the other two".

Now he would need all his aplomb, for on 9 April, the private correspondent of *The Freeman's Journal* was reporting from London that the opposition to the Maynooth grant increased "with the heat of the weather

.... This you would hardly expect, the dog days being yet so distant".
He went on to say that many small meetings, inaccessible to reporters,
were being held in back parlours and that a number of inflammatory
placards had been posted throughout the city during the past few days.
He sent on a copy of one which he had found stuck to a pump:

'Endowment of Maynooth'
'Protestants of England, are you prepared to pay out of your hard-earned
savings for a Popish Establishment ?'
'The second reading of the Maynooth bill stands for Friday next'
'Sir Robert Peel has refused more time'
'Send up petitions to London and Demand it'

A deputation, led by Sir Culling E. Smith, had called on Peel asking for
more time but was refused.

It is hard to convey the extent and vehemence of the anti-Maynooth
campaigners. *The Freeman's Journal* said: "We perceive, from the provincial journals, that in several dioceses meetings, under the auspices of
the clergy of the district, are advertised. Petitions lie for signature in
different parts of the metropolis; and, in every imaginable way – from
the pulpit, the press, and the platform an opposition unprecedented in
zeal, extent and concentrated energies, will be brought to bear against
the bill. The scene which will be exhibited in the House of Commons
on Friday next, will, we venture to predict, be unexampled".

A good example of the kind of thing that the newspaper had in mind
occurred on the very day that this report appeared. At a public meeting
at Yarmouth a speech (later printed by the *Norfolk News*) was delivered
by the Rev. Wm. Brock castigating the endowment of Maynooth. There
was "immense cheering" when he said: "How singular, how passing
strange, how utterly incredible, that whilst the constitution shudders
from its extremities to its heart at the damnable doctrines which are
inculcated at Maynooth, Maynooth should be sanctioned with its patronage, and provided with a princely income from its funds". And there
was a "profound sensation" when the Reverend Gentleman went on to
say: "I want words to express the musings of my spirit, as I see my
country thus waiting, like a jackal, upon the roaring lion, which is going
about amidst the beauteous scenes of verdant civilization and incipient
christianity, asking whom he may devour". Well might Maynooth shudder
at such eloquent and profound animadversions ....

For his part, Peel was addressing the Queen. He wrote to her on 9 April
to inform her that he would move the second reading of the Maynooth
Bill on Friday, 11 April. He considers the bill so vital as to be ready to
risk the fate of the Government on it. He has had an interview that
morning with Mr. Blake, who showed him a letter from Archbishop
Murray expressing entire satisfaction with the measure. The Queen was

quite gratified. She wrote: "We are anxious to hear the effect which has been produced by the Maynooth Bill in Ireland. The Queen anxiously hopes Sir Robert does not feel uneasy about the result of the debate. The measure is so great and good a one, that people must open their eyes, and will not oppose it". At last the Queen was thinking of her Irish subjects. In Ireland, at least some of those who were aware of what Peel's step entailed were also delighted. On 10 April, Bishop McNally, of Clogher wrote to Renehan: "you can, I suppose, think or speak of nothing at Maynooth but the astonishing Bill of Sir Robert Peel, which is pregnant with such important consequences and which will in all likelihood be, in a few days, the Law of the Land".

Simultaneously, *The Freeman's Journal* was reporting from its London correspondent that both the Maynooth grant and Peel's Ministry were in danger. The big hazard was an amendment proposed by a Conservative member, Henry George Ward, to the effect that the finances necessary for the grant be taken from the funds of the established Church of Ireland This could easily topple the Bill. *The Globe* for 10 April said that all depended on Ward's motion going through. Sir Robert Inglis warmly supported it. Before the debate opened on Friday, the 11th, however, it had emerged that the Liberals, or at least their leaders, would not support it. This should clinch the issue, thought *The Freeman's Journal*. And so indeed it did. Ward withdrew his amendment and despite hectic activity all day in the Commons by petitioners against the Bill and *The Mail*'s conjecture that evening that the downfall of Peel was a *fait accompli*, the second reading of the Maynooth College Bill was moved. The public securities, which had become depressed during the day due no doubt as to how things would go, had not yet returned to normal.

During the debate the Prime Minister said of Maynooth: "This institution, whether good or bad, is, beyond all dispute, a very important institution. Its office is to form the character of those who are to form the character of millions". The Bill was designed to help it to do just that. Nay more, it would "promote the real Union of Great Britain and Ireland". He replied to three categories of its opponents, those who objected not to principle but to the amount of money involved, those who objected in principle to all grants to a Church which they regarded as corrupt, and those who objected in principle to all grants to all Churches whether corrupt or pure. On the night of the 11th, ten or eleven English Catholic Prelates who were then in London forwarded their thanks to the Prime Minister on his conduct of the Maynooth affair.

The debate went on for six protracted nights. It was sometimes acrimonious, as when Mr. Grogan, a member from Dublin, attempted to read out extracts from the Maynooth textbooks and the House became impatient. The Liberator spoke in favour of the Bill. After all, he had fortified himself at a meeting of the Loyal National Repeal Association held in the Conciliation Hall, at which he had squared his conscience about accepting endowment, for the circumstances, he said, were such, with the Protestant Church in Ireland established by Catholic money, "it is deemed no infringement of the voluntary principle to receive, by way of restitution, the means of educating the Catholic clergy". John Bright spoke against the measure as bad for religion; Lord John Manners gave it his support.

Another speaker was Gladstone, M.P. for Newark, who had opposed the introduction of the Bill, yet who now in the end supported it. He seemed entirely inconsistent to those present. Sir Robert Inglis had even expected him to lead the opposition to it. Few could understand his attitude. It seemed at once both political prudery and political suicide — he who had resigned office because of declared opposition to the Bill now to be supporting it. Disraeli said it appeared from this that Gladstone had no principles at all. Cobden, after listening patiently to his reasons for his action, declared: "What a marvellous talent is this. Here have I been sitting with pleasure for an hour listening to his explanation, and yet I know no more why he left the Government than before he began". It appeared to many that he supported the Bill out of political expediency. Gladstone himself said later that his resignation had been absurd. On the other hand, in his book on the State and the Church, he had attacked even the then existing Maynooth grant, declaring it to be a weak display of tolerance, and he had never repudiated his book.

One of the most famous speeches was that of Macaulay, delivered on the second night of the debate. His words are forever remembered by Maynooth: "When I consider with what magnificence religion and science are endowed in our universities; when I call to mind their long streets of palaces, their venerable cloisters, their trim gardens, their chapels with organs, altar-pieces and stained windows; when I remember their schools, libraries, museums and galleries of art; when I remember too all the solid comforts provided in those places for instructors and pupils, the stately dwellings of the principals, the commodious apartments of the fellows and scholars; when I remember that the very sizars and servitors are lodged far better than you propose to lodge those priests who are to teach the whole people of Ireland; when I think of Oxford and Cambridge — the display of old plate on the tables, the good cheer of the kitchens, the oceans of excellent ale in the buttery, and when I remember from whom all this splendour and plenty are derived; when I remember the faith of Edward III and Henry VI, of Margaret of Anjou and Margaret of Richmond, of William of Wykeham, of Archbishop Chicheley and Cardinal Wolsey; when I remember what we have taken from the Roman Catholic religion — King's College, New College, my own Trinity College and Christ Church — and when I look at the miserable Do-the-boys Hall we have given them in return — I ask myself if we and if the Protestant religion are not disgraced by the comparison". It was powerful and it was effective. When the second division was taken, on 18 April, 1845, there were 323 'Ayes' for the motion, 176 'Noes' against.

It had been a hectic few days. An account of the proceedings was given by *The Globe* on 12 April, describing the previous day's session: "The scene within the house was one of considerable excitement. The table and floor around it, became covered with heaps of petitions, which were removed by the messengers from time to time, to make room for successive heaps. The number of petitions presented last night amounted to the immense number of *two thousand, three hundred and seventy-two* — a far larger number than was ever presented against any measure on one night in the history of parliament ... The lobbies were filled with numbers of clergymen, ministers and gentlemen, principally members of deputations from the country..... The appearance of the neighbourhood of the house, in the vicinity of which there were congregated large numbers of well-dressed persons, also showed the interest excited by the measure. Knots of persons were seen in earnest discussion. Frequent bursts of indignation issued from these sections of the multitude ...".

All the stops had indeed been pulled out in an attempt to block the Bill. In the middle of the debate on 14 April, there had been a great demonstration in the city and a mammoth meeting at Covent Garden Theatre. Another had been held in the London Tavern, chaired by the Lord Mayor, in response to a petition from two hundred of the principal merchants, bankers and traders. Not to be outdone, English Catholics had held a meeting in favour of the grant in, of all places, the Freemasons' Tavern. Amongst those present were the Earl of Arundel, the Earl of Shrewsbury, Lord Beaumont and others. The Earl of Arundel, who chaired the meeting, reminded his hearers that "for nearly fifty years the College of Maynooth had been the nursery of the Irish Catholic clergy" (Cheers).

The provinces had not been wanting in mounting their protestations. On the eve of the second reading division, a great meeting had been held in Birmingham, opposed to the grant, under the secretaryship of a Mr. Bull and given publicity by a Mr. Ragg. It had opened with the recitation of Psalm 67 and had been interspersed with "immense applause", cries of "hear, hear", and "laughter". In Ireland, the Rev. Josiah Wilson saw "a gleam of hope from Dingle" and "a gleam of hope from Birr" for Protestantism.

The English press had been hostile, although, strangely enough, *The Standard* came out in favour on the grounds that the Bill might strengthen church establishment as such in Ireland. Strangely too, *The Northern Whig* announced a petition in favour of the Bill forwarded from Belfast. But perhaps it was not so strange. It was a riposte to *The Banner* of Ulster, which had announced a petition from thirty-seven Belfast ministers against the Maynooth grant.

The atmosphere in London was electric. On Tuesday, 15 April, *The Freeman's Journal* printed a private letter received from London the day before: "As I passed along today from Charing Cross to Westminster, I may say I walked between two lines of 'No Popery' placards. They all partook of the same character though somewhat varied in their phraseology..... The moral of all was, no endowment for Maynooth".

While the debate on the second reading raged, some interesting views were also being expressed off stage. On 12 April, George Beresford, Protestant Primate of Armagh, had communicated with his opposite number in England, Archbishop Sumner the English Primate of Canterbury. He was both for and against the Maynooth measure, torn no doubt both by religious and political considerations: "The priests who have been trained in that seminary have been the promoters and instigators of all the violent political agitation and disturbance that has taken place in Ireland. To increase the influence of the Roman Catholic bishops by increasing their patronage in nominating students to this college, and to add to the number of pauper candidates for admission into the priesthood by increasing the fund that is to be appropriated to giving them a gratuitous education, seems to me to be more likely to aggravate than to diminish the evils which would lead one to conclude that there is something radically wrong in that system (I mean viewed politically and socially, leaving out of sight its extreme religious bigotry) when those who receive the benefit of it prove to be so turbulent, disaffected and intolerant". Yet, because of his loyalty to Peel, he was not opposing the grant. "I have thought that it was not becoming my station to lend any assistance to a movement that might have the effect of removing the present ministers of the crown from their seats". He would support Maynooth itself if he thought it would produce better priests. It was an honest and forthright statement.

Even the Queen had become caught up in the events, as, writing from Buckingham Palace on 15 April, she conveyed to the King of the Belgians: "My Beloved Uncle — Here we are in a great state of agitation about one of the greatest measures ever proposed". It was ironical that on the 18th, W.B. Ferrand Esq. M.P., should have ended his speech in the Commons against the Bill with the words: "I solemnly believe that if Her Majesty's present Government can induce Her Majesty to attach her signature to the Roman Catholic Maynooth Bill, she will sign away her title to the British crown". We are told that there were "ironical cheers".

For the moment the debate was over. But it had left its mark. European opinion had become attracted by it. The *Journal des Debats* had reported on it, weighing the opposition of the Established Church (in the person of Sir Robert Inglis) against that of the Dissenters. The *Presse* and *L'Univers* had denounced the opposition, while *Le National* feared that the agitation could cause greater trouble, and *Le Constitutionel* found the whole thing remarkable for the devotion of public men like Peel, who sacrifice themselves for the vindication of their principles.

The consol market had now improved following the termination of the second stage of the debate. As *The Morning Chronicle* for Saturday, 19 April, put it: "The public securities opened firm this morning, owing to the large majority in favour of the second reading of the bill for the permanent endowment of the College of Maynooth". *The Evening Freeman* brought out a special edition, and *The Waterford Chronicle, Tipperary Free Press, Mayo Constitution, Connaught Ranger, Wexford Independent* and *Waterford Mail* were all glad. It was reported that Peel had received "a highly complimentary letter from sixteen out of seventeen Professors of Maynooth, expressing their grateful feelings for what he is doing". *The Morning Post* could not refrain from commenting: "These very professors .... are the teachers who have turned out upon Ireland its mischievous bands of parochial agitators". By and large, it was Peel's supporters who were most vociferous. Lord Brougham passed on to him the sentiments of satisfaction of a French lady friend: *"On est ici dans une grande joie de la grand majorité de Peel; et M. Guizot, tout malade qu'il est, en a été bien réjoui".*

Guizot in fact congratulated Gladstone as well as Peel on having given justice to Ireland. Much later in the century, Gladstone declared that he was not at all sure that he deserved this. He recalled his original opposition to the Bill and said that this was due to his tenacious adhesion to the basic principles of his book *The State in its Relations to the Church* (published in 1838), namely, that loyalty to the Anglican Church entailed an obligation not to establish Popery in any way. He confessed that he had been somewhat confused at the time that he wrote the book. Perhaps he does merit being better understood for his stance in 1845, although most people thought that he was still confused then.

His book does certainly seem to have been central to his position when he resigned rather than support the Maynooth Bill. At the end of April, he wrote to Archdeacon Manning, who had advised against his resignation. He quoted a letter from Newman, giving an imaginary reconstruction of his position before an interlocutor. Newman had summed up the reason for his retiring as follows: "The public thought they had in his book a pledge that the Government would not take such a step with regard to Maynooth .... Had he continued in the ministry he would to a certain extent have been misleading the country". Newman could see no principle for the resignation even though he believed Gladstone to be conscientious. Interestingly enough, Newman found Peel to be religious but unclerical and anti-Church.

Between now and the end of May, when the third reading of the Bill was expected, opposition to the measure mounted. On 22 April, Peel wrote to Mr. Croker: "The opposition to the Maynooth Bill is mainly the opposition of Dissent, in England; partly fanatical, partly religious, mainly unwillingness to sanction the germ of a second Establishment, and to strengthen and confirm that of the Protestant Church. Oxford and Cambridge are quite well represented by their respective members, Goulburn and Estcourt, opposed to Law and Inglis. We have with us almost all the youth, talent, and real influence from public station in the House of Commons. Many of our opponents there merely yield to the wishes of Dissenting constituents".

The Unitarians, in a letter to The *Tablet* (22 April), had dissociated themselves from the anti-Maynooth agitation. Those of Dublin even sent in a petition in favour of the grant, arguing that it was only right that the most numerous body of Christians in Ireland should participate in the funds which they largely contribute. But not many more Non-Conformists favoured the Bill. Meeting after meeting was held, speech after speech delivered, denouncing Maynooth; as *The Greville Memoirs* for that week put it, "the steam had been getting up in the country" about the matter. Queen Victoria, however, was pleased. She wrote again to her uncle on 23 April: "Our Maynooth Bill is through the second reading. I think if you read Sir Robert Peel's admirable speeches, you will see how good his plan is. The Catholics are quite delighted about it .... The Protestant establishment in Ireland must remain untouched, but let the Roman Catholic Clergy be well and handsomely educated".

As if to herald dire consequences unless it were listened to, the Central Anti-Maynooth Committee held a big meeting in Exeter Hall on Wednesday, 23 April, the very day on which the Commons resumed debate on the Bill. An extraordinary scenario was developed outside, with "placards posted on walls, waggons, carts, men's backs, etc." *(The Freeman's Journal*, 25 April, 1845). Proposals for putting down Popery were received, Mr. Mortimer recommending "Signing" and Rev. Mr. Burne "a small anti-Maynooth catechism".

Aubrey de Vere was on a visit to England and stayed the following night with Wordsworth. They talked about the Maynooth affair. De Vere wrote in his diary: "Drank tea with Mr. Wordsworth at Moxon's. (Moxon was a publisher). Mr. Wordsworth in great force — had borrowed Mr. Roger's court dress, and Dr. Lang's sword for the Queen's Ball. Spoke against the Maynooth grant, and said that what Ireland wanted was protection for life and property, reverence for labour, and the moral improvement of the people, especially in habits of self-respect, and regard for the comforts of life. He was very eloquent.....". On the 25th de Vere had the following to say: "Breakfasted with Mr. Wordsworth at Moxon's....... Went to the House of Lords, and heard a speech from Lord Lansdowne, in favour of the Maynooth Grant, seated next to me two smooth and meek, not unobservant Maynooth Professors......". It is a pity that he does not tell us who they were.

As far as the Irish Bishops went, it would seem that some of them at least were taking it for granted that the battle had been won. The Bishop of Achonry wrote to Renehan: "I am delighted at being able to congratulate you and the College on the altered condition of Maynooth. The grant has been made in the most gracious and unexceptionable manner. It has been more liberal than the greatest friend to the institution could anticipate". *The Freeman's Journal* thought it well to warn the Premier that he need not expect the clergy to respond politically in return for the increase.

Just then Mr. Ward of Sheffield resurrected his amendment, which proposed that "it is the opinion of this House, that any provision to be made for the purposes of the present Bill, ought to be taken from the funds already applicable to Ecclesiastical purposes in Ireland". This was something that few of even the Conservative opponents of the Bill wanted to contemplate. The amendment was lost by a large majority.

The Bill was by now in the House of Lords, which was the last hope of the Protestants. On 29 April, *The Freeman's Journal* jokingly ran a heading 'The Maynooth Bill in the House of Lords — How to bait a bench of Bishops'. Peel was recommending Forbes Mackenzie for a lordship of the Treasury for his having supported the Maynooth grant. He seemed to have been elated by his success to date. At the end of April, when refusing to see a further deputation from Sir. C. E. Smith about Maynooth, he snorted that "that subject has undergone the consideration of the House of Commons during ten nights' debate." But he must have been gratified to read a letter to *The Freeman's Journal* from Archbishop McHale of Tuam, expressing his satisfaction and thanks.

It was against this background that a militant gathering was convened at the Crown and Anchor Tavern on Wednesday, 30 April. This was the famous 'Anti-Maynooth Conference', the biggest of 1845. Made up of representatives from all over the United Kingdom, it went on for four full days. From it came the establishment of provincial machinery for the prosecution of opposition to the grant.

A whole host of pamphlets began to be issued. The fashionable reviews joined in. In April, *The Congregational Magazine* carried an article 'The Popish College of St. Patrick, Maynooth, Ireland" with excerpts from Inglis and Noel. In the same month and again in May and June, *The Electic Review* also carried articles on the College — "The Maynooth Endowment Bill continues to agitate the country. It is the one subject about which a large portion of the people think and talk. It has awakened deeper feelings, has led to more ominous trains of thought, and is clearly destined to work a greater change in the convictions and public course of the more reflecting portion of the community, than any other event which has happened for many years".

In May, *Blackwood's Magazine* took up the hue and cry: "If this endowment prospers, Protestantism will receive a deadly wound in the empire which is, and has been, and by Providence was appointed to be, its main bulwark". Some questioners might be pardoned for asking what part of the anatomy was the empire. *Blackwood* went on regardless. The endowment of Maynooth would mean the ultimate separation of Ireland from the British empire. In similar vein *Frazer's Magazine* for May. And then, of course, there was *Punch* which castigated Peel unceremoniously:

> "He has baffled our every hope
> He's surely in league with the Pope
> We thought him a friend of the Church
> He is leaving her now in the lurch
> I'll bet that he shortly obtains
> A cardinal's hat for his pains,
> To punishment let us denounce him
> Will nobody venture to trounce him ?"

At this stage, Popery, Maynooth, O'Connell and Repeal had all become lumped together as the common enemy. The bigotry was such that the Queen was embarrassed by it: "I blush for the form of religion we profess, that it should be so void of all right feeling, and so wanting in Charity". There was some consolation for Irish Catholics to be found in the remarks about the Maynooth Bill made in the French Chamber of Deputies, where a M. Berryer described it as a most liberal measure, in harmony with freedom of conscience. Consolation too could be derived from a letter of the Rector of Kilmore, Church of Ireland Diocese of Meath, who, writing from Kilcock to Sir. C. E. Smith, had curtly informed him that he would not allow the introduction of any anti-Maynooth petition into his parish. At least some neighbours were holding together.

In Ireland as a whole there were mixed opinions about the grant and the success of the Bill met with some reservations. The Bishop of Ardagh remonstrated with O'Connell about it: "Much has been said about the gratitude we owe for the grant to Maynooth, but I confess that I for one (and I am joined in the sentiments by the priests and people of this diocese) feel no gratitude whatever. In the first place, our own energies and determination wrung that paltry sum from a bigoted and anti-Irish cabinet, nor shall we ever thank the rich glutton when he disdainfully flings us the crumbs from his table. Secondly, the grant is so miserable in amount, that it can be looked on in no other light than as a sheer mockery and insult".What is wanted, he avers, is the repeal of the iniquitous Union.

Likewise, Bishop Francis Patrick Kenrick wrote to Peter Kenrick: "It is generally thought that the English Government is forging a chain of gold for the priests by the appropriation made to Maynooth." And the Archbishop of Cashel wrote to Renehan: "I look upon the Bill as virtually passed, and sincerely hope it may be productive of all the good that is expected from it, but unless there is an increased spirit of piety and humility, I apprehend it will be more difficult for the authorities to manage the students and certainly still more difficult for the students to govern them after leaving College, with the notions of rights and of independence that this measure is naturally calculated to engender".

In Britain, as the time for the third reading of the bill approached, the pace of opposition hotted up. More and more meetings were held; it became impossible to keep track of them. *The Freeman's Journal* gave an intriguing account of one of these, held in Exeter Hall on 14 May:

"Fully three-fourths of those present on either side belonged to the gentler sex; and the galleries on either side of the platform were filled with beautiful and young ladies, most of them in Polka jackets. The quarter part of these amused themselves by working samplers; in which the revered orators may find themselves done in Berlin wool tomorrow morning by some of the softest and most delicate fingers in London. Others of the ladies more carnally given devoted themselves to sandwiches and biscuits, with considerable gusto, and several bottles of liquid, not the colour of water, were emptied during the proceedings".

On 19 May, *The Freeman's Journal* declared that "the anti-Maynooth agitation has reached its zenith". So indeed it had. All sorts of things had been said about the College: even though called 'Royal', it was really a 'Papal' college; Jesuit 'secret societies' had been introduced into it (This would appear to have been a reference to the Sodality of The

Sacred Heart) and so on and so forth. It was anything but funny. The *Journal* intimated that the extent of the intolerance in London had become unimaginable.

In actual fact, the controversy had broadened and had now become a question of Protestantism versus Catholicism. This can been seen from some of the anti-Maynooth pamphlets in which, although entitled 'anti-Maynooth', the College is scarcely mentioned at all. Some of them were quite amusing. One such was *The Anti-Maynooth Petition: A Tract for the Times*, by one of the delegates to the Anti-Maynooth Conference, which sold for 1 penny or six shillings per hundred. It conducted its argument by way of a conversation between William and John. William: "Good day, John. Are you going to sign the Anti-Maynooth Petition?" John is not interested but is gradually brought around by quotations from the Maynooth class books.

When the debate did resume, on Monday, 19 May, it continued for three nights. During this debate, Mr. Spooner distinguished himself once more for his anti-Maynooth sentiments; and Peel found it necessary to counter the old charges about the role of the College during the 1798 rebellion by proving that the Trustees and President had taken measures to stop disaffection there.

Finally, on Wednesday night, 21 May, the House divided and the Bill was carried — 317 for and 184 against. It only remained for the Bill to finish its course in the House of Lords, where it was read for the first time on 24 May, without discussion. On 2 June, the second reading was moved by the Duke of Wellington, who, amid shouts of 'hear, hear', supported the College warmly. The Earl of Roden was against, and conveyed information on the College received from some persons who had been educated there and which had been collected at a Priests' Protection Society meeting in Dublin at which he had been present. He reported one of these as saying:

"A diocesan of mine told me he always contrived to get sick at the approach of the sessions, and thus evaded, during five or six years' residence at Maynooth, taking the oath of allegiance. On Christmas and Patrick's night, the best singing students are supplied with wine. The best singers are called on to sing in the dinner-hall, whilst the others are drinking their wine. A certain gentleman, now a priest in the county of Kerry, was selected to show off his vocal powers on one of these nights. He chose from among his collection of songs one composed by an R.C. bishop of America. Of the loyalty or disloyalty of this poetic effusion I leave the meeting to judge".

The reference here was to the celebration following Catholic Emancipation, when the students had sung the rebellious song composed by Dr.

England of Charleston. Happily, the Marquis of Normanby who may have remembered the great reception given to himself by the students in 1835, when seditious utterances were also said to have been made, stoutly defended the College and all it stood for. For a moment there was real embarrassment, when a petition came in, signed by three hundred non-resident members of the Senate of the University of Cambridge, disavowing one that had been presented in favour of the grant by seventy-eight resident members of same.

There must have been lighter moments too, as when the Lords doubtlessly heard that the Reverend Vicar of Cheltenham had met one of his parishioners leaving church who had asked "if Maynooth was to be built in Cheltenham?". The good lady was so confused by all the talk about Maynooth as to be forgiven for thinking that. She reminds one of the Irish lady at the time of the foundation of the Maynooth Mission to China who inquired whether Maynooth was in China. The second reading ended eventually with a majority of 157 for the Bill (226 to 69). Suddenly, it was all over. The third reading of the Bill in the House of Lords took place on 16 June. After a short discussion, the division took place – giving it a majority of 131. On 30 June, despite having been presented with four hundred and seventy petitions against it, Queen Victoria gave her assent to the Bill.

Peel must have been elated; the going had been difficult. Macaulay said years afterwards that the strain had shown on him during the debate: "How white poor Peel looked while I was speaking". He had indeed been brave. At one stage he had confessed that he would carry on regardless, "very careless as to the consequences which may follow" the passing of the Bill. At another time he had said that he felt "a sense of fatigue on the brain". Now it was over and he could be pleased. To use the words of Dr. Russell of Maynooth, he had surely been "a noble fellow". The Archbishop of Dublin called to the Castle to express his thanks.

SOVEREIGNS GALORE

In more ways than one, the Maynooth Act of 1845 marked a new period for Maynooth. Dr. Montague having died, Dr. Renehan was appointed President on 25 June. He had been Vice-President since 1834, having been 'forced' by his Bishop to accept the position. Now he entered office on the crest of a wave. Not only had the grant to the College been increased from £9,000 to £26,360 a year but, by placing it on the Consolidated Fund, the Act had removed it from the polemical area where it had previously been discussed during every session of the House of Commons. In short, it had been made 'permanent'.

It was welcome for a lot of reasons. Fr. Healy of Little Bray said later that but for it the people would not have been able to pay for their priests. Needless to say, the professors were also pleased. Prior to its

Canal at Maynooth

Maynooth Village

Entrance to College

St. Patrick's

College Cloister

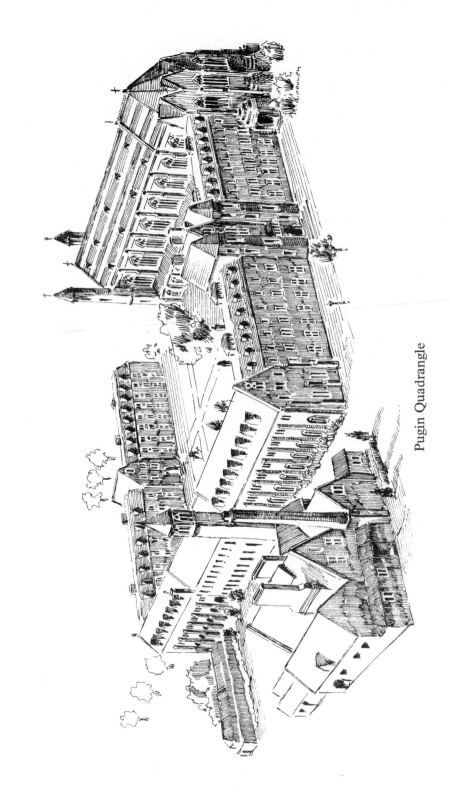

Pugin Quadrangle

College Chapel

THE RECENT FIRE AT MAYNOOTH COLLEGE – VIEW OF THE BUILDING ON THE DAY AFTER THE CATASTROPHE

Aula Maxima

Dunboyne House

advent, they had been tending to complain even if mutedly. One of the newspapers had carried an account by a visitor to the College: "The only complaint, if complaint so gentle a murmur could be called, that the professor to whom I had the honour of an introduction made on the subject of salary was, that he had not the means of purchasing those works which he thought necessary to the conscientious fulfilment of his duties, or the financial ability to make that use of the vacation which he desired". It was a refrain that was to be heard again long afterwards.

Some people had reservations about the grant. One was the Reverend James Maher, who wrote to Cullen on 9 June: "Professors with £300 a year may be excellent men, good theologians, distinguished scholars, but certainly not the best to introduce the ecclesiastical spirit into the young mind.......£26,000 a year. What a propensity to pay a few priests to educate youth for the ministry, to fit them to preach, amongst other things, a love of poverty and mortification, a contempt of riches and worldly pomp .... Secular priests ought never be employed as professors in the education of ecclesiastics (unless they become like the men of Castleknock)."

The deceased President would have been in a quandary as to how he would cope with the increased grant. Of him Fr. Healy had this to say:

> "Dr. Montague, the President, was in the habit of conveying from Dublin — in an old post-chaise by which he travelled — the entire amount of each quarterly instalment of the Government grant, and he never lost, nor was in dread of losing, one farthing, although his route lay through Lucan, passing close to a tablet on the roadside recording the murder of a priest in 1807 by highwaymen."

Perhaps this is why "the College trap" was held in such awe in much later times?

The Bishops lost no time in meeting to assess the implications of their good fortune. They assembled in the College on Tuesday, 24 June, but we are also told that they discussed their topics — as they still do — "in the halls and groves of Maynooth". A certain anxiety seems to have prevailed. The basic question was "What will be done with the present college — will it be enlarged or abandoned, and a new one erected?" Or so we are told by *The Freeman's Journal* for 23 June.

There was a rumour amongst the students that "the College of the Foreign Missions may be benefitted, if it may be done under legal sanction". This was a reference to All Hallows and goes some way towards indicating just how close the relations between Maynooth and the Irish Vincentians always have been. There was said to be agreement (although the press then as now might be queried as regards reliability) that if

71

it were put to the students that the College should be changed from its site, "it would be carried, not only unanimously, but with acclamation". The majority of the professors too, if not all of them, "would, it is believed, desire a change of locality", for "they too are susceptible to the influences of atmosphere". The paper had no doubt that, during the next four years, "the facilities will be much greater for experimenting upon building than on philosophy". It summed up therefore: "Let the old building be sold. It would make an excellent barracks; it would answer as a model farm, for there are 65 acres of land attached".

The *Journal* at this time devoted much space to Maynooth. There were leading articles, and subleaders and letters — one of these urging the creation of a Chair of Ecclesiastical History, because "the idea of the divinity professors, already overpowered with matter, attending to this gigantic branch, is out of the question". Again the kind of thing that was to be heard much later in the history of Maynooth. "It is true that divinity may be studied without a professor; that is, *totaliter qualiter,* as they say. That philosophy, classics, geology, the abstract and physical sciences, may be acquired without a professor, may, perhaps .... but that classes of students can get even an entrance in ecclesiastical history, without a professor, is certainly a thing not possible". As things turned out, a Chair of Ecclesiastical History was quickly instituted and Dr. Russell appointed to it.

The new salary structure was excellent — £500 for the President, with an allowance of £90 for wine, £322 for the Vice-President and £304 for the Prefect of the Dunboyne, £260 for the Senior Dean and Profs. of Theology etc., £237 for the Profs. of Natural Philosophy etc.

It is only natural that even more visitors should have been attracted to look at Maynooth. Early in July, 1845, one of these, W.W. Carus Wilson, an evangelical polemist, whose letters on Maynooth were later carried by *The Times* in 1846, privately published his impressions of the place:

"After having heard so much of their poverty and wretchedness, we were all surprised with what we saw. The students are all dressed in black, with long black gaiters..... We were told that the students had everything they wanted, (indeed we went into the kitchen and saw the very best fare preparing), and that they had as much beer and drink as they liked, (we saw the brewery, a good sized building, standing by itself), and as much to eat as they wished; and on Fridays the food is altered in quality (that is, fish instead of meat) though not in quantity, as they were not, on that day, restricted at all. This is rather singular, for surely a fasting does or ought to imply an abstinence. Then as to the beds: Sir R. Peel talked of 'three sleeping in a bed'. Now our guide told us that he never knew of such a thing as even two sleeping in a bed, all the time he had been there, twelve years; indeed we saw the beds, which, though very good, were not large enough for two; much less three..."

One thing at least was certain — there was no shortage of students for the College. In August, the Bishop of Ossory was able to appoint fourteen to the fifteen places available to him; the Bishop of Killaloe even sent up a student whose father was a Protestant, and the Rector of the Irish College, Rome, which institution's funds were low, feared there would be a big rush of students to Maynooth but comforted himself with the thought that "Rome will always be Rome". Cullen told him that he thought that at Maynooth "the great wealth will not do much good. All are anxious to have as much of the grant as possible. There is no regard at all for such money. No one cares how it goes". Just imagine, he says, one young man no more than twenty-two years old, has just been appointed Professor of Philosophy with £240 per annum. "What an elevation for a young lad of humble family", particularly when one remembers that he was not all that able. Cullen had assisted at his concursus and "never heard a worse exhibition in Latin and Greek than the candidates made". He thought that many of the Roman students would be able for them, not only in this but in Metaphysics and Theology.

In some ways Cullen was quite right. The new wealth of the College — then as much later — did not help in every respect. Before long, Bishops would be complaining that their students were being corrupted by it. Even as early as the beginning of October, the Bishop of Kildare and Leighlin was writing to the President, seeking an appointment for one of his young priests on the staff of the College: "His taste is not for a missionary life".

But, for all that, Irishmen generally were disposed to see the outcome as a great victory for faith and fatherland. On the announcement of Peel's concessions, Thomas Davis, the most important of a new and vigorous band of young Irishmen, remarked to a friend in a letter that "the events at Maynooth will greatly weaken our enemies".

Writing later in his *Young Ireland 1840 - 45* (Dublin 1884), Gavan Duffy all but gloated over the fact that so many petitions against the grant had failed, although in true politician's fashion he also recalled that there had been some notable examples of support for it among Protestants, including some from Ulster.

As might be expected, the general attitude of Protestants was one of frustration and a determination to follow the matter up. M.P.'s who had supported the Bill began to lose their seats. At an election for the County of Edinburgh, one of the candidates was asked 'Do you or do you not approve of the grant to the Catholic College of Maynooth?' When he did not receive an answer, the questioner asked the crowd: "Is such a man as that a proper representative for this country?" — to loud cries of "No, No", mingled with a hiss. On the whole though, the mood was one of Catholic triumphalism. *The Freeman's Journal* was unashamed in publishing doggerel with the title 'The Marvellous Dream of Dr. Robert McGhee':

"Of all the doctors in this town,
The accoucheur for me, Sir,
Of Hall of Exeter renown,
Is Dr. Bob McGhee, Sir.

He dreamt a dream — a fearful dream —
Of Popish machinations,
Of Dens, Maynooth, Sir Robert's scheme,
And Rome's abominations".

Suggestions for the improvement of Maynooth were quick to emerge. One of the most exhaustive was contained in *Thoughts on Academical Education, ecclesiastical and secular,* by a Catholic Priest (Dublin, James Duffy, 23 Anglesea St., 1845). While arguing that jointly with the improvement of Maynooth, a portion of the funds should be applied to some diocesan seminaries (although by what legal process he does not say), he put forward four points in respect of the College:

"First, to add to the present buildings a college-chapel, a library, a museum, a laboratory, an observatory, and such other improvements as may be required for the better accommodation of professors and students.

Second, to provide for the library a large and select stock of books, in every department of learning; allowing also a yearly sum for the purchase of valuable works — to furnish a superior apparatus for the hall of experimental philosophy ....

Third, to improve the physical condition of the students..... Among these sanitary improvements, so to call them, might be included the endowment of a resident physician..... The same person could also be professor of Chemistry, though inconvenience might now and then arise from merging the two offices in one person.

Fourth, to improve the status of the president, vice-president, professors and officers of the establishment. To omit other matters, the salaries of the professors should be considerably augmented, so as to make their chairs more desirable than benefices. This would be a double service to the house; it would attract men of first-rate talents, and it would fix them in their chairs perhaps for life......A professor, who knows not when to vacate his chair, who, perhaps, each day of his

74

occupancy has before him the prospect of some desirable office in the church, will not, it is plain, labour with the same assiduity in his particular walk of science as they who are fixed to their chairs, as one may say, for life".

The professors found themselves well off. In October, Russell sent a contribution to Cullen for the Irish College, Rome. That month, Russell was greatly delighted by the news of Newman's conversion. Newman himself had made sure that Russell was one of the first to be told. He was confirmed shortly afterwards and Wiseman, as President of Oscott, wrote to Russell on 1 November giving him a full account of the proceedings. At that stage, Newman was thinking of transferring from Oxford to Oscott, but all was hush-hush about that. Wiseman asked for Russell's opinion about Newman's future: "You will be able, after consulting Dr. Murray, to give me your opinion about the question how far he is allowed to continue the sale of 'Tracts for the Times' ". And he gives an account of Newman's forthcoming book on the development of doctrine. He encloses some letters also which will let Russell know how the Oxford "movement is going forward". Shortly afterwards he wrote again. Newman is doing well and is in great form. Many more are coming in. He requests prayers for "one first-rate Oxford man" who is quite shaken by events. Towards the end of November, Russell sent on to Newman a little volume of Canon Carl von Schmid's Tales which he had just translated, and on 7 December, Newman acknowledged receipt of the gift: "I shall value it ten times as much coming from you". Indeed he was thinking just then of visiting Maynooth. Writing to J.D. Dalgairns on 16 December, he told of how he proposed to visit Ushaw and Stonyhurst around the Christmas period and "I shall *like* to get to Maynooth to Dr. Russell". When his book on 'development' did appear, he wrote to his friend James Hope just before Christmas that he was gratified at hearing that some people at Maynooth had a good opinion of it.

Back in the College, preparations were being made for a new start. On 7 November, Sir Edward Bellew wrote to the President reminding him that Lord Ffrench, Mr. Hussey and himself had been appointed on a committee to draw up a report in relation to the better internal management of the house "under the new order of things". He asked for Renehan's views and got them:

"That all the rooms be provided with suitable furniture which should never be removed from the room to another.
That servants be employed to supply the students' rooms with water, to remove it in the morning and brush out the rooms.
That a laundry be provided and all the washing done at the public expense.
That the students be supplied with academic dress — cap and

gown, every second year, and be obliged to pay for them if ordered by the Superiors at other times.

That the College halls and corridors be lighted with gas — or with oil lamps, and sufficiently.

That the galleries be scoured down every week or fortnight, except from November to March and a servant employed solely in attending to the cleanliness of the outward precincts. That the walks, greenhouses, flower pots etc. of the garden be kept in decent order".

A copy of this memorandum is to be found among Dr. Renehan's papers in the *President's Archives* at Maynooth. In those days as in later ones, the President had to busy himself with small things as well as with large, too many of which were not statutorily under his control. Just then, he had 504 undergraduate students in the College, together with 19 "Dunboynists", of which number about 250 were lodged in single rooms and the remainder in rooms containing from two to seven beds. He would like a direction as to who should enjoy free places. Also, the allowances to the Dunboyne students "under the new system — the alterations, if any, to be made in the dietary, attendance and comfort of the students, require to be determined. Under the firm conviction that I was only complying with the wishes of the Board, I ventured at my own risk to supply the sugar necessary for breakfast and supper during the last month". The President's duties were surely comprehensive.

Renehan's difficulties were compounded by complaints from Maynooth which reached the Castle early in December about the 'non-execution' of the new Act. The Archbishop, Dr. Murray, was called to the Castle to give an explanation. He asked Renehan to forward to him any explanation he could furnish on the subject. On 9 December, Murray did present himself before the Lord Lieutenant who communicated these complaints to him and he in turn let Renehan know immediately. The complaints related to the expense allowance to the students made by the Act (only portion of which had been received), the fact that they had waited for an improvement for three months and that there was no court of appeal to which they could turn. The young gentlemen were certainly being impetuous. That very same December, the President made a technical error in writing a letter concerning the character of a former student — Denis Layne Brasbie — of whom we have already heard, to the Anglican Bishop of Worcester. It was to be fraught with serious consequences, of which more later.

Despite all that, at the end of 1845 Maynooth College had every reason to face the future with confidence.

Chapter III

As Famine Stalked

As the middle of the century approached, Ireland began to experience a traumatic disaster — the Great Famine of 1846 - '47. With a population of some 8 million, subsisting mainly on potatoes, and with fever rife throughout the country, the conditions for plague were present when partial failures of the potato crop occurred between 1816 and 1845. A similar failure took place in 1845 which led to a national tragedy. The famine, with its accompanying diseases, reached its height during 1846 and 1847, when, whether by death or emigration, the country lost over a million people.

The College, and most of the area around Dublin, did not suffer anything like the rest of Ireland. In fact, directly owing to the increased grant of 1845, it was in a position to flourish rather than stagnate. Nevertheless, it was affected by the famine indirectly.

January, 1846, broke hopefully for Maynooth. That month, the President was informed that Sir Thomas Freemantle would pay a visit to the College, before his departure for Parliament, in order to be more informed and better able to answer any questions that might be raised concerning it.

Before long, however, there were certain premonitions that a crisis in the domain of health lay ahead. In mid-February, Dr. Dominic Corrigan, Physician to the College, replied to a request by the President for suggestions as to what improvements might be made in the medical arrangements for the place. Strangely enough, he had none to make; he thought the existing system to be satisfactory. But if, perchance, a new infirmary were to be erected, the architect should consult with the medical people. This was to be only the beginning of protracted discussion on the matter.

FOREBODINGS OF DISASTER

Dominic Corrigan, the College Physician, was himself one of the most distinguished students of the Lay College at Maynooth. Born in 1802, in Thomas Street, Dublin, Corrigan, after having completed his classical studies at Maynooth, had been apprenticed to the then College Physician, Dr. Talbot O'Kelly, during which time he also attended lectures in the Royal College of Surgeons, Trinity College and the Apothecaries Hall. In 1824, he had gone to Edinburgh for further training and graduated there the following year. Success quickly attended his career, and by 1830, at the age of twenty-eight, he had been appointed Physician to the Charitable Infirmary, Jervis Street, and a year later Consulting Physician to Maynooth College. By 1846, he had attained quite a reputation, having already published half-a-dozen important papers, one of which established him as an authority in particular areas of heart disease.

This then was the man whom the President of Maynooth, Dr. Renehan, again consulted in April, 1846, about improvements in the medical catering for the College. This time Renehan had made his own suggestions, requesting Corrigan's comments on them. The suggestions and comments run as follows: 1. "That an apartment be fitted up in the Infirmary as an Apothecary's Shop where all necessary medicines shall be kept and compounded according to the directions of the attending medical officers". Comment — It is not of consequence where the medicine is kept or compounded; 2. "That the attending Physician or Surgeon be requested to visit the College at least once a fortnight". Comment — This is not necessary; 3. "That the attending Physician and Surgeon shall write their prescriptions in full, in separate prescription books; the name of the patient being set forth at the head of each prescription". Comment — Not necessary; 4. "That the resident medical officer be required to enter, in a book to be called 'The Infirmary Registry' the names of all inmates and to state *in general terms* the nature of their complaints, when commenced, how long continued and the termination of the cases". Comment — Such a document would be objectionable. It would be hurtful to students and injurious to their families. Further suggestions were similarly treated and one does get the impression, that, even though they had been made by someone who was not a physician, they might have been more sympathetically received.

Beyond the walls of Maynooth, health conditions began to worsen, and that some intimations of this had begun to penetrate the College emerges from a letter of April, 1846, from Dr. Egan, Bishop of Kerry, thanking the President for having forwarded £25 in half notes from Dr. Callan, Mr Farrelly (Bursar) and Mr. Kelly (Professor) for the needy in his diocese. He will give it, he says, to the parish of Brosna, but disease and destitution is so widespread that it is hard to know which parish needs help most. "It is painful as you pass thro' the streets, or on the high roads to behold the emaciated countenances, the sunken eyes, the faultering steps of those who last year were young and athletic ..... The disease is not confined to the destitute. It is fast extending to all other orders of society. The Priests are absolutely exhausted having to attend so many sick calls and in many instances are obliged to walk, their horses being unable to carry them, thro' want of sufficient feeding and the Priest not getting as much as would purchase oats for his horse".

Still the College itself was proceeding well. That same April, a Visitation was held, having been postponed for a week by the Castle to enable the professors to return after the Easter vacation. Prior to it, the Secretary to the Trustees, Mr. Flanagan, wrote a long account to the President as to how it would be conducted. It is an interesting citation of the nature of a Visitation:

"As a matter of course the Superiors, Professors and Students will be assembled before the Visitors in the Great Hall and their names called and answered to. It would be most desirable that you would be able to announce at the list that all have taken the oath of allegiance and for that purpose, if there are any newcomers who have not taken it, it would be well if they should take it before the Visitation.

The names, duties and salaries of the Superiors and Professors will form an essential part of the report of the Visitation to Parliament, the description of the duties of the Professors to comprise the number of Lectures each given in the week, the duration of each lecture and the number of students in each class ....

As far as I could collect from the Visitors, enquiry will be made into the lodging and dietary of the students and I apprehend a searching investigation will be made into the extent of the course of Mathematics and Natural Philosophy.

On allusion being made to Lodging and Dietary.......I remarked that the Visitors could be perfectly informed on the lodging of the students by having a classified list of the rooms of the College put into their hands, the number of rooms containing, say, 5 students, the number containing 4 and so on to the number containing one student, of which they can select one of each class for Visitation.

On the subject of the Dietary of the Students, they can satisfy themselves by visiting the Refectory at 3 o'clock and on this point Dr. Murray approved of my suggestion that nothing should be added to the usual table, lest it may be said that the dinner was made up for the Visitation......."

The Visitation — in accordance with the Act of 1845 — was duly held on 20 April. The Visitors were the Duke of Leinster, Dr. Crolly of Armagh and Dr. Murray of Dublin, Lords Rosse and Lincoln and Mr. R. Pigot. It began at 11 a.m. in the Great Hall — 19 professors (one was absent on leave) and 512 students (ten were absent because of sickness) being present. The President was closely interrogated as to whether he had any complaints to make against the professors or the students. These in turn were questioned likewise about him. There were no grave complaints on either side. It emerged that there were 346 rooms for the students, also that the Oath of Allegiance had been taken by all students except two (who had been ill at the time), at the last Quarter Sessions held in Maynooth village. The evidence was in due course laid before Her Majesty and presented to both Houses of Parliament by Her Majesty's command. It was published in the *Parliamentary Publications: Accounts and Papers,* vol. *XLII* (1846). Following the Visitation, the Trustees ordered the supplying of butter at breakfast to all the students and the attendance of servants to sweep out their rooms.

If things were not at all bad in the College, they were certainly shaping up badly outside. By August, famine openly stalked the land. Indeed the College too began to feel the pinch when, on commencement that Fall, classes had to be reduced because of it. *The Achill Missionary Herald,* however, had no difficulty about attributing the famine to the endowment of Maynooth, seeing in it the hand of God by way of chastisement: "The Protestant members of the House of Lords and Commons... have concurred in passing a Bill to endow a college for training priests, and defend and practise and perpetuate this corrupt and damnable worship in this realm. The ink wherewith the signification of royal assent was given to that iniquitous measure was hardly dry when the *fatal rot* commenced its work of destruction".

Some of the Irish Bishops were disposed to see things differently; and viewed the endowment as a danger to the Catholic religion through its materialistic influence on the Maynooth-educated clergy. Thus, in December, 1846, the Bishop of Derry, Dr. Maginn, wrote to the President recommending "a young man of the name of Logue of respectable but indigent parents" for what was called the McDevitt Burse in the College, the young man in question being related to that family. It would be good, says the Bishop, if Logue could get the burse rather than that it be added

80

to the "Peel douceur" presently enjoyed by some gentlemen at Maynooth. Indeed to give it to any of them would only be injurious. He himself had recently been to Dublin but was unable to call to Maynooth on his way back. He had caught influenza and, as it had the symptoms of the typhus fever, he had hurried home to Derry "to have my bones gathered to my fathers".

The Bishop's closing words provide a good picture of the way the then prosperous Maynooth was regarded by many outside: "Wishing you every success in your arduous and exalted mission, to prepare the young hope of Ireland for the trying times that are before them by reconciling affluence with piety and making our young levites, regaled by seven or eight years at the *lauta mensa* of Maynooth, *agréer* (as the French say) with the scanty fare of the wild mountain passes and deep ravines of Donegal". Even Dr. Haly of Kildare and Leighlin, who earlier had assured the President that he welcomed the increased grant as "favourable to the interests of religion in your *Leviathan* Establishment", was by now also beginning to wonder how it would dispose students for life on the mission. Writing at the same time as Dr. Maginn, he admitted that he found it hard to call out any student from Maynooth "during this afflicting time", for a student's condition there is so much better off than it would be amongst the people "where nothing but desolation in its most fearful and alarming state presents itself to his view every day, every hour".

WHILE ACADEMICS FIDDLE

Despite the fact that they came from the ordinary people throughout the country, the students seem to have been rather oblivious to the plight of the masses. The Trustees themselves, even though undoubtedly aware of the general state of things, continued to direct College affairs with an open hand. In July, 1846, they decided that "every student in future, on entering Maynooth College, is required to provide himself with 8 sheets, 6 pairs of stockings, and 3 pairs of shoes, which supply he shall keep up during his residence in the College". Their Secretary, Rev. Mr. Flanagan, conveyed this at once to the President.

For his part, Dr. Renehan was at that time more concerned with the way in which the recent Visitation had been reported. He had noted discrepancies between the account of the Visitation which he had supplied himself and that which had appeared in the newspapers, finding that "not one single sentence of the original papers has been left unaltered", even though his name had been attached without his consent. The bad grammar and "gross blunders of punctuation" in the printed version must redound to his shame and the discredit of the College. My, my: some commas must indeed have been omitted, although by today's most widely accepted syntax, they would surely only have looked funny

81

if included. Famine was far from his thoughts. Could Flanagan let him have the originals as soon as possible ? Yes, he could, and would send them by the Clerk to the Office in Lucan, which he is told is a safer mode of conveyance than sending them "by the carman".

The professors, while not blinkered to the condition of the country, were not over-distressed either. Earlier in 1846, Dr. Patrick Murray had issued the first of a series of dissertations on Catholic subjects for the enlightenment of laymen. which he hoped to prepare regularly during the vacations. This first was on the divine institution and obligation of confession and in the form of *A Letter addressed to the Rev. Dr. Pusey.* It was published in Dublin by Thomas Richardson of Dawson Street. That June, he published *Prose and Verse,* a little collection which included such bombastic material as that in the essay 'On Puns and Punsters': "Let no one pun until dinner is over, or nearly over. But here is the peril. In the company of a practised punster you are never secure. He is worse than the bore in Horace, or the frogs in Aristophanes, or the old man of the sea in the eastern story, or Lord Brougham in the House of Lords. Like a shower in April his nonsense pours down on you, when you least expect and are least prepared, when you are without cloak or umbrella; when you are in solemn contemplative mood, while your mind is soaring upwards, he sends his intangible arrow after you, and brings you down, like a heavy bump on the black earth. While you are discussing politics or metaphysics with a friend, and working out the big idea, he shoots his tiny missive at it, as children crack soap-bubbles at the touch of a pin. Whenever an opening presents itself a pun enters, as air rushes into a vacuum ...... Perhaps we would have no puns in our utopia. But in the real world there is, after all, a large number of people, grave and good, and able, who really love puns, who entertain an exquisite relish for this sort of amusement. Critics should not overlook this fact ...." It is hard to avoid the thought that Murray had some colleague in mind. But it was all pretty frivolous stuff while Rome was about to burn. That September he followed it up with a piece in *The Dublin Review* about 'Pictures from Italy' by Dickens.

Dr. Russell, the review's editor, was thinking of relinquishing the editorship just then. Wiseman lost "not a post" in writing to him "not to think of such a step". He informs Russell that Newman and the Littlemore community are coming to live at the old college, Oscott, sends his regards to Murray, "to whom I will write in a few days", and asks when Russell is coming to visit them at Maryvale ? That he was to do later on.

Wiseman was really co-editor with Russell, because the latter did most of the work. In another letter at this time he told Russell: "We are short of matter, especially light. Cannot you get Mr. Kelly or Dr. Murray or others to do something?" Wiseman actually was not feeling too well just then. That Autumn he was complaining to Russell about his health, fearing that he might not be able to carry on. In Ireland shortly before, an old friend of the College had gone to his reward: the Bishop of Cloyne, Dr. Crotty, had departed from 'Cove', soon to be known as Queenstown after Victoria had visited it.

That same year another professor, Dr. O'Reilly, was all agog about a visit to Rome. In June he wrote to Cullen to expect him, saying that he hoped to make the journey in eleven days. In today's perspective the route he took is intriguing: "From Kingstown to Liverpool — London — Brighton — Dieppe — Paris — arriving in the last place ...... in less than 48 hours from Kingstown — then on by Marseilles ...... Once at Marseilles, we could of course take the next packet for Civita Vecchia". By August he was in Naples, having trouble about saying Mass and annoyed by the nonsense of having to get a document signed by Monseigneur the Vicar. At the same time, Cullen was hearing from his nephew, H. J. Cullen, that the Dublin and Cashel railway was open as far as Carlow, and from Dr. Cantwell, Bishop of Meath, thanking him for having got a Doctorate in Divinity for Mr. Whitehead of Maynooth. The College Trustees were busy otherwise, demanding compensation from the Great Western Railway Company for the ground occupied by it adjacent to the canal at Maynooth.

The students were so comfortable in the College as to be anything but anxious to leave it at the end of their course. In June, 1846, Dr. Coen of Clonfert, former Dean at Maynooth, was quite short of priests and for two or three years had been unable to allow any of his students to complete the fourth year's theology. One gathers that they resented this strongly, prompting him to protest that, even though he understood that the theologians were allowed £20 per annum, which might be an inducement to some to prolong their course, still he *must* have them out, through need of priests. Clearly, they were reluctant to go.

THE DANCE OF DEATH

As 1847 came in, the effects of the famine became more pronounced. By 13 February the Bishop of Killaloe was writing to Renehan: "I feel quite nervous. We are so overpowered with the distress and clamours of the multitude. May God relieve them — the Clergy and Bishops of Ireland never experienced such times !!" Bad they were all right. The *President's Archives* at Maynooth is a veritable mine of information, to be found in letters from various Irish Bishops, about the state of the country just then. One of these correspondents in particular, Dr. McNally of Clogher, had been a colleague of two successive Presidents on the staff of Maynooth and was in the habit of interlacing his letters about his students there with vivid descriptions of conditions in his diocese. There is an extraordinary contrast between what he wrote to Dr. Montague in October, 1844, and to Dr. Renehan in March, 1847. In 1844 he had nothing special to report:

"I dont know anything in this part of the country worth communicating. The people are quiet and peaceable. The crops are generally saved and good and abundant. Even the potatoes, about which apprehensions were entertained, are on the whole in this part of the country a fairly average crop. The emigration from this part of the country has been considerable and yet the population of the Parish cannot, it appears, be much diminished for on Thursday last, I confirmed twelve hundred and fourteen persons, all belonging to the parish of Clogher".

By March, 1847, all had changed completely. Writing to Dr. Renehan, the Bishop says:

"It would be impossible to give an idea of the deplorable state of our poor afflicted people. In this neighbourhood fever and famine are making frightful ravages among them. They are lying out in the fields and the people are so terrified that none but the clergy can be induced to approach. I yesterday sent out a coffin for a poor creature who died in a field of fever and have just heard that no person could be persuaded upon to put the body into it. While I write the inquest is going on. The terrible visitation which the Almighty has sent upon the country fills the strongest minds with terror and dismay. Fourteen deaths in this parish, on yesterday, were reported to me last night. It is wonderful how the clergy can bear their increasing labours, attending on the sick and the dying. Such, I believe, at present, is the deplorable state of every part of Ireland".

Such was certainly the case not far from McNally, in the neighbouring diocese of Derry. There, on 10 March, Dr. Maginn penned self-explanatory words to Renehan: "Our misery is daily accumulating. God only knows where it will end." A week later he wrote again:

"We have set aside tomorrow, Friday and Saturday, as days of fasting, humiliation and prayer for this diocese, joining in communion with the good Bishop of York, Dr. Briggs, who made a particular request to that effect. Our country has been reserved for terrible trials. May God in his infinite mercy grant her children that Christian fortitude so necessary in their unparalleled tribulations. We require the prayers of these young levites under your spiritual superintendence who, removed from the world's perplexities and contaminations, can raise their pure hands and hearts with confidence to an offended heaven. They could not be employed in a better work than prayer for their unhappy country".

Things were just as bad in the South of Ireland. A month before, Archbishop Slattery of Cashel, in acknowledging receipt of fifteen half-notes from Renehan for the relief of the poor in Thurles and the Ursuline Sisters, referred to the priests too who were suffering as a result of "the general calamity that has befallen the People". He is "quite upset" by the "trying times" and quite incapable of the "energetic exertions" which they call for, "so that I cannot but regret having ever been placed in so prominent a position, or having ever seen the day of which next Wednesday is the Anniversary (of his consecration as Bishop). But this is now a vain regret and ought not to be indulged by me, if I had either Religion or Philosophy enough to sustain me but alas I have not".

On 25 February the good Archbishop received the second instalment of Renehan's half notes to make up £15. He was quick to thank his benefactor and his second letter is as illuminating as his first on the famine as it hit the town of Thurles:

> "The distress of the People is every day increasing and persons who three months ago were able to do without assistance are now run out and seeking for relief. For some weeks past the deaths in this Parish alone average from 15 to 20 every week exclusive of the Poorhouse where in some days there have been 10 and 12 dead together, and although it could not perhaps be said that any one died of actual starvation, it was nearly as bad, they died of inanition and want of enough to sustain life...."

He went on to say that, even though the public works were undesirable and tended to demoralise the people, they were better than nothing. Permanent measures for the future were not contemplated by the Government. And yet, he went on too to talk about the Jubilee which was to be preached in the diocese the following Sunday and enclosed a copy of the rescript proclaiming it ! Were it not for fortitude like this, one supposes that the nation would have perished.

In the far West, things were no better. That March, Archbishop McHale of Tuam acknowledged to Renehan receipt of £10 "for the suffering poor of this diocese". He had been expected in Dublin by the Archbishop —

> "But the truth is that we are both so occupied in continual business and anxiety regarding the awful distress of the people that I understand from him his Grace cannot attend. Fortunately the business did not require my presence as it was a distribution of charitable funds from America which can be done by an equitable proxy. Again accept my sincere thanks for your sympathy for our poor people".

In thanking Renehan for the help which he had forwarded, McHale

85

expressed the hope that the grant to Maynooth will not be "called back", a step which he would regard as "attended with serious embarrassment to your community". In truth, it would have been an embarrassment also to the various dioceses of the country, so dependent were they, in those stringent times, on governmental succour.

It is gratifying to find the College so ready to be liberal with its Queen's largesse. Letter after letter came in thanking both President and staff for their generosity. One came from Kerry, from Bishop Cornelius Egan, whose place of residence, Killarney, was feeling the full brunt of the hunger. There, he says, all available space in the Workhouse and Auxiliary Workhouses was crammed. The air was bad. There were twenty to thirty deaths per week. especially among children and the old. One can meet a father who went in with four or five children leaving with one on his back. The story was the same in Killala. From there, the Bishop to Renehan: "We are here in an awful state of destitution, Clergy as well as laity", but he thanks "the Superiors and Professors of the College for your very liberal and charitable contributions for the relief of our starving people". Clearly, the Queen's gold was being put to some excellent use.

As the terrible year progressed, death began to claim the priests also. From Thurles the Archbishop of Cashel: "The priests here are harassed to Death by duty and the distress of the people which is rapidly on the increase. Fever and dysentery are making frightful ravages — one of the Nuns in the Presentation Convent is just being interred. having died of fever". He reports that Dr. Murphy of Cork had on the previous Tuesday declared that his own time would come soon, "for my soul is sorrowful unto death". And so indeed he died, eloquent testimony to the frightfulness of those days. Not long afterwards, the Vicar Capitular of Cork — Thomas Barry — called out as many students as possible for ordination "in consequence of the mortality of Priests in this Diocese and the great necessity of having a sufficient number to attend to the great multitude of the dying".

From the Midlands — from Athlone — came another cry, this time from the Bishop of Elphin: "The famine is daily increasing in this diocese, the deaths innumerable. May the Lord have mercy on us and spare our People". Again from Clogher (6 May): "The new much named relief has, as yet, done nothing for us. The public works are stopped and our people starving. The delay and formalities of relief Committees, as they are called, are beyond endurance and yet it is to such that contributions for the fund are remitted, and not, except in a few instances, to the C. clergy, who are compelled to see the people dying off of starvation — of diseases brought on by want of food, without having any means of affording relief". And once more (25 May): "Our afflictions are great and heavy and they have been increased immeasurably by the distressing rumours of O'Connell's death, which have just reached us".

O'Connell had indeed passed away — mourned a lot by some such as McNally, not so mourned by others, then or afterwards. But it was hard for any Irishman to find *The Times*, in 1847, asking: "What is an Englishman made for but to work ? What is an Irishman made for but to sit at his cabin door, read O'Connell's speeches, and abuse the English ?".

Came June, 1847, and there was no let up to the plague. Rather were its side-effects being felt. The Archbishop of Cashel to the President of Maynooth:

"We are still struggling with famine and fever, and what is more than both the demoralisation of our people consequent on the system of relief that this incapable Government has inflicted on the country. Every feeling of decent spirit and of truth has vanished, and instead there is created for us a cringing lying population, a Nation of Beggars. It would actually make one's blood run cold to be an eyewitness of what we are obliged to submit to, the ablebodied obliged to leave their work and the youth their schools and spend their time congregated about the gate of a Soup Kitchen where their scanty rations are doled out, mixed up with all manner of persons good and bad. It is enough to bring a curse on the country to have the poor of the Lord degraded as they are and that in a land calling itself Christian".

These were hard words. But in 1847 both bishops and people were very glad of any port in the storm. There is a letter in the *President's Archives* from much later — Cullen to Russell — which tells us that during that year a collection was made at Ivrea in Piedmont for the poor of Ireland. When sending on the proceeds to Dr. Murray of Dublin, the Italian Bishop mentioned that an Irish Bishop had died in Ivrea in the 15th century and was still venerated there. His name was Thadeus Maher or Meagher. Renehan had told Cullen that he could not discover any Irish bishop of that name. When writing later to Russell (in the 1860's), Cullen was still hopeful of finding out more about the matter. He would like to get a copy of the Bishop of Ivrea's letter which, he thought, must be among Dr. Renehan's effects.

We have already had occasion to note the reluctance with which some of the Maynooth students of this time approached what should have been their task in life whether at home or abroad, in spite of the grave need for priests expressed by many of their Bishops. Early in 1847, Dr. Denvir of Down and Connor referred to the scarcity of priests in his diocese. In April, the Bishop of Elphin spoke about the lack of readiness on the part of young men — whether at Maynooth or not — to take up foreign missionary work, even for a time. He wrote as follows: "Alas, it is too bad that the Apostolic spirit which ever animated the youth of Ireland and prompted them to go to every region and clime to propagate the

Kingdom of God, should have so degenerated in these our days as to render it so extremely difficult to procure priests for foreign Missions". In fact, it was now the turn of the missionary territories to try to do what they could for the physical benefit of Ireland. India, even with its own intermittent famines, was notably generous with aid. In Calcutta, Archbishop Carew launched a relief fund, his *Bengal Catholic Herald* carrying many letters from past Maynooth contemporaries seeking help for their unfortunate parishioners. We gather that the Irish in the army in India were unstinting in their generosity.

In face of a certain shortage of priests which, as has emerged, began to characterise these years, it is somewhat surprising to find quite a number of Bishops specifying that they wanted only Irish-speaking clergy. Well, perhaps the request was not so strange for, if the Irish language was spoken widely in their dioceses, as indeed it was, it was obviously important that the priests be able to speak it. And so we find the Bishop of Clonfert in February, 1847, asking the President of Maynooth to make arrangements for the ordination of two of his students who spoke Irish, which was so necessary for his diocese. In like manner Dr. Maginn of Derry: "I earnestly solicit your attention to the necessity of obliging the Derry students to attend the Irish class so as to render themselves capable of hearing confession and imparting some instructions through that language. At present it is a matter of extreme difficulty with me to properly provide for the mission in consequence of the ignorance of the Irish language which I may say almost universally prevails among our young clergymen. For the future I will make Irish a *sine qua non* for all our young men coming out in our mission". The Bishop of Cloyne wrote to Renehan on 10 May, 1847, to tell him that he had made up his mind "never more to consent to the ordination, *under any circumstances*, of any Cloyne or Ross student, who shall not be able to speak the Irish, the language of the great majority of the People of their Diocese, knowing well as I do, the grievous inconvenience that has resulted to the Administration of the Diocese as well as the positive injury that has accrued to Religion from the too great facility with which my Predecessors have from time to time consented to the Ordination of young men, who whatever might have been their qualifications otherwise were on that score alone totally unfitted for this Mission. The Missionary to China felt it his duty to learn the language of the People amongst whom and for the benefit of whom his ministry is to be exercised, and I see no reason why for an Irishman the language of his Country should not be at least as easy an acquisition."

By mid-1847 the scourge of the famine had really begun to be felt over most of the land. In May, typhus fever had spread through the country — Cork, Sligo and Belfast especially. Mr. Magennis, former Professor in the College, was struck down by it. Crowds were leaving for America. So told Dr. Dixon, Primate of Armagh, to Cullen. Sometimes they never made it;

a few days before, a ship from Derry with 251 people on board was wrecked after three days out. All were lost, except three sailors. In the College, things remained calm. In June, the Trustees resolved "that the sum of Eighty eight pounds be divided equally among the superiors and Professors of the College to improve their commons and particularly to encourage the most regular exercise of hospitality to Strangers who may be invited by any of them to their table."

It must be said that the professors had been generous to the needy, insofar as those records that have come down to us testify. Dr. Callan was amongst the most generous, and if one had to decide whether his great charity or his electrical genius was his greatest characteristic, his charity wins out. During the famine he continuously gave to those in want. Repeatedly, he enabled the Presentation Sisters of Maynooth village to provide food and clothing for the poor of the locality. But it is a measure of the general Maynooth situation that it could be said by the Reverend Mother of the convent that as "there was not much distress in the district, so there were not such extensive claims on the kindness of the sisters".

SURVIVAL OF THE FAT

Maynooth survived the famine better than most places. How could it have been otherwise, given its privileged position ? During the terrible year of 1847 itself, a Catholic magazine had fulsomely bespoken its flourishing: "Vigorous be the growth, and clustering the superabundance of virtues that vegetate in the bosom of our own dear Maynooth College ! Verdant be the literary laurels that are to deck, in thick and honourable profusion, her children's brows ! *Lucet et ardet* be her perennial motto ! a light to the nations of the earth − a furnace of glowing charity and ardent zeal in the service of a grateful world ! So may she be the exalting parent of generations of saints − so may she best fulfil the godlike mission assigned to her".

A Visitation of the College was held on 22 June. It showed only a slight diminution in the student body, to 515. The effects of the 1845 increase in the grant had begun to be felt − the allowance for Dunboyne students now being £62, an increase of £20 per annum for contingent expenses. The Visitors commented on the excellent state of the larder and the kitchen. Breakfast consisted of cocoa, bread and butter; dinner was beef or mutton, boiled or roasted, on alternate days, also bread and vegetables, including potatoes, as well as beer or water at the choice of the student. On Friday it consisted of bread, butter and eggs, together with a pie (of apples, gooseberries or rhubarb) or occasionally rice pudding. Fish was also served occasionally, especially during Advent and Lent. The Visitors could not fail to be impressed by this. They were

89

particularly interested in Callan's continuing experiments: "Since the last Visitation he has made a very important improvement in the construction and use of the galvanic battery, by substituting for platina, platinized or gilded lead, or platinized or cromed cast-iron; and for nitric acid a solution of common nitre. He has found that the platinized leaden battery is the most powerful battery yet constructed; that it is more powerful than a platine one, even of the same size; whilst the cost of the platinized lead for the former is not the sixtieth part of the cost of the platine for the latter." In general, though, the Professors were far from being overworked. Dr. Russell, Professor of Ecclesiastical History, was found to be giving one lecture of an hour and a half and two lectures of an hour, each week, to 160 students. His salary was £260 per annum.

The Visitors, however, were more than satisfied. Before leaving, the Chief Baron expressed a desire to be present at the closing exercises of the College, that is, to assist at the defence of a Thesis. Once a year six or eight of the most distinguished Dunboyne students used to hold, in the presence of the Trustees and the entire Collegiate body, a public disputation on certain subjects, set forth in a printed document called 'Thesis Theologica'. It is not clear whether that for 1847 was in fact attended by the Chief Baron. More than likely, he was satisfied with having secured the Report on the Visitation. The Secretary to the Trustees this time took no chances about the submission by the President being misreported. He had the matter written up before the departure of the Visitors from the College and sought verification of it by them. But he was furious when the Chief Baron and the Duke of Leinster picked at his notes until near twelve o'clock before agreeing to them. The next day he had to dictate it all over to a clerk and then employ a scrivener to enter the matter into a book. He was irritated by the Chief Baron; unless that kind of thing stopped, he would have to give up the Secretaryship.

Renehan's humour too could not have been the best when, towards the end of June, Flanagan informed him that he was in trouble with an "unfortunate former inmate" of the College. This was the Reverend Denis Brasbie, one time Catholic priest now a parson. In December, 1845, Renehan had furnished the Anglican Bishop of Worcester with a statement concerning Brasbie's character, to which the latter took exception and on the head of which he now brought an action for libel against the President claiming £5,000 damages because of the loss of a post which the statement had cost him. The case was to be tried before the Chief Justice and a special jury. Flanagan assured Renehan that everything possible would be done to make sure that jurors of unprejudiced character would be chosen to act in the case.

The trial was fixed for Monday, 21 June. Prior to it, a practical joker (very likely from the College) played a prank on Dr. O'Reilly, Professor of Moral Theology. He was served with a *sub poena* by somebody

90

unknown as he passed through the town, as a result of which he had studied English Law and Canon Law for a week, only to find that his services were not expected by the court. Dr. Dixon was taken in also in the same way and conveyed his annoyance about it to Cullen in no uncertain terms: "It was a cruel hoax and the author of it would richly deserve to be employed in breaking stones in New South Wales for one month at least". When the case did come up, the jury was locked in for the night. Then came the verdict. Renehan was indeed found guilty but the damages awarded were small — £25. The costs, however, which were also awarded against him, were quite high, something in the region of £300. The whole affair is set out in a pamphlet brought out at the time entitled *Trial and Conviction of the Rev. Dr. Renehan, President of Maynooth College, for a gross and malicious libel against the Rev. Denis Leyne Brasbie,* published from reports in the *Dublin Evening Herald* by the Priests' Protection Society. It was a heavy enough blow for the President, whose health was not improved by it. Indeed he passed a bad Summer vacation that 1847, and not because of the famine.

In the middle of July he received a letter from one Thomas O'Reilly, a student who, had the intention of leaving the College, complaining that Drs. Renehan and Whitehead had snubbed him in the street, Dr. Whitehead treating the town to "something like a drunken brawl", calling him a "renegade villain and similar opprobrious terms for which that gentleman will yet have to tender a suitable account". The recent lawsuit had apparently left a taste for litigation.... This time the College authorities were quick to prepare their defence. Within twenty-four hours they had secured the signed testimony of a Malachy Duggan of the town of Maynooth, stating that he was ready to swear that on the 14th. at 11 o'clock at night, he was roused from his bed to save a person who was said to be about to throw himself into the canal and also said to be a student of Maynooth College, Mr. Thomas O'Reilly of Kerry, who was followed by a large crowd of people. He had quickly ascertained that O'Reilly had no intention of drowning himself. He was not mentally deranged, except perhaps by whiskey of which he smelled strongly. O'Reilly had come to the hotel with him but had then refused to go in. He had gone rather to Carton Gate, saying that he intended to go into the demesne. He had scaled the College wall with a view to spending the night out but had been met and recognized by the President and Vice-President and would now not be allowed to continue in the College. He had refused to let Duggan leave him and, repeatedly used improper language regarding the President and Vice-President, threatening to blow the head off "the bloody Whitehead". Duggan had finally got away from him. A similar affirmation was secured from Luke McMahon, tailor, of the town of Maynooth. He confessed, on being interrogated by the President, to having been paid by O'Reilly on the evening of 12 July to bring whiskey to him in the Infirmary. His son had brought it there — a pint of it — next day.

Luckily, both the President and the Vice-President escaped being arraigned before the courts. But they did have their hands full of administration. The Trustees and individual Bishops were exacting in their demands. In spite of his poignant experiences with the famine, the Archbishop of Cashel was ordering in the Autumn of 1847 that those students of his who did not attend the singing classes should be excluded from orders, also asking about whether new buildings would soon be available so as to provide better accommodation and make for better discipline. The President too had quite a lot of work to do by way of assisting an episcopal sub-committee in the drawing up of new College statutes. In November, the third Visitation following the 1845 Act, was held, but had nothing special to report. Immediately following it, a meeting of the Trustees directed the President to contract for the printing of a fifth edition (one thousand copies) of Delahogue's treatise *De Ecclesia*.

There was no shortage of food or of time for writing. The horrors of the famine cannot but have been far from Dr. Russell's mind when, during 1847, he produced articles for *The Dublin Review* on 'Antiquarian Finds in Lycia', 'Tales of the Black Forest', 'Turkish Sieges of Vienna' and the 'Novels of Lady Fullerton'. Dr. Kelly, though, thought that the members of staff did not write enough, and complained about the inadequacies of the library which, he said, inhibited writing. "Besides, the professors of Maynooth could assign quite as satisfactory a reason for their silence...... (the fact that) unless they had previously obtained permission, they were absolutely prohibited from publishing anything under pain of expulsion. We believe this law, which we cannot trust ourselves to characterise, has been either actually repealed, or is in the way of being abolished, or modified in some way which will render it less injurious to the interests of the country and the character of the college". He did agree that there had been many anonymous writings of great merit from the staff. Kelly himself, in an article in the *Irish Catholic Magazine*, gave some words of encouragement to his countrymen "in these awful times"; let them not forget that the Dark Ages begot the Middle Ages; glory had succeeded decay.

Tight although the times were, no serious effort to cut the grant was made during these famine years. True, in the Spring of 1847, there was some criticism advanced about the College finances, but nothing came of it. It was rather the other way round, in that the President made representations to the Treasury for even more money. He himself, in spite of all the difficulties that had come his way, was busily building up his collection of manuscripts. He got a windfall in January, 1848, when James Murphy, brother of the deceased Bishop of Cork, wrote on his own behalf and that of his brothers, Daniel and Nicholas, to say that they had decided to present the Bishop's collection of MSS. to the Royal

92

College of Maynooth: "We shall ship them in a case on the steamer for Dublin next week." Renehan replied at once, thanking the brothers for their "splendid beneficence", a "munificent" present which would entail the "deep and enduring gratitude of the College". He will give "this Collection the most distinguished place of honour in our new and magnificent library" and will be happy if the whole collection, which should grow over the years were to be known as 'Bibliotheca Murphyana'.

In actual fact, Renehan became an obsessive collector of manuscripts. Alas for the man who gave him the loan of any. One has to suppose that it was only a reverential fear of his Archbishop that caused him, in early 1847, to return to Dr. Slattery of Cashel five packages of papers which the latter had lent to him. The 'Black Book of Limerick', lent also to him by Bishop Ryan of that diocese, for the purpose of enabling him to write his history of the Archbishops and Bishops of Ireland, fared differently. Renehan still had it when he died and it passed with some of his papers into the library of the College. In 1848, Joseph O'Longain, Gaelic poet and son of Michael O'Longain, admirer of Paul O'Brien, the first Professor of Irish at Maynooth, dedicated a book of poems entitled *Duanaire na nEascop* to 'An tAthair L. F. O'Renechain'. He had written this book, he said, for the bright and happy priest without fault, him of the seed of warriors, who now ruled daily over the youth of the College that blessed our gentle and prosperous land:

Do sgriobhadh an leabhar so don Athair geal shuairc gan chaim
Do shiol na bhfearachon meanamnach O'Renechain
Ta ag riarugha air sagairt is macra chliar gach la
A ccolaiste an apstail do bheanaigh ar n-iath mhin bhlath".

BACKLASH 1848

On 6 March, 1847, O'Connell had left for Rome for health reasons; he died on the way in Genoa on 15 May. Back home in Ireland, they did him proud by way of obsequies, although one cannot help feeling that Irish ecclesiastics had mixed feelings about him. Shortly before he left for the continent, he had paid a surprise visit to Maynooth where he made a speech that may have advanced his own concerns but only embarrassed the authorities there. That it left some of the audience uncomfortable is not in doubt. A student who was present recalled afterwards that O'Connell's idea was to introduce his son, John, to the students. There was a suggestion that he had invited himself and was not all that welcome by the authorities who were still nervous of the Government. The students were respectful but not enthusiastic. Some even thought for a while of taking the horses from under his carriage. This was understandable when he was overheard "apostrophizing" the bust of George III in the hall and Pitt's good intentions towards Ireland.

In any case, many of the students had sympathies with The Young Irelanders, a title which was given to a group of young men who were members of O'Connell's Repeal Association and who had banded themselves together as a discernible entity around the year 1841. Thomas Davis was their most important leader. Another was Charles Gavan Duffy. Whatever O'Connell said, it was unlikely to get much hearing at that time in Maynooth. Of the visit the Archbishop of Cashel said to the President: "O'Connell's visit took you quite by surprise, but just now it is rather a harmless proceeding, the address notwithstanding, which as you observe was inconvenient as a President, but perhaps not worth noticing. It is likely that some of the Board might be disposed to make more fuss about it than the Government". Still, O'Connell commanded the loyalty of many. On 25 May, Bishop McNally of Clogher wrote: "Our afflictions are great and heavy and they have been increased by the distressing rumours of O'Connell's death, which have just reached us. There is scarcely a hope but we will fondly cling as long as possible to the little that remains. I had been arranging to have a day's public prayer for him throughout this diocess." Maynooth paid him its respects. As Dr. Dixon put it in a letter to Cullen: "We have not been wanting in our duty to poor Dan, although this has not been noticed in the papers. We had our solemn office and Mass for his repose".

O'Connell's passing in many ways opened up a new approach in Irish politics. Young Ireland came into its own. Before his death they had abandoned the Repeal Association, his own 'new initiative' for the ending of the Union peacefully. That the Maynooth students could easily be drawn into politics emerges from a letter of Slattery of Cashel to the President, as early as September, 1845, concerning a meeting that had been held down there and to which he had advised his Maynooth students not to attend "lest some evil minded persons might make a report to the Government .... and perhaps great inconvenience might result either to the lads themselves or to the College". Slattery did not have all that much time for O'Connell. A bigger attraction to the students was constituted by Young Ireland. That they were ripe for 'mischief' can be gathered from various Bishops' views of them to the President a decade afterwards when they were 'out on the mission'. Thus Murphy of Ferns: "I have remarked that the young men coming home from College, these last fifteen or twenty years ..... are more inclined to dabble in Politics than the Priests of former times. I do not know how to account for this: but observe, Very Revd. Sir, I do not insinuate the least blame to Maynooth, but I feel it is owing to the progress of the Times" (December, 1854). Vaughan of Killaloe: "Some of the young priests who came home since I became a Bishop are not at all as *humble* as they ought to be". (March, 1855). Vaughan again: "Some of the young priests who come home these two or three years.... practise more argumentation than theology" (February, 1857). These were the men who, in Maynooth in the late

94

forties, had sympathies with the Young Irelanders or the O'Connellites.

It was Gladstone who said later that O'Connell could believe anything he wanted. In 1823 he had said that the great body of the people would be quite contented with the Union and that reference to its dissolution was only for the purposes of rhetorical excitement. In 1840, however, he went on his campaign for the repeal of it, a campaign that reached its zenith in 1843.

That year, another visitor, the German, Herr J. Venedy, toured the country. Venedy (1805 - 1870) was a popular historian who had written a life of Frederick the Great. He was the author of three travel books, one about his visit to Ireland. His book was published in translation in 1844, by James Duffy of Dublin. Entitled *Ireland and the Irish during the Repeal Year 1843*, it maintained that the Catholic clergy were *democratised* even apart from O'Connell's influence, by coming mainly from the ranks of the peasantry. At the same time, he had to recognise that Maynooth required such a knowledge of Latin, Greek and Mathematical subjects as to make it impossible for the humblest class of the country (as indeed of any country) to have it because of incapacity to pay for it. He recalled too that one half of the students at the College paid for their education and that no student could be on the establishment at less outlay than fifteen to twenty-five pounds per annum, so that while the Catholic Church in Ireland, as well as all over the world, exalts the humble, "her ranks are actually recruited by those who might have attained to any other of the liberal professions at less cost". It was an exaggeration,yet it had a degree of truth in it. Nevertheless, says Venedy, these clerics mixed well with the people as a whole and played a large part in the movement for repeal.

But destiny was to have things otherwise. The Young Irelanders held out great attractions, dedicated as they were to noble ideals for the nation, the implementation of which they saw as requiring the status of an independent sovereign State, an army, a flag and a language. In October, 1842, the first issue of a weekly paper called the *Nation* appeared, under the editorship of Gavan Duffy from Monaghan. Interestingly enough, George Crolly, Professor of Moral Theology at Maynooth, who had come up as Professor in 1844, had before that, while a priest in Belfast, assisted Duffy to establish the *Vindicator,* a kind of predecessor of the *Nation.* The Young Ireland group were the only people who took seriously O' Connell's loud talk about forcible resistance, but, when it became apparent that it was only talk, they had become critical of him and, as it were, swung to the left. As the Repeal Movement sagged and finally collapsed, the Young Irelanders mounted their attempt at rebellion. The resulting fiasco only showed how much out of tune they were with the people.

Many of the people after O'Connell's death were swayed for a time by his son John. With him and his followers, the *Nation* came in for a hard time, the epithet 'Godless' being regularly thrown at it. Why this should be, one can only speculate, although, in 1843, Dr. Murray of Maynooth had written to Daniel O'Connell protesting against an article which had attacked *The Dublin Review* as being "written by Saxons", "anti-Irish", "printed in London".

The Dublin Review was definitely orientated towards the English establishment. One has only to read Wiseman's letters to Russell to realise this. Indeed, given the royal endowment of 1845 and the atmosphere which prevailed there during this time, one can only marvel that Maynooth managed to keep its contacts with the grass roots of Irish life and did not sell its soul. In truth, it was a touch and go affair. But there were many in the College who were close to the soil. Dr. Murray had a number of friends among the Young Irelanders. When a Bishop charged him with having expelled the nephew of one of his priests because of the uncle's opposition "to your friends, Duffy, Mitchel and O'Brien", all Murray could do was to say that administrative business was not his affair. He was not the only one at Maynooth, or among the Irish clergy in general, to have leanings towards the Young Ireland cause. Even Dr. Russell, in the said *Dublin Review* itself, struck a nationalist note in reviewing 'The Ballad Poetry of Ireland' and insisting on the need to encourage the creation of a national literature.

During the State Trials of 1844, which led to the imprisonment of both O'Connell and Duffy, Murray took a keen interest in the proceedings and contributed several letters to the newspapers. Under the signature of 'Irish Priest', he had protested in the columns of the *Nation.* An open letter to the Lord Lieutenant was published: "Let your Excellency bear in mind that deeply as the root of the deadly hatred of English domination that festered in the hearts of the great mass of the Catholic population since that domination was first established over them, is a feeling of utter distrust, and, in the State Trials, of utter despair of an impartial administration of the law". Lord Clarendon attempted to reply but was answered scathingly. And when James Duffy, a Monaghan man and relative of Murray's, launched the *Irish Catholic Magazine* in 1846, he could rely on the support of both Murray and Crolly, themselves close friends. They were equally close to Gavan Duffy, of the *Nation*. The latter's description of Murray is "a man of vigorous intellect and many accomplishments, peculiarly familiar iwth the English classics, and master of a style which has been rarely excelled for poignancy and lucidity". He had wished to become "an Edinburgh Reviewer", and Gavan Duffy, during Carlyle's Irish visit of the Summer of 1846, had asked him to see to this, "which he did promptly and cordially".

As 1848 approached, restiveness became manifest throughout the land. For a while, John O'Connell managed to secure support. As regards Maynooth, Dr. Murray of Dublin had this to say to the President in June, 1847: "I have heard that several students of Maynooth have signed a political address. I beg to express a hope that none of the students for this Diocese have been guilty of such a violation of College Discipline. I pray you however to call the Dublin students together and inform them that any one among them who has done so and will not withdraw his name, or shall hereafter do so, will be visited with my marked displeasure." Murray succeeded in quelling any budding political drive but only by the skin of the teeth.

Dr. O'Reilly wrote to Cullen on 13 July, giving him a good picture of the state of affairs in the College: "By the way we were near having a Maynooth demonstration for Old Ireland. An address was prepared and unanimously signed by the students to John O'Connell promising I suppose adhesion to him and against the other party. It was however fortunately denounced in time to the domestic authorities and suppressed. Afterwards the Board of Trustees passed a resolution reprobating and forbidding all political demonstrations of that nature. They were right, for it is hard to tell the extent of evil that would result from such proceedings at Maynooth .... The state of the country is deplorable. The people are still in great distress ...."

Years later, at the investigations of the Royal Commission of 1853, the Reverend Walter Lee, Junior Dean, gave evidence about "some few students having used strong language during the time of the great excitement that prevailed in 1847 or 1848" and about their having attempted to procure an address to O'Connell. But the President had suppressed it. Or rather it was suppressed by the Senior Dean, Dr. Gaffney, the President being ill and the Vice-President away.

That this political agitation in the College was far from being just a flash in the pan is attested to by the serious way in which quite a number of Bishops viewed it. The Primate, Dr. Crolly, was quite pointed in his attitude:

> "I have heard with much sorrow and surprise that some imprudent and misguided persons have induced a considerable number of the students of the Royal College of Maynooth to sign a political Declaration, which may produce an improper excitement in the important institution over which you at present preside. You are aware that such conduct is contrary to the instructions which I received from the late Pope Gregory XVI and I can assure you that the present Pope has given me a similar injunction for the direction of the clergy of Ireland. I need not tell you, that any person who attempts to introduce any political excitement among the students has violated the Statutes of the College. I therefore request, that you will without delay, assemble the students, who are under my juris-diction, and desire them in my name to withdraw *immediately* their names from any political Document, that they or any of them may have been induced to sign, under pain of incurring my severe displeasure. Their proper compliance with this injunction may enable me to protect them and others from just censure at the approaching Visitation of the College".

This was a tough approach, like that of Dr. Murray. These men were old and able to lean on their advanced years. The Bishop of Kilmore (Dr. Browne) was equally intransigent:

> "I have been informed that political party questions have been introduced into our National College and that a number of students have been induced to sign an address to John O' Connell approving of his political views. I never imposed the slightest restraint on any one touching political opinions, but I think the agitation of political opinions in the College will be very injurious to study, to peace and order and possibly end in the subversion of the establishment. I hope that the subjects of Kilmore have had the good sense to remain neutral on this occasion, but if unfortunately they have joined in any political demonstration, I have to request that you, with my authority, do order them to withdraw their names and co-operation now and in future whilst in the College from all such dangerous proceedings".

Likewise, Cornelius Denvir, Bishop of Down and Connor, expressed his "unspeakable regret" at having heard that some students for that diocese had "at the instance of some persons in your Collegiate community signed some political declaration". This is contrary to the directions recently laid down by the Bishops of Ireland for the conduct of their clergy. He too requests the President to call the students together at once and inform them that he — Denvir — requires each "to withdraw his name from the document in question without a moment's delay".

If ever anything were 'orchestrated', surely it was this episcopal response to John O'Connell's effort to get open support in Maynooth. It was swift and firm and co-ordinated and it worked. On 17 June, the Archbishop of Dublin is writing to the President saying how delighted he is that "the misguided project was checked", and adding: "Do not on any account venture to come to Dublin on Saturday. Any business you may have to transact could be done by letter without the risk of a premature exposure". There was no trouble about the matter at the Visitation of 22 June, except that the Trustees at their meeting "resolved that the President be requested to communicate to the Students of this College, at the earliest opportunity, our decided disapprobation of the introduction of any political subject for public discussion in the College, or of any political document for signature, and that any member of this College who shall directly or indirectly aid or concur in such political proceedings, shall be visited with our heaviest displeasure".

If anything, it was the Government that was in trouble, as witness a remark of Bonham over the fortunes of the Peelites in the general election of 1847, that "Maynooth has certainly destroyed several of our friends". Quite a number of M.P's had lost their seats by reason of having supported the Maynooth Grant in 1845. A titular neighbour of the College, Lord Lucan, had narrowly escaped defeat because of the opposition of the Free Kirk and other Dissenters.

Throughout the trouble about the student political involvement of 1847, the Archbishop of Tuam remained more aloof than the other Bishops who had come down so heavily. Speaking of McHale's role at this time, his biographer says that he was a great patriot who kept alive the hopes of the nation, "asking in tones of thunder, that justice shall be done to Ireland." There is or was in the library of the College a copy of this biography, on the margin of which a student — opposite the sentence just quoted — noted simply: "Ireland sees to that herself (1920)" ....

In 1848 she was thinking in like vein, or at least the Young Irelanders were. Thoughts were turning to violence. There can be no doubt but that, whatever may have been intended by the Crown in establishing Maynooth, whatever may have been intended by Peel in richly endowing it, and whatever may have been intended by the Bishops in striving to see that it remained loyal, the College had turned out and continued to turn out a great stream of nationalist students. Inglis, on his visit to Ireland in 1834, had remarked that whenever a liberal priest of the older generation was appointed to a parish, "straightaway an assistant, red-hot from Maynooth, was appointed to the parish and, in fact, the old priest is virtually displaced".

At the time of Repeal, there were references by Irish Protestants to "blood-stained Maynooth", a place described as "an infernal machine, plied by the Satanic sons of Loyola", whose products were "rank rebels", "case-hardened, sneering, profligates", who were "immersed in a whirlpool of seditious politics". As D. Croly had put it in 1835, in his *Inquiry into the Principal Points of Difference between the Two Churches:* "Reckless of consequences, they interpose between the tenant and his landlord, and endeavour from the altar, at the time of mass, to persuade the poor man that if he does not place himself in hostility with the lord of the soil, to his own great detriment, and that of his poor family, he will violate the most sacred duties and run the imminent risk of eternal damnation". They must have gone fairly far when even McHale was driven to comment about "the arrogance and pride of some of the young men from this house" *(Sermons and Discourses).*

In addition to many students and at least some members of the staff, one can speculate too at times about what the real thoughts of the President were in political matters. After all, he was passionately devoted to Irish history and literature. That he did not always 'toe the line' in the way the Castle expected is very clear from a letter to him of 18 February, 1848, from Dr. Murray, Archbishop of Dublin:

"Dear Dr. Renehan — Observations have lately reached me from different quarters expressing surprise and regret, that the President of the Royal College of Maynooth was not among those, who, on a recent occasion, thought it right to testify their respect for Her Majesty by appearing at the Levee of Her Representative. I could not, of course, offer any explanation of the omission. There was however an observation added which would not, I am sure, have the least foundation in truth. It was said, that when it was remarked to you that your absence, on the occasion alluded to, had been unfavourably noticed, you replied, that you would not, if you attended the Levee be able to govern the College. This, if it had a shadow of truth in it, would be a sad tale for Maynooth. Having heard the above observations, I thought it only fair that you should be put in possession of them. I remain, Dear Dr. Renehan, Yrs. + D. Murray".

As usual, the position of the President was unenviable. Sure, he had a powerful protector, but it was hard for him to be his own man. Immediately on receiving Archbishop Murray's admonition, for it was hardly less, he sat down and wrote a reply, of which he retained a corrected copy. He asks Murray to accept his humble thanks "as well as for your disbelieving the motive to which my absence was ascribed as for your enabling me to contradict the unintentional misstatement". He cannot remember ever saying what had been attributed to him concerning the government of the College:

"In grateful and devoted loyalty to our gracious Sovereign, in profound respect for her eminently dignified and talented Representative in Ireland, I need not tell your Grace that I do not yield even to those whose duty or privilege it may be to assist in the public courtly exhibitions of such respect. But I am free to confess that it never once occurred to my mind that I would be expected or that I ought to attend at the Levee and that I therefore was absent merely from habit and without any very distinct motive. I did not attend last year or the year before and I neither heard of any remarks on my absence nor was aware of any reason for alluding this year more than those. My revered predecessor, so distinguished for intense veneration to even the most Tory governments, during his many years here of office, never attended at a Levee. I am under the impression that *no* President of the Royal College of Maynooth since its first establishment, ever appeared at a Levee, except perhaps (for I am not sure of the fact) on one very extraordinary occasion. While therefore, I was solicitous that the late Levee be most respectfully attended, with this uniform practice to guide me and these numerous precedents, the idea of thrusting myself personally into the honourable cortege did not even occur to my mind and I felt about it pretty nearly as I would about a Levee at St. James' or a Birthday Review in the Park, or a Play by command or any other public testimonies of respect to her Majesty, suited to the different ranks and classes of society. But should Your Grace or the Trustees advise me to the contrary, and authorise me, notwithstanding the resolution passed by the last Summer Board to join in what some may consider a manifestation not of loyalty or respect only, but to some extent also of politics, I shall feel a pride and a pleasure in following whatever course your Lordship may recommend as most becoming the President of a purely ecclesiastical College and most expressive of loyalty to the Queen and of respect to the Irish Viceroy."

It was a clever letter, respectful and yet unbending, particularly adroit in recalling the resolution of the Trustees about political manifestations. His was in truth a difficult position, caught between the establishments and the students.

As the year wore on, the unrest in the country developed. The Bishop of Down and Connor was writing to the President about the insubordination of the young priests towards their Parish Priests, tending to do things as they wanted to. Word was coming in to him too of the "hotheaded" publications of Fathers Bermingham and Kenyon, who were fully in the Young Ireland camp.

Priests of the Diocese of Killaloe, Fr. Bermingham was Parish Priest of Borrisokane and Fr. Kenyon Curate of Templederry. Of the two, Fr. Kenyon was the more notable. He was a native of Limerick City, where his father was a prosperous merchant. He was educated for the priesthood at Maynooth and ordained in 1836. He had held two curacies before his appointment to Templederry in 1842, where he was to die ultimately as Parish Priest in March, 1869, not too long ago after the Fenian Rising.

In the 1840's, Fr. Kenyon was a staunch supporter of the Young Irelanders, becoming a close friend of John Mitchel and others of their leaders. In 1846, just before the split between them and the O'Connellites, he had published an essay on 'Physical and Moral Force', which openly asserted that the people had the right to arm and to fight for their liberties. It was by no means the most scholarly production, yet it is interesting, if only because of the scarcity of material from Irish writers at the time on the ethics of revolt. Dr. Patrick Murray of Maynooth, friend of Gavan Duffy's though he was, remained silent on the subject until 1853, and when he did write his position was so hedged round with qualifications as to be of little practical help. Kenyon was very direct in his views, too much so, his Bishop thought. The matter came to a head after Fr. Kenyon wrote to the *United Irishman* (its first number) in February, 1848, seeming to suggest the desirability of armed resistance. Many thought that he should be dealt with harshly.

His Bishop, Dr. Kennedy, wrote to Renehan saying that he had consulted a theologian, who laboured to convince him that "a case may arise in which resistance to constituted authority would be lawful". He says that he had never doubted this; even the British Government, he has no doubt, would not object to it as an abstract principle.

Indeed, he is one of the many who feel indignant against the late Mr. O'Connell for his treatment of the Young Ireland party for refusing to forswear that principle. Still, he is against acting on that principle now, knowing that few people really want to endure the horrors of civil strife, except those in misery, who are easily led to hope for a change. He then goes on to explain the Kenyon affair. The moment he had read in *The Clare Journal* about Kenyon's letter in *The United Irishman*, he had written to him, expressing surprise and disappointment that he should have contributed to that paper, and requiring him to have no more to do with it. Still, Fr. Kenyon had gone on afterwards to make a speech in Templederry more or less repeating the same sentiments. So the Bishop had acted again. Kenyon had promised to give up writing or speaking on political matters while under his jurisdiction but the Bishop was not satisfied with that. It would not be enough on the part of an ecclesiastic who had pledged himself "to support John Mitchel, T.F. Meagher and Mr. W. O'Brien, in any way, or anywhere. Some expression of regret for his stance was surely necessary. The Bishop had held up De Lamennais for Kenyon's warning. He is anxious about Kenyon who, even when suspended, had tried to stay on in his parish for four months. Was this, the Bishop asks, in order to have the people in his hands when "the Commissariat" was formed — in other words, until a rebellion ? At this time, Fr. Bermingham was also involved in the same kind of thing. The Bishop suspended both until, in one way or another, they came to heel.

Rebellion, however, was in the air. But the Government was on the alert. On 21 May, Mitchel, who wanted a Republic, was tried and sentenced to fourteen years transportation. In July, Duffy and some other leaders were arrested and lodged in Newgate. Smith O'Brien, Meagher and others resolved upon a rising but what took place — a few incidents especially in Co. Tipperary — was a non-event. It quickly fizzled out. The Queen, however, imagined "risings in all directions" in Ireland; "Really they are a terrible people". William Smith O'Brien was subsequently transported to Australia.

The Maynooth students appear to have taken no part in the rebellion, such as it was, although that September, Dublin Castle sent in a query as to whether a certain John Kelly was a student of the College and, if so, where did he come from and where was he on the previous 9 August ? The generality of the students were occupied with other things. In June, the Board had agreed "that black Pantaloons, short black garters and the standing clerical collar to the Coat, be the universal dress of the students". Russell must have been pleased; he liked elegance. He certainly cannot have had much time for those who sought revolution. A year afterwards, when he was mentioned for Armagh, a correspondent of Cullen's had been very blunt: "The fate of our Church and nation is in the balance ... If Dr. R——l of M——th be the man, VQ nobis. He is a courtier and no mistake".

The Queen was expected to visit the College soon after, during the course of a trip to Ireland. She needed a change. In 1848 she had been worried by revolution. Then in Feburary, 1849, there had been an intruder at Windsor, leading *The Times* to print remarks reminiscent of 1982: "Let the Queen of Great Britain be able to sit down to her piano or sketch-book with the same security against intrusion as any other lady in the land". On 19 May, a fourth attempt had been made on her life, by a mad Irishman named William Hamilton.

In August she came to Ireland, landing at Cove and changing its name, disembarking also at Cork and then going by sea to Kingstown and on to a Levee in the Phoenix Park. She was accompanied by the Prince Consort, together with the Prince of Wales. On 6 August, the day of the Levee, she noted: "This morning we visited the College". One does not have to ask which College ? It was not the Royal College of St. Patrick. In any event, the Archbishop of Dublin made very sure that the President of that College would be present at this important Levee. When the latter visited him two days before, he had hurried him off to the office which issued tickets for it as he was afraid that it would close at four o'clock and was anxious that the President got there before then. He inquired as to whether he was in time and had got an admission card. To make doubly sure, he announced that on the day previous to the Levee some Bishops were to dine with him and he invited Dr. Renehan along also.

There was a possibility that the Queen might go to the College: "I find that Her Majesty is to visit the Duke and, if so, it is very likely that she may drop in on you". The informality recalls Percy French's song about the visitor from Dromcollogher who dropped in to see King Edward VII: "Said the butler, he's out; he is'nt about; for I don't see his hat in the hall". The visit to the College was not to materialise, although Archbishop Murray was holding out hopes for it even on the eve of her trip to Carton. To Renehan on 9 August: "I am requested to be at Carton tomorrow from half past twelve to five o'clock. I must beg therefore to intrude on Mr. Farrelly for a bed. I am far from thinking it improbable that some of the Royal Party will look in on the College. Perhaps even the amiable little Queen may take it into her head to do so".

On Friday, 10 August, Carton demesne was thrown open to the public and there were special trains to Maynooth. It was a good day, with bright sunshine, as the report in *The Freeman's Journal* tells us. It tells us too that among those present to meet Her Majesty was Dr. Renehan, President of Maynooth College. She was cheered by a number of College students assembled near Leixlip, while the College displayed "handsome flags". One wonders what they were; Carton flew the royal standard.

Even after this, it was hard for the President to allay suspicions about the loyalty of his institution. That October, the Secretary to the Trustees sent him two cuttings from *The Times*, in case he had not seen them. One was a letter reproduced from *The Tipperary Star* about trouble in Dungarvan as a result of which many had been arrested. The other was one reproduced from *The Clonmel Chronicle* which was more startling. It ran: "We learn that the arrests which have recently taken place at Dungarvan implicate certain students of the Romish Colleges of Waterford and Maynooth in connection with secret societies. A few of the students of the former are already fugitive, and it is rumoured, we know not how truly, that 50 or 60 youths at Maynooth will have to be expelled, for being connected with the recent conspiracy".

Flanagan was apologetic for having to raise this matter with Renehan:

"I hope you will not think it obtrusive to suggest that in these times it might be well to caution the Students not to make any allusions in their correspondence with their friends, especially in the disturbed places, relative to these riots, unless to condemn them". There were other complainants too. A one page tract, *Maynooth and the Colonies*, published in London in 1850, tells of how complaint had been received in 1849 by the Protestant Association concerning the activities of Maynooth men in the colonies, notably in Melbourne. Messages, it said, were on their way to bring out more dissidents: "More are coming from Maynooth".

And yet, for all the accusations of nationalism levelled at the College, there was little interest there just then in the Irish language. Ulick Bourke, later author of the *College Irish Grammar*, entered Maynooth in 1849 for the Diocese of Tuam and was disappointed with the state of Irish there: "In Maynooth not one student out of a hundred learns, during his course, to spell, to speak, and to write Irish as a language. There is an Irish class, but the language of the Gael is treated as the language of the Hebrew race, as something foreign, not the language of thought of the country, of life, of business". His later grammar was "designed chiefly with a view to aid the students of St. Patrick's College, Maynooth, and the Catholic University of Ireland in the study of the National Language". That there was need for a knowledge of Irish by priests continued to be attested to by many Bishops. In the same 1849, Dr. Delaney of Cork declared that the number of parishes there that required a knowledge of Irish was large.

After famine in 1847 and abortive revolt in 1848, the year 1849 was a tough one. Some idea of the rigours of the times can be gleaned from a letter by a Derry priest, following the death of Dr. Maginn in January. The Bishop had travelled from Buncrana to Derry, getting drenched in an outside car. "The arm which was most exposed to the wet became quite black and had clear marks of mortification". The doctors had not been able to agree as to what precisely had killed him. So poverty-stricken were the times, that many Bishops could not provide support for their priests.

Clonfert: "I am not able to provide for the support of any more priests this year, however important their services certainly would be to the mission".

Cork: "We are suffering exceedingly not only thro' the misery and poverty of the people, but also thro' the infirmities of several of our older clergymen and from the unceasing efforts of the enemies of. the Church to destroy the faith of the flock. In the wildest districts of the Kingdom they are erecting new churches where there never was one before, opening new schools and increasing the number of Protestant clergymen; effecting as a matter of course that the Priests cannot live there and that the people must be their prey. Thank God the spirit of our poor priests is admirable, and the Faith of the people little short of miraculous".

Killaloe: "Those few parishes which, before the famine, required the assistance of a curate, are now so wasted and almost depopulated, that they are not able to support even one priest".

And so on and so on — from Armagh, Ossory, Raphoe, Kilmore and other dioceses. Either the people were too poor to be able to support what priests they needed, or too few to need many priests. Emigration had reached startling proportions. Thus French of Kilmacduagh and Kilfenora on 8 May 1850:

"As melancholy Starvation, heartless extermination and unexampled Emigration of our People to the shores of the United States of N. America, have rendered this poor diocese (in common with the West of Ireland) a Wilderness !! ... my poor Parish Priests are obliged to dismiss their curates, owing to the scanty means of sustenance for themselves. Already three of my poor Curates have called for their 'Exeat' and went to America. May the Almighty in his mercy spare both Clergy and People !! 'Parce, Domine, Parce populo tuo'."

And from him again on 14 May, 1850:

"But the Almighty is good and our hopes are great that the Potatoes will be abundant near harvest. There is no other Salvation for the West of Ireland !!! "

Chapter IV

The Phoenix Rises

It is quite amazing how quickly the College, which Peel so generously endowed in 1845, began to apply its new-found wealth. The year had not ended before an architect had been appointed to produce plans for an extension to Maynooth. Augustus Welby Pugin was an Englishman who, converted to Catholicism, had already made a name for himself in both England and Ireland for the soaring spires and tapering arches of his Neo-Gothic. Sponsored by John Talbot, 16th Earl of Shrewsbury and Waterford, he had secured quite a few prestigious contracts and had also published a book on architecture. Some of his earlier work had been in Ireland, where he had designed the Chapel of St. Peter's College, Wexford (1838) and the Church and Convent at Gorey (1839).

A MASTER BUILDER

During the Summer of 1845, Pugin was invited to visit Maynooth and to submit a design for a new building. It is thought by some that Peel had a hand in securing the commission for him. In any case, Pugin's plans were affirmed by the Trustees on 12 September. Cullen reported to Kirby: "He will make it Catholic enough. The board of public works is to do all". In addition, the sum of £18,500 was to be spent in repairing the old buildings. This is a lot, said Cullen, but then "everything done by Government must be a big job". The said Board of Works itself found the sum (£30,000) granted by Parliament for building, repairing and furnishing the College to be inadequate and appealed to the Treasury through their agent Mr. Ratcliffe. On 21 November, a building committee was appointed "to confer with the Board and Mr. Pugin on all necessary occasions and to supervise the execution of the works of the College". It was undoubtedly a new beginning.

When Pugin received the commission to work for Maynooth, he was only thirty-three years of age. In spite of the 'Catholic commissions' which he had got to date, his conversion to Catholicism in 1835 had not helped his professional prospects. It had caused him to lose the commission to rebuild the Houses of Parliament, although he did get a secondary commission in connection with them from the architect that was appointed. His first Government commission was the Maynooth one, although one must suppose that it was with the consent of the Trustees.

From the start he was at loggerheads with nearly everybody. It was hard to blame him. The original figure of £30,000 for the new buildings was proposed to be reduced to £18,000 even before he began. After his appointment, he wrote to Shrewsbury giving out about it. His letter is not dated — they seldom were — but it does date from that Summer:

"I have just returned from Ireland, and to all appearances, everything is arranged about Maynooth, but after the great experience I have had about the uncertainty of human affairs, I shall not calculate on it until we have actually begun. I was very kindly received both by the authorities of the college and the Lord Lieutenant, who invited me to a grand state dinner on Tuesday. There are great difficulties about Maynooth; the grant is quite insufficient for the building. And it appears that the Government will neither give any more, nor consent to Dr. Crolly's proposition to take a sum from the yearly grant for its completion, so I am quite at a stand and have no idea how it will end".

That he resigned in a huff is clear enough, however obscure the circumstances surrounding it. For sixteen staff-members, headed by the Senior Dean, Mr. Gaffney, addressed a memorial to the Board of Trustees, deeply regretting "that Mr. Pugin has ceased to be the architect of the College". They said that the reasons which induced him to resign were not insuperable in nature and could be overcome by co-operation. Early in April, 1846, Gaffney wrote to Pugin, enclosing a copy of this petition, and expressing the hope that he would be architect soon again. In Gaffney's opinion, it was best to start with the money that was available and hope for the best in the future. It was good advice, and of a kind that was to prove valid too for later times. Gaffney, who seems to have had a good relationship with the erratic Pugin, calculated his words: "Who will build our new church or college ?" The staff are most anxious since they heard of his pull out. They had waited on Dr. Murray, the Archbishop, who had advised them to canvass each member of the Trustee body. There will be a meeting of these latter on 22 April for the sole purpose of coming to a decision on the buildings. "We have £30,000; let us begin with the sum. and when exhausted, Providence will not be wanting. The new church and buildings will not remain unfinished".

As the date for the meeting approached, Mr. Flanagan, Secretary to the Trustees, began to be disturbed. The burden of his job seems to have been weighing on him for some time. On Easter Tuesday, 1846, he wrote to the College President, his spelling and grammar not perfect:

"I had a long conversation with Mr. Pigott one of the Visitors on Mr. Pugin's plans and the embarrassing Position in which the Trustees are placed, being called together on the Wednesday after the Visitation to receive the plans of the Board of Works, which they say, they were directed by Government to submit in place of the plans of Mr. Pugin which were found impracticable for want of means. Mr. Pigott is of the opinion that the Trustees may still adopt Mr. Pugin's plans, if on his plans, they can, with the building fund, make the requisite Buildings and improvements for the accommodation of the students etc. As we are all agreed about the desirableness, in fact, the necessity of following his plans if at all possible, perhaps you could do something effectual before the Trustees meet."

Flanagan argued that it would be good if Pugin could come over and confer with the President about the matter, also with Dr. Murray and some others of the Trustees. If satisfied, they could tell the Board of Works that the Building Committee had referred the Board's plans to the Trustees, who were of the view that Mr. Pugin's plans were practical and that they preferred them. This is exactly what they did when they met. As always, the Trustees were crisp and explicit in their recording of the decision (23 April, 1846):

"Resolved that the Building Committee or any three members of it comprising an Archbishop be commissioned and hereby empowered to adopt such part of W. Pugin's plans as will afford the requisite accommodation to superiors, Professors and students, provided that W. Pugin will prove that such Buildings can be executed with the available Building fund or thereabouts and that, if Mr. Pugin fails to prove that such Requisite Buildings can be so executed, the said Building Committee or a Quorum of them be hereby empowered to confer and co-operate with the Board of Works in carrying out their proposed plans, having previously required such alterations to be made in said plans as they may deem necessary".

One has to have admiration for the Trustees. They covered themselves in every way and yet retained flexibility. On 27 April, Pugin met the

Building Committee in Dublin; and it was agreed that the work should go ahead but with the projected quadrangle being left unfinished and the chapel omitted for the present. It was later agreed to omit the Aula Maxima also.

Again the minutes are very clear (27 April):

> "The Building Committee, they say, met with Mr. Pugin, at 10 a.m. and established that "by leaving out the Church but retaining the Continuation of the Cloisters and diminishing the Quadrangle, the requisite accommodation may be afforded to the Superiors, Professors and Students and that such Building can be executed with the available Building funds".

Hence the Trustees declared that "they agreed to and adopted his reduced plan". One is tempted to ask: 'Whose plan ?' There is a note, though, signed by the Secretary, Matthew Flanagan, that Pugin himself had indeed ascertained from the Board of Works that it was possible with the funds available to erect three sides of the quadrangle and that he was happy enough for the present to leave out the Great Hall and the Church.

Thereafter, discussions with Pugin were about details only, even though sometimes they were very recriminatory. Such, for example, was his adjustment in November, 1846, to provide another entrance to the Professors dining room at the West end, one that quickly came to be unused afterwards. By the end of the year, he was in a state of "most severe illness produced by anxiety of the mind". So he himself wrote to a friend.

The Maynooth undertaking obviously took a lot out of Pugin; the Building Committee kept pressurising him and everything had to be approved by the Trustees, as when it was agreed in March, 1847, to prolong the South Side of the Quadrangle by 52 feet so as to make the sides equal. This appears to have been Renehan's suggestion. They were magnanimous and forthcoming on this occasion, for "to meet the cost of it, we hereby guarantee the payment of a sum not exceeding two thousand pounds if necessary, out of College funds". They had got a way around the implementation of Dr. Crolly's original bright idea.

Pugin himself was away ill in the Spring of 1847, and his affairs were looked after from Ramsgate by John H. Powell. Sometimes Pugin wrote himself, mainly to bemoan the scantiness of the funds. He was delighted when the Trustees undertook to pay for the extension of the South Side. Quite a number of these undated letters of his are to be found in the *President's Archives*. They show that five lecture halls were planned for the basement of the Library, that the later St. Mary's Oratory was to be a Study Hall and that the Board Room was also intended to be one of the rooms on the South Side. At one stage, Renehan made another suggestion — to turn the West Side to the North — which infuriated Pugin. This would open the quadrangle and ruin the collegiate character of the building, as well as destroy all the great features of the design. He was not in favour of this open-ended complex but he would dearly like to make an extension to the West Side. If that could at all be done, the chapel might later be relocated

Pugin's health deteriorated swiftly. We find Powell writing to say that he has been very ill with an inflammation of the head, which deprived him of his sight. He did retain his senses at that stage, stressing that any extensions agreed by the Trustees must be cleared with the Board of Works lest he be suspected of only wanting to get more money. He shot an arrow now and then: "Indeed the whole building must be considered as the best way of making the cheapest possible design and not at all to be regarded as a specimen of what a pointed collegiate building ought to be". Powell rubbed the salt in: "Mr. Pugin gave up the work originally foreseeing the impossibility of producing a good thing for the proposed amount and was only induced to undertake the present work by several of the trustees in order to make the best of a bad job and prevent a much worse building being erected. Anyone who expects therefore a very fine building under these circumstances must be disappointed and he expects that the building will be the cause of much disappointment". Anybody who knows the building will have to agree that, for all its magnificent exterior, the greater portion of its interior leaves much to be desired.

In May, 1847, Pugin arrived in Rome, for a long holiday on the advice of his doctors. He was appalled by the "paganism" of Rome's classical architecture. It should not be forgotten that at Maynooth he had wanted Stoyte House replaced by a Gothic building, indeed all of Maynooth if possible. On 10 July, he wrote to Renehan from Dijon, expressing regret at hearing that the work was progressing so slowly. He will come to Ireland as soon as he can. "If this building had been in England and with my own builders it would have been half up by this time".

In August, 1848, he found time to marry his third wife; and for a while things went well. A back entrance and road to the new buildings, especially the kitchen, was planned but unfortunately never executed. In October, preparations were made for the future gas lighting of the College, Pugin being reported as having recommended that the pipes for this should be laid in the new building beforehand. He also prepared a plan for the fitting up of an "experimental hall" for Dr. Callan.

Still, Pugin always managed to be somewhat undiplomatic in his handling of the Irish Bishops. And his handwriting was quite impossible. A letter from the Bishop of Derry to Renehan is amusing in this connection: "I received yesterday a letter almost as hard to be deciphered as an old Gothic Church Tracery. The initials only of the writer were subscribed,

111

but I think they were meant for the name of Mr. Pugin. It was said of the Martello towers (by Curran, I believe) that they were built to humble posterity and I venture to promise that if Mr. Pugin's letters be all such as what I ascribe to him and if they reach posterity it will require a Champollion or a Dr. Wall to decipher them". The one he has just got "has neither date nor time nor place". He found the matter, however, interesting; it was on the new Catholic University project, and he sought "the illustrious architect's address".

Before the Pugin building at Maynooth was finished, there were many more *contretemps* with the architect. The original plan included 60 rooms for professors in the new quadrangle. Before it was completed, the President wrote to Pugin to say that all these were not required as "there are only 19 Priests in the College". He felt that some should live else- where than in this quadrangle; thirteen rooms for professors should be sufficient there. Indeed, if the professors of the Junior House were to live in that place, only nine professors quarters were necessary in the new building. It does seem that the President's recommendations were followed, and happily, because even if the staff quarters, and corridors in them, that emerged are perhaps too spacious, the other thing would have been exceedingly cramped. In like manner, Pugin had envisaged 300 students'rooms for the quadrangle; only 270 were asked for by the Board.

For all his volatile temperament, Pugin put up with his clients' require- ments quite well. At times it must have been hard, as when the Clerk of Works (Jacob Owen) wrote to him complaining that padlocks had been put on the doors of the new building which prevented free access to them. His reply was caustic: "I never meant to clap a great Padlock (on it). It must be something peculiar to the Emerald Isle. I think a padlock outside an ecclesiastical college would give great scandal and a very bad idea of its inhabitants". It did happen though, not only then but much later too in the history of the College. He asks that it be removed. But then comes a real rub: "I know you are a good judge of locks both of Prisons and cellars". He is in good fettle all the same, for he asks Owen why he does not come to London to see "all our fine work at the Exhibition?" He, Pugin, has been commissioned by the Government to choose works for the exhibition that will adorn the arts in England. He has selected several Irish gold brooches, which should make him a popular man in Dublin. And he concludes with an air of abandon: "Hurra for the Curragh of Kildare and the blue sky over it". In more than one letter to the President, he expresses his thanks to the "gentlemen of the College", who were "so zealous" on his behalf. In one of these he confesses that he never really thought that the full, or almost full, project would get off the ground.

By the end of April, 1849, the front of the new building was being roofed. Dr. O'Reilly, who had begun to be scrupulous and could not say the office alone, in writing to Cullen seeking a dispensation from it (he

112

was shortly afterwards to enter the Jesuits), told him that "the whole thing will be a handsome and remarkable Gothic Pile". He also informed Cullen that Primate Crolly had died on Good Friday.

The Trustees carried on regardless, as is their custom and their strength. On 27 June, they resolved "that it is desirable to enlarge the dining room in the new Building by adding to it a portion of the adjoining room and throwing the remainder of that Room into the entrance Reception Room, making one enlarged dining Hall, and one Reception Room: the detail to be submitted to Mr. Pugin". Those who are acquainted with the geography of Maynooth College will guess that what was in question here was the Professors' dining room and will have been glad of the decision. That dining room was to see many an illustrious occasion, hear much good talk and banter, be host to many distinguished guests. In the 20th century, one of these was Eric Gill, who came down to Maynooth on Friday, 24 October, 1919, after Mass in the Dominican Church in Dublin. He has left us a pen-picture in his *Essays* (London, 1942):

"Friday 24 October, 1919. To communion at Dominican Church. Breakfast and then by 9 o'clock train from Broadstone Station to Maynooth to meet some of the professors at the College. A great place — Pugin at his best — except the chapel, but even that would have been good if left plain ..... Dinner in professors' dining hall 12.30 — not much puritanism either about the dinner or the conversation".

Pugin must have been annoyed when, in December, 1849, the Trustees postponed the gas lighting of the College, because of the difficulty of conveying tubes through solid walls, and associated dangers. By June, 1850, he was able to report that the new building was completed according to contract, although he furnished a list of additional works and requisites that he deemed indispensably necessary. The Trustees agreed and set in motion the process of providing them, the first being the glazing of the cloister and the staining of the internal woodwork. The 1850 *Report of the Irish Commissioners of Public Works* had it that the Pugin buildings "are nearly completed and will, we expect, be ready for occupation early in the ensuing Summer".

The College was riding on the crest of a wave. In December, 1849, the Trustees authorised the President to contract, with the Duke of Leinster for all or part of the nearby farm of "Lar O'Brien", lately occupied by a man called Palmer. This was done at an annual rent of £2.5.0 per acre. Plans were also pressed ahead for converting the existing Brew House into Stables, supplied by Nathaniel Jackson.

The post of Bursar in the College was vacant and was hotly contested, Archbishop McHale of Tuam being interested in his nephew, and the Bishop of Clonfert in his brother. Clonfert urged that dioceses that were not already represented on the staff should get some preference over those that were. The Trustees were more disposed to look for extra funds from the Government, resolving at their meeting in October that, as the new buildings were still so unfinished as to be unfit for habitation, an additional outlay was necessary. A "College Church" also needed to be erected. And not only had the Parliamentary Grant been spent, but £3,700 "from other resources now entirely exhausted". They resolved that a memorial be drawn up by the President and Bursar and forwarded to the Lords of the Treasury seeking an increase of the grant for "indispensable purposes".

Pugin was then thirty eight, but was already worn out and did little work from then on. By 1852, he was suffering from delusions, and had to be confined in Bedlam asylum for some months. He was disillusioned with the "Oxford men", who were leading a revival of classical architecture — among them Newman. He must have been disappointed too with the reception given to his new buildings at Maynooth by some of the staff there. Dr. Murray was to comment sarcastically to the Maynooth Commission of 1853: "I doubt not the Goths would have been greatly pleased at them". On 14 September, 1852, Pugin died at Ramsgate after a long illness. He was only forty years old.

WHEN GOLD CORRUPTS

It is evident from the internal records of the College that the years immediately after the 1845 endowment were not at all noted for student discipline. There is a letter to the President, of 30 November, 1848, from Mr. Simmonds, a farmer at Collinstown, near Leixlip, complaining about how a number of students from the College had forced an entrance into the lawn in front of his house: "I consider this a very indecent and outrageous act". He asked for an assurance that it would not be repeated. The President replied courteously at once, regretting the annoyance and promising that he would do everything possible to prevent a recurrence of this "mistake". He also defended his students: "You may rest assured that self-respect makes them as solicitous as you can wish them to be, to observe this prohibition, which must inconvenience them the less as there is no other farmer within the range of their walks whose owner thinks it 'a very disgraceful outrage' that they should once or perhaps twice a year pass through his land". In any case, they were newcomers and unacquainted with the neighbourhood. Simmonds insisted that it was no mistake; some of the students had left the public road and climbed over a gate.

Then there was the case of the student who, on 1 February, 1849, wrote a love letter to his "ever dearest Kate" from "yours eternally J.M.D.". It had undoubtedly been intercepted. The President certainly had his hands full. In December, 1849, he received an anonymous epistle — one of those missives so dear to all in authority — signed, as so often by 'A Friend', informing him about the papers and liquors that were being brought into the College "by the Gates", and delivered to the students through the Gateman. If such doings are not soon put a stop to, they shall be hearing about it in the House of Commons.

Bishops were writing too, such as Dr. Murphy of Ferns: "I find that many of our young priests have contracted the nasty habit of smoking. I do not know where they commenced this practice, it cannot be in Maynooth. I would feel obliged if you would take the trouble to caution the Young Men from this Diocese against such an unpriestly fashion". And a priest in Phibsboro wrote about the conduct of a student during the holidays. But on the President's requesting for details, he did not have much to say against the student:

"The particulars are:
1st. The levities were a forwardness of manner in conversing with the ladies who stopt in the house and joining in their dances habitually;
2nd. The dances were Quadrilles, not Waltzes nor Polkas;
3rd. The ladies were pretty much advanced in years;
4th. He was spoken to and said that not being in Holy Orders he considered it no harm".

Whatever about such 'extenuating circumstances', many were of the opinion that the situation in the College was not good. It would not be the last time that it would have to face up to such reproaches. The Irish College, Paris, was thought to be no better. Cullen, appointed Archbishop of Armagh in December, 1849, wrote from Paris to Kirby in Rome in April, 1850: "Altogether this College is in a bad way. Poor Ireland has much to fear from its future ministers. We must endeavour to keep up the Roman College". In October, he sent some students, "but the position of M. has put such ideas in people's heads that no one now wishes to pay for the education of their children". His attitude towards Maynooth was already hardening and bore signs of things to come. In October he again wrote to Kirby: "Castleknock going on well. Carlow has lost nearly half its numbers. Derry and Belfast seminaries are closed. Thurles also is nearly abandoned. Maynooth will be everything. God help Ireland when this will be the case".

That December, the fifth Visitation since the Act of 1845 took place in the College. There were now 500 students. Only two rooms with five beds remained and three with six. Still, the new library did not have shelves, the halls benches, the kitchen grates, or the refectory tables. There was no heating of any kind available, such that the rooms might be unsafe during the Winter months.

115

There was also a major upset. On 15 October, 1848, Dr. Whitehead had gone missing. Fr. Maher of Dublin wrote to Dr. Cullen — then still in Rome. "Dr. Whitehead has not been heard of". On 20 October, Dr. Russell followed up with a letter to say that all in the College were anxious about him. He had gone away in June in poor health, and nobody knew anything about him since his sister had learned from him in August that he was going to France. The saga was to go on — Dr. Dixon writing to Cullen about it on 17 November (thanking him for a statue of the Virgin and a book, which he had raffled for £24.5 and £10 respectively to relieve distress in Dingle at Cullen's request). He too had no word of Whitehead. The news about his absence had by now percolated around. In November, Dr. Delaney, Bishop of Cork, wrote to the President of Maynooth: "I hope you have some satisfactory explanation of the afflicting absence of poor Mr. Whitehead, which has excited the liveliest sympathy of everyone".

As Pugin's buildings began to soar, "rising in Gothic grandeur", as Dr. O'Reilly put it in a letter to Cullen of 21 December, 1848, the cloud of the Whitehead mystery hung over the College. O'Reilly does not fail to refer to it: "Dr. Whitehead is still missing". He himself was "thinking of a trip to Limerick as usual". It was the Bishop of Clonfert, Dr. Derry, who perhaps was most explicit about the problem which Dr. Whitehead's disappearance constituted:

"It is painful to speak or write about poor Doctor Whitehead. I suppose all hopes of tracing him are now abandoned. A heavy responsibility is connected with the appointment of his successor. There certainly will be great difficulty in effecting a proper appointment. It would be disgraceful to the College to have a headless or an ignorant Vice-President. Yet I fear that good sense or great learning does not characterise some of the aspirants. I suppose all possess a fair share of piety: a talkative piety is not necessarily more solid or fervent than that of others".

116

Dr. Whitehead had been "written off", but he was not finished. In February, 1849, he surfaced. His old colleague, Dr. McNally of Clogher, was amongst the first to write to the College expressing his delight: "I have been much gratified to learn that favourable intelligence has been received of the V. President and that he is well and soon expects to join your community." As we gather from a letter of O'Reilly to Cullen much later (3 July), he had been located in the U.S.A., after shipwreck.

The news had come only just in time. The Board, says O'Reilly, was about to appoint a new Vice-President. On hearing of Whitehead's re-appearance, they had given him four months more during which to return, and ordered £100 to be sent to him. But all was not yet over. At the April Visitation, the Duke of Leinster queried Whitehead's continued absence. The President put up a good show, saying that the Vice-President was away since last Summer owing to indisposition; but that he himself and the Deans had been supplying his duties. The old Duke really does seem to have been a bit of a pest.

During this time, the Bishops in general were more concerned about national affairs than those of Maynooth College. They were about to confirm their rejection of the recently introduced plan for provincial university colleges — the famous Colleges Act. They were also engaged with the Synod of Thurles. As far as Renehan was concerned, the one really bright light must have been receipt of a message from the Bishop of Cloyne, Dr. Walsh, to the effect that he was dispatching Dr. Crotty's library to the College. His books — 2,000 in number — had been left to the Cloyne Diocesan Seminary, if this were established within four years, otherwise to Maynooth. As there was no prospect of such a seminary materialising "in these awful times", Dr. Walsh forwarded the books in cases by steamer to Dublin. The Archbishop of Cashel, Slattery, congratulated Renehan on this acquisition, as indeed on others too: "I see by the Papers that you bought largely at the Repeal Association's auction both for the College and for yourself. I think you got Columbanus's Scriptores which I believe is his best and most valuable work and very rare at present as also is Colgan, of whose two volumes there is a copy (1645 Louvain) in the Library here .... Dr. Crotty's books with those of Dr. Murphy must make a large addition to your library in the College".

Other Bishops were more preoccupied with trying to get students into Maynooth. Clonfert was hoping for this although he was not sure that his candidates would secure admission "even without the intervention of good Doctor Callan". Apparently Callan used to try to be helpful in the matter, spiritual man that he was. Yet many students failed to gain admission. Applicants from Clonfert were particularly unsuccessful, so much so that their Bishop felt quite frustrated: "It is provoking to have the good Royal Commons of Maynooth lost upon me, to whom its educational and devotional facilities are equally useless". In Cloyne, so great was the desire of candidates to get into Maynooth, that Bishop

117

Murphy decided to place an advertisement in the "Cork Journal" to the effect that all Cloyne places in the College could be filled only after a public concursus. Dr. Callan fell ill towards the end of 1849 and suspended his professorial duties. He spent some time at spas in France and Savoy and portion of 1851 in Rome.

A PARADISE OF WRITERS

During this time the College experienced one of its most fruitful — if not its most fruitful — literary periods. The staff was brilliant in the extreme. Apart from Callan, whose genius ran in a different direction, there was Russell, Murray, Crolly, Kelly, Renehan, Dixon and others.

These must have been given quite a fillip by the publication, during the years 1842 - 44, by Pucinelli of Rome, of the four volumes of *Rome, Ancient and Modern,* by their former colleague, the Professor of Rhetoric, Dr. Jeremiah Donovan. It had been quite a distinguished performance, well in the tradition of his predecessor, John Chetwoode Eustace, whose *Classical Tour of Italy* had captured the imagination in Georgian times.

Scientists and humanists to one side, the great theologian then at Maynooth was indisputably Patrick Murray. Crolly, Murray's colleague and close friend, was probably a better thinker, or at least so we are told, but he was said to be heavy and dull as a lecturer, over given to logical sequences, corollaries, sorites and the like, whereas Murray was said to be always clear in statement, even if sometimes too vehement.

On Friday, 6 July, 1849, Carlyle, the eminent Victorian writer, met Murray. It was in O'Hagan's house in Dublin, at breakfast, those present including "2 young Fellows of Trinity and others Hancock the Political-Economy Professor, one Ingram, author of the Repeal Song 'True Men like you men' " and "Dr. Murray, Theology Professor at Maynooth, a big burly mass of Irish Catholic Irishman" — Gavan Duffy too. The talk was 'England versus Ireland'. "Dr. Murray, head cropt like stubble, red-skinned face, harsh grey Irish eyes, full of fiery Irish zeal, too, and rage, which however he had the art to keep down under buttery vocables: man of considerable strength, man not to be 'loved' by any manner of means ! ..... Not a pleasant breakfast in the mood I was then in".

Thomas Carlyle (1795 - 1881) was seldom in the mood to appreciate Ireland or praise Irishmen: "The whole country figures in my mind like a ragged coat; one huge beggar's gabardine, not patched or patchable any longer". He resembled Thackeray in his paucity of compliments for the country and, like those of Thackeray also, his descriptions of Irishmen were generally unpopular in Ireland. Still, some years later he did help Dr. Murray to become one of the influential group of contributors to *The Edinburgh Review.*

It took some time for Murray to establish himself. In 1849, in early July, when his namesake, the Archbishop of Dublin, might well have been writing to him, he was communicating rather with Renehan about the definability of belief in the Immaculate Conception. At the time there was great discussion among theologians about this matter, including those at Maynooth. Crolly had written two essays on it in *Duffy's Magazine*, Russell and Murray had composed poems, and it was generally taught in class at Maynooth. Now the matter had been taken up in Rome, which sought to ascertain the view of the Catholic world. When Archbishop Murray's query arrived, there were only between forty and fifty students in the College and many of the professors were on vacation. A reply was sent which quite a number of them did not agree with. A later writer says that it "was not seen by the superiors or the theological faculty. It had gone to the ironmongery department and was replied to by a crank, who declared that Maynooth did not believe that the doctrine was one to be defined". The reference is vague, but at least it is clear that the reply was not regarded as satisfactory by the generality of the staff. We are told that when those absent returned, "they were pained and grieved and hastened to reply for their College. One of them was very angry". This, it would seem, was Patrick Murray.

The questions that the Archbishop had asked the President were: 1. as to whether belief in the Immaculate Conception of the Blessed Virgin Mary was general among the people, and 2. as to whether it would be desirable to have it defined as an article of faith. The President's view deserves to be preserved. Owing to so large a proportion of the superiors and students being absent, he had not been able to get an answer to the questions that could purport to be the answer of the College. He did, however, consult nine of the superiors collectively, the largest number in the College together since 3 July. His testimony is important:

119

"From the perfect unanimity of their declared opinions as well as from my general knowledge of the opinions of the absent Professors and their devotion to the Immaculate Virgin, I feel quite confident in stating that 'the belief of the Immaculate Conception of the B.V. Mary is very general' indeed, if not, as I believe, thoroughly universal amongst us. Of those whom I could thus consult, several declined to offer any opinion on the 2nd query. But while all of us felt our inadequacy to offer any opinion on so momentous a question, and are prepared to embrace with dutiful and cheerful docility the decision of the Church whatever it may be, only one person expressed as his opinion that it was 'desirable to have the doctrine of the Immaculate Conception now defined as an article of Faith', three others avowed that if left solely to their own lights, they would think such a definition at this juncture neither necessary nor desirable".

The majority "was not aware of any evil that called for such a remedy". Against it also was the "temper of the present times, the struggles of the Church, the oscillation and rocking of political Europe". Then too, "the Church in every age seems to have abstained from defining new articles of faith without necessity". It should be remembered as well that Trent had discussed this matter but, though the great majority of the Fathers held it, the Council deliberately abstained from defining it. In Maynooth just now the majority felt that devotion to Our Lady is progressing quietly and that such a definition would not make it more intense. In fact, a definition might only cause controversy in the Church:

"Simplicity of faith and docile submission to authority are unfortunately not the characteristic of these unhappy days. Multitudes of professing Catholics are less disposed to embrace reverently new articles of Faith than to forget and disregard some of the plainest and most essential truths already defined. In several countries heresy and infidelity would be likely to seize on the new definition as an occasion for blaspheming the Holy Mother of God, for impugning the Infallibility of the Decrees of the Church, for falsely imputing to Catholics novelty and change of belief, for contrasting the defined doctrine with the writings of St. Anselm, Bernard, etc. ...."

"In these British Islands, moreover", what many of those recently converted feel to be an excess of devotion to the Blessed Virgin Mary is their biggest difficulty in coming back to the Catholic Church. A new article of faith might shake their belief and put off others.

There is a distinct impression that Renehan is here talking about Newman and it is hard to avoid the conclusion that Russell was against the definition. That November, Russell gave the inaugural address to the first general meeting of the Irish Ecclesiological Society, of which he was President. The purpose of this society was to promote the study of Christian art and antiquities and to encourage the practice of ecclesiastical architecture in Ireland. As well as a number of Irish Bishops, the society's patrons were Wiseman (then titular Bishop of Meliopotamus) and Montalembert. Its Vice-President was Dr. Matthew Kelly of Maynooth and its honorary members included Pugin.

Matthew Kelly was an extraordinary genius. In 1841, after being examined in Moral Theology and Philosophy as well as in English and French, he had been appointed to the Chair of English Elocution and the French language, or, as it was sometimes referred to, the Chair of Belles Lettres and French. He was to make his mark quickly. In 1842, an essay by him on 'St. Etienne du Mont' appeared in *The Dublin Review*. In 1849, he edited White's *Apologia pro Hibernica*, as well as the three volume *Cambrensis Eversus*. In 1850, he followed this up by editing O'Sullivan Beare's *Historiae Catholicae Hiberniae Compendium*. And, in 1851, he translated Gosselin's *Power of the Popes during the Middle Ages.*

He was well matched by others in the College at that time. But he at least was plain Irish in his interests. Some colleagues, if one may say so, were rather precious – contributing to *The Dublin Review* on the most esoteric and effete subjects – Murray on 'Irish Eloquence' and 'Hood's Poems', and Russell on 'Huc's Chinese Empire'. At least Kelly had the common sense to write on 'The Church of St. Patrick', and Crolly on 'The Irish Insurrection'. Russell was a step ahead of the others. At that time, he published Leibnitz's *Systema Theologicum*, with an Introduction and Notes, translated the tales of Canon von Schmid in three volumes from the German, and also prepared a report on the Carte MSS. in the Bodleian Library. He wrote as well for the *North British Review*, the *Encyclopaedia Britannica*, the *English Cyclopaedia*, and the *Academy*. During 1850, one issue alone of *The Dublin Review* carried five long articles by Russell on subjects as diverse as 'Peter the Cruel', 'The Authorship of Thomas a Kempis', 'Cambrensis Eversus', 'Denis Florence MacCarthy's Poems' and 'Dr. Newman's Discourses to Mixed Congregations'. In 1851, he contributed an article of forty pages to the same review on 'The Sign of the Cross'. Wiseman got the credit of being the review's editor, but, subsequently, in a letter to *The Tablet*, Mr. T. Placket testified: "During my apprenticeship as compositor, from 1851 - 1858 (and before and after), it was printed by Richardson and Sons, Derby. During the period that I worked upon it, it was practically edited by Dr. Russell of Maynooth College". Dr. Russell, he said, "wrote a flowing hand", with small script and the lines close together. After the publication of his Leibnitz, Russell sent a copy to Newman, from whom he received a gracious letter of thanks dated 2 October, 1850. In the preface Russell had explained that he had made the translation in 1841 "in the hope that the *System of Theology* might contribute to the diffusion of those Catholic views which at that time had begun to make sensible progress in England and had just received a strong impulse from the publication of the memorable Tract XC ....".

Around this time, despite his many administrative problems, Renehan was also active in the literary domain. He became a member of the Council of the Irish Archaeological Society — the President of which was the Duke of Leinster. He was also President of the Celtic Society, founded in 1847 for the publication of material for Irish history. Dr. Kelly was said to have been instrumental in funding it. The memory of Paul O'Brien, first Professor of Irish, was still green in the College. In March, 1850, arrangements were being made for an epitaph for his tomb (and that of the first Vice-President, Dr. Power) — preferably in Irish. Dr. Denvir of Down and Connor asked Renehan to prepare the epitaphs. As far as the Bishop could remember, Dr. Power had died in 1817, a day or two after ordinations in the College, Dr. Murray of Dublin having consecrated the new graveyard while Dr. Troy was ordaining in the chapel. The idea was to have the graveyard ready when Dr. Power died. Denvir was not sure when Fr. O'Brien had died; the medical doctor's books should be checked.

In the early 1850's, Murray was one of the great litterati in the College. He was quickly coming to be recognized too. In May, 1849, he had preached the sermon at the month's mind for the deceased Archbishop Crolly. October, 1849, saw the visit of Fr. Rootham, General of the Jesuits, to Maynooth, where he entertained the staff to an account of the expulsion of the Jesuits from Rome and was noted down by Murray. He was quaint in his animadversions: "History testifies that, from time immemorial, there has always existed in Rome a nest of atrocious characters"! Carlyle's visit had been in July, and between it and that of Rootham, Murray had nearly quit this world. He was very ill after the Summer vacation and had made his will on 10 September, 1849, George Crolly and Matthew Kelly being witnesses. But he was to rally and live for more than thirty two years after. In December of that year, he was making preparations for the publication of his first *Irish Annual Miscellany* by Bellew of Grafton Street. A prospectus about it was circulated to the Bishops. Slattery of Cashel had no time for him: "I don't like either Murray or his book and I won't pay 6 shillings for it".

By March, 1850, Murray was in full flight following the publication of the *Annual Miscellany*. This had been attacked in certain Protestant quarters as an irruption of the Goths, which the author had taken as a sly poke at "the new Gothic College at Maynooth". Not that he was really in a position to give out about this, given his attitude to Pugin's Gothic. But he did let fly in reply — in letters to *The Tablet*, the *Nation* and the *Freeman*, all later published together as *Letters on the Philosophy of Plain Speaking* (Dublin, 1850).

He had started his *Irish Annual Miscellany* rather ambitiously to remedy the dearth of Catholic literature in English, especially in matters connected with religion. There was particular need for this, he thought, in view of the "new fact" that had arisen in "the provincial College in Cork", with its "flippant, ignorant, arrogant and most anti-Catholic" lectures. He planned five or six volumes. The *Miscellany* ranged over almost every imaginable theme, from a discussion of W. H. Maxwell's 'Wild Sports of the West' to William Carleton's 'Shane Fadh's Wedding'.

1850, was a year of some notable events. On 1 May, Prince Arthur was born. On 27 June, the Queen was struck on the head by a retired Lieutenant of the Royal Hussars. On 2 July, at a half an hour after midnight, Peel died. Despite their early differences, Victoria was very upset.

At this time, Murray seems to have been in trouble with Rome about some of his views, for Cullen wrote to Kirby: "Dr. Murray of M. sent a long defence to the Propaganda of his book and opinion. I got it from Mgr. B' O who requested my opinion on it. I have just written twelve pages to answer him". On the other hand, Carlyle, in 1852, secured a commission for Murray, at the request of Gavan Duffy, to write for *The Edinburgh Review*. On 30 January, he wrote to Duffy: "I have described Dr. Murray and his project to the editor in question this morning, and I put the question to him: '*Will* you deliberately read his paper if he send one? ' By this means, taking part of the risk upon myself, I think the problem may perhaps be a little abridged, and the risk of the other parties less. You shall hear at once what answer there is; till then, keep silence, please. My conviction is that any deliberate essay of Dr. Murray's would decidedly deserve the trouble of *reading* by an editor ....".

Murray did contribute to the *Review* for a brief period during the editorship of Mr. Empson. When Cornewall Lewis succeeded Empson, according to Gavan Duffy "he made objection to something in an article submitted to him, and Dr. Murray seized the occasion to retire altogether" (C. Gavan Duffy — *Conversations with Carlyle*, London, 1896).

At the end of April or beginning of May, 1852, Murray had sent off an article on Carleton to the editor of the *Review*, who had asked him previously to name some of the subjects he would like to write upon. This one, on Carleton's novels, maintained that Carleton (for whom he had a soft spot) was the best among Irish writers for depicting contemporary Irish life. A week later it was back, printed, with some small changes suggested. Murray agreed to all but two. But he was not prepared to accept dictation indefinitely. In a message to Gavan Duffy he said: "A strong religious scruple got into my head about being connected with *The Edinburgh Review*. Though professedly a literary and political journal, yet of late years especially, it had become rather theological — the theology being, of course, of a very bad stamp. It occurred to me that there was an impropriety in my contribution to such a periodical. I reasoned myself out of this — still I felt very uncomfortable, though keeping my uneasiness

123

all to myself. There were four articles out of nine in the January number, and two in the last number, more or less of this character. Lewis's note took a heavy weight off my mind."

Then there was Crolly, who published *The Life and Death of Oliver Plunkett* in 1850, brought out by James Duffy of Dublin and dedicated to Russell. It was a proper performance by a Northerner. In the same year he wrote a number of letters to the *Dublin Evening Post* in defence of the views of his uncle, the Primate, on mixed education, expressed to the Parliamentary Commissioners on Education in 1825. The then Primate, Dr. Cullen, thought little of them. He wrote to Kirby: "Have you seen Crolly's letters ...? There are the filthiest composition you ever saw ... What a beautiful thing it is to have such a man teaching theology and giving example to students. See what £300 of Government money per annum effects".

INTIMATIONS OF MORTALITY

The beginning of the year 1850 had seen a dramatic event that was to have momentous implications for the future of Maynooth. On 4 January, Cullen wrote from Rome to the President announcing his own appointment as Archbishop of Armagh. He knew nothing about the place, he said, and would be depending a lot on Renehan for assistance. He would also deem it his duty to aid the President in every way possible in "maintaining discipline and order in the important establishment over which you preside ....I know how important it is to support the authority of the superiors". He was to take this very seriously as Bishop for the rest of his life. Renehan sent his congratulations immediately, and invited him to Maynooth as soon as he arrived back to Ireland.

Shortly after Cullen had left Rome for Ireland, Wiseman was writing to Russell, telling him in great confidence that he is to leave England for ever in August; he is to be named Cardinal and, in the circumstances of Catholic England just then, will most probably have to stay in Rome as a member of the Curia. He is not pleased at all at the latter idea "for I own that, consulting one's human feelings, to stand at the helm in the capital of this Empire ... is a nobler position than to be one of a Congregation in which one may have the power of giving one vote in favour of the right".

The College began to have financial difficulties once more. In November, there was question of preparing yet another memorial to the Treasury seeking funds. On the other hand, enemies of the College were bitterly opposed even to what it was already getting. A Belfast clergyman recalled the famine which, as other Protestants before him had also suggested, he thought had resulted from the Act of 1845, because, "in that very year, that very month, the land is smitten, the earth is blighted, famine begins, and is followed by plague, pestilence, blood". Handbills began to appear

124

denouncing "Vice-Pope Paul Cullen", and members of proselytising societies mounted the College wall and threw bundles of tracts into the grounds.

Dr. Cullen began to become more actively interested in the internal affairs of the College. In January, 1851, he complained again to Kirby about "the a priori arrogance of Murray's writing and also that of Crolly". He had a special aversion to Crolly. Writing about the latter's life of his uncle, which had just appeared, he said: "It is a precious specimen of biography. The Maynooth men have disgraced themselves, but good will come from it, as it will give us an excellent opportunity of speaking of the matter at the board."

He was not the only Bishop who took a poor view of some of the College productions. Slattery of Cashel, who had no great opinion of Murray, had some reservations about the elimination in the new statutes of the old regulation forbidding publication by staff members, for "it were to be wished that some of the publications emanating from the Maynooth Doctors had been suppressed for they are specimens of bad taste and worse temper that are unbecoming nay disedifying in the extreme". In March, Cullen was concerned about the filling of the See of Dublin. He has heard that Renehan's name or was it Russell's?, may be on the list and is doubtful about the wisdom of it: "The Holy See will find it difficult enough to make a good choice. I fear Dr. R. would not be very safe".

Lawrence Renehan of Cashel dominated Maynooth for many years. There is an extensive pen-picture of him (although not a very flattering one) in the Diary of Archdeacon John O'Sullivan (1806 - 1874) of Kerry:

"Renehan was infirmarian when I entered college and as repulsive, forbidding a fellow as needs be. He was evidently in the greatest distress as might be inferred from his patched clothes, mended shoes and darned stockings, a hungry, half-fed, ill-conditioned fellow. With his grey eyes starting from under his thick red eyebrows and his red furry hair standing on end he was about one of the most repulsive characters to be met any-where".

O'Sullivan was very critical of Renehan for the way in which he badgered students during his year as Infirmarian:

"The consequence was the whole house was in arms against him. He could not cross the walks or the square without being shouted after and whistled at. His hair was the very colour of the red paint called Raddle with which they mark the sheep, and he went by no other name, and however they contrived to procure some of it they did not leave a wall in the house on

125

which they had not written 'Raddle' in most conspicuous characters. Even in the refectory they would rise simultaneously as if they were done, that he may say grace, and then sit down in shouts of laughter at having deceived him".

He had to admit, however, that Renehan was very able. At the concursus for a Chair of Theology in 1826, he had run circles around the Reverend William Higgins, his opponent. Higgins "was evidently far and away behind Renehan, who was and is a man of powerful intellect and more powerful memory". But Higgins had played it cool, and Renehan became disconcerted when "the students would rise in a body and applaud Higgins not from any regard or admiration of him, but from the intense dislike they entertained for Renehan". He had failed on that occasion to get the Chair but had later become Professor of Scripture and then President, "where he stays I hope". This last was written in 1851, just when the President was being mentioned for a Bishopric. O'Sullivan was concerned that he might become Bishop of Kerry, as a paragraph had appeared in late 1850 in a Limerick newspaper to the effect that Dr. Egan (of Kerry) was going to get a Coadjutor and naming Renehan of Maynooth as a candidate. O'Sullivan thought that he himself could be in the running. He was horrified at the idea that Renehan might be Bishop of Kerry; it is clear that at no time was there any love lost between them.

In February, 1851, O'Sullivan had occasion to visit Dublin and Castle-knock, and took the occasion to return by Maynooth, dine there and come down to Cork by the night train, where he would spend a few days with the Bishop, Dr. Delaney. Things worked out differently:

"I had a car at the door to take me over from Maynooth to Salins, but Renehan the President became so importunate that I could not refuse staying for the night. After dinner he and I and Dan McCarthy (Professor of Rhetoric since 1845 and Bishop of Kerry towards the end of the century) walked for a while and then adjourned to the President's room. We had tea, coffee, Madeira, Port, Sherry, Whiskey, sugar, hot-water. Renehan was evidently determined to do the hospitable".

It is not surprising that a heated argument quickly ensued. O'Sullivan continues:

"Had I not known Larry of old, and had I not been convinced of his non intention to insult, I protest I would have walked out of the room. The Madeira etc. satisfied me he did not mean offence ..... (Eventually, however) I stood up and moved off to my bedroom. He still followed me, took a chair and made himself at home, argued and crossed and was rude and insolent

126

for near another hour, until I had to turn him out by taking up the chamber pot and saying I could hold out no longer".

Scabrous material some high-minded critic may say, but it is human stuff, down to earth, and evocative of a side to Maynooth which exists as it does in all similar institutions.

In May, 1851, the Great Exhibition opened in London. This was the show piece of mid-Victorian Ireland, but it is unlikely that the Maynooth Trustees were all that interested in it. Their immediate concerns lay elsewhere, notably in defending the College once again. In June, they inserted a notice in *The Freeman's Journal* and *Evening Post* denying a charge made by W. Anstey, Member of Parliament for Youghal, that it was the regular custom of some of their members, and notably Dr. McHale, to speak against the Maynooth Grant at the Bishops' own annual meetings. There would have been no reason for such a posture, as the College was turning out a lot of fine priests and it needed the grant in order to so do. Indeed that September, the Bishop of Cork wrote to congratulate the College on the conduct of the young men who had recently come from it. It afforded much consolation and "if, as there is every reason to hope, their successors continue like them, little fear need be entertained for the interests of religion".

In 1851 too, Newman became Rector of the newly established Catholic University even though the University itself was not to be set up formally until 1854. He had met with a deputation of Irish Bishops about it and had got their queries answered by Monsignor de Ram of Louvain, Dr. Dollinger of Munich and Dr. O'Hanlon of Maynooth, who, for all his petulance, does indeed emerge as an extremely capable man. Newman himself visited Maynooth on Tuesday, 7 October. The Pugin buildings were still unfinished.

One is forced to wonder what the thoughts of some in Maynooth were at the prospect of the new university. It can hardly have seemed anything other than a danger to Maynooth. This would have been all the more so because of the renewed opposition to the Maynooth Grant. In 1852, Vansittart drove Pusey out of county representation in England on the issue of his support for it. In London was published an anonymous attack on the College entitled *Maynooth: In Three Letters to Mrs. Hardaway*, by Simon Scribe, Senior (actually one Adam Black, M.D.). The Archbishop of Dublin — then quite old and near death — was worried. He wrote to Renehan (28 January, 1852):

"I met Dr. Whately at the Levee today, and he informed me, that a Friend of his in England, a constant supporter of the Maynooth grant, has been startled by all the atrocious things which are circulated so widely against that Establishment, and has written to him for information as to the course of Studies there carried on. Finally, it was agreed that his Friend should be referred to you for authentic information on the subject. You, of course, hear quite enough about what is said against us. However, I may as well send you a couple of extracts from the London *Morning Post*. The Catholic University is brought forcibly to bear against us. I always thought it would. The latter would be a very poor substitute for Maynooth."

The *Morning Post* of 26 January had carried a report from the *Hull Packet* of a meeting held some days before to protest against the May-nooth Grant, a meeting described as "one of the largest and most enthusiastic we have ever witnessed in Hull". Newman was watching the proceedings with interest. That April, he noted that Lord Derby had replied to those who were urging the withdrawal of the Maynooth Grant that he had no such intention at present. A couple of days later, he also noted that *The Times*, in a leading article, had supported Derby but had added that if a rival to Maynooth, namely the Catholic University, were founded, the State might fairly consider itself absolved from aiding Catholics who chose to act independently. Newman kept up his interest in the matter, noting again, towards the end of April, that there had been a debate in the House of Lords about the continuation of the grant. He made no bones about suggesting that there was a certain incompatibility of interests as between Maynooth and the Catholic University: "I cannot help suspecting that the Debate about Maynooth has for a time checked any very active operations about the University, for the Maynooth interest must not be roused against it".

In May, 1852, the College came under violent attack. *The Eclectic Review* ran an article on the 'History of Maynooth College', viewed with a jaundiced eye, and a Dr. Dill, in a pamphlet entitled *The Mystery Solved, or Ireland's miseries, their cause and cure* (of which 4,000 copies were sold in six months), traced all the country's woes, including once again the potato blight, to the endowment of the College: "There you find 500 students, generally of the lowest class; their cabin costume exchanged for a black suit with long black gaiters; and themselves from having in their humble homes 'cultivated letters on a little oatmeal', now amply supplied with smoking joints and portions of ale, and receiving besides £20 a year of pocket money". Really, it said, the Reverend Mr. Goold was right when, at the Edinburgh Anti-Maynooth Meeting, he had declared the College to be "a cauldron of seething horrors around which are squatted the old hags of treason, disaffection and agrarian outrage".

A copy of Dill's pamphlet was presented to the English Parliament. During the second week in May, that Parliament debated Maynooth. The Irish members tried beforehand to establish what the questions would be so as to be in a position to answer Spooner, and Cullen asked Renehan to go to London to be present at the debate and be able to assist the

M.P.s. The idea of an inquiry into Maynooth had surfaced. One of the M.P.s had written to Cullen saying that he thought there was a majority in favour of it. It must have been galling to those who were concerned about the College to find another inquiry looming less than thirty years after that of 1826. Some were more irritated than worried. Writing to Kirby on 13 May, Cullen said: "M. has been assailed on Tuesday. I send you a copy of the debate. It would be better for us it were at the bottom of the sea than to have it made the instrument for attacking us every day. Whether it stand or fall, it is not a matter for which we can sacrifice our religion".

Chapter V

A College Under Siege

In 1852, Sir Francis Head published his *A Fortnight in Ireland*, in which there is a long account of the College of Maynooth. Head (1793-1875) had previously been a successful Lieutenant Governor of Upper Canada from 1835 to 1837. He was famous for his books on travel in South America and a biography of Bruce, the African traveller. Also well known as a 'Quarterly' reviewer, he was a clever and versatile writer. He was meticulous in his description of the journey to Maynooth, of the College buildings and the courses of studies, and his account deserves to be read in its entirety by anybody interested in the place. Unfortunately, it is too long for full reproduction here.

He took a second-class return ticket to Maynooth, travelling in a well appointed train. He was very much satisfied by this; it was so different from all that he had learned in his youth about travelling in Ireland — "of thatched postchaises and of hostlers running with red-hot pokers in their hands to 'start' the horses":

> "On reaching the platform I found a train of dark rich blue carriages, equal, if not superior, to any I have ever seen on the continent of Europe. Each was composed of a first-class coupé, handsomely lined with blue cloth, and (between them) of two second-class carriages, painted in the interior drab-colour. In both were four seats, comfortably furnished with well-stuffed cushions covered with new glossy morocco leather. The glass windows, above which were Venetian shutters painted in two

shades of light blue, had neat lined curtains chequered in blue and drab. From the roof of the carriage, which was painted white, there protruded two round black iron ventilators, about nine inches high, pierced with holes like a colander. In the coupes there was scarcely an inhabitant, but the second-class compartment was nearly filled with a clean well-dressed and respectable class of persons. As soon as a sudden and loud whistle, which I particularly remarked had no peculiar Irish tone, ordered us to start, a general commotion or rather a series of general commotions, began ...."

Eventually they arrived at Maynooth:

"The village of Maynooth, which is about a quarter of a mile long, is composed of one long, very broad street of low houses, two stories high, some of which are white, and the rest from age a drab colour. At several intervals are to be seen very slight indications of a bygone intention on the part of this quiet village to turn itself by three of four streets at right angles into a town, but the abortive attempt soon dwindled into huts and cabins that in a very few yards come to an end. At the eastern extremity of the main street there is a low wall with iron railings, and a park-gate communicating with a broad road and greensward upwards of a mile long, and the breath of the main street, of which in fact it is a prolongation. This road and park are the approach from Maynooth to Carton, the splendid residence of the Duke of Leinster".

At the other end of the village, says Head, "stands the Royal College of Maynooth, looking like something between an old-fashioned English country-house and a French chateau":

"The central portion is inhabited entirely by Professors. The middle window of its second story was wide open, displaying to view two very large school globes, separated by twelve extra-sized folio volumes with red leaves, standing on their edges, with their lettered backs uppermost ...... Accordingly, walking up to the central door, I rang the bell, and, on a servant appearing, I desired he would give my card to the President, and say I begged leave to speak to him. The man told me that the President was away, but he would go to the Vice-President; and in the meanwhile he begged me to walk into a comfortable small room of three windows, handsomely furnished with a scarlet and black carpet; scarlet curtains edged with yellow lace, with white muslin curtains underneath; a round table, covered with a scarlet and black cloth; ten dining room chairs,

131

with black hair bottoms, a dumb waiter; brass fender; common grate; a painting of a man, with both hands uplifted, on his knees before two friars, one standing, the other sitting on the ground close to a cross surmounted by Alpine scenery. In a spacious carpeted adjoining room, the door of which was wide open, was a large dining hall (standing on a scarlet and black carpet), four silver decanter-stands, a large full-length picture of St. Francis on a pedestal, and about a dozen and a half of plain hair black-bottomed chairs".

The Vice-President, who appeared quickly, was, of course, Dr. White-head, described by Head as being of about forty years of age, tall, light, and active, with a countenance that was both exceedingly clever and particularly pleasing. He had Head's card in his hand and remembered that he had been Governor of Canada, leading Head to mutter to himself that this man read *The Times*. Taking out his notebook and pencil, he proceeded to make copious notes about the College. He was entertained to dinner before he left, something not done in the case of many such visitors:

"As it was now on the point of four o'clock I returned to the Professors' Department, and, obtaining there the little I wanted for the arrangement of my toilette after so long a stroll, I entered the small reception-room where, by the Vice-President, I was introduced successively to his colleagues — the Principals of the College. I need hardly say that in appearance and in reality they were exceedingly clever-looking men, and the usual preliminary formalities of society were scarcely over, when the door of the dining room was thrown open, and we took our seats at an oblong table, at the head of which was, of course, the Vice-President. Our dinner was exactly what it had been described to me, plain, simple, and homely. It consisted of a large joint of mutton, a great dish full of fowls, ham, and vegetables of various sorts. We had then one immense fruit-pie with cheese, butter, and a slight dessert. The wine consisted of super-excellent port and sherry; and as soon as the cloth was removed, a large jug of hot water, a couple of small decanters of whiskey, a bowl of white sugar, and a tray of tumblers, each containing a little ladle, were successively placed on the table".

Head deserved good treatment. He later wrote well of the College, one of the best and most respectful accounts of all the 19th century visitors. He was critical of some things, "chimneyless rooms", with no arrangements "for the entrance of fresh air, and for the exit of foul", and found the students "more serious and taciturn" than he expected. But he was

132

delighted to find the statue of King George III, "the founder of the institution", in the library, where he also came upon a number of students, each "in his black gown and black stock, edged with white". He was intrigued by a notice there which announced that "whoever takes a book out of this library incurs excommunication ipso facto". The students' refectory also fascinated him. It was a large room, lighted by ten windows, with a raised gallery at the end, "like the orchestra of a country ballroom". In its centre was an elevated pulpit or desk "from which prayers are read very loudly to the students during the whole of their dinner time", as well as some "historical works of the Church of England, some Saint's life, and lastly, the Roman martyrology of the day in Latin".

The building spate commenced by Pugin was not yet over:

> "I was standing on the grass looking at some students, who, in their black College caps and loose flowing gowns, were strolling about, when I heard an explosion, and, casting my eyes towards the direction from which it proceeded, I saw a black mass about the size of a 13-inch shell rise from behind the buildings, pass over their roof, and, after going high into the air, fall heavily on the grass. Two or three workmen happened to be near me, and as they also had watched the parabolic course of the lump, and as the eyes of almost every student had, I believe, been similarly engaged, I said to them 'What's that ?'. 'From the quarry!' they replied, as cooly as if it were just a common occurrence".

The students were probably used to explosions of all kinds ! Writing home during these years, one of them told how they sometimes emanated from Dr. Callan's laboratory: "We have a priest here from Co. Louth, Dr. Callan, the Professor of Science, and many are afraid he will blow up the College. Yesterday in St. Joseph's Grounds we heard an explosion that was like the end of the world. It is believed his health will not hold out, and many say he should be given a good rest". It is thought that Cullen even doubted his spirituality; in another age he would probably have faced an inquisition. Head was quite interested in everything and would have been underterred by the dangers of Callan's den. Nor did the explosion distract the student from whose room he heard "the notes of an accordion plaintively and well played". Later "inmates' will be amused to hear that he also found "hanging from one of their domitories ......
a yellow cage containing a starling", and observed many benches scattered about the grounds "probably to encourage meditation".

And so he left. Dr. Murray, in his 1853 *Annual Miscellany,* is rather unfair to him when he comments that the visit was laced with "a little whiskey Punch, of which most ungratefully, no record is given (good whiskey, by the way, is not so easily procurable in and about Dublin as at Cork) ".

The year 1853 also saw the publication in London of *Memorandums made in Ireland in the Autumn of 1852,* by John Forbes, M.D. Sir John Forbes (1787-1861) had many medical publications to his credit. In 1845 he had been made a fellow of the London College of Physicians and in 1852 received an honorary degree of D.C.L. from the University of Oxford. He was knighted in 1853. His account of Maynooth is not as thorough as that of Head, but, like the latter, he too mentions that the students' rooms had "no provision for the admission of warm fresh air, or for the escape of fowl." Clearly there was need of the new Pugin blocks which were not yet occupied, although Head had felt that the students, in their new one roomed "monastic severity", would miss the companionship of their fellows in the old system. Forbes was quite complimentary to them:

"Not having an introduction to any members of the College, we threw ourselves on the kindness of the first gentleman we met with, and were most courteously received, and kindly shown over the whole place by one of the senior pupils, a very intelligent and gentlemanly youth of eighteen or nineteen. There was no reserve or restriction on his part, in showing me whatever we desired to see, or in giving us whatever information we sought at his hands. In his conduct and manner, there was the same good breeding and the same open cheerfulness which we might expect from an undergraduate of Oxford or Cambridge, doing the honours of his College to strangers. And I may here remark that the bearing, dress and address of the students generally, were decidedly those of gentlemen; though here and there a critical eye might detect indications of a humbler fortune and breeding than are to be met with the English Universities".

Forbes's conclusion, when it appeared, must have been welcomed by the College: "On the whole, from what I myself saw at Maynooth, and from what I have since learned respecting it, I am bound to conclude that it is a well-planned and well-managed institution, calculated to communicate to its students a good secular as well as religious education, and to send them forth, amply qualified for the discharge of their sacred functions as priests; and as well-informed gentlemen, to set an example of social propriety to their flocks ". Forbes had fallen in with particularly affable students, for we gather that experience had taught the body in general to be careful of strangers who, we are told by Dr. Murray, often asked "impertinent and grossly offensive" questions: "Five or six weeks ago a batch of emissaries from the Priests' Protection Society, I was sorry to hear with a few clergymen among them, entered the College and,

C. W. Russell

R. Ffrench Whitehead

A. Welby Pugin.

Cardinal Newman

Nicholas Callan

Sir Robert Peel

Patrick Murray

Matthew Kelly

The Empress of Austria

Lawrence Renehan

George Crolly

Eugene O'Growney

running into the library, commenced to belabour the students reading there with objections against clerical celibacy, etc.: some of them had the modesty to ask one of the professors of theology, without introduction of any kind, for leave to enter his lecture hall, and remain there, and probably open a public discussion, during the lecture hour. If half a dozen of Irish priests assailed the University of Dublin or of Oxford in this way ?....." *(Essays, 1853).*

Murray has left us a marvellous picture of Maynooth during the Summer vacation:

"Maynooth, during the Summer vacation, that is from near the end of June to the beginning of September, must be a dull place to visit: I know it is shocking dull to live in. Deserted halls, deserted corridors, deserted rooms, deserted squares: the Board of Works in full operation, repairing the dilapidations of the past, and anticipating the wants of the coming academical year — scrubbing, sawing, plastering, boring, hammering, painting, glazing, and so forth: the hum and stir of life that fill every nook and corner during the season of study, subsided into stillness and stagnation. But a very small proportion of the students remain in College during vacation ...... The College has a drowsy and dusty aspect, and looks not very unlike a large house with but one or two care-takers living in it. The lecture halls are filled with forms and tablets stowed away and crowded together ....The professors' pulpits, in which those 'great Dons' are, after a few weeks, to pour out their stores of erudition, and weave webs of mimic sophistry to catch their unwary pupils in, look like a room out of which a dead man was just taken to be buried .... The battery of spits, on which a whole army of sheep and bullocks are to be roasted before next Christmas,moves lazily round with its diminished burden — as if the College had lost its appetite in the hot weather. The long gravel walks and large fields, over which, by and by, so many hundred of gowns and caps will swarm, present the show of a few small knots ...... The College is a kind of syncope, and nothing seems really to live in it except the old carpenter with his great brown paper cap and wallet of nails ..... the painter, the mason, and the rest of that class. The Summer vacation is not the time to see Maynooth, at least to see the living, breathing Maynooth ....".

GATHERING CLOUDS

The accounts of Head and Forbes could not have harmed the place when, in the early 1850's, Maynooth came under siege. When Paul Cullen arrived from Rome as Archbishop of Armagh in 1850 empowered as papal legate to convene a national synod, the anti-papalists in Ireland had become alarmed. His translation to Dublin in 1852 had only increased their state of unease. The Church, especially in its concretisation in Maynooth, began to come under the sustained kind of attack that it had not experienced since 1845. Lord Derby's shortlived conservative Government was put under renewed pressure to discontinue the Maynooth Grant. A broadsheet appeared entitled *The Withdrawal of the Grant from Maynooth College,* printed at the steam-press of Purden Brothers. Bachelor's Walk, suggesting a form of petition against the College and giving the rules for memorials to the Queen and Parliament. It was issued by a Committee of the Dublin Protestant Association.

Divisions between the Bishops themselves did not help matters. There is a letter from Bishop Murphy of Cloyne to Renehan, of May, 1852, bemoaning this "for had we religiously banded together, guided by moderation and prudence, giving offence to no man, and having our Acts stamped with firmness and disinterestedness, neither we nor our people should ever be spat upon, buffeted, and persecuted as we have been — but no, *division* the Evil Genius of our unfortunate Country is still in the ascendant". Archbishop Cullen, as would appear from a letter of that month to Kirby, seems to have revelled in the "discussion on the College of Maynooth". But he is unlikely to have been got to support the idea of a Royal Commission of Inquiry through the inducement of a higher grant. He knew rather that he had no option but to work with the new Government of Lord Aberdeen. He may have seen it as a way of finding out exactly what was happening at Maynooth, especially as regards its teaching. He had become very suspicious of the College when Crolly and Murray and three or four other members of the staff had criticised the pastoral address that was issued after the Synod of Thurles. He seems to have been persuaded that, as in the case of the Irish Church as a whole, a great deal needed to be put right at Maynooth.

In point of fact, the area of student discipline seems to be one that could reasonably have given cause for worry just them. One hopes that Newman did not come across this during his visit in May, 1852, when he appears to have stayed a couple of days, or later on 5 June, when he went down there — "over to Maynooth" to use his own words — for an ordination. Right then, the President had again received an anonymous letter, signed by 'a friend', bringing to his notice that "Mr. Coates is still trading in his Bookes and Sweetes, together with Shooses and Cloths of all descriptions on Sundays at the time you and Mr. Whitehead is engaged at the Masses. This work was not carried out when McNamara was alive ... The people of the town of Maynooth wonders at you to allow such worke. If the Scotches paper catches this or Lord Naas, they would make a great deal of it". Coates, goes on the complainant, also brings in bad books and "what do he have in his pockets where he do have 2 coats on him ?".

"Whiskey and cordals" are suggested. After all his name was Coates, if Dr. Murray would have pardoned the pun. When the President did nothing about it, the same 'friend' wrote again to "enform" him of a "Great blow-out intended by Mr. Coates when the students is going out" — on vacation evidently. If they go in his cars and stop at his house, they are to get roast and boiled and the best of Port and old whiskey that is doped so as to keep them from getting out of order as they had done last year at the "Station House", when they had to be put in the "Turf house" until the Dean came along. A note appended by the President to this message suggests that it is from "Kennedy, letter carrier", but there is a question mark going with it.

That August, another Kennedy — one Kennedy McNab — wrote from Inverness. Announcing himself as "an entire stranger and Presbyterian", he sought information on Maynooth for a pamphlet to be published anonymously, entitled *A Plea for the Catholics of Ireland in connection with the Maynooth Grant*, designed, he said, "to counteract the prevailing bigotry in Scotland on this subject". Renehan replied carefully to him: "As far as I can judge, by comparison of the average with the pupils that have come here from the London and Dublin Universities, I should think a higher standard of preparatory information is required here than in most of the universities". He gave a long account of the educational system at Maynooth and one cannot but admire him for the trouble which he went to in order to help his College in any way possible. He referred McNab for further information to the 1826 Report. The latter replied during the following February thanking the President, but even with the help of Lord Lovat he has been unable to procure the report in question. Could he have a copy — a tall order in view of the size of the volume. Yet Renehan sent him one — on loan !

During 1852, the storm clouds were gathering. On 14 August, *The Tablet* had defended Maynooth and in words that deserve recording:

> "The main object of the College is to provide an efficient national clergy for Ireland. That she has happily succeeded, the zeal, piety, and uncompromising energy of the Irish priests is a sufficient proof. But, owing to circumstances special to some of the dioceses in Ireland, where for instance, there might not be an immediate want of clergymen, Maynooth has from the first year of her establishment down to the present, contributed her glorious contingent of priests and bishops to break the bread of life to those who yet sleep in the shadow of death; and from the wild highlands of Scotland, and the more civilized shrines of England herself, to the fertile pampas of the Andes, and the remotest bournes of China and Japan, the faithful, generous, Irish missionary may be found exercising the functions of his sacred ministry, and perpetuating the virtues

and glories of the dear old fatherland."

—A bit of an exaggeration there, certainly as far as Maynooth was concerned. However, it was not unwelcome. So concentrated was the attack on the College at this time that, in September, *The Dublin Review* carried a notice of Dr. Dixon's *General Introduction to the Sacred Scriptures* which was much more devoted to defending Maynooth against attack than with a serious evaluation of the book. It was strong in its defence of the teaching at Maynooth and of the political conduct of persons educated there. It hit out angrily at the many tongues that "are being sharpened like swords against it" by people like the Spooners. Who, it asked, has heard tales about "its Proctors and their bulldogs, or of the necessity for such functionaries", unlike certain universities everybody knows about ? "Who has celebrated, in prose or verse, its rows between 'town and gown' ?" "Who has learnt of Maynooth wine-parties, and ruinous bills run up with tradesmen, or indorsed by youngsters, for their spendthrift elders, to Jews ..... ?"

Defend Maynooth though the *Review* might do, Dr. Cullen was uneasy lest Dr. Dixon might be appointed to Armagh in succession to himself. To Kirby (9 August, 1852): "The only doubt about him (Dixon) arises from his connection with Crolly, Murray and others of that kind in Maynooth. They are dangerous and may exercise influence on him". Yet, as so often happens, on 4 November, 1852, Dr. Cullen wrote: "Dr. Dixon is to be consecrated on 21st in Maynooth. I consecrate him". Cullen was later to exercise an undue influence over Dixon, to the detriment of Crolly and Murray.

Dr. Cullen need not have been worried at all about Murray. He was always orthodox. In 1852, he canvassed his first arguments in favour of papal infallability, which brought a rejoinder from *The Catholic Luminary*. It was during that year too that he defended Carleton's novels in *The Edinburgh Review*. Cullen might not have liked that every much, as Carleton was likely to have been somewhat of a *persona non grata* with the Irish Bishops. But he was from the same part of the country as Murray who never forgot that.

William Carleton (1794-1869) was born in Co. Tyrone, the youngest of fourteen children. He had been destined for the Church but did not persevere. Indeed the experience of a station at Lough Derg even led him to the resolution never to enter a church again. He became the writer of a huge output of tales about the Irish peasantry, in which he strove to give a faithful picture of the people at that time.

In December, 1852, we find Carleton writing to Murray to thank him for the article in *The Edinburgh:* "I cannot esteem you and love you more than I do". Murray replied in February, 1853, in rather maudlin terms:

"Dreadfully hurried as I am, I must tell you an anecdote about your 'Poor Scholar'. I was spending the summer vacation in the upper part of Co. Cork some eight or nine years ago. I brought down your 'Traits, etc' with me as a present to the family I was stopping with — they had not seen them before. One beautiful day I began to read the 'Poor Scholar' in the drawing-toom for them. When I got near the end — at the death of Lanigan, I think — I had to give up, the tears were too strong for me. Then one of the young ladies tried, but with the same success. Then the old gentleman (he was near 73, and a fine intelligent man); he too had to give up; we all got into a state of such passionate weeping that the book had to be closed for that day — and I believe the last scene was never read aloud".

As 1852 came to a close, the attacks on the College reached a crescendo. In December appeared a pamphlet entitled *A Beacon Light: Maynooth tried and convicted*. It appealed to the original intention of the Irish Parliament in founding Maynooth, namely, that loyal priests should be produced which, it argued, had not happened. On the contrary, this College was productive of much evil: "Here we have a corporation of bachelors receiving authority, at the cost of the nation, to overthrow the most endearing domestic relations — disturbing domestic peace". The author recalled the efforts of the Irish Parliament to knock down "this Babel of its own rearing" in 1799; now "phoenix-like we still see this College — and we feel it like a nightmare — an incubus upon the social system of Britain and its dependencies".

Richard Whately had, however, defended the College, saying that, whatever one might think of it; the country was now stuck with it; to withdraw or diminish the grant would be "spoilation", tantamount to passing "an Act for the sale of the Colleges and the estates of Oxford and Cambridge, and the application of the produce in reduction of the national debt". His efforts were to some extent in vain. That year saw an item 'Repair of Maynooth College' omitted from the Estimates, following a vote in the House of Commons in which its enemies had prevailed. As the yearly endowment had to be used for specific purposes as laid down by the 1845 Act, this left the College in great difficulty.

At the same time, progress was being registered in respect of the Pugin complex. In May, the Board of Works had informed the President about the new kitchens: "The progress made is very respectable — one of the roasting grates is put together, another nearly so". In July, the Board had written again in reply to a suggestion from him to convert the top of the Staircase Tower in the Pugin Quadrangle into a belfry and to construct connecting passages between the new and the old buildings. The trouble, said the Board, was whether there was enough money to effect these changes. The belfry was ultimately done; and one cannot but be glad that the connecting passages were not attempted.

GOVERNMENT SUSPICIONS

1853 saw the launching of a great movement both in Ireland and England against Maynooth College in every respect. Undoubtedly, the change-over the previous December from Derby's to a Government under Aberdeen, had something to do with it. It would be tedious to trace in detail the pattern of events that unfolded; a sketchy outline will suffice. In January, Philip Dixon Hardy produced a long tirade, *The Maynooth Grant considered religiously, morally and politically,* 'with documentary proof that it was originally obtained by Fraud and Perjury and that its continuance is a subsidy to Disloyalty and Sedition' (Dublin, 1853). From Brighton the Reverend William Hanson delivered himself of another epistle, *The Maynooth Endowment and nunneries bills,* in which Wiseman, Cullen and McHale were attacked: "Popery cannot be reformed any more than Maynooth" and both should be destroyed. A head of steam was being worked up and was sooner rather than later bound to blow up in the face of the College.

Life had to go on there nevertheless, and early in 1853, the President began to be pressed by Bishops about their own immediate concerns, i.e., the provision of priests for the mission that were properly qualified for it. It would not have helped the temper of Messrs. Dixon Hardy and Hanson to know that the Bishop of Killaloe was emphasising that, if his young priests knew no Irish, "they will have an unpleasant time of it. I cannot make towns for them. I was obliged to learn Irish in a mountain district and had no alternative but one I could not adopt, viz. to leave the mission altogether". The Bishop of Clonfert was also worried about an insufficiency of Irish on the part of his students coming out from Maynooth, although the Bishop of Limerick accepted the fact that some of his students could not speak it.

The President had also the normal disciplinary problems. In June, the Acting Superintendent of the Police contacted him from the Castle Yard to inform him that four volumes of the breviary (with P. Cullen written on them) had been found near the Grand Canal on the 15th inst., together with a black frock coat and a "sutan". The Superintendent had learned that a gentleman of that name had been ordained in the College about the same time. He wondered where he now was. The President replied that Mr Cullen left Maynooth on the 13th by train due in Dublin at 10 p.m. On the 16th he had written from Athenry to a friend in the College, saying that he had directed the Maynooth railway porter to keep a trunk for him until his return from Dublin, but which by mistake was sent to Dublin, and being unlabelled, was either lost or stolen. Mr. Cullen could probably be found in Athenry. Fears of a major crime or tragedy were allayed. Towards the end of the month, the Trustees directed the Bursar to procure appropriate paintings for the new professors' "dining Parlour" at a cost not exceeding £100. Some Italian paintings, including a fine view of St. Peter's square, which now grace the antechamber to the Professors' Refectory, may have been acquired at that time.

The threatening storm burst on 19 September, when a warrant for a Royal Commission of Inquiry into Maynooth was issued. There were to be five Commissioners — The Earl of Harrowby (Chairman), Travers Twiss of the Church of Ireland (a lawyer), Mountifort Longfield, also of the Church of Ireland (and also a lawyer), together with two Catholics, Baron Pigot and James More O'Ferrall. Henry West and John O'Hagan were appointed Secretaries to the Commission. The first meeting was held in Dublin Castle on the very next day (20 September, 1853) and was to be followed by 39 more, until 8 January, 1855, the last being in the Office of the Treasury, in London.

During the sitting of the Commission, there was much correspondence between the Secretaries and the President of the College. Very quickly the Commissioners decided to visit the place, and the Secretaries wrote from the first meeting to Renehan to say that they would do so on Thursday, 22 September. In a private note, O'Hagan assured the President that the purpose of this visit was primarily to see the "locus in quo". Renehan bade them welcome and was ready to co-operate in every way. This first visit was an informal one but the formalities began soon after. On 24 September, the Secretaries sent on to the President a copy of the commission under which they acted as well as certain "interrogations" on which his written answer was requested. On 25 September, they were looking for any written compositions that may have formed part of the students' examinations, if such were kept in the College. The 'trial' had begun.

The Bishops were concerned about the outcome. The Primate of Armagh wrote expressing the hope that the College "will come through this new ordeal of a Royal Commission with honour, as I have no doubt it will". Dr. Cullen feared that the business would prevent him from going on a visit to Rome, although he was not at all pleased with Maynooth where, apart from anything else, "the bribery is so great ... that no student can be got to go to any other College". Everybody had his own preoccupations. Writing to Henry Wilberforce at the end of September, Newman feared "that the Maynooth Commission would throw back matters" as regards the promotion of the Catholic University.

The Commissioners quickly got down to business. Dr. Henry Neville was questioned on 6 October. He was critical enough of some things. There was little intercourse between students and professors apart from class, something he thought could be improved. So also did Dr. Moriarty. The President was said to be against their dining together, because of the lack of space, the frequent presence of visitors and the "different avocations, condition and ages of the professors and students". The dampness of the College was also referred to, Dr. O'Kane saying that he had seen shoes in some students' rooms covered with green mould. The system of attendance by the physicians, Drs. O'Kelly and Corrigan, and Surgeon Ellis was explained.

Gradually, the structure and life of the College was unfolded – the method of appointing professors, the routine of the deans, the courses of studies. Dr. Murray thought that "the Professors of theology are greatly over-wrought", by their lectures and the necessary preparation for them, as well as by "incessant reading, incessant wear and tear of mind, working like a mill, from uprising till bed-time day after day". Dr. Denvir made a plea for more chemistry teaching "because a portion of it has reference to the improvement of agriculture; and were the priesthood, by a knowledge thereof, enabled to tender sound advice to the farming portion of their flocks, such advice would be assuredly acted upon". The Bursar was quite concerned about the drainage which "is executed in a very excellent and permanent manner, and with the addition of a few traps ..... which are now being made ..... cannot fail to be of great importance in draining not only the foundations of the buildings, but also the ground in the immediate vicinity".

The Commissioners were not to be deflected from their main purpose. They invited views from people outside the College. The Archbishop of Cashel, Dr. Slattery, received an invitation but declined it. Privately he expressed the hope that the sessions were "proceeding fairly and not in the spirit of that ferocious Bigotry now so prevalent and are not giving much annoyance".

The Bishop of Clonfert also declined to be interviewed. O'Hagan sent on to the President a catalogue of priests from *Battersby's Directory,* asking him to mark the names of Maynooth-educated priests. On 18 October, he

142

wrote again, requesting Renehan to appear before the Commissioners on the following Thursday, 20 October, and saying that he is enclosing a list of the subjects on which the Commissioners are anxious to receive information. Renehan replied that he had found no such enclosure, to which O'Hagan answered that the reference to an enclosure should have been erased as no particular heads of examination had been determined upon. He did say that the President was liable to be asked whether there existed within the College any tendency to political manifestations, "and that it will be very important to establish that the authorities of the College do not tolerate such manifestations and are watchful upon the subject". O'Hagan — a Catholic — was trying to be as helpful as he could. However, the Commissioners were quite exigent. They required to see some of the textbooks in use at Maynooth, notably *De Obligatione Statuum* and all Delahogue's theological work. And they pressed the President and the Professors about the priests in Irish politics.

The President was not too happy about some people's recollections (particularly those of Dr. Farrelly) of political indiscretions that had occurred sometimes in the past. He contacted Dr. Derry of Clonfert, who had been a student with him at the time of Earl Mulgrave's visit to the College, to try to establish what he could recall had happened on that occasion. Derry had replied:

"I was in the Refectory the night that was kept festively in honour of Lord Mulgrave's visit — I heard Dr. Whitehead speak but only recollect allusions to the shamrock and love of country. I heard Dr. Dixon speak and one of his points was the superior professional knowledge of the Irish Priesthood, or rather of priests educated at Maynooth as compared with any other professional body in Ireland. Dr. Gaffney spoke, so also did your humble servant and what makes me believe you were present is the decided impression on my mind that you were pleased to say I had got on well. I recollect my observations had reference to the relations of Deans and students .... and shortly afterwards Dr. Montague and, as I always thought, yourself, Dr. Gaffney and myself, went to the Lay house refectory and in the same way joined in the festivity ...... This is all I said to Mr. Farrelly when, on the day of your examination in Dublin, he asked me had I any recollection of what occurred. I did not say a word about your singing 'Dear Harp of my Country' or anything else. Dr. Farrelly was amusing himself by that little interpolation".

Then came the turn of the students, first the Dunboyne students and some other seniors, who were directed to present themselves before the Commission on Friday, 21 October, at 12 noon. There were further "summonses" to other students to attend at the Castle on the following day. They were conveyed to them through the President of the College. Needless to say, the students did have certain complaints, given an opportunity for discussion *in camera*. Some of them wanted more exercise, as Mr. Hurley, one of the Divinity students put it: "I think that if an hour was given for a run, or a walk, before dinner, it would be very useful". Another, recently ordained, thought that the study of Latin, coupled with the great discipline and the extraordinary hours of silence, was "calculated very much to produce stupidity and dullness generally in the minds of the students". Others still were dissatisfied with Dr. O'Kelly, arising from what one of them said was his want of knowledge. They were unlikely to have been dissatisfied with the allowance of beer, the expenditure on which had increased from £630 in 1844 to £1,035 in 1852.

Mr. Farrelly, the Bursar, was not at all happy with some of their replies, just as the President himself had not been with Farrelly's own recollections. Writing to the Primate on 1 November, he showed some apprehension as to the damage which some of them, particularly the members of what he called the Committee of Grievances, might do. "Three of the leading members of that body, Flannelly, Hurley and Slattery, were at their own request examined by the Commissioners on Saturday, 22nd ult. They did not give a very flattering account of the Government and Management of the College, of which, of course, they consider themselves infallible judges. I fear there is neither 'peace' nor 'happiness' for the College till some of its present inmates are removed from the restraints of College discipline and placed in a sphere more congenial to their ideas of human liberty ... While I deplore these proceedings, of course, I take care to have no interference in them".

Farrelly, like so many Bursars, was in favour of 'an modh direach', while preserving a distance personally from the business. As the Autumn wore on, the inquiry became tedious, also probably for the Commissioners. The President had to supply the names of all the students then in the College and, once again, to go through Battersby and mark off the names of the clergy of Great Britain who had been educated at Maynooth. The respondents were at least given the opportunity of correcting the written version of their submissions. This was particularly important in the case of those professors who had given evidence that might have left them open to the charge of Gallicanism, something in which Dr. Cullen was intensely interested (Letter to Kirby, 18 November). The Commissioners went so far as to request from the President a translation of the Roman correspondence regarding the College that had been printed in the 1826 Report. Then, in January, 1854, came a request for a list of the Maynooth-educated priests in "British India, the British Colonies and America". And the long process continued of collating and correcting the evidence.

In September, 1854, the warrant of the Commission was extended to enable it to complete its work. Finally, on 8 January, 1855, all was done. The printing only remained, and that, as was the custom in those days, was done quickly. The Crimean War was in full swing.

ROMAN PRESSURES

If Maynooth was under scrutiny at home on the part of the Government, it was also under scrutiny in Rome.

Dr. Cullen was at the beginning, middle and end of this, for he thoroughly distrusted the teaching of some of the college Professors, just as much as he disliked them. As early as January, 1853, before the Royal Commission had at all been established, he had succeeded in getting the Trustees to resolve "that the Theology of Bailly, dogmatical and moral, having been prohibited by the Sacred Congregation of the Index, *donec corrigatur,* the President is instructed to have such parts of the said work withdrawn as are used in the Classes of the College". He took advantage of the occasion to warn Propaganda that Delahogue's work might also need to be replaced: "This author .... wrote his work for the use of the college". Perhaps Propaganda could find from its files whether it had been censured earlier in the century. Then, to give him his due, he added: "Meanwhile in all these matters there is need to proceed with caution, because just now the government is about to appoint a commission to examine the position of Maynooth College, which could seize on every trifling circumstance to attack the institution". Nonetheless, it is likely that he saw the Commission as an opportunity for Rome as well as for the Government to find out precisely what was being taught in Maynooth. In April, he informed Mgr. Barnabo, the Secretary of Propaganda, about the forthcoming investigation, noting that one of the objectives of the Commission would be the maintenance of Gallicanism. This was the body of ideas incorporated in the 'Four Articles' drawn up by the French clergy in 1682, and which included the tenets that in secular matters kings and princes are not at all subject to the authority of the Pope, that his authority is limited by that of a General Council, that it must respect the ancient 'liberties' of the Gallican church, and that it is not final unless confirmed by the consent of the universal church.

Dr. Cullen had a fixation about the danger of Gallicanism at Maynooth. It is hard to see how he had developed it. While he was still in Rome in 1839, ten years before his appointment to Armagh, Kirby could have told him what Dr. O'Reilly of Maynooth had written that year about his experience on the staff of Maynooth. O'Reilly had said that, even though he had re-entered the place with many prejudices, after a year he had to admit to a change of mind. He had declared that Gallicanism was almost dead and "papal infallibility is not looked on in any odious light and is certainly inclined to by many of the professors".

145

Yet Cullen was not at all content. On 3 May 1853, he complained to Kirby about some pieces by Russell and Crolly which had appeared in *The Dublin Review*, saying that "altogether the periodical is not very strong on the Catholic side". He was particularly annoyed by some of the sentiments concerning politics that had been expressed by some of the Professors before the Commission. On St. Charles' Day, he wrote to Kirby: "One thing appears certain that unless Murray and Crolly are removed the College will become a regular nuisance. They are eternally agitating, Young Irelanders, enemies of the authority of superiors and yet at the examination they denounced all the priests who interfere in politics. They will inspire a sad spirit into the minds of students". That same year he had high praise in a pastoral for a paper by Dr. Kelly on 'The Reformation in Ireland', which had appeared in the *Rambler*. In 1854, though, at the time of the declaration of the Dogma of the Immaculate Conception, he is said to have been very disappointed at the attitude of many of the Maynooth staff. Certainly, towards the end of February, that year, he was convinced that Maynooth was Gallican.

Russell was not suspected of Gallicanism, but Cullen did not favour him for all that. When, in mid-February, the question arose of the possible appointment of Russell as Bishop of Dromore, Cullen urged Propaganda to the contrary:

> "Father Charles Russell is .... an able man. He was nominated some years ago as a coadjutor for Ceylon, but asked to be excused from that burden because he had several sisters who depended on him for their support .... Moreover, although a professor in the college at Maynooth, Father Russell spends little time there, but is found visiting here in Dublin, or travelling here and there through other parts of Ireland. This mode of behaviour makes one fear that he would not be fond of being at home. Furthermore, although Father Russell is very fond of literature, he has as yet never taken part in the movements recently made in favour of the Catholic University .... Notwithstanding, therefore, the learning and good conduct of Father Russell, I should not expect good results from his promotion".

It was calculated to be effective, even if a little unfair.

On February 24th, 1854, the fourth anniversary of Cullen's consecration, he wrote to Kirby:

> "I got a peep at the Maynooth examination yesterday. It is perfectly Gallican. Mr. Crolly is a little way more than Gallican. When a Pope confirms a general council, the council becomes infallible because it is to be supposed that a majority of the

146

Bishops agree with him. He is the organ of the majority. Rescripts and bulls if not received do not bind — temporal power responsible to no one on earth. I wonder can a King or prince commit a mortal sin in his administration which would expose him to the penalties of the Church. Mr. Furlong now in Rome is also thoroughly Gallican. He explains he says what is meant by the Pope's infallibility and then tells the students to think as they like — of course on the temporal power's independence he agrees with Crolly ... Dr. Moriarty was examined on the system of discipline adopted on the Continent and recommended that it be introduced into Maynooth. ....Crolly among other things stated that no bishop could remove him from his place as professor because he was engaged in teaching theology in a public school or College — Such a privilege applies to Universities but I suppose not to a private unapproved College like Maynooth. Inquire and let me know ... Dr. Russell was not exercised as to Gallican questions. He merely stated that he admitted no temporal power of the Pope direct or indirect. It appears that the professors gave in the questions they wished to be asked. Crolly and some others were determined to crush Ultramontanism. Crolly brought his answers ready written and read them. There was an air of intriguing in the whole business".

Who were the "some others" mentioned ? It would be strange if Murray were among them, because already he was becoming famous — infamous in the eyes of those opposed to it — for his defence of papal infallibility. In the Preface to his *Theological Essays* (the new name he gave to his *Miscellany*) for 1854 he himself had written: "I shall not be at all surprised to find myself denounced by certain doctors of the new theology as a heretic". *The Catholic Layman* was one of the sources that denounced him: "We pity poor Dr. Murray, for we greatly fear his lamentations are in vain; and that his 'old theology' is in a fair way of being superseded by the 'new theology' of his dangerous associates". This journal carried on its attack in 1856, when it berated Murray's defence of infallibility in an article 'Black Heretics and White Heretics', in which (Pat Murray of Westmeath' was castigated. It was difficult for Murray, yet as an aside it should be said that both his genius and, at least at that time, his unflappability, were demonstrated by his giving two lectures in Cork just then on 'The Poetical Genius of Thomas Moore'. Behind his back, however, ominous things were happening.

It is thought that, by the end of February, Cullen was in possession of all the evidence given before the Commission. He certainly had it in July, in print but before it was published, given to him by one of the commissioners. That month he wrote to Kirby to that effect, saying that he wanted it to be examined in Rome. The word got out that he had been given the proofs of the report as it was produced, by one of the Catholic Commissioners, More O'Ferrall. Three Maynooth Professors wrote to Lord Harrowby protesting about this. Where, then as now, was confidentiality? But Harrowby refused to see anything remiss about the matter. A question about it was raised in the House of Commons, but to no purpose. Already, Dr. Cullen was in contact with Propaganda, through Kirby, expressing the fear that the expositions of some of the Maynooth Professors before the Royal Commission were tainted with Gallicanism. Kirby added his own voice to the same effect. The *Archives of Propaganda* contain a lot of material that throws light on all this affair.

In December, 1854, Cullen was in Rome for the defining of the Immaculate Conception on the 8th. A number of other Irish Bishops were there also. The Archbishop of Dublin took the opportunity to call a meeting in Propaganda devoted to the question of the teaching at Maynooth. At the meeting he made it clear that he had some of the evidence in his possession. They divided 3 and 3 —McHale of Tuam, Derry of Clonfert and McNally of Clogher (all former members of the staff) took the side of the College; Dixon of Armagh, Murphy of Cloyne and Cullen himself were critical of it. The matter was referred to Propaganda for its decision, and on 18 January, the first meeting of a special sub-committee of the Cardinals of Propaganda was held about it. Meanwhile, there were bad relations between the Irish parties to the dispute. In early February, knowing that Mgr. Barnabo supported Cullen and without doubt feeling themselves outnumbered, McHale, Derry and McNally left Rome. On 18 February, a special meeting of the Congregation was held before the Pope on various Irish questions, including Maynooth. On 1 March, the Report of the Royal Commission was published in Ireland.

148

That Dr. Murray was fully *au fait* with what was happening is clear from a letter to Gavan Duffy of 16 March. In it he maintains that Mgr. Barnabo of Propaganda is a "mere creature tool and partisan" of Dr. Cullen. Murray was not above playing politics. He told Duffy that "before Dr. McHale left Rome, Dr. C. addresséd a letter of accusation against him to the Pope — in which among other things he charged him with having assisted ..... at a dinner with ..... Mr C. G. Duffy, the Mazzini of Ireland". McHale had tried to defend himself as best he could. But Murray would have Duffy "draw up a document addressed to the Pope himself, containing a full, circumstantial decisive refutation of the slander ... If you wish, I will draw it up for you in my own hand, in orthodox Latin and form ... This must be kept a profound secret".

He goes on:"Dr. C. has made desperate efforts to ruin Maynooth and get it *entirely* into his own personal hands. I have no doubt, from circumstantial evidence, that the Catholic part of the commission have been in conspiracy with him — I include J. O'Hagan. I have no doubt that Aberdeen was in the conspiracy .... Nothing will save us but a parliamentary inquiry in which the whole scheme must be ripped from top to bottom. Spooner will be our best friend — 'Truth is stranger than fiction' .... You need not fear about attacks on my Church Tract. I am Ultramontane except as to the Temporal Power of the Pope. Besides I mean to send each sheet, as it is printed off, to Rome for revision — corrections to be inserted at the end of the volumes before publication". "P.S. Drs. Dixon and our friend Moriarty are strong with Cullen *against* Maynooth !!!".

At this time, Cullen, still in Rome, presented a *relatio* on the state of his diocese. This he did on 27 March, in a long Latin document which pointedly raised the question of Maynooth. To accompany it, he again, on 27 March, wrote to Propaganda from the Irish College, explaining it in great detail. He refers to the importance of Maynooth. Its course of theology had been irrevocably affected by Delahogue, whose work was not worthy of being retained as a textbook in any major seminary. Crolly's replies to the Commission deserve attention and indeed also Murray's and Neville's — all three Professors of Dogmatic Theology. He lists the Gallican points in their evidence and for good measure submits an Italian translation of the relevant extracts. Back at home, the Bishop of Clonfert (Dr. Derry) was taking the thing with great *sang froid:* "I have been startled or amused by the many changes suggested in Maynooth affairs. The Report of the Commissioners is I suppose duly sustained by the evidence. I fear the priesthood of Ireland will not think the higher of the wisdom or the learning of the witnesses".

The Archbishop of Dublin's time in Rome just then was enlivened by an unusual happening. He told about it in a letter of 14 April, to his cousin, Hugh Cullen, of Liverpool. It concerned an accident which had taken place during a papal audience:

"The Pope was receiving all with his usual affability and goodness, when on a sudden the main beam of the room broke across in the centre, the floor nodded for an instant, then precipitated Pope, cardinals, bishops and generals, students and all, one hundred and twenty in number, to the ground floor seventeen feet below, literally covering them with a coat of rafters, bricks and mortar and enveloping them in a dense smothering cloud of dust. Fortunately, however, neither Pope, cardinals nor bishops sustained any hurt or damage .... The Pope fell on a student (an Irishman I think) whilst two other students came down on the poor Pope. It was an Irishman that pulled his Holiness out of the ruins and another from Drogheda that whitewashed the Pope outside with a bucket of water, much to the amusement of Pio Nono. The French commander had his sword smashed to pieces, as it fell from the scabbard; he himself was very much damaged, as two or three persons tumbled down on top of him. The Austrian general had his sword also broken and lost his boots whilst endeavouring to extricate himself from the ruins."

Cullen was impatient for action by Rome. He returned to the struggle on 23 April, with a full account of the Maynooth problem as he saw it. In this he describes the College as one of the most important in Europe, because it forms almost all the priests and bishops of Ireland and of many of the British colonies. But he gets on with haste to the problem – Crolly, whom he describes as Professor of Dogmatic Theology. In those days the distinction was blurred between dogmatic and moral theology as understood later. He believes that Crolly is Gallican in his teaching but, fortunately, with two exceptions, his views are not shared by the superiors or other Professors. It would be good if the Congregation could intervene – better than leaving it to the Irish Bishops as this could easily cause complications; some of them might even agree with the opinions in question ! It goes without saying that the Maynooth Professors are in his diocese and depend on him for their faculties, but to date no Archbishop of Dublin has ever used his powers to regulate the internal affairs of the College. He has no complaint about most of the Professors and students but some Professors are suspect of Gallicanism. Most notable among these is George Crolly, but there is also Patrick Murray and Henry Neville.

The world went on. That 17 April, Lord Raglan sent off a despatch from the Crimea announcing the bombardment of Sebastopol. The same day, Bishop McNally of Clogher, now returned from Rome, wrote to Renehan regretting that, on his way back home, he was not able to call to Maynooth: "Maynooth is now so much assailed by some persons in Rome as it is by Mr. Spooner and his adherents in the English Parliament". The present writer remembers with pleasure his days as a student in

Oxford in the early 1950's, where he was a regular visitor to the home there of the Misses Spooner, for Sunday afternoon tea and a piano recital !

Propaganda was not to be rushed. On 30 April, the Congregation referred the matter, as usual, to an expert, Signor Perrone — a famous theologian who, years later, was to congratulate Murray for his *De Ecclesia* — seeking his considered opinion on it. The extracts supplied by Cullen were furnished to him. At this stage, another player entered the contest, Dr. Dixon, Primate of Armagh. He wrote to Kirby from Drogheda on 15 May, 1855:

> "My Dear Dr. Kirby — I have never asked you to execute a commission for me at Propaganda in which I felt a deeper concern than I do in the present one. I know not if you have seen a copy of the Maynooth report and evidence since it was given to the public in this country. I have gone through the two vols., and I need not say what pain it has cost me to read such statements made by Professors of the College. If our episcopal body here were united, I should insist on one of two things — either that those professors should be removed from the College or that they should be obliged to publish to the world an expression of their sorrow for the insolence and extravagance which characterise those statements. But in the present state of our body such a course presents such difficulties that the very attempt might do much more harm than good. Then I have concluded that I ought to take the strongest step which one man acting by himself can take, to mark my sense of this evil and that is to resign my place as a Trustee of the College. Of course, as one of the Bishops of the country I should still take a deep interest in the College and exert myself for its improvement and the correction of abuses in it — a matter to which all the bishops of the country have a right to look. At the same time I apprehend that many well-meaning persons in this country would call this proceeding on my part imprudent and injurious to the College. But if I had the conviction that this course would not dissatisfy Rome I should not mind what these people would say ... I do think that what I here propose would be the most effectual step which I could take to awaken the pious Catholic public here to the conviction that evils were to be dreaded from other quarters as well as from Spooner and his friends".

He added that, if the Archbishop of Dublin were still in Rome, his opinion should be sought. Dr. Dixon must have been quite embarrassed by the fact that two old colleagues — and Northerners to boot — were involved in the affair. His letter shows him to be rather torn between a

151

feeling for them and a consciousness of his duty. His views were duly lodged by Kirby with the Prefect of Propaganda.

Then on 18 May, Perrone published his opinion. In typical fashion, he notes that there are two sides to the dispute, one doctrinal, one prudential. From the doctrinal point of view, he has found Crolly's views ultra-Gallican — even tending to heresy — and has found an anti-Roman bias in the Maynooth replies in general. One example is their reiteration that it is not an article of our faith that the Pope, acting with all the Church, is infallible when he solemnly declares the divine and natural law. Is he then merely speculating? Was Pius IX not infallible when he defined the dogma of the Immaculate Conception? As regards the prudential question, there were various possibilities, one of which is that the Congregation could declare itself dissatisfied with the teaching in question.

PALAZZO di PROPAGANDA

On 14 June, the Congregation met again in special session to decide on what was now called the 'Crolly affair'. To Perrone's question as to whether they should disapprove of Crolly's teaching, the answer was: *"Affirmative in omnibus"*. But they added immediately that Mgr. Dixon should be asked to remain at his post and also that an effort should be made to find a quiet way to convince Crolly to retract, asking him to come to Rome to see how he could be got to change his mind. Cullen's view had been thoroughly taken into account and the Report of the Royal Commission also. Even the Report of 1826 was adverted to, McHale's views at that time being noted as strange.

On 27 June, the Trustees met at Maynooth and, on its being moved by Dixon and seconded by McHale, resolved that "the Trustees are deeply impressed with the necessity of taking into consideration the late Report of the Commissioners of Enquiry with the College and the Character of the evidence submitted to the Commissioners by some members of the College, but that, for grave reasons, they deem it advisable to adjourn this matter to their next Summer meeting". The idea, presumably, was that by then the dust would have settled. Cullen was sarcastic about their deferral of action until a year hence and wrote to that effect to Kirby: "I think they will find that the business has been done for them".

In July, he was on retreat in the College with his priests. He reported to Kirby: "The Professors at the College of Maynooth are much engaged in defending themselves, and they have a large enough party, but this is now the opportune moment to give a blow to Gallicanism". It would be interesting to know what he thought of an article on The Maynooth Commission in *The Edinburgh Review,* which appeared that month, and which had been critical of the discipline at Maynooth, describing it as more suitable for girls in a boarding school than for men who have later to mix in the world. He would have been more put off by its favourable contrast of the courses for the ministry at Maynooth with those of Oxford where greater reliance seemed to be placed on "the light of nature", the "intercourse of undergraduate life", and the "boat-races".

That July, he was also at work blocking the possibility of Dr. O'Hanlon's appointment as Coadjutor to the Bishop of Elphin, enclosing an 1846 letter to his predecessor by Dr. Renehan saying that O'Hanlon was not remarkable for "piety, prudence, zeal, edification and respectability". Cullen adds that O'Hanlon's views on clerical agitation are as strong as the Archbishop of Tuam's, so that his promotion could cause difficulty in this respect. Towards the end of August, he is again writing to Kirby complaining that nothing has happened at Maynooth about the Gallican charge. The Professors have returned to their work without having received any rebuke, and continue with confidence to teach the same ideas which His Holiness reproves so much. No instruction has been received by them as the matter is under judgement by the Holy See, from which he hopes a directive will come shortly. To clinch the issue, he wrote along the same lines to Barnabo. And when that did not bring a response, he even wrote to the Pope — through Kirby — who did not deliver the letter becuase, by the time it arrived, Propaganda had issued its judgement on the question. Cullen's frenetic anxiety could subside — at least for the time being.

On 6 September, 1855, the Congregation conveyed its decision to the four Irish Archbishops. The matter, it said, is a serious one because of the nature of Maynooth and one that must be cleared up. Crolly must be warned, and asked to retract and amend his teaching, and the Bishops should take the opportunity to reform clerical life in the College. A separate letter was sent to Cullen, spelling out the views of the special Congregation meeting of 14 June. He hastened to tell Kirby about this and is obviously gratified that at last the Archbishops have been ordered to see to it that Crolly retracts his views and repairs the scandal that he has given, also that books which "smell badly" be removed. The Archbishops, he says, will decide what to do immediately.

In October the Trustees in general were still not very alarmed. At their meeting they dealt with the amount to be paid annually by the Professors for wine in the Parlour, ordering no change to be made, "whether any gentleman partake of the wine or not". Following the meeting, Cullen wrote to Kirby:

"We did not talk about the Propaganda letter. After the meeting the archbishops of Armagh and Tuam and I (the archbishop of Cashel being seriously ill was absent) dealt with the said letter. As soon as Professor Crolly was informed of Rome's decision about his views, he submitted and declared himself ready to make whatever act of reparation would be required of him. He promised also to go to Rome immediately after Christmas. We did nothing about the other professors, but it was decided that the four archbishops would meet in Maynooth on November 15, to oblige these gentlemen to retract ..... The Propaganda letter has effected a wholesome fear among the professors, and they are in trepidation, fearing something worse. I hope in this way Gallicanism will be banished from the College".

According to the historian Emmet Larkin, "what was really bothering Cullen about Maynooth, of course, was its independence ..... He decided, therefore, to intimidate them by demonstrating that he could reach them, however indirectly, if necessary. His choice of the issue of Gallicanism ... was masterful, for it .... raised a question of doctrine ..." More credit for a genuine concern for orthodoxy should be given to Dr. Cullen.

He was calculating without the agreement of McHale, who, having learned that Slattery of Cashel would be unable to attend because of an indisposition, wrote to Cullen on 8 November, proposing that, as the Maynooth business which they had been asked by the Congregation to look after is so important, "in deference to the Holy See as well as in justice to the great National interests involved, we should not proceed in the affair of any general inquiry into the state of the College of Maynooth until we have the assistance of, at least, the four Archbishops". He had written to Armagh to the same effect. Cullen sent on his letter to the Congregation. McHale covered himself against any Roman misinterpretation of his action by writing personally to the Prefect of Propaganda, Cardinal Fransoni, on 11 November, saying that, although Cashel is sick, the other three Metropolitans can do what is needed; however he still expresses himself as being in some disquiet about the absence of one of their colleagues. It is a matter that is of much interest to the other Trustees of Maynooth.

As planned, the meeting of Archbishops took place in the College on 15 November. Just prior to that, the Primate had written to the President announcing it and hoping that the Professors would be "at home" as "it may be necessary to speak to them". There are a number of accounts of

154

this meeting, all of which are worth recording. After it (on 29 November), Dr. Cullen wrote to Kirby of the Irish College. Dr. Slattery, he says, was ill and could not come, so he and Dr. Dixon had taken matters in hand. McHale had not been present either as he had been held up and was late in arriving. McHale himself hastened next day to report to Rome to Fransoni (whom he spelt 'Fransonio', most likely to the latter's chagrin). He had arrived by train at 1 p.m. after a long journey. By then the other two Archbishops had already got the whole work done, even before 2 o'clock. He gathered that it had only taken about a half an hour. This is surely most unusual as no hour for the meeting had been fixed. Still, he is happy to say that Rev. Dom. Crolly had assured the two Archbishops — and himself later — that he was quite ready to do whatever the Holy See required. McHale also reported his version of events in a letter of 2 January to Slattery. If Pugin's script were difficult to unscrabble, this defies all undoing, but the salient points can be established. He had come by the one available train. As it was passing the College, the professors were being assembled by Dixon and Cullen and, "in the space of twenty minutes, about the time it took me to walk from the station to the College, the meeting broke up and all the members were about the hall door at my arrival. You may guess my surprise". It would be a pity if the uniform understanding between the two metropolitans should conduce to sowing the seed of lasting discord.

Cullen's own version of what happened is contained in his letter to Kirby of 29 November:

"We called Crolly in the first instance and he signed a most humble retraction, expressing his regret for what he had done, retracting the opinions he had uttered and promising to do everything in his power to repair the scandal given. Dr. Dixon and I are to communicate his retraction to the Bishops and I will send a copy of it to the Propaganda. Mr. Crolly also engaged to publish his retraction among the students. After this first step we assembled all the superiors and professors and Dr. Dixon gave them a good lecture for their published evidence and said that they had incurred the displeasure not only of the Holy See but also of every good Catholic in Ireland. I also gave them a lecture and I stated that the letter of some of the professors to Lord Harrowby was so anti-ecclesiastical in character that I had made up my mind to withdraw all faculties from the author of it and would have carried this determination into effect had I not within the last few hours been assured that those engaged in the transaction were heartily ashamed of what they had done. I think that all were greatly humbled and that their Gallican propensities have received a severe shock. Everything passed off in this way very quietly and I was about to return to Dublin when, lo, Dr. McHale arrives at about half past

155

two o'clock contrary to what he had intimated to me. I went to him immediately and informed him that we had settled everything before he had arrived and he said he was very glad of it. Whether he was really pleased I know not, for I immediately started off for Dublin and have had no opportunity of seeing anyone since. I think however that it was most providential that he absented himself, as had he been with us there would have been discussions and discussions and probably the professors might have been provoked to say something in their defence. It will be well to explain how matters happened lest the Propaganda imagine that we excluded Dr. McHale."

Kirby as usual lost no time about forwarding this to Propaganda. Cullen himself wrote to Fransoni on 2 December: "The professors who feared some stronger measure were very pleased to be left without further punishment. I hope that they will profit from the lesson which they have been given and I am convinced that in the future they will not be so ready to show their tendency towards Gallicanism. I believe this to have been the first time that the authority of the Holy See was demonstrated in Maynooth College ...."

Dixon likewise had written to Kirby to the effect that Mr. Crolly had made an admirable submission and was preparing to go to Rome at the beginning of Lent, 1856, in compliance with the wishes of the Congregation. A short while later, Cullen dispatched Crolly's signed retraction to Kirby for delivery at Propaganda − "Let me know if it be sufficient" − together with a covering letter to same. In this he goes over again the circumstances of the retraction. Crolly's retraction is there in the *Archives of Propaganda* − one page, signed by him and witnessed by Dixon and Cullen. It is a copy − vouched for by Cullen − who urged that it be inserted into the *Acta* of the Congregation.

Dr. Patrick Murray made notes of the proceedings, which are kept in the College Library. These *Notes* are full of human interest and give another slant on the whole thing. During the meeting, he says, "neither Cullen nor Dixon looked straight at anybody while they were speaking but kept their heads down". At the general interview with the staff, all were present except Mr. Crolly, who had been interviewed already, and Mr. Tully "who was out hiding". Dr. Cullen had brought up the matter of *several* (Murray underlines this) Professors having written to Lord Harrowby against him, objecting to the evidence provided to the Royal Commission being submitted to the Holy See. It could do him no harm, he had said, but was an appeal from ecclesiastical to secular authority which was not good. Murray notes that none of those present uttered a word.

Later he added many postscripts to this account of what had happened on 15 November, mainly insinuating that what Crolly had been charged with was unacceptable more to Dixon and Cullen than to the Holy See. Dixon had evidently waffled. He had excused himself profusely; all he was interested in was to save the good name of the College. Murray found his attitude "wanting in the respect due to so learned, virtuous and every way so respectable a body", especially as he had been a member of the staff himself. "His temper was occasionally warm" and his tone throughout "so offensive and arrogant" that Murray refrains from going into it: "He was our parlour fool". On the other hand, "Dr. Cullen's *tone* was by no means of this kind". He suspected Cullen, though, of being prepared to expel himself and others from the College or at the very least suspend them. He lists an entire catalogue of Cullen's transgressions in delating Crolly to Rome, etc. He has heard that Cullen was "highly incensed" at some of the things he himself had said about the way the Maynooth Board conducts its business, but he has "nothing to retract or modify"; he was only telling the truth and, if it were critical, that was as it had to be. He has heard too that Dr. Cullen was out to get him for his teaching that Protestants could be saved because of invincible ignorance. But Rome had not followed that up. Murray's *Notes* do not make pleasant reading.

After this, little came from Cullen about Maynooth, its Professors or its teachings. In Dublin there was more excitement about the trial of the Redemptorist Fr. Vladimir Petcherine, accused of burning Protestant Bibles, than there was about the doctrinal situation at Maynooth. O'Hagan was now involved in this and was busily defending the Russian *emigré*. He was primed by Dr. Russell, while Murray coached Curran, the Junior Barrister. Murray had sat throughout the trial in Green Street Courthouse, which some criticised as "undignified for a Maynooth Don". This was in December. That same month, Cullen wrote to Kirby expostulating that Crolly and his friends were criticizing him for having acted for reasons of personal animosity, having gone over their heads to Rome and in a matter which involved only small inaccuracies. He must have been pleased, when at the end of December, Propaganda wrote to him expressing satisfaction at the visitation and in particular with the way Crolly had been dealt with. He was asked to communicate this to Armagh.

In March, 1856, Crolly himself was busily explaining to Kirby, for the benefit of Propaganda, that he could not go to Rome just then because of family affairs. The Board of Maynooth were preparing to examine the evidence of the Professors before the Royal Commission. But, as Cullen had rightly estimated, their work had been done for them. Even though a Rescript from Rome of 16 May authorized the Archbishop of Dublin to call a meeting of the Bishops about Maynooth affairs in general, when it took place it did not amount to much. The meeting was held on 20 and 21 June, in Dublin, in Cullen's house. The Bishops as a whole insisted that the doctrine taught by the Maynooth Professors in general was sound. Several disciplinary matters were discussed. On 13 July, Dr. Cullen began

157

his report on Maynooth for Propaganda. After copying it, he sent it off on 3 August. It was the end of the matter as far as he was concerned, and even today, it is hard to know whether he was right or wrong in his approach.

Once only, afterwards, he returned to the thing. That was in 1861, when he wrote to Barnabo concerning the possibility of a granting by Rome of a doctorate of divinity to George Crolly. Crolly, he said, had expressed Gallican, almost Jansenistic, views before a government commission and had not published his retraction of them. A degree should not be conferred on him until he removed the impression created by his evidence. It was the last swish of the tail ....

Once things are started in Rome, it is difficult to know where they will end. In January, 1857, Propaganda was inquiring why Mr. Crolly had not yet come out. According to Kirby, an Irish priest in Rome had reported Cardinal Barnabo as saying: "Why does that Crolly not come to Rome ? He was ordered to come and was to be here in Lent, but now it is Winter and he is not here yet". Kirby thought that he would indeed come eventually, even though he had not been 'ordered' to. Dr. Dixon was hoping that when this happened, he would get a very kind reception. Propaganda did not let up. In February, the whole Crolly business was discussed at a General Congregation. This time Dr. Neville was also introduced, but they did not proceed against him as the Bishop of Cork had promised that he had amply retracted his opinions. At home, Cullen was in a quandary about the candidature of Dr. Furlong of Maynooth for the See of Ferns. He is a good and pious man, who can hardly be passed over. There is nothing against him "except the Gallicanism of his examination" before the Royal Commission. He was appointed and made a fine Bishop. The entire Maynooth episode was eventually lived down. January, 1857, also marked the arrival of news of Cullen's elevation to the Cardinalate.

When one thinks of what Maynooth had to endure by way of Protestant attack all through 1855, the more one begins to understand the impossible situation in which attacks on another front put it. On 21 March, 1855, *The Witness*, an Edinburgh newspaper of the Church of Scotland, had called for a day of intercessory prayer that God might direct Parliament aright to disendow Maynooth. On 10 April, the Reverend M. Hobart Seymour had published a pamphlet, *The Disendowment of Maynooth as a question of national, social and civil policy*, being the reproduction from *The Bath and Cheltenham Gazette* of a speech to the Protestant Alliance in Bath. The speech had not exactly been original in its approach, even if regularly interspersed with 'laughter'. One portion of it merits quoting. "We learn that we are providing Romish Priests for Australia, for America, for India, for China, in fact for every part of the world. Thus we find that England is providing Romish missionaries for the Pacific, Romish priests for China, Romish priests for India and Roman Archbishops for the States of America. Now, Sir, I am sure that this was not the original intention of the endowment of Maynooth". China may have been irrelevant to it then, but it was to come into the Maynooth picture later.

On Saturday, 5 May, *The Lady's Newspaper* turned its attention to Maynooth. True, it was more concerned with events in India: "Accounts from the North-Western Frontier still continue unsatisfactory. There have been some successful operations against the Brusse Khail men; but the Hazara country is represented as being in a disturbed state .... The Bedurs of Deodroof and adjacent districts recently assigned by the Nizan to the British Government, have been creating a disturbance ... Lieutenant Frankland, commanding the Lingsagoor field force, received early intimation of these proceedings, and surprized the insurgents by a well-managed forced march ... The Naib was given up, the rebels dispersed".

This passage gives a striking insight into the world of the Victorian Empire. We can be sure that in garrison quarters in Dublin and the Curragh of Kildare, in Limerick and Tipperary and Buttevant and Fermoy, there were ladies to whom it was very meaningful. What did *they* think of Maynooth ? Their newspaper went on to say that the good sense of the English people had been outraged by the Maynooth Grant. It cited a certain 'Mr. Horsman' as having said in the Commons that it simply had to be ended. A couple of paragraphs on, it was referring to a ' Mr. Horsfall ' as being of the same opinion. The same man or another ? — quite a problem for those proof readers who get so worried about such things .. *The Lady's Newspaper* gave a long coverage to Maynooth — as critical as could be. It was in vain that, in June, John Francis Maguire endeavoured to rehabilitate the College; *The Eclectic Review* was straightaway off the mark to renew the attack on it, maintaining that the Report of the Commission of 1853 had been "meagre, superficial and unsatisfactory to the last degree". In fact, for a couple of years there was a plethora of articles and pamphlets, all very critical of Maynooth.

In December, 1856, there was a fire at Carton, which the students of the College helped to put out. The Duke conveyed his thanks during the following January, on their return from vacation. A letter of this period from the Bishop of Killaloe gives an idea of how one of his students might have travelled up to the College: "The sooner he goes to Maynooth the better and he can go by the steamer to Athlone and will be in Maynooth the same evening by travelling in the Galway railroad carriage which goes by the College".

Writing on non-theological subjects by the Professors continued unabated. In all likelihood, C. W. Russell was working towards a paper which he delivered the August of 1857, 'On the inhabitants and dialect of the barony of Forth, in the County of Wexford', which he represented as "one of the minor curiosities of the ethnographical map". According to *The Freeman's Journal,* examples which he gave of the peculiarities of the old Forthers "afforded not a little amusement to the audience". That was to be in August, the following year, just before the Presidency fell vacant. It can hardly have helped his candidature with some Bishops. That September, most people were more interested in *The Freeman's* announcement that there were high hopes for a successful attempt "to connect Europe and America by the electric wire".

SHADOWS OF A RIVAL

Maynooth was getting a hard time of it. If it was caught between London and Rome on the one side, it was also caught by the promotion of the Catholic University. It is hard to know what Newman thought, but there is little doubt that he regarded Maynooth as a rival. In April, 1853, he had written to Ambrose St. John: *"Entre nous,* for it must not be mentioned, I feel no doubt the Government is intriguing with Dr. Cullen about the University. Maynooth will be held up *in terrorem.* I don't see the end of it. One does not see how the University can be given up, considering how much has been subscribed. I may be kept in suspense an indefinite time".

Later the same month, he wrote to Dalgairns that he suspected the Government was cool about the University because of the Maynooth Commission. And in May, he was asking the opinion of James Hope Scott on what was to happen to the University: "Is Dr. Cullen so hampered with the National School Question that he can determine nothing else? Or is the new Primate afraid of Maynooth suffering ? Or is the great Archbishop of the West afraid of an incursion of Saxons ?" He was beginning to be bitter and Maynooth was part of the reason. In June, he complained to Robert Ornsby that nothing was happening and again we get the refrain: "Is the new Primate and the Maynooth Commission the difficulty ?" By November, though, he was telling Ornsby that he is seeking as Lecturer in Astronomy a Dr. Daniel William Cahill who had studied at Maynooth; Ornsby said he was a "quack". At times, Newman could be big, as when, in 1853, he offered Orestes Brownson a Professorship, even though he had criticised the *Essay on Development* in 1845 something which Newman had described as "rudeness".

In June, 1854, Newman was in Maynooth, for the purpose of getting the Hierarchy to approve the acquiring of the Medical School and also a list of Professors to be appointed to the Catholic Univeristy. He wrote to Henry Bittleson from Dublin: "I was in Maynooth yesterday to meet the Bishops. The Archbishop of Tuam shook his hand with so violent a cordiality, when I kissed his ring, as to punish my nose".

It was so like Gladstone's visit to Corfu, a few years later, when, as Viscount Kirkwell tells us, he "excited the perhaps illiberal disgust of the English by publicly kissing the hand of the Archbishop. ... Mr. Gladstone, having taken and respectfully kissed the Bishop's hand, leaned forward to receive the orthodox blessing. The Bishop hesitated, not knowing what was expected of him .... At last, however, bending forward, he hastened to comply with the flattering desire of the representative of the British Crown. But, at this moment, unfortunately, Mr. Gladstone, imagining that the deferred blessing was not forthcoming, suddenly raised his head, and struck the episcopal chin. The resident and other spectators of the scene had considerable difficulty in maintaining the gravity befitting so solemn an occasion.....". One wonders whether Newman had any such sense of humour.

J. Lewis May, in his biography of Newman published in 1930, quotes him as saying about the Catholic University in 1854: "As to Maynooth, the President, Dr. Kenehan, was distinctly cold towards the project of a University, while Dr. Russell, under date of July 2 wrote to me, I explained to you, when we last met, how I myself have felt the subject of the University and how despondently I have looked upon the prospects". Obviously, Newman was not very close to Renehan, whose name he had even spelt incorrectly. Was he thinking of Kinahan's whiskey, so popular at that time ? He appreciated Russell, as being "of the most cultivated class in Ireland", but, in spite of his encouragement, Newman "had a more desponding view than ever of the University, from things which came out of the Maynooth commission".

Ward in his biography says that Newman found the majority of Irish Bishops not at all alive to the importance of university education for Catholics. The policy which prevailed at the Synod of Thurles was, he says, what Newman used to call that of "the political and devotional party" as opposed to the champions of intellectual interests, the party of Dr. Cullen as opposed to that of Dr. Murray and Dr. Russell. Ward says of Newman: "It is idle to speculate as to what use he might have made of such gifts and talents among his colleagues had the circumstances of the country been different ..... and had Dr. Russell instead of Dr. Cullen, been Archbishop of Dublin". He believed that Murray and Russell, in common with the ablest and most cultural members of the Irish clergy, regarded some *modus vivendi* with the Queen's College as the only practicable course. Cullen has been regarded as being opposed because, in the words of the historian McClelland, in his biography of Manning, "it would exclude his beloved Maynooth"! How hard it was for Dr. Cullen to be understood.

Around this time, Newman appears to have enlisted Russell's help to win over the President to the new University. Russell was in London just then and replied that the moment he returns he will show his letter to Renehan. He has a feeling that this job could be done better by others, especially those who think differently. It would be great if Newman could "conciliate" those who have been hostile.

161

"It is difficult but, I think not impossible. I wish very much that you would win over Revd. Mr. Crolly, one of our professors of Theology, whom you know, or at least have met at the College. I am not sure that you would succeed but if you do not fear to encounter a failure, it would be worth the trial. I hardly like to propose it, but a letter from you, written frankly, and openly admitting your knowledge that he had hitherto regarded the project as unfeasible, might have the effect of inducing him to co-operate in carrying it out, now that it has been seriously taken up and that we are committed to its success or failure".

Russell was clearly sceptical of the outcome — even of the University *in se* — and did not want his own name mentioned in connection with his suggestion. He arrived back in Maynooth in mid-July, having visited Ely, Peterborough, Lincoln, York, Ripon, Durham and other churches "which lie along the great Northern line". He saw the President and in August informed Newman that Renehan's feeling "is that in his position, considering the present public position of the Maynooth question, it is better for him not to take any step which could bring his name into discussion". The President, says Russell, hopes that Newman will not misunderstand his feelings. Newman should know "where his real feelings are". A Delphic utterance indeed, not out of character with Renehan, who at that time had his hands more than full with the task of presiding over Maynooth.

Cullen, for all the suspicions that lay on him, was more open to the University than Newman thought. In the Autumn of 1854, however, he was worried by other matters. Cholera had hit the country. In September he wrote to Kirby that it was very severe in Limerick and Belfast and other places in daily communication with Dublin, although it had not yet hit the city. But in Finglas, "quite close to us", over twenty persons have died. He himself left for Italy in October, where he was put in quarantine in Civita Vecchia, confined in what he called a horrid place, after having experienced a terrible storm. The captain could not get in and had to turn back to the Gulf of Spezia, which they had reached after seven or eight hours tossing.

It was in 1856 that the name of Robert Ffrench Whitehead, Vice-President of Maynooth, came up in connection with the vacant see of Galway. Dr. Cullen had his views on the matter. Whitehead, he said "is a very worthy ecclesiastic, but unfortunately he is very excitable, and those who know him intimately assure me that he sometimes runs the risk of going mad by such immoderate excitement, or at least of doing strange things. If it were not for this weakness, he would be a good Bishop". Newman, for all his donnishness, was no fool in practical affairs. That same year he wrote: "Poor Dr. C. ! I should not wonder if he is quite dragged down with anxiety. The great fault I find with him is, that he makes no one his friend because he will confide in nobody, and be considerate to nobody. Everybody feels that he is emphatically *close*, and, while this repels friends, it fills enemies with nameless suspicions.....".

In 1856, Richard Coyne, who for decades had held the title of 'Printer to Maynooth College', died. With him the title became extinct. In a way, this was a mistake and a loss to Maynooth's academic trappings. His bookshop in Dublin had been a great place for foregathering and discussing. During the early days of the Catholic Association, O'Connell used to hold its meetings in rooms over it, and it was said that on one occasion, having only a small attendance, he pressed into service to make a quorum two Maynooth students whom he found browsing in the shop below.

The University was to survive for some time. In 1862, Cardinal Cullen would lay the foundation stone of what were to be magnificent new buildings for it in Drumcondra. But in 1864 the site was to be leased to a railway company.

Chapter VI

A President with Panache

On 20 October, 1857, the death of the President of Maynooth, Dr. Renehan, was announced to the Board of Trustees. He had carried a heavy burden for many years and had gone to his reward. *The Freeman's Journal* was generous to him in its obituary:

> "Nothing in the shape of public bereavement or affliction had occurred for a long period calculated to throw a deeper gloom and sadness over the hearts of both clergy and laity alike than the loss of this truly pious priest, gifted scholar, and illustrious Irishman, whose solid learning and exalted virtues have not confined their influence within the walls of his college, or within the shores of his native land, but have fructified far abroad in the missionary success of the many who have studied under his auspices, and have benefited by his teachings and example".

The Board proceeded immediately to elect his successor. Charles William Russell was elected, the only other candidate being Robert Ffrench Whitehead, whose application was not taken seriously by many, although he got five votes to Russell's nine. He had not canvassed for the position, but his relative, Lord Ffrench of Bunowen Castle, Clifden, wrote to

Primate Dixon on his behalf, without his knowledge. Right after the election, on Archbishop McHale's proposal, Whitehead was given a year's leave of absence "for the purpose of recruiting his health". He was senior to Russell but had been regarded as unreliable and incapable of holding the office of President. Sir Francis Head would surely have been displeased. In actual fact, Russell had been a compromise candidate. The Trustees would have preferred Matthew Kelly, whom Cullen described to Kirby as "a very good Holy Roman", but his health too was not great. Interestingly enough, only four days before Russell's appointment as President, Newman had written to the Archbishops suggesting his name for the vacant Vice-Rectorship of the Catholic University.

Russell had entered Maynooth at the age of fourteen and began his post-graduate studies at the age of twenty. He was appointed Professor at the age of twenty-two, the same year that he was ordained priest. He had come from Killough, Co. Down, of solid merchant background. Having been educated at Drogheda and Downpatrick, he had completed the Maynooth courses with considerable distinction. Appointed to the Chair of Humanity in 1835, he became the first Professor of Ecclesiastical History at Maynooth after this was established in 1845 following the increased grant of that year. By 1857, when he acceded to the Presidency, his literary output had been very considerable. Kelly succeeded him in Ecclesiastical History, moving to it from Belles Lettres and French. Whitehead prepared to spend the Winter in Rome.

At Maynooth just then there was little news other than what came in about the Indian Mutiny. Farrelly, writing from there to Kirby that November, says: "There is no news of any interest here nor any news of importance from India since the taking of Delhi — none of the troops from this country have yet reached the scene of action — when they do 'tis likely the war will not last long" — a curious mixture of loyalty and patriotism.

Dr. Kelly was soon afterwards invited by Newman to accept the office of Vice-Rector of the Catholic University but, his health failing, was unable to do so. That year he published *The Martyrology of Tallaght*. The year previous to it he had also done important work for the College in providing a new structure for the courses in French and English. On Kelly's declining the post, it would appear that the Vice-Rectorship was offered to Edmund O'Reilly, who also declined. Dr. Kelly was eventually persuaded to accept it.

AUSPICIOUS BEGINNINGS

On Russell's appointment as President, Archbishop Dixon wrote to Kirby that everybody was satisfied with it. Archbishop Cullen must have been among them, despite his interest in Kelly, because Dixon says that

165

he was all powerful at the Board. The lay Trustees, in particular, had assembled in great force ready to do whatever he wished. One feels that at this stage Dixon was having a spot of sour grapes — too late though that now was. Russell entered his new position with great elan; he was congratulated by the Editor of *The Edinburgh Review,* who declared himself glad that the Bishops had selected "a gentleman whose tolerant and liberal sentiments are not exceeded by the rarity and extent of his attainments". Newman complimented him too and he replied on 12 November, saying how immensely gratified he was. What Newman had said about him was "one of the greatest satisfactions of my life".

One of his first tasks was to try to salvage for the College what he could of Renehan's library, which was to be sold on Monday, 2 November, at 1 o'clock in the Literary Sale Rooms, 13 Anglesea Street. There were very nearly two thousand items, including 17th and 18th century theological works — all listed in a catalogue entitled *Bibliotheca Renehaniana.* Shortly afterwards, Russell was pleased to receive from P. Ellis of Waterford Christian Brothers the walking stick of Dr. Hussey, the first President of Maynooth and later Bishop of Waterford. Ellis hated to let it go, as Hussey had been almost one of their founders and he stipulated "that Maynooth is never to part with it". He also sent on Hussey's portrait — for an artist to copy it: the original had been painted by Collopy of Limerick. He need not have worried at all about Maynooth not parting with the cane. The law of inertia alone would have seen to that. It went eventually to the College Museum in the 20th century and happily escaped the attention of robbers on two occasions.

Russell's promotion did not mean an end to his writing. He continued his researches for a life of Cardinal Mezzofanti, which he had begun as an article for *The Edinburgh Review,* also on a *Report on the Carte MSS.* in the Bodleian Library, which he later edited with J. P. Prendergast in 8 volumes, as well as the *Calendar of State papers of James 1* (4 volumes). He must have found administration irksome when he was approached by his old friend the Bishop of Clonfert to see what he could do about getting his brother appointed as Dean in the College. Neither the Trustees in general nor Russell were keen, as the man in question had no experience of office at Maynooth. It passed and Russell continued with his writing. Some of this was curious to say the least, such as 'Hawkers' literature in France', which appeared in *The Edinburgh Review.* In March, we find him writing to O'Hagan — now Lord O'Hagan — agreeing to become a member of a committee set up to help the widow of Hogan the sculptor. He was also dealing with a suggestion by some Cloyne priests that a "likeness of Dr. Crotty" be lithographed, so that each of them might have a copy. They asked Russell to help them with this project. A suitable miniature was found and directions received from Cloyne as to the manner of its reproduction: "But the artist begins to work, let the magnifying glass be applied, and the apparent harshness will be smoothened down so as to bring out the very best and truest expression of Dr. Crotty's countenance". The Cloyne priests were faithful to their deceased Bishop.

Any matter of a cultural nature seemed to be referred automatically to Russell. In May, the Bishop of Ardagh and Clonmacnoise contacted him immediately after he came into the possession, "for a small consideration" to the Protestant sexton, of a very ancient crozier that had been found beneath the ruins of St. Mel's Cathedral, in the parish of Ardagh, Co. Longford: "I shall take it up to the College in June and you very probably will be able to trace its date to some very remote period of the Irish Church".

Around the same time, Dr. Cullen was asking Russell whether he could find for him a map which had been prepared by Dr. Kelly, then near death if not dead: "I wrote some time ago to Dr. Murray about poor Dr. Kelly's ecclesiastical map of Ireland. Mr. Petra who is publishing an ecclesiastical map of the world is most anxious to have it. All the other maps are ready except that of Ireland. Will you be so good as to send a copy without delay ? The first volume of Petra's work has appeared. It is in huge folio most inconvenient for any useful purpose. It contains only Italy and is accompanied with a history of each diocese. I suppose the whole work will cost some hundreds. Italy of course is very accurate, but when the author will come to Denmark, Sweden, Ireland and other remote countries, I fear it will be anything but free from error. Padre Passaglia's defection from the Jesuits made great noise. He is at the English College". This reference is to the break with the Church by the noted Jesuit theologian of that name — a colleague of Perrone who had examined the Maynooth teaching in 1855 — who had become involved in political affairs beyond the limit, and had fallen under ecclesiastical censure. He died reconciled to the Church in 1887.

Early in 1858, Russell published his *Life of Cardinal Mezzofanti*, the celebrated Italian linguist, on which he had worked for so long. It was printed in Dublin and published in London. All reviews of it were laudatory, from *The Tablet, The Rambler* and *The Literary Gazette*, to *John Bull, The Guardian* and *The Globe*. It was also reviewed with praise by *Etudes, Civilta Cattolica* and *The Augsburg Gazette*. Wiseman wrote in May to congratulate the author, as did Dean Milman of St. Pauls, Fr. Faber, Dean Stanley of Christ Church, Oxford, and R.R. Madden, author of *The Lives of the United Irishmen*. There was a letter from Newman, thanking Russell for his complimentary copy and praising the book effusively but with a dig — "So you would not give us a Vice-Rector" — and some queries as to how he might obtain certain theological and other works. Manning also wrote, requesting as well that Russell would contribute a Preface to a translation of Hunter's *Life of Innocent III*. Overnight, he had become quite famous.

Just then he had to address himself to a problem that had arisen concerning *The Dublin Review*. Acton was developing plans to take it over, and Wiseman and Russell were none too happy because they did not wish control of it to pass into such liberal hands. They were hoping for an amalgamation with the *Rambler*. Dr. Dollinger was on the side of Acton, which did nothing to relieve their unease. Yet, in spite of all these preoccupations, Russell was not forgetting the foreign missions. Perhaps he remembered his call to Ceylon. He found time to petition the Work for the Propagation of the Faith in Paris for aid to the Missions in Hyderabad.

We can be quite sure that he was in his element when, on Wednesday, 8 September, 1858, he welcomed Wiseman to Maynooth. This account was published later:

"His Eminence proceeded on Wednesday by special train from the Broadstone at a quarter before ten o'clock, a.m. to May—nooth for the purpose of paying a visit to the Royal College of St. Patrick .... At the Maynooth railway station he was received by the Very Reverend Dr. Russell, President, and a number of clergymen, and conducted to the carriage in waiting to convey him to the college, where suitable preparations had been made for his coming. There was a large concourse of townspeople assembled, who cheered heartily, and the band belonging to the town played appropriate airs during the progress to the College. The reception given to his Eminence passing through Maynooth was most cordial. The professors and the students, over five hundred in number, in full academic costume, were in waiting without the college grounds, and accorded to their illustrious visitor a thoroughly Irish welcome".

The Cardinal presided at Mass in the college chapel, at which he preached to the congregation, and afterwards gave a solemn Pontifical blessing.

"At half-past two o'clock the students assembled in the new library, a large and very fine building, for the purpose of assisting at the presentation of an address. The whole body of students were present, and at the head of the hall were seated the professors. On a dais was erected a throne for his Eminence, surmounted by a handsome canopy. Chairs were placed on the dais to the right and left of the throne for the bishops. The hall was decorated with festoons of flowers. His Eminence, on entering the hall, was greeted with hearty and renewed bursts of applause".

Amongst those present was the Bishop of Bombay. In the evening there was a banquet in honour of the Cardinal: "Upwards of seventy prelates, clergy, and gentry sat down". And that night "the college and also the town of Maynooth were handsomely illuminated in honour of the visit... A band paraded the town playing favourite airs, and there was general rejoicing."

After this it must have been hurtful to the polished Russell to get a strongly-worded complaint from Dr. Moriarty, Bishop of Kerry, about the appearance of some of his students. He got this before the end of September. They were, said Moriarty, generally "unpromising subjects." The absence of clerical propriety in dress and address, the vulgarity of appearance in some and their untamed demeanour made me most anxious to get rid of them. We are too far gone into the 19th century to admit into the Priesthood men who would not be admitted into the Police". This must have been doubly nettling to Russell, seeing that the previous June the Trustees (doubtless at his instigation) had resolved that, after September, the students be required to provide soutanes of uniform colour and texture and that a uniform overdress for cold weather be a short black cloak, reaching to the knees. Simultaneously, the Dunboyne students were ordered to resume the cloak formerly worn by them. However, he may have banished his annoyance by busying himself with the procuring of portraits of all the deceased Presidents, Superiors and Professors of the College — at a cost not exceeding £8 each — which had also been decreed by the Trustees in June.

That October, he was greatly disturbed by the news that Newman had offered his resignation from the Rectorship of the Catholic University. This emerged from a letter of Newman's to Dr. Gartlan, which had been produced out of the blue by Dr. Cullen. In actual fact, already in April, 1857, Newman had sent a letter of resignation to the Bishops, but they had asked him to continue, part-time at least. He would if he had a proper Vice-Rector. Now he was again pulling out, and even though at that very time Dr. Kelly, who had spent the Summer on the Continent on medical advice, was hoping to take up the Vice-Rectorship, it was to prove abortive and Newman was to go.

Even when appointed, Dr. Kelly had been in poor health. On 21 October Russell wrote to Newman to say that the Maynooth Trustees had agreed to Kelly's resignation from his Professorship there. The latter hoped to see Newman soon at Maynooth and had asked Russell to tell him that. Kelly himself was then too ill to write. In the event, Newman did not join them in the College, and Kelly's condition deteriorated. He was in great pain, worn out with sleeplessness and only able to sit up for a little while each day. Russell kept Newman informed.

On Friday, 29 October, Dr. Kelly received the last rites from his brother and died next day at 11 a.m. at the age of forty-four. Despite his frailty, at the time of his death he had been preparing the *Ecclesiastical Map of Ireland*, referred to by Cullen, also superintending the publication of Renehan's *Collections on Irish Church History*, and was planning to edit a new printing of Colgan's *Acta Sanctorum.* A memoir of him said that "he was fond of music, and played and sang sweetly sacred and national airs, but even this, his only relaxation, he rarely permitted himself in his own room". *The Quarterly Review* paid a remarkable tribute to him: "Mr. Matthew Kelly of Maynooth .... must be named as one of the most independent and inquiring minds that have yet taken in hand the mysterious lore of ancient Erin ".

He had had a habit of writing notes on the margins of books that he was reading. One of his favourite notes was: "We all die; and like waters that return no more, we fall down into the earth". Russell told Newman of his death. It was a big shock to all, he said. He will not ask Newman to come to so gloomy a place as Maynooth now is but he may like to assist at the funeral office. He hopes he will be able to come on Monday and remain for the funeral on Tuesday. Newman did indeed come. As Russell told Dixon of Armagh: "Dr. Newman was here for the last few days till this evening. He spoke to me very anxiously about a Vice-Rector for the University. It occurred to me to mention Dr. Gartlan of Salamanca..." Gartlan became Vice-Rector that November but Newman himself got out of the University.

New vistas began to open up for Russell. A new college chapel began to be seriously mooted. Some Bishops were confident that they could help it, others afraid that collections in their dioceses might be difficult. The Bishop of Ardagh was one of these, pointing out that he had twelve or fourteen chapels in the course of erection, together with several school-houses. Russell found it hard to give it the attention he would like, owing to the pressure of his literary and cultural interests. In November, John Edward Pigot, a Dublin barrister, was trying to get him to help in founding a Catholic club in the city, to be called 'The Irish Athenaeum Club', the committee of which should include Drs. Murray and Farrelly of Maynooth and the Vice-Rector of the Catholic University. Though favourably disposed towards the idea, Russell found himself unable to join the committee. Murray wrote his poem 'Sponsa Christi et Mater', published by his relative James Duffy, and Renehan's *History of Music* came out, published posthumously at his own expense and a copy presented to each of the students in remembrance of their charity and prayers for him. Gladstone wrote to thank Russell for a copy of his *Life of Mezzofanti;* he invited Russell to meet him again "if you visit town next year".

Early in 1859, Patrick Francis Moran, Kirby's successor as Rector in Rome since 1855, also wrote to Russell. His account of the Rome of this time is fascinating, even adding to historical knowledge in some respects. The French were in occupation of the city, as they had been since 1849, when they had come in to push out Garibaldi. They were to stay until 1870, whether or not the Pope approved of it, and were not without their deviousness. In July, 1858, at a secret agreement at Plombières between

170

Cavour and Napoleon III, an alliance for war with Austria had been entered into, to drive the Austrians out of Venetia and Lombardy and establish a North Italian kingdom. The war started in 1859. It is against that backdrop that Moran wrote to Russell:

"Many in Rome are just now alarmed at the prospect of war between France and Austria. Did such a war take place, there is no doubt the position of Rome would be rather perilous for a little while. The Emperor Napoleon had lately decided on sending an increase of 20,000 troops to this city; however the Holy Father protested 'by Telegraph' and though they were being embarked at Marseilles, an order from Paris changed their destiny elsewhere. Sardinia seems bent on war as it has no other way to distract the attention of the world from its present bankrupt state. All good people here sincerely hope that the Emperor will not allow himself to be involved in war by his late family ties: but let things be as they please. I am sure that after a little while Rome will return to the *status quo,* as it has the interest not only of one State but of all States for its guarantee. The Prince of Wales is enjoying himself exceedingly at the Carnival. For all I hear, it would seem that he is winning golden spurs for himself, while his *contorno* are showing themselves to be the rankest bigots possible. At the interview with the Holy Father and Antonelli and on other occasions they gave offence by their vulgar rudeness, and I heard that when visiting the traditional objects of sacred curiosity in the portico of St. John's, they joked and laughed the whole time, whilst the Prince himself remained quite steady and attentive ! All attend the Protestant Conventicle outside the Porto del Popolo with great regularity every Sunday and the minister, once an ardent Puseyite, has deemed it a good opportunity for showing his advancement and I hear makes most fierce onslaughts on Rome and the Catholic Church. However, *Dominus irridebit eos.* The people of Rome are, thank God, very peacable and quiet. A conspiracy was discovered a few days ago and about 40 persons arrested, ... The head conspirator arrested was proved to be a spia of the French General of this city. Such are the means employed to bring the Papal Government into discredit".

The reference to the Prince of Wales is interesting, as not much is known of his movements at this time. He worried his mother a lot: "Poor Bertie ! He vexes us much" (November, 1858). "Bertie continues such an anxiety" (April, 1859). It was that very Spring that he was in Rome, for at the end of April the Queen was writing: "If matters go smoothly in Italy, Bertie will not go to Germany till August". From Moran's letter to Russell it

171

is evident that Bertie was doing fine in Italy. There is a note in the papers of the Irish College, Rome, which indicates that he visited the College on 17 March, 1859, sporting a shamrock! His ostensible reason for being in Rome was to study Roman art and architecture. It did not really improve his style, for a year later Victoria was still complaining that "he is not at all in good looks; his nose and mouth are too enormous and he pastes his hair down to his head, and wears his clothes frightfully". At least he wore a shamrock that St. Patrick's Day and, apart from looks, had apparently profited from his stay abroad which ended in the early Summer following it. As the Queen wrote: "Bertie is improved" (June, 1859). Shortly, though, in the 1860's, accompanied by the 'Marlborough House Set' — some of its members had in all likelihood been with him in Rome — he was doing the night rounds in the less reputable parts of London.

Russell was now being suggested as coadjutor to Dr. Denvir of Down and Connor. As 1859 drew to a close, not everybody liked the idea, even when they were on Russell's side. In early December, Moriarty of Kerry wrote to him:

> "I had news today from Belfast which in other circumstances would have given me great joy but which now fills me with alarm. I hope the Almighty will never let you down so low as to make a Bishop of you. On one condition I would approve of it — viz: that you would continue President of Maynooth during the time of your co-adjutorship which for the sake of Maynooth and of my very dear friend Dr. Denvir I hope may be very long".

Russell was engaged in the routine matters that fall to every President of the College — dealing with Bishops about their students, working on a memorial to the Government (Lord Carlisle) for a grant for repairs, and so on and so forth. During one Summer, Cullen (always with his eye on the Continent) had informed him that a namesake of his (son of Thomas Russell of Mountjoy Square) now in France had distinguished himself in the Papal service at Perugia and had been decorated by the Pope with the Cross of St. Gregory. Soon afterwards he had reported that the Pope was not very well and prayers were asked for his recovery. In Cullen's words: "Things are going from bad to worse in the Romagna".

Russell was still orientated towards the literary field, producing his 'Graffiti of Pompeii' for *The Edinburgh Review*. Indeed that year saw the publication also by Thomas Webb of Dublin of 'The Wars of Wellington', a narrative poem in fifteen cantos by 'Dr. Syntax', which was said to be a pseudonym for Dr. Russell. What warblers they were in those days ! Murray had every reason to be happy, as the Trustees had agreed to pay £100 for the purchase of his *Annual Miscellany*.

Clonliffe College had been started by Cullen and by now had some thirty-five students. The reality of its challenge to Maynooth does not seem to have registered with Russell. In any case there was nothing he could do about it, although the number of students at Maynooth had fallen to 367. Russell was occupied with his task of getting portraits made of former staff members. It was not easy as most of them were dead. We find Dr. McNally of Clogher telling him that a portrait of Dr. Slevin might perhaps be produced from a photograph of one of his nephews who, he has heard, bears a strong resemblance to his uncle. Cullen was suggesting that the Trustee body was too unwieldly and that the College could more efficiently be governed by "an archbishop and his suffragans". That Autumn the famous Father Tom Burke O.P. gave the retreat at Maynooth. Whatever he may have meditated about then, Russell did not change his mind about declining a mitre, for when the Coadjutor-ship of Down and Connor came his way, he again refused the appointment.

In 1859, a London publisher brought out *A Little Tour in Ireland,* by an 'Oxonian'. Its reference to Maynooth is priceless: "We passed the station at Maynooth, but did not see the 'Royal College of St. Patrick' and are therefore unable to vituperate that establishment, as otherwise it would be our duty to do". Nevertheless, under Russell's enlightened guidance, the College was set fair for distinction.

THE GHOST ROOM

In January, 1860, Wiseman was in Rome, during the course of his litig-ation with Dr. Errington. He wrote to Russell giving an account of himself. At this stage Russell was beginning to realise that his Presidency was not going to be a sinecure. At the start, it might reasonably have been expected that he would preside over a settled institution. The grant had been secured, the buildings largely finished, and the College put through the Roman hoop. Surely it was now time that it had a head who could preside peacefully over what had been built up before him. In Dr. Russell it had a candidate for that role, cast as he was in the mould of a Renaiss-ance humanist. But he was not to be allowed to reign like one. That the enemies of Maynooth were still ready and willing to make difficulties surfaced early on in his career at the top. The Parliamentary session had scarcely opened in February, when Mr. Spooner denounced the teaching at Maynooth and declared the State support given to the College to be a "national sin". A couple of years later, the Chairman of the Liberation of Religion Society was to say to W. J. O'Neill Daunt that Spooner's attacks had nothing to do with enmity towards Maynooth as such, but were aimed at the whole system of Church establishment in the Kingdom. That indeed is very likely true. Whatever of it, in the same February, Dr. Murray began his essay on 'M. Thouvenel's Circular: The Temporal and the Spiritual Orders'.

A collection for the Pope was taken up in Ireland, £15,000 being raised in the Dublin Archdiocese, around £315 from Maynooth. In March, Cullen requested an acknowledgement of the latter by Rome, saying: "Their contribution is generous enough". Antonelli had already sent on a general acknowledgement, but on 10 March the Vatican sent a letter to Kirby expressing thanks for the homage of the students of the College in donating the sum of £314.1.0. At the Vatican thoughts must have been much occupied with events in Italy from where, Cullen told Russell on 7 March, the news was very bad, although Rome itself appeared to be in no danger.

In Maynooth, the President had to address himself to securing funds, unsavoury though he might find this to be. No monies had been voted for maintenance since 1852, and, even though the splendid new Pugin complex was now in full use, a lot of repairs needed to be effected in the house as a whole. On 14 June, previous notice of a forthcoming memorial about this was presented by Russell to the Chief Secretary for Ireland in London, Edward Cardwell, M.P., and, on 22 June, the memorial of the Trustees to the Lord Lieutenant followed. They were prepared to accept "any reasonable expedient, by which the College may be saved from falling into decay". At the Visitation of 20 June, there had been a number of complaints, especially about the sanitary condition of the College. The President had to admit that during the past year the sanitary condition "had not been so satisfactory as in former years; that three deaths had occurred during the year, one in the College, the result of insanity ..... He regretted too to add that the general condition of the senior infirmary was so bad as to render it entirely unfit for the reception of the sick, and that independently of its ruinous condition, the building was of itself utterly inadequate in size and accommodation for the wants of so large a community".

Actually, on the day of that Visitation, no fewer than thirty students were at home as a result of ill health; from January to April cold and influenza had prevailed to a great extent. The new buildings were damp and, despite painting having been done, the plaster on the walls required renewal and new window frames were called for. The library needed fitting with shelves and there was also need for an assembly hall and a college chapel, as well as for the gas lighting of the entire College. It was a tall order, however justified it might be. Perhaps Russell thought that his 'Anglified disposition' would procure what was needed without too much difficulty. In the meantime, the students were 'contained' by a resolution that, "in addition to having a vocal or instrumental concert on Christmas and St. Patrick's Day, some instructive and entertaining exhibition be provided for them on these occasions." The Visitation also ordered that Scavini should be substituted for Bailly as a College text. How relentlessly the mills had ground .....

174

If Russell had expected a good response to "his" representations to Government, he was not disappointed, for as quickly as 10 July a Bill was introduced by Parliament to enable the Trustees to make provision "for certain necessary Buildings and Repairs", also "to complete the unfinished Royal College of St. Patrick at Maynooth". This was obviously a reference to those aspects of the Pugin plan that needed to be finished. The Bill was enacted on 20 August.

On the 22nd, Cullen wrote to Russell that "the news from Rome is bad. It is feared that a revolution will soon explode in all the towns of the Pope's Italy". He repeated this on 25 November: "The news from Rome is very bad. I fear the Pope must leave. He has no means of paying the national debt and if he remains he will be persecuted for payment. I do not know how he can get on in Rome ".

Russell had his own fears at home. They were presaged by the reference in his report at the Visitation that there had been a death in the College during the previous year as a result of insanity. That October (on the 23rd), the Trustees passed a resolution: "That the President be authorized to convert the room No. 2 on the top corridor in the Rhetoric House into an oratory of St. Joseph and to fit up an Oratory of St. Aloysius in the prayer hall of the Junior Students". Why these two should have been conjoined is now anybody's guess. The conversion of the bedroom, in a rather inaccessible part of the students' living quarters, into an oratory — in which capacity it never seems to have been used — was unusual to say the least of it. A writer on Maynooth in the *Irish Ecclesiastical Record* for 1940 says that for some the unexplained resolution was bound to conjure up the vision of ghosts. And so indeed it did, the story of 'the Ghost Room' going down in the folklore of the College.

To date, the best-known account of the ghost room is that contained in Denis Meehan's *Window on Maynooth* (1949):

> "The story, as it is commonly now retailed, for the edification of susceptible Freshmen, begins with a suicide. The student resident in this room killed himself one night. According to some he used a razor; but tellers are not too careful about such details. The next inhabitant, it is alleged, felt irresistibly impelled to follow suit, and again, according to some, he did. A third, or it may have been the second, to avoid a similar impulse, and when actually about to use his razor, jumped through the window in Rhetoric yard. He broke some bones, but saved his life. Subsequently, no student would be induced to use the room; but a priest volunteered to sleep or keep vigil there for one night. In the morning his hair was white, though no one dares to relate what his harrowing experiences may have been. Afterwards the front wall of the room was removed and a small altar of St. Joseph was erected".

175

There was supposed to be a footprint burned into the floor of the room and blood marks on the walls ! Of course, the story lost nothing in the telling. Rolt, in his account of Maynooth which appeared also in 1949, develops the theme somewhat. As he has it, the third victim, on recovering from his injuries, told of how "he was standing before his mirror shaving when he saw, reflected in the glass, a figure standing behind him and gazing over his shoulder. As he looked, this figure raised its arm and drew the extended index finger across its throat, whereupon, without being aware of what he was doing, he was impelled to make the same gesture with the hand in which he held the razor. After this, it is said, the party walls of this grim chamber were pulled down so that it is now an open lobby. Was the room haunted? Or did the first student take his life for some extraneous suggestion and leave behind him some powerful force of auto-suggestion ? We shall never know". It is rather surprising that Rolt's account has been missed by those interested in the happening. One of the fullest and best known versions is that contained in Joseph O'Connor's *Hostage to Fortune*, which was published in 1951. He was a student at Maynooth at the turn of the century and writes vividly about the 'ghost room'.

"The room is on the top floor of the larger of the two buildings which constitutes the Junior House. A long corridor runs through the centre of the floor from end to end, having on each side a vista of doors, the doors of the students' rooms. They present an unbroken line on the east side of the corridor, but on the west, three doors from the end, there is an open gap where a door and the room it served should have been. The door is gone and the open space has been converted into an oratory with a neat carved wood altar standing where the window used to be. On the wall above the altar ran a legend in Latin which told its own tale. "A morte subito et improviso salve nos, Deus", O Lord, preserve us from a sudden and unprepared death .... I have better a reason for remembering the haunted room than most Maynooth students. When Mike O' Brien (later Bishop of Kerry) and I and the seventy or so other freshmen had signed our names at the gate lodge on that dusky September evening 1895, under the supercilious eye of Cerberus the college butler, he led us through the shrubbery path to the Junior House and into the Hall of Rhetoric. There he counted off twenty of us and said, 'Ye are for the top corridor. Take up yer trunks with ye and wait for me....'. Up the stone stairs, three flights of them ... We were a mixed lot from Ulster, Munster, Leinster and Connaught. Simon Prendiville, Frank Crowley and I were the only Kerrymen in the bunch and we stuck together ..... Cerberus gave Frank and me the room on either side of the little oratory at the end of the corridor, and

176

to Simon the room opposite. To us it was just an oratory, a natural thing to find in an ecclesiastical college ... On the third day.... the old students returned in their hundreds and swamped us. After supper they took us under their wings, patronized us and put us wise to college slang, tabus and musts until the last bell rang. On our way to .... Rhetoric House, Tim Houlihan asked me on which corridor I was. 'The top — near that little oratory', I told him. 'Holy Moses', he exclaimed in horror, 'that's the ghost room' ".

The present writer remembers that he too lived his first year at Maynooth in close proximity to it. It used to be visited then regularly by those visitors to the College who were well in enough to be treated to a glimpse of it. Hans Holzer, in his *The Lively Ghosts of Ireland*, which came out in 1967, tells about his visit, with a companion who was psychotic, and who felt a sense of "animal fear" in the room, with a desire to run and a dreadful headache. She had, she said, "a feeling that an animal had followed us down to what is now an oratory" and "for a moment I was integrated into whatever had happened there and I could have gone out of the window". She felt that something unresolved was still present. Holzer thought that maybe a dog had died in the vicinity during the Middle Ages and "became incorporated into the later edifice" — this because he had recalled hearing that the third student in the story had seen 'a black shape' in the room. "Shades of the Hounds of the Baskervilles" was his comment. Holzer had been told about the Maynooth room by Patrick Byrne, who had brought out his *Irish Ghost Stories* not too long before that. He had nothing to add to the story, nor did John J. Dunne, who published his *Haunted Ireland* in Belfast in 1977, even though he does carry the story of 'The Room at Maynooth'.

It was some time in the 1960's that the most authentic account of what happened was discovered. Strangely enough, it was found in Belfast. It consists of notes made by Dr. McCarthy:

"April 20, 1860. This anniversary was saddened by a strange event which I hope God will seldom permit — the death of Thomas Maginn of Kilmore (the name is spelt in Greek lettering) by his own hand. This poor fellow entered the College last Sept. for Logic and ever since was remarkable for deficiency in class. This seems to have weighed heavily on his mind and a month ago he resigned his place to the President. On reflection however he withdrew the resignation and was called by his professor but with no better success than before. His fellow students noticed that altho' exposed to be called again at any moment he did not apply himself to study in the last week, nor did he give any intimation to the professor. It seems he slept occasionally during the year, perhaps on account of sickness. The inability to study does not seem to have been always as great. At any rate before entering College he was regarded as rather a good student and passed I believe the Entrance Examination without being noticed. For the last few days a new idea seems to have seized him, as he spent nearly an entire hour the evening before the said accident with one of the monitors seeking advice and complaining very much that the devil was tormenting him. I may observe that in his room which was on the second floor of the rhetoric house in front at the *now* refectory end, were found open on his desk a Bible, Butler's lives of the saints and some MSS. on class business. On this morning (April 20th, Friday) he put an end to his own life but the means adopted were very singular. He imitated as far as could be the sad death that occurred in the Junior house before exactly 19 years on the first *Friday* in Lent. This poor fellow had leave to sleep for the last few days and slept this morning also. Immediately after the other students went to *Mass* he left his own room went upstairs into the place where the unfortunate example (No. 2. Upper Corridors back over the *now* refectory) was given. Cut his throat in 4 places and then flung himself out through the window. The evidence that he went into this room is first the fact of his cap being found on the bed there, secondly some desks being removed and thirdly complaining after of a pain in the ankles. The first point would be conclusive if well authenticated which I believe it is. Immediately or a few minutes after the fall a servant passing by saw him weltering in his blood with the throat gashed through, so as to cut the epiglottis, still he swallowed a little water then and afterwards, but little more. The servant went at once for the priest and doctors and he was attended by both before he left the spot. As he was speechless however and as danger did not appear imminent, the last rites were not administered then. Surgeon Ellis came down by 12 o'clock and pronounced the case hopeless – his impression was that he must die at least of starvation. By this time the young man's own confessor Father Mulloy administered Extreme Unction and immediately after he spoke, made then we have every reason to hope a good confession and continued in a more or less reasonable state up to 4 o'clock. The night was dreadful, because Surgeon Ellis strictly prohibited food or drink of any kind. Nothing could be done except sponge the lips from time to time".

"21st. This day again this poor fellow had intervals of reason from about 8 in the morning up to 2 o'clock, which he employed almost constantly in prayer. He even heard Mass in the morning and asked for a prayer book to read out of it. But after 2 p.m. the death struggle began. He spoke still incoherently up to ½ after 4, after which time he was not heard to utter a distinct word. At 3 minutes before 8 he expired — the President being with him at the time and reciting for him the prayers of the departing soul".

"22nd. This morning at 5 o'clock, the coroner was sent for to Naas. He did not arrive until 4½ p.m. when the jury, Coats, Green, Deane, Furlong, etc., in all 15, were collected to see the body. They came after to the Logic Hall where the Enquiry was held. The chief witnesses were the servants who first found him lying on the ground, another servant who saw him walk downstairs, the Vice-President, Dr. E. Kelly, Mr. Finnegan Monitor from Kilmore, Mr. O'Reilly, dt. from Dublin, Mr. Smith — a class-fellow from Kilmore. His evidence and that of Mr. Finnegan were most important. Mr. Smith swore that they had both slept in the condemned room, No. 2, without knowing it to be such at the beginning, that he had learned this fact after and that Maginn had spoken to him repeatedly of the bad luck which threw them into that room above all others. Mr. Finnegan was told by him after the event how the whole occurred — He also came to seek consolation under many troubles he said. After the accident he spoke of the devil suggesting to him that he should destroy himself, that however he (the devil) put it off because the various plans appeared impracticable, that the devil would not allow him to do it he said, because it was impossible as yet. After a few words however he appeared as reconciled and so well disposed on the first occasion, added Mr. Finnegan, that I did not think it necessary to say more about it imagining it was no more than ordinary depression. Of course the reason was entirely gone when he admitted these suggestions on the part of the devil. It is un-necessary to add the verdict — died by his own hand, being of unsound mind at the time".

"23. We had high Mass today (absente corpore) in both houses at 9 o'c. At about 11 ½ we proceeded to the infirmary to meet the corpse and amidst considerable rain we proceeded to the grave yard — Mr. Mulloy officiating. Benedictus being sung and blessing given, we arrived in rooms at 12½ just before the heavy rain began to fall. It continued very wet up to 2½ p.m."

There is one other account which should not be passed over. It is that of C. W. Russell, Maynooth's President. On 20 April, 1860, he wrote to

H. R. Bagshawe, then Editor of *The Dublin Review:* "There is a fate over me this time. This morning a most shocking and painful event — an attempted suicide — has occurred here. I am in momently attendance on the poor fellow and cannot possibly do anything at my paper".

He wrote to the Archbishop of Dublin two days later:

"Your Grace will be dreadfully shocked by the sad occurrence... it is a most extraordinary case. Just nineteen years ago a poor young man from Limerick committed suicide here by cutting his throat and throwing himself from the second storey. By one of these fatalities which occasionally arise it chanced that the poor fellow (named McGinn from Kilmore) who has just put an end to his life, slept in the room in which the act was done, on the first night of his coming to college. This circumstance it appears took a deep hold of his imagination and he frequently recurred to it as unlucky for himself. It happened too that the poor fellow proved very deficient in his studies and was much dejected in consequence. Latterly, however, he had been more cheerful. But on Friday morning, during Mass, the poor youth, haunted by the old impression, actually went to the illstarred room of the former suicide and here exactly repeated the act of poor O'Grady. He was found in a few minutes below, strange to say with limbs unbroken, but the injury to the throat was so fearful that he died last night. The poor fellow perfectly recovered his speech and his consciousness and made a most holy preparation for death. It is a terrible shock to the community but God's will be done.

That is the true story; they say that truth will out. A College tradition referred to by Meehan that the first tragedy occurred between the years 1842 and 1848 is incorrect; from Dr. McCarthy's notes we know that it happened in 1841. From these it is also pretty clear that two and not three students were all that were ever involved. The verdict of the jury in 1860 appears quite justified.

THE STIFF UPPER LIP

All of Russell's *sang froid* was required for the next few years of his presidency. 1861 began with news that one of the professors of theology, Dr. Molloy, had been given leave from the College for health reasons. That kind of thing, though understandable, always creates problems for a President. In April, he was probably gratified at receiving a letter from Montalembert, thanking him for having sent on a copy of *The Dublin Review*, which contained a review of his *The Monks of the West*. He has read this "with great interest and satisfaction", and is grateful to the author; he has not been treated so kindly by the French press, whether "infidel" or "clerical". In a few days he hopes to send Russell his answers to Cavour's speeches on the freedom of the Church. In May, there were other letters from France, from the Irish College, Paris, by Cullen in connection with his students: "Everything is quiet here, but no one knows what is coming on"; "Nothing new in Paris, but probably the Troops will be kept in Rome".

In Ireland there was some excitement by reason of another visit by Her Majesty, the Queen. At the time, the Prince of Wales was on a tour of duty with the army at the Curragh Camp. Indeed, there is reason to believe that the Queen's visit to Ireland just then was for the purpose of reviewing the troops — the Grenadier Guards — with whom he was stationed. As he marched past with his company, her thoughts were that he "did not look at all so very small". On 23 May, he visited his mother at the Vice-Regal Lodge: "Bertie came for luncheon yesterday". Whether she realised it fully or not, he had been introduced at the Curragh to what his father feared — "the objectionable life of cavalry officers". Later in the year, she was to be upset by one of his amorous escapades while there.

In June, preparations were under way at Maynooth for the building of a new Infirmary, for lighting the College with gas and for heating the apartments of the students. They were none too soon in coming, for during the previous season the health of the entire community had been below average. Since the previous June, there had been forty-five cases of serious illness, with five deaths, three in the College and two at home. On one day during the previous December, seventy-eight students had been sick. Nobody could blame Dr. Whitehead for refusing to take up residence in the Vice-President's new quarters in the Pugin quadrangle. Things must have been difficult enough for the President, even though the improvements which he had sought were now underway. This was the year that Peadar O'Laoghaire came up to Maynooth, and in *Mo Scéal Féin* he confirms the prevalence of sickness there:

> "It was the rule of the College at the time that a person had to spend eight, seven or six years there .... If the examination showed that it was not necessary for a youth to spend eight years in there, a year would be remitted; and if the examination showed that it was not necessary for him to spend seven years inside, two years work would be remitted. I was let off two years. That was of great benefit to me, as the air of the place is very severe on the health of the boys who go there from the country. Whatever in the world it was, they found it severe ... Fine, big, strong boys went in the same year as I did. No sooner had they spent a year inside than they were quite emaciated ...

I recall one who came the year I entered. He was over six feet in height .... He had astonishing strength ... A couple of years afterwards, I saw that man and he had very little strength. The air and the food of the place adversely affected him and he collapsed. He had to go home ... He wasn't long in the house with his people when he went to his eternal home ... I said that the air of the place affected him. It did, but that was no wonder. The place is too low and the canal, that goes west through the middle of the country, runs outside the wall of the College, and the mist from the canal dampens the air so that it is unhealthy to a person's chest ... But I also said that the food affected him ... The food inside was very good — but it wasn't on such we were reared and we were not used to it. It didn't suit us."

O'Leary himself, as might be expected from that, did not have the greatest health at Maynooth. Russell must have had to endure a lot of bickering about health and related matters. In August, Canon Quinn, P.P. of Athy, transferred an endowment, set up in Maynooth by his late uncle, to Clonliffe. The President also had the inevitable dose of complaints about students during vacation time. In July, Mr. John Ferguson, of Hollymount, Drumshambo, Co. Leitrim, wrote about one of them who had trespassed on his land while out shooting: "Entertaining as I do such veneration for your College, the great nursery of the Irish Priesthood, I was more than astonished at the ribaldry he displayed on that occasion. After abusing me in high Billingsgate style and endeavouring to provoke a quarrel by using all the irritating and scurrilous language which his vocabulary or ingenuity could suggest, I even feared he would shoot me... I think the law will look after him ... Retaining proper sentiments for myself and my religion, I am Very Rev. Sir, Yours respectfully".

The President most likely received some comfort from the publication that year of *Logicae seu Philosophiae Rationalis Elementa* by William Jennings, Professor of Mental and Moral Philosophy. He was an able man but only lived for two more years. In 1861 also, Patrick Murray, now fully recovered from his illness, published a lecture which he had given to the Catholic Young Mens' Society — 'The Divine Origin of the Supremacy of the Roman See' — one which was full of auguries for his future work. He also published a commentary on a booklet by Passaglia on the 'Roman Question'. During August he addressed himself to another pressing matter, the prevalence of souperism in the country.

In June, a Mr. G. K. Browne had written to him from Warwick, inquiring whether the charges contained in the organ of The Irish Church Mission Society were true, namely, that "the steward of Maynooth College, accompanied by fourteen students, had formally apostatised". The story had been that, on a visit to Dublin, the steward was given one of the

182

Society's tracts and was thus led to inquire about Transubstantiation and eventually to lose his faith, whereupon he had been requested to resign his position and was now butler to a naval gentleman, but not before he had induced fourteen of the students to leave the College. Murray rebutted this vigorously in *The Mendacity of Souperism in Ireland:* "I am fully thirty years a member of Maynooth College — eight as a student, twenty two as a professor. I have made diligent inquiries among the other heads of the College, some of whom are forty years members of the establishment. Not one of us ever knew or heard of the existence of the alleged facts in the above statement".

But students had been leaving Thurles, if not for the same reason. In October, the Archbishop of Cashel, Dr. Leahy, was quite incensed with Maynooth when one of his candidates was rejected at entrance examination. He had lost a large number from Thurles, far more than he could afford to lose even though he had more than enough before that: "A great evil that was staring me in the face everyday was the immense number of Ecclesiastical Students in our College, not by any means the most desirable as subjects for the Church. During the years of comparative prosperity following upon the famine, the farmers of these counties (Tipperary and Limerick) ran their sons in upon us in great numbers, who had better many of them be in the track of the plough. The sanctuary was opened with a golden key ... of eighty that came in our College a short year ago I could in five years provide for not more than twenty. It was not easy to see what was to be done with so overwhelming a number, or what check could be put to the existing evil and how — when, lo, one fine morning they all or almost all quit the College in a body on the pretext of not being well fed. This was, no doubt, a grievous scandal and has left a stigma on our College and Diocese".

Russell was being got at from all sides. In September, Moriarty of Kerry was urging that the Christian classics should be read only during the Rhetoric year, indeed that his own students be dispensed from reading them at all. In his opinion, they might even be flung out of the window as they are of little interest to lay people and therefore not needed in the secondary schools. On an entirely different level, Keane of Cloyne was writing about the Maynooth students having had a Requiem Mass for Terence Bellew McManus. A former Young Ireland veteran, whose funeral was exploited by the Fenians, McManus had died in America in November. His body had been received in St. Patrick's Cathedral, New York, where he was eulogized by Archbishop John Hughes, who presided at Solemn Requiem Mass. On arrival in Queenstown, the remains had also been brought to the Cathedral there where another Mass was offered. In Cork, however, Bishop Delaney had refused to have any function or to allow the body into any of the city churches. Much the same thing was to happen when it reached Dublin, where Cardinal Cullen refused to cooperate. In these circumstances, the President of Maynooth had felt that he would have to do something to show his disapproval of the students' action. The Bishop of Cloyne did not disagree with what they had done in itself, but he had some fears that the enemies of Maynooth would make propaganda out of it:

"I regret to learn by your last note that what has occurred in Maynooth cannot be so easily passed over by you ... For political reasons the Church neither gives nor refuses her ministry to any sinner dying in her Communion. Hence, the course I would recommend in the case of any one who had received the last Sacraments, whether Christian, Pagan or Jew, is the course adopted in Queenstown. To some of the Parish Priests, who spoke to me on the subject, I said the same — that is, if they were asked to say Mass in their Chapels for the soul of Mr. McManus, to do so as they would *pro quocumque fidei defuncto;* but, on no account to sanction or permit any political demonstration within the Church or in the Chapel yard. When, however, young men in a Royal College like Maynooth volunteer a Service, the proceedings in that case have a significance which the enemies of the institution will not fail to turn to account. It is not unlikely that during the next Session of Parliament the public will hear of it again".

Dr. Cullen was, as always, in touch with Rome. In November: "I have had very late accounts from Rome. The Pope is quite well and the city perfectly quiet. One of the Brigade, Captain O'Keeffe, nephew of Dr. Delaney of Cork, is commanding a detachment of the late King's party in Naples".. And in December Wiseman was sending Russell a Latin inscription which he was not able to make out, as well as his own epitaph in the same language, which he had got examined by one of the best lapidarists in Rome, who would not change a word of it ! It had been carved in Rome on an immense marble slab.

Early 1862, saw Russell in touch with Lord Rosse, Chancellor of Dublin University, about works in Algebra, Trigonometry, Geometry and the like. He was also interested in Lord Rosse's 'giant telescope'. Truly, he cast his net widely. In March, Acton, who wished to convert *The Rambler* from a bi-monthly to a quarterly doubled in size, tried to head off opposition from *The Dublin Review* by reasuring Russell that his proposal would not injure it. The latter replied in a friendly way but asked him not to do anything just yet. Then he wrote immediately to Wiseman and Bagshawe urging them to merge *The Dublin Review* and *The Rambler*. Newman, consulted by Acton, thought that an amalgamation of the independent review with one sponsored by a Cardinal was an impossibility. He was right. Wiseman once again was reluctant to deal with *The Rambler*. As a result, the following October there came a change in the editorship of *The Dublin Review*, when W. G. Ward took over from Bagshawe.

Russell had more than enough to occupy him in College administration. At the end of December, 1861, a big meeting had been held in Dublin to prepare plans for a concerted renewal of attacks on Maynooth. A Rev. Mr. Wallis declared its endowment to be "subversive of civil and religious liberty" and a Mr. Nunn "blessed God" that it was given to him to protest against that great iniquity. The meeting had resolved to petition Parliament to withdraw the grant as "the prolific cause of degradation and misery of the country". The petition was framed accordingly:

"Humbly Sheweth — That your Petitioners respectfully remind your Honourable House that the British nation solemnly protests against the principles and practices of the Church of Rome.

That your Petitioners thoroughly acquiesce in that national decision, believing as they do that those principles are the prolific cause of the degradation and misery both spiritual and temporal of every country in which they are prevalent; that they are hostile to and utterly irreconcilable with civil and religious liberty; and that their propagation in these countries must in time produce the same lamentable results which they do elsewhere; and that, consequently to endow a College for the dissemination of such doctrines is suicidal, inconsistent and dangerous.

Hence your Petitioners most humbly pray that your honourable House may withdraw all State endowment from the Roman Catholic College of Maynooth.

And your Petitioners will ever pray".

In fact, the College cannot have been too well off at the time, for in June, 1862, the Trustees decided to reduce the salaries of the Superiors and Professors somewhat in the case of future appointments. Russell's scholarly activities must have been seriously interfered with by all this. So too by the endless student complications, as when in February that year one of their body wrote to the *Nation,* dissociating himself from a political declaration that had the backing of the College authorities. The President had remonstrated privately with the editor, A. M. Sullivan, for having ordered its insertion. Sullivan retorted in typical media fashion; a journalist had no other course. He had gone too far in the past, he thought, in vetoing such correspondence, so much so that the independence of his journal had been laid open to suspicion. The student's letter had been accompanied by an endorsment by an ecclesiastic outside the College. Anyhow, it appeared right to him for a student to dissent respectfully from a political declaration put forward in this name: "A newspaper is a vehicle of public information and any communication reaching it, referring to a matter of legitimate public interest, fairly stated

185

and accompanied by sufficient authentication, cannot be rejeceed because of its fairly expressed opinions". Interesting too is the decision of the Bishop of Derry, Dr. Kelly, communicated to Russell that January, that he had cautioned his people against attending the Derry Model School, under pain of exclusion from the sacraments. This school had been set up against his wishes but, thank God, the Christian Schools and those of the Sisters of Mercy are all well attended by Catholics.

Before the year was out, it is said that Dr. Murray of Maynooth was being sought as Coadjutor by McNally of Clogher. How the scene had changed since his own elevation. The priests wanted Murray at any rate, or at least a very considerable number of them. He was backed too by *Frazer's Magazine* of London ! But appointed he was not to be. Nobody wrote a lament, unlike when Father Sheridan, Parish Priest of Kingstown, died around that same time. The elegy ran as follows:

"He entered Maynooth College in eighteen hundred and nine,
And curate of Maynooth was made before all in his prime.
This zealous, young, and holy priest was ordained by Dr. Troy.
Who by his ministrations he pleased his God on high".

THEOLOGICAL INVESTIGATIONS

These years saw considerable literary output from Maynooth. New arrangements for the editorship of *The Dublin Review* had been made in October, 1862, and Manning wrote to Russell expressing the hope that he would be satisfied with Ward. He selected three 'assessors' for theological and general Church articles — Manning himself, Russell, and a Jesuit Father. Russell did not give up his work either for the secular *Edinburgh Review*, which that month published a piece by him on 'The Herculaneum Papyri'. One can only guess his thoughts when Dr. Dixon wrote to him from Armagh seeking whether the College tailor could make a mitre for him after a Roman model, indeed along the lines of "Dr. Cullen's grand Roman mitre". He was likely to have been more at home when the College held a festivity on the occasion of the marriage of the Prince of Wales. Of this McNally of Clogher wrote to him: "I see with much pleasure that your celebration of the marriage of the Prince of Wales at Maynooth was admirable. Our demonstration here was in every respect much grander than in such a place could be expected. For the poor in the workhouse, in the jail, in the reformatory and in their own houses, ample provision was made to secure their comfort. Our seminary which was splendidly illuminated was, on account of it, one of the most beautifully attractive objects. The day was kept in strict holiday. The town was, from an early hour, filled with many thousands of our people, whose conduct was above all praise. Every sort of amusement was prepared for them — music, races and an admirable display of fireworks and these were kept until a late hour without, thanks be to God, any accident of any kind or the slightest appearance of disorder. I write as much because I know you will be glad to hear of our people, especially, looking to what has occurred in Belfast and elsewhere ...."

This was in March, 1863. Just then Russell, was excited by an offer of two thousand volumes to the Maynooth library by the Abbé Migne in return for some Mass stipends. The latter was forever involved — perforce — in financial deals to keep his presses going. This one, attractive though it was to Russell in one way, was not to everybody's liking. But he was assiduous in working for the expansion of the library. In September, we find him writing to Marshal Vaillant, Ministre de la Maison de l'Empereur, asking for a copy of the book *Les Catacombes de Rome* for the College, and to this end reminding him of the hospitality extended by France to Irish clerical students during difficult times in the past.

He did not forget ordinary administration, however much or little he may have liked it. In 1863, he succeeded in getting more money from the Treasury for repairs to the College and also got the new Infirmary fitted for occupation. All the time he was harried by student lapses, as when Bishop Moriarty of Kerry sent on a complaint which he had received about one of them who was teaching catechism in Glenflesk during the holidays and who had "made up to a girl". Indeed he had sent her an "extraordinary letter", enclosing his photograph, "and mind you, in worldly costume, with a profusion of gold chains etc. about him". Then there was Bishop Furlong of Ferns, who complained a short while later about two students of his who "engaged in a wild adventure last Summer — a visit to the Exhibition and then to Lille and travelling through Belgium and France on foot!" One of them on a previous occasion had behaved in such a way at a party that two of those present on the way home said he would never be a priest. Also a young lady had confessed that she was attracted to him and that, having charged him once with being the author of some amorous poetry in the *Nation* he did not disclaim this, though the Bishop had no proof that the attachment was mutual.

In 1863, on Tuesday, 10 March, Dr. Murray began a diary. It was to go on until September, 1882. *Murray's Diary* constitutes an important and interesting source for life in the Maynooth of his time. He was also busily at work on his treatise *de Ecclesia*, which he had started in March, 1859. In early January, 1863, having just finished No. 158 of D. 14 of the treatise, he had been seized with the most dangerous attack of sickness he ever had — brain fever. He was delirious for a week, full of imaginings, and received absolution from Mr. Tully and extreme unction from Dr. McCarthy. He had recovered towards the end of February, and gone to Clones, his native place, to recuperate. It was there that he started his diary.

His recovery marked the beginning of a long spate of articles, particularly for *The Dublin Review*. These extended from Spiritism (1867) to Ritual

187

(1869), Atheism (1872), the Vatican Council (1873), and a sheaf of shorter articles. Despite all this activity, he does not appear to have been happy. In May, 1863, after returning to the College, he declared: "I am heartily tired and sick of Maynooth", and had left again for a holiday in Bundoran. From there he went to Sligo where he had heard that the soupers were active. He had a fierce antagonism to souperism. He got a full account of "the attempts of the Presbyterian parsons to keep their prey".

He spent nine weeks in Bundoran, during which time he met the Parish Priest of Cushendall in Co. Antrim, and heard from him about the progress of souperism there — a new form of it having emerged, called "The Mothers' School": "The mothers bring linen etc. and sell it to destitute females at first cost, and assemble them together to work it up. At these meetings there are prayers and the bible reading". On his return to Maynooth, he went to Dublin, and by previous arrangement met a girl, aged twelve, who had been four years in the Bird's Nest. "I interrogated the girl. The children get beef for dinner on every Friday: did not get meat commonly on other days. Were told that the B. Virgin is not Mother of God, etc. etc. A sham controversy carried on every Monday before the children between a Protestant and a pretended Catholic". In October, he noted that *The Times*, in an obituary on Dr. Whately, who had died a few days previously, had said with what amounted to pride that his family had helped Catholic waifs and strays but with due regard to their Protestant convictions. It was no wonder that in 1856 Archbishop Cullen had issued a pastoral on proselytising societies, listing no fewer than twenty-one in Dublin.

By November, Murray was strong enough again to resume work on his *Tractatus de Ecclesia*. He had not written a word on it since the previous January. Now he was hoping to have it completed before the Summer of 1865. Within a couple of months, he suffered a bereavement, or rather the College did. He had just returned from Clones on 1 January, and had met Dr. Callan in the dining room. The next evening Callan was struck down by apoplexy, while hearing confession. He had lingered on until the evening of Thursday the 14th, when he died of a stroke, having been in almost unbroken half-consciousness during that time. He was buried on 17 January. He was then aged sixty-five. He was much loved by many people. Murray says that he himself did not know how much he loved him until he was gone. Dr. Cullen was unable to come to the funeral; he had a severe cold; he had also just heard of the death of his Vicar General, Dr. Yore. Many paid tribute to Callan, "a small, dark, delicate man, with a sweet and amiable countenance, his outward appearance revealed the true marks of his inward character — saintliness, simplicity, humility and self-effacement". Another recalled "the old lecture hall with its blackboard and the little man, chalk in hand, vigorously at work in front of it ... the central figure ... the aged Professor ... whose childlike simplicity and saintly example could not fail to make a lasting impression on all".

Meanwhile, Russell continued his literary work, being thanked in May, 1864, by the editor of *The Edinburgh Review* for another article of "extraordinary learning and interest" — 'De Rossi's Jewish and Christian Inscriptions'; his taste moved in strange directions, but that kind of thing was an affectation of the Victorian period. Cardinal Cullen may well have wanted to steer interest and ability in the direction of more substantially Catholic and Irish themes when, in October, 1864, he founded the *Irish Ecclesiastical Record*. 1864 also saw the issuing of Pope Pius IX's decree encouraging Neo-Scholasticism. Nothing tempted Russell from the esoteric. That August he is writing to the Ambassador of Russia in London — Baron Brunnow — thanking him for a copy of the *Codex Sinaiiticus Petropolitanus*, which His Imperial Majesty Alexander II had kindly presented, at Russell's request, to the College library.

Other members of the staff were active also, busily building the reputation of Maynooth for theological and general learning. In 1864, Dr. McCarthy edited Dr. Kelly's *Dissertations Chiefly on Irish Church History* and Dr. Murray finished the second part of his treatise. His diary for the day (13 December) was nevertheless lugubrious: "How little to note in the life of a laborious and retired student, like myself. Day follows day, as wave follows wave, on, on, no shore beyond; and to which I am so rapidly and silently hastening".

The students continued their usual capers, the Seniors complaining to the Visitors of that year that they were not receiving all the allowances to which they had a strict right from the Act of 1845. They were given a full statement of accounts by the Bursar, showing that for the last fifteen years the total unexpended surplus of the funds to which the senior students were entitled, only amounted to £16.13.6. To counter this disappointment, the entire College had now been lighted with gas and arrangements made for heating all the apartments "by means of a hot water apparatus". So says the *Parliamentary Publications*, Vol. *XLIII*, 1865. It was a development that should help the cause of scholarship. And a group of people from Donegal who came down to see Maynooth that January were so impressed that their Bishop, McGettigan, wrote to Russell: "Their visit to Maynooth is an Epock in their lives and for the long winter nights they have pabulum for stories that will astonish the natives."

In August, Murray was dissatisfied with an article in the *Irish Ecclesiastical Record* which, in his estimation, overstated the case about *all* the legislation of the country for centuries having been directed to the destruction of Catholicity. It is this kind of thing, he says, which "contributed largely to foster and extend the madly rebellious spirit, which has so deeply leavened large masses of the Irish Catholics". He finds the occasional denunciation of Fenianism by Catholic sources as irony, "very stupid irony too". On the last day of December, he is writing in his diary that, even though he had hopes to go to press with the entire manuscript of his 'treatise' at the beginning of the New Year, he now realises that he cannot. "The delay in sifting the difficulties against the Supremacy from certain Patristic passages and historical facts is much greater than I anticipated. But I have been determined to shirk nothing – to meet every difficulty worth meeting, full in the face – to sift everything to the bottom, till I come at the pure and solid truth". Before long however, he was bringing the first roll of MS., commencing the second Fasciculus of the third and concluding volume, to Gill, the publisher. On 16 June, 1866, "near nine o'clock" in the evening of a Saturday, he finished the third part "de S. Pontifice". One can almost see him watching the clock – and who could blame him? He had now taken in to consideration all the objections to the primacy of the Pope that had been posed to him by Ward, as the latter had strongly maintained that these were the great weapons of the 'Oxford party'. He is happy that he has disposed of them and is now engaged in the 4th part of his work, at which he proposes to remain until 16 July.

On Wednesday, 1 August, the great work was finished: "Last night, at a quarter before nine o'clock, I closed the labour of so many years, and finished the 22nd and last Disp. of my Church Tract". Once, jocosely, he had told James Healy, pastor of Little Bray, that, when preaching in Clones, coming near the end he had said:" 'One more word and I have done !' 'Oh, my darlint', exclaimed an old woman, throwing up her hands, 'that you may never be done' ". Now he was 'done' indeed. He wrote immediately to inform Ward and "told him of the tumult of emotions that rushed upon me, as my hand trembled on the concluding lines. I have a bounding sense of freedom, such as I do not recollect to have ever felt before". He celebrated the occasion with a poem, published in his *Prose and Verse* in 1867:

> "At length is realized thy dream –
> That cherished dream of other years:
> And toils, though but just ended, seem
> Long past, like boyhood's joys and tears.
>
> Lay gently down thy weary pen,
> And the last page press softly on,
> With lowly bended forehead then
> Thank God for all that He hath done"

It may be that he wrote this while travelling, as was the case with many of his "versicles", pencilled in such unlikely places as the top of a coach. It was a cause for rejoicing when, towards the middle of August, Murray received the congratulations of Perrone on the completion of his work. It is possible that Perrone was the Roman theologian to whom he had sent it, as it was written, for checking. If so, it is indeed absorbing, for it was Perrone who, in 1855, had found fault with the views of Crolly, Murray's friend. Though slightly indisposed in September and worried by a somewhat violent outbreak of cholera in Dublin, he was able to see his work through the printers, and on 17 November the sixth and concluding Fasciculus of the *de Ecclesia* was published. He notes in his diary that he himself was born on 18 November, 1811 — "So, I, this day, complete my 55th year". He was not old but spoke and acted as if he were. The *De Ecclesia Christi* was dedicated to Pope Pius IX, as the Pope destined to define the dogma of Papal Infallibility. *The Quarterly Review* was enraged at this. Murray's work was to stand; it was much used, we gather, later at the Vatican Council. Murray, though, must have had his head a bit turned by it. He was wont to say: 'Quid docet Murray', 'Sic docet Murray' and 'I am a tub of theology' !

Newman was not at all pleased with Murray's work. In April, 1867, he wrote to James Hope-Scott:

> "There is a great attempt by W. G. Ward, Dr. Murray of May-nooth, and Father Schrader, the Jesuit of Rome and Vienna, to bring in a new theory of Papal Infallibility which would make it a mortal sin, to be visited by damnation, not to hold the Temporal Power necessary to the Papacy. No one answers them and multitudes are being carried away — the Pope, I should fear, gives ear to them, and the consequence is there is a very extreme prejudice in the highest quarters at Rome against such as me. I cannot take Oxford unless I am allowed full liberty to be there or here".

He does seem to have fancied himself as *the* leader of an Oxford movement to Roman Catholicism. It is hard to see how Murray's teaching could have been offensive. In June, 1867, Murray wrote in his diary: "The two great enemies of social and ecclesiastical order, of the temporal and spiritual well-being of man, are tyrants, on the one hand, and rebels and revolutionaries on the other. They act as cause and effect. Tyranny begets rebellion, and rebellion begets tyranny. The Church has always condemned both".

But there were lighter moments in Murray's life, even at this stage of his professional career. That Summer, he spent a holiday up North, with his sister and a friend. They did some mountain climbing in the rain and sought refuge in the house of a local farmer. Murray sounded the occupants as to whether they had any poteen, and, right enough, soon after the woman of the house "brought us a flask of the 'real native', which had been buried in a bog at some distance. It was all they had just then; and most delighted did they seem to be in having it for us ... I never tasted better stuff ... What a fine Catholic people these are in those secluded lake and mountain homes, with their simple hearts and simple lives, so contented and joyous withal. 'Of such is the Kingdom of Heaven'. The baleful breath of Mazzini, Cavour, Palmerston and the rest has never tainted their atmosphere". It is good to know that Murray was human enough to have such comprehensive spiritual interests .....

In January, 1868, he sent a copy of his treatise to the Pope, also one to Cardinal Bilio, whom he had heard to be one of the ablest theologians in Rome. He continued to be rather melancholy:

> "Another year has gone forever ... In the beginning of next September I shall be 30 years professor in this College. All these years and those that preceded them seem now to me as if they had never been, or like a dream I had long ago, and remember now but dimly. The tumult of these years is all hushed ... There are, however, two things, in my retrospect of those strifes, which I cannot regret. The first is the active part I often took in every vacancy I can now remember ... The second is the part that I took at the time of the Maynooth Commission of Inquiry ... and was the cause of my not having been made a Bishop. I mean not the part I took, in itself — for I by no means approve now of everything I said or wrote or did on that occasion — but this *result;* which I take to have been a special grace from God; and for which I often thank him, when it occurs to my mind".

Murray's diary, 31 December, 1868:

> "Clones. The last day of the year. Rain almost incessant since I came here. For three days could not put my nose outside the door — sighing all the time for my grand corridor in Maynooth. Piercing cold, too, all the time".

LET DONS COMMUNE

During these years, Russell and Newman exchanged many letters. In

192

April, 1864, Russell was looking forward to the personal portion of the *Apologia.* Well he might, for when this ultimately appeared, it was most complimentary to him. That April, Russell wrote to Newman suggesting that "in fact our little correspondence, such as it was, would, to any fair mind, be a most complete and most satisfactory history of the several stages of your relations to your former communion and to your present one". Newman replied that he was "writing from morning to night" and requested that he be let see the letters that Russell had referred to. He quoted from the letters in the *Apologia.* This appeared, as was frequently done at the time, in parts, the third part coming out in May, 1864. Russell sent on the correspondence that Newman had sought, although he says that he misses one of them, which is a pity because he feels that it contained a declaration of Newman's immovability in the Anglican Church, even more than the others. He wants them back when Newman is finished with them, but the latter can publish anything he wants from them including Russell's name if he wishes.

When the sixth part appeared, Russell was gratified and moved by the references to himself. He had always felt a high degree of affection towards Newman, of a kind he can hardly explain – a sort of sympathy of which he can remember only one other instance in his life and the recollection of which brings tears to his eyes. It had been his wish, he tells Newman, to "let you alone", feeling that it would "almost be intruding in God's own work to push rudely upon the struggle which I saw in many of its results in what you were writing from time to time". He had always felt too "that with God's grace, your own mind worked out its own problems". Newman found this letter encouraging, a stimulant which helped him over a distracting respite from the *Apologia,* while he was penning his *Letter to the Duke of Norfolk.* That was finished towards the end of June and Newman's hand was "tired".

In March, 1865, after Wiseman's death, Newman told Russell of how he saw him shortly before. He had not seen him more than six or seven times in thirteen years. He thought it considerate of those who made the funeral arrangements not to ask him to attend. Still he had to admit that the Cardinal had done great work; and said he was pleased about his great funeral. "He always meant kindly, but his impulses, kind as they were, were evanescent, and he was naturally influenced by those who got around him – and occupied his ear". Just a month before he died, Wiseman had been asking Russell to verify a quotation from Byron criticising Shakespeare which he, Wiseman, had referred to but could not find.

Newman now began to recast the *Apologia* and Russell provided him with further material, notably a letter from W. Monsell which was important for a certain period. He would also like to see the piece "General Answer to Mr. Kingsley" modified. Newman had already attended to this, but only for the purpose of exposing his own meaning more clearly. He felt that he should speak out on such matters and that Russell was really more tender towards others than displeased with him. At times Russell did prevail on him to leave out or modify some passages, but in May he insisted: "I do not see my way to withdraw my statement that the Pope in Ecumenical Council is the normal seat of Infallibility or to throw doubt upon my convictions that certain Italian devotions to Our Lady are not suitable to England". Russell retorted: "Would you not say that 'The Pope, in conjunction with the Body of Pastors', whether 'in Council' or 'dispersed' is the normal seat of infallibility ?" Russell is quite insistent about this and seeks to mollify Newman's vanity by adding: "I wish further to say that *no one* is aware of my having written to you or of my taking any exception to the *Apologia* except indeed, as to the latter, one very dear friend, whose opinion I asked for my own greater security". Newman would not give in. On 17 May, he replied: "I will only say, that still, with my best lights, I do not see that the Pope's judgements out of Council are other than extraordinary utterances, and therefore, if they are extraordinary, they are not normal. If a Council were held now, I conceive one of its first acts would be formally to receive and repeat the condemnation of Jansenism and the definition of the Immaculate Conception. It would be natural for it to do so anyhow, but I think it would consider it a duty." Hence he will not change his passage. Russell wished he could speak with him, but his sister was ill. He cautioned Newman again about the piece on Infallibility, pointing out the need to be careful about the language used and the danger of being misinterpreted. When, early in 1866, another distraction from the *Apologia,* his *Letter to Pusey,* appeared, dealing with some Anglican misconceptions about Catholic excesses in devotion to the Blessed Virgin, Newman was congratulated by Russell. Before the *Apologia* finally was published, he omitted some passages about Catholic discipline to which Russell had also objected; but he did not budge in his idea of Papal Infallibility.

In 1866, Russell came second in the voting of the Parish Priests for the then vacant see of Armagh. It was the third see for which he had been mentioned, following those of Ceylon and Down and Connor. The Government was supposed to favour him, and Dorrian of Down and Connor wrote to try to get him to put away his "dislike of a position full of troubles from priests and people". However, he was not appointed to Armagh, to which Dr. Kieran succeeded. Whether or not he was anxious for a change, is debatable. If he were, he must have been consoled by the publication of Newman's *Apologia.* Years later, his nephew, Fr. Matthew Russell, S. J., composed some lines on first reading a certain page of it. '*Il prétend*', as the French would put it in their inimitable way, to have known nothing of his uncle's influence on Newman's conversion until he read about it in the *Apologia.* Even though he had attended Russell's class

in Ecclesiastical History at Maynooth, he had been unaware of it until
then, so close a secret had the uncle kept it. Therefore:

"Again betrayed! Another of thy deeds,
Performed by stealth to help a brother's needs,
Divulged by happy accident at last ...".

COLONIAL PERSPECTIVES

The dependence of the College on the Treasury, and the import for it of
political unrest on the part of Irish Catholics, continued to dog its days
all this time. The dependence on the Treasury was very real. In June,
1864, butter at breakfast had to be discontinued, owing to the state of
the funds; in October, the withdrawal of beer at dinner was substituted.
In November, the Trustees sent in their now almost annual memorial,
which was straight away passed to London. There was not much that
could be done in the second city of the Empire without sanction from the
top. The memorial was addressed to His Excellency, John, Baron Wode-
house, Lord Lieutenant and General Governor of Ireland. It sought
general funds but also a grant for the erection of the fourth side of the
unfinished quadrangle, "comprising the Chapel and Common Hall, so that
the College may be completed according to the original design" — of
Pugin. The Secretary to the Trustees (the Reverend Mr. Flanagan was
still in that office) undertook also to write to Peel about it, as he had
already done to the Chancellor of the Exchequer. It was Russell who
had drawn up the original version of the memorial. In February, 1865,
he visited London, possibly with a view to helping it on informally.

The health of the students was still giving concern. Eleven of those sent
home had died during 1865. That October, the Visiting Physician submitted a lengthy report dealing with the ventilation, the water supply,
and the provisions supplied to the College. The "crude material" provided
was said to be of unobjectionable quality but its "manipulation" left
much to be desired. Some filtering fountains with drinking vessels might
be provided at convenient positions in the corridors. Dinner water should
be "allowed to repose" for twenty-four hours in glazed earthen jars. To
remedy it fully, it should have an admixture of some kind, to ward off
constipation: "I shall content myself by briefly stating that I believe it
quite possible that a plan could be matured for supplying the students
a ration of good and wholesome Vin Ordinaire .... without embarrassing
the finances of the College". This 'dietary' was wonderful re. eggs: "In
the almost innumerable modes of preparing eggs, which even a slight
acquaintance with the elements of modern scientific cooking produces,
we have a never-failing reserve for a wholesome and palatable as well as
a substantial diet". Whether or not the finances permitted this or the

wine, the Trustees were happy when the Duke of Leinster offered to enclose the College grounds with a wall and also build a boundary wall cutting off the castle grounds.

In December, Russell and the four Archbishops were received quite favourably by Gladstone. They very likely raised the question of new grants. Shortly afterwards, Dr. Cullen was in Rome, where he "feared that a revolution will soon be attempted". At home many dioceses were short of priests while others had more than they needed. The President got his quota of letters from foreign parts — Montreal and the like, mainly in the Colonies — seeking students from Maynooth. In December, 1866, Dr. William Lanigan, who had done his higher studies at Maynooth, was appointed the first Bishop of Goulburn in Australia. There was a distinct air of 'Britishness' about. In 1866, when Dr. Dorrian wanted a preacher for the opening of St. Peter's new church in Belfast, he endeavoured to get Manning to do the needful. Failing this, he got the Bishop of Birmingham. Cardinal Cullen attended also, and Dorrian was glad to be able to tell Russell that there was all attention to him at the station and not the slightest insult came from any quarter at any time. A week earlier, Russell had been invited by Cullen to a dinner in honour of Gladstone's son. In November, there was an awe-inspiring spectacle when a meteoric shower entered the earth's atmosphere. In less than an hour, several hundred meteorites cut their way through its upper layer in lines of five. Dr. Lennon, Callan's successor as Professor of Natural Philosophy, took a special interest in the phenomenon; many years later, as an old Professor in 1910, he was to write an article about Halley's comet.

Then came the Fenian Rising of 1867. Fenianism had really originated in America, on 17 March, 1858, under the leadership of Michael Doheny, John O'Mahony and John Mitchel, who had escaped from Tasmania in 1853. James Stephens organized the movement in Ireland and was quickly joined by O'Donovan Rossa, founder of the Phoenix Society in Skibbereen in 1856. The Fenians were formally known as the Irish Republican Brotherhood and were committed to total separation from England, if necessary through the use of physical force.

The Government had things under close surveillance. As early as September, 1865, the paper *The Irish People* had been suppressed and O'Leary, Luby, O'Donovan Rossa and others arrested. The authorities had been keeping tabs on them since October, 1858, when the Parish Priest of Kenmare, whose name was Sullivan, had furnished the Castle with particulars relating to the young men who were drilling in the hills around there, followers of James Stephens and O'Donovan Rossa. Bishop Moriarty of Kerry is said to have been warned by the Lord Lieutenant, when at the Castle on other business, that the Government had the names and addresses of the members of the Fenian-inspired Phoenix Society. As a result, the Bishop is said to have got A. M. Sullivan of the *Nation* to write an article counselling non-involvement in the conspiracy.

Sullivan, a native of Bantry, had been given charge of the *Nation* by Gavan Duffy before the latter had gone to Australia. It was ironical that the name of the first of the prisoners to be tried, in March, 1859, had also been that of Sullivan. They had been told to plead guilty and that they would be released, which is in fact what happened.

The Church had not come out of the affair with much appreciation on the part of the Fenians. The sequel to the arrival home of the remains of Terence Bellew McManus had not been forgotten either. In actual fact, the question of clerical-Fenian relations is a very vexed one, involving not only the Irish clergy at home but also Bishops and priests in North America and the Antipodes. It is true that the Irish clergy as a whole did not support views such as those expounded by Maynooth-educated Fr. Patrick Lavelle of Tuam, in a paper entitled 'The Catholic Doctrine of the Right of Revolution', delivered in the Rotunda, Dublin, in February, 1862. Indeed the Irish Bishops not only warned against such views but against secret societies of the kind the Fenians were. But Dr. McHale of Tuam had consistently dissented. In January, 1870, Rome unreservedly condemned Fenianism and pronounced its members open to *ipso facto* excommunication. There were many Irish Bishops and priests withal who were reluctant to outlaw the Fenians, and many of them had good personal relations with individuals in the Fenian camp. Nevertheless, the Fenians on the whole turned sour against the Catholic clergy. There was a good deal of anti-clerical writing, particularly in *The Irish People* before its suppression. One contributor even blamed St. Patrick for the defects of the Irish character.

The Government had pre-empted the Fenian designs by the arrest of the leaders. The Fenians still hoped for success, aided by thousands of Irish volunteers from the United States, in the wake of the American Civil War. Only a few came and they too were arrested. The Rising, when it did come on the night of 5 - 6 March, 1867, in bitter cold, was a fiasco. There were widespread little engagements but they amounted to nothing, even though some 4,000 Fenians were said to have turned out in Cork alone.

The authorities at Maynooth were concerned. The memories of 1798 had not died there, and the students of the end of the 1860's showed, to use the words of Dorrian, "a spirit of independence". But then, he also complained about their practice of smoking, a habit which, he heard it said, was "winked at in the College" ! But joking apart, the superiors must have been somewhat nervous. They remembered the students' condolences for T. Bellew McManus. They were probably aware too of Fenian activity in the neighbourhood of the College — a Fenian circle at Leixlip is believed to have had 2,000 members. They had little sympathy for the revolutionary brand of nationalism, unlike the evolutionary constitutional policy that had been espoused by Murray's friend, Gavan Duffy. The latter had visited the College in 1867, after nearly ten years in Australia. He was an able man and had done well there. Murray and he had agreed to meet again in Kingstown, on 28 June, to have a long chat about old times, doubtless including Young Ireland days. They met a third time in Dublin in August, and Murray had been deeply touched after they parted. He hoped that Gavan Duffy could leave Australia for good after seven more years, and settle in Ireland as he intended. Murray recounts it all in his *Diary*. It is tantalising that, in that section of the diary, the very next nine lines are scrubbed out with pen and ink. What did Murray say in them ? Was it, perhaps, something about Gavan Duffy and their earlier aspirations to national independence ? Technical methods may yet find out.

The College administration could never be sure of the extent to which the nationalism of the students might go. This was particularly true whenever the country was in political turmoil. Old priests who were students there in 1916 have told of similar worries then. A lot of it had to do with their origins. S. C. Hall in his *Retrospect of a long Life,* discussing the priests of the mid-nineteenth century, says that the Maynooth men of that time were of humble village origin, with narrow views. In 1867 itself, 'An Irish Peer' — whoever he was — in a pamphlet entitled *The Irish Difficulty,* made out that, in general they were the sons of small farmers or shopkeepers, raised above their former equals without getting the social habits of the higher classes, creating in them a social resentment which often caused them to become demagogues. Frantz Fanon would surely have recognized the syndrome; and there is no denying that it was relevant in particular cases.

Signs on, as they say, a Father O'Connor, writing from Boston in 1868 in the Fenian newspaper *The Irish Republic,* defended Maynooth against the charge of being anti-Fenian: "The professors or students there would not swallow the rigid doctrines of Cardinal Cullen or Dr. Moriarty regarding secret societies. As long as the Church declines to condemn Fenianism, so long do all the Irish priests, Maynooth students especially, claim the privilege of interpreting theology, scripture and canon law for themselves ..." The Decree of the Holy Office, of 12 January, 1870, which did condemn Fenianism, had not yet been promulgated.

It is little wonder that the *Report of the Oaths Commission* in 1867 covered the oath taken at Maynooth by the President, although it is peculiar that it gave no formula for that of the students. The President's oath was the following:

> "I, ---, having been elected and approved as President of the Roman Catholic College, or seminary, of Maynooth, do swear that I will diligently, faithfully, and conscientiously execute the said office, to the best of my skill and judgement, and that I will as far as in me lies enforce a due observance of the bye laws, rules, and statutes made for the government and discip-

The Russell Collection

Callan Letters of Patent

8° & 9° VICTORIÆ, c. 25.

An Act to amend Two Acts passed in *Ireland* for the better
Education of Persons professing the Roman Catholic Religion,
and for the better Government of the College established at
Maynooth for the Education of such Persons, and also an Act
passed in the Parliament of the United Kingdom for amending
the said Two Acts.   (30th *June*, 1845).

C A P. XXV.

'   WHEREAS by an Act passed in the Parliament of *Ireland* in the
'   Thirty-fifth Year of the Reign of His late Majesty King *George*
'   t   the Third, intituled *An Act for the better Education of Persons* 35 G. 3. (I.)
' *professing the Popish or Roman Catholic Religion*, it was amongst other
' things enacted, that the Lord Chancellor or Lord Keeper of *Ireland*, the
' Lord Chief Justice of the Court of King's Bench in *Ireland*, the Lord
' Chief Justice of the Court of Common Pleas in *Ireland*, and the Lord
' Chief Baron of the Court of Exchequer in *Ireland*, for the Time being,
' together with certain other Persons therein named and the Persons there-
' after to be elected in the Manner by the said Act directed, should be
' Trustees for the Purpose of establishing, endowing, and maintaining One
' tholic Religion, and that the said Trustees should have full Power and
' Authority to receive Subscriptions and Donations to enable them to
' establish and endow an Academy for the Education of Persons professing
' the Roman Catholic Religion, and to purchase and acquire Lands not
' exceeding the annual Value of One thousand Pounds, and to erect and
' maintain all such Buildings as might be by the said Trustees deemed
' necessary for the lodging and Accommodation of the President, Masters,
' Professors, Fellows, and Students who should from Time to Time be
' admitted into or reside in said Academy; and it was further enacted, that
' it should and might be lawful for any Popish Ecclesiastic to officiate in a
' Chapel or Building to be appointed for that Purpose by the said Trustees
' or any Seven or more of them, any Law, Statute, or Provision to the
' contrary notwithstanding: And whereas by an Act amending the said Act
' and passed in the Parliament of *Ireland* in the Fortieth Year of His said
40 G. 3. (I.)   ' late Majesty King *George* the Third, intituled *An Act for the better*
' *Government of the Seminary established at* Maynooth *for the Education*
' *of Persons professing the Roman Catholic Religion; and for amending*
' *the Laws now in force respecting the said Seminary*, after reciting that
' a College or Seminary had been established at *Maynooth* for the Educa-
' tion of Persons professing the Popish or Roman Catholic Religion, and
' that large Sums of Money had been granted to the Trustees named in the
' Act herein-before recited, to enable them to improve and extend the said
' Institution, and that it had become necessary to make further Provision

Bishops at College Centenary

Freshmen

Student Types

my impression of
Maynooth Professors
during Entrance Week

all
seemed
at least 6 feet 7'
fearfully black
awfully severe
oppressively dignified.

the miserable
worm who
had to undergo
the examinations

Professorial Types

College Examinations

College Rules ?

"Good Students"

"Radical Students"

Work And Play

line thereof; and I will bear faithful and true allegiance, and to my utmost endeavours, inculcate the duties of faithful and true allegiance to Her Majesty Queen Victoria, and Her successors, in every member of the said college or seminary.

So help me God".

The Government was unquestionably aware that this was easier said than done. Possibly because of this, and in order to prevent the law from falling into disrepute, the Commission had recommended that the oath of allegiance, taken by the students, officers and servants of Maynooth College, should be dropped. *The Promissory Oaths Act, 1868 (*31 and 32 Victoria, c. 72), enshrined this by implication.

1868 saw the visit to the College of His Royal Highness, the Prince of Wales. On Wednesday, 21 April, he set out at 3 p.m. from the Castle, via the Broadstone Station, for Carton and Maynooth. Royalty had finally decided to look in on the place. The Princess remained in Dublin. Perhaps she thought that the place would be too masculine for her. *The Times* gave a detailed account of the journey, which "was performed" in about eighteen minutes, the engine driver being the chief locomotive superintendent. At Maynooth the party was provided with a carriage from the station, through the "eastern archway", to the "principal gate of the new building" — most certainly St. Patrick's arch. Before this the students were already mustered and "gave the Prince a vociferous welcome". He then passed into the "great northern cloister", between "double lines of students in academic costume", to a dais prepared for him. There was an address of loyalty from the President (extended also to the Princess in her absence) after which nine of the senior class were presented to the Prince. He later inspected the dinning hall and the library. He was gracious enough to send a reply to the President, some days later, through Sir William Knollys, which said that the Princess was especially grateful.

The Freeman's Journal of 22 April 'went to town'. There had been, it said, several flags erected on various prominent parts of the buildings. The College doctor for sixty-four years (Dr. O'Kelly) and his two doctor sons had also been presented, as well as the Parish Priest of Maynooth. It gave the text of the President's address. He had been grateful for the honour of the Prince's presence. He recalled with pleasure the previous royal visit to Ireland and to Carton. That had been during the long vacation. This one had given an opportunity for the "living homage" of the College to be extended. As the Prince left, the students renewed their acclamations and he "bowed several times in a marked manner". The students did not lose out themselves: an application from them to have the June examination 'allowed' to them as a gesture to the visit was quickly received. The administration 'passed the buck': "the application would be laid before the council". Cullen writing to Kirby in Rome was relieved to be able to say that there had been no Fenian disturbance during the visit of the Prince to Ireland. The fleet deployed outside Kingstown had put up fireworks when he was leaving.

Dr. Murray's journeys were usually between Maynooth and some part of Ireland. In January, 1869, he travelled by rail from Clones, in incessant rain, amid the "endless, shrill, nonsensical prattle" of children in the carriage. At the middle of the month, he went to Dublin with Crolly to hear Dickens at the Rotunda. They managed to get a seat in the gallery:

> "He came out exactly at the appointed time, 8 o'clock. He is decidedly a bad *reader*. Distinctness, strength (especially for a large room and crowded audience, as on this occasion), modulation — these are essential for a good reader. In none of these did he show any excellence: nay, he failed in them all. His first piece, 'Boots in the Holywell Inn', I had not previously read. The two next I had almost by heart, 'Sarah Gamp and Pecksniff', 'Bill Sikes and Nancy': yet I hardly heard a single sentence distinctly. As an *actor*, he did Old Fagan to perfection throughout: it could not be surpassed. Nancy he also did very well. Crolly says he did Bill also very well: but I could not agree with this. Sarah was very poor: but Picksniff was an utter failure — and all the rest failures. In this Crolly fully agrees with me. There could not have been less than two thousand persons present — I should say near three thousand. I never witnessed more perfect decorum in any assembly outside a church. I have heard on good authority that Dickens himself stated that he never appeared before any audience so orderly and well-mannered as that of Dublin, save only in Manchester ".

On 30 January, 1869, Murray's friend, the Irish writer, William Carleton, died. He had been a rakish character, whose writing about Maynooth had not been appreciated there. Murray wrote of him in his diary for 1 February: "I fear he died, as he lived, 'without God in this world' ".

Their last meeting had been accidentaly in Dublin in May, 1868. Carleton was then in his seventy-fourth year. Shortly after his death, Murray found out that "during his last illness, he was constantly beset by two parsons, who regularly relieved each other 'turn by turn about ?'". Father Carbery of Milltown Park had written to Mrs. Carleton to inquire whether her husband was disposed to die a Catholic, to which Carleton had replied in his own hand "no doubt the last lines that unfortunate hand ever traced": "2 Woodville, January 6th, 1869. My dear Mr. Carbery — Believe me I thank you from my heart for the interest you take in my eternal welfare. Mrs. Carleton has told me of the desire you feel that I should receive the last rites of your Church from your hands. For half a century and more I have not belonged to the Roman Catholic Religion.

I am now a Protestant, and will die such. I shall not add one word calculated to give you pain, and I trust that, notwithstanding this difference of creed, as Christians, you and I will be allowed to meet in the presence of him who created us and who is the Father of us all. Believe me to be, my dear Carbery, most affectionately and faithfully yours, W. Carleton".

Murray could not get himself to accept that Carleton really believed in Protestantism, and commented that this letter was without doubt dictated by the parsons. He was sure that, long before his death, Carleton "had ceased to believe in any religion whatever. Many years ago he told Gavan Duffy that, if he were to believe in anything, it would be in polytheism. On another occasion, in Duffy's (the bookseller's shop), he spoke to Crolly of Protestantism in terms of ridicule and contempt". It seems that he was constantly tortured by religious doubts. Yet, on 23 December, 1862 — only six years before he died — Carleton had written for Christmas to Murray, thanking him for a gift, and praying: "God grant you many happy returns of this sacred season". May he rest in peace.

Ireland, during the Spring of 1869, was upset about the repeal of the Party Processions Act. This was the repeal of an Act passed in 1850 prohibiting such manifestations, which was unpopular with many Catholics and Protestants and was in any case being widely ignored rather than enforced by the Government. Even though the Bishops opposed its repeal, it was finally erased from the Statute Book in June, 1872, by which time the Bishops were more concerned about other matters, particularly the university question. In 1869, however, many of them were agitated about it.

The North was especially open to trouble if parties could parade with impunity. Dr. Kieran, Archbishop of Armagh, wrote to Russell that there would be great danger of collisions between Catholics and Orangemen, indeed of a repetition of "the sanguinary riots which have so often disgraced the North". Dr. Dorrian of Down and Connor echoed the same thing; it was not at all unlike the 1970's: "In Belfast we are not afraid, for, at worst, we can defend ourselves. But, in remote parts, the Catholics are often weak as well as foolish".

There had, he said, been six "Catholic murders" in one parish in Co. Antrim, all of which had gone without punishment because of the corruption of "the old bitter partisan Magistrates". Some of these "who, in the Belfast riots, were standing by looking on while girls were dragged by Orange ruffians by the hair of the head, still hold the Commission and this, after a liberal Inquiry and with a liberal Government". The Bishop of Derry, Dr. Kelly, was also opposed to the repeal of the Act, fearing a renewal of displays offensive to every Catholic. How history repeats itself !

At Maynooth there were no such fears. A different climate prevailed.

In March, a student by the name of Daniel J. Lawlor, finished reading Newman's *The History of My Religious Opinions,* and wrote from the College to Newman sending some lines that had come spontaneously to him. The previous year, he had consulted Newman on the subject of English reading and had got a courteous reply from him. No doubt the connection between Russell and Newman loomed large in the consciousness of the Maynooth students. Lawlor had written eight stanzas, some of which merit reproducing:

> "Oh! Newman, thou whose soul long sought
> Midst error's dreadful ways,
> The path of truth, which God had wrought
> For man to work his praise.
>
> From Him, the Great, the God of might,
> Thou ask'd a guiding stay,
> Which from the Catacombs of night
> Might lead thee to bright day".

One can only imagine what Newman thought about his being described as having been amid the dreadful ways of error in the catacombs of the night, but at least he paid the author the compliment of retaining his lines. Nor should it be forgotten that, after his death, the memorial slab over his grave, at his own desire, was inscribed: "Ex umbris et imaginibus in veritatem". But that was years later. In 1869 both Russell and Newman had many years left in them. Russell was seeking some rare books on Macaronic poetry from Sir John Simeon of London.

Then came another royal visit; that of the Prince of Wales must have gone down well with the royal family. Now it was the turn of Prince Arthur. He arrived in Ireland on 5 April and visited Maynooth no later than the 8th. *The Times* covered the event with its usual thoroughness. The weather in the morning had been bad and "in a spirit of resignation rather than of hope the Royal party prepared for their intended journey to Maynooth, but as the day advanced they were rewarded for their patient bravery by observing some auspicious symptoms". In fact, there was a "lucid interval in the weather" and they set out at 11 o'clock, the Prince "in a barouche drawn by four horses and preceded by outriders". They reached Maynooth at 1 o'clock, to be greeted by a hearty cheer from the students.

The Prince was received by Dr. Russell, and the Dean and Professors were presented in the reception room. The President expressed the gratitude of all in the College for the visit — the second within a year. It gave evidence, he said, of Queen Victoria's interest in Maynooth, as did Prince Arthur's other name (his middle name was Patrick) of dedication to Ireland. *The Freeman's Journal* adds that this took place in the Prayer

Hall; obviously the long awaited Aula Maxima was not yet there. The students wore "their academic caps and gowns". Present also were a number of gentlemen residing near Maynooth, including the Parish Priest, a representative of the Dunboyne Establishment and representatives of the different undergraduate classes. The Hall was "beautifully adorned for the occasion" with a scarlet and gold canopy over the "State chair".

While the address was being read, the Prince stood uncovered. Then, in reply, he thanked them especially for the allusion to his name and said he would report well to his mother. *The Times* reported that "the students testified their sympathetic pleasure by hearty cheers". Then he visited the library, one of the refectories and the kitchen which, *The Freeman* said, "is, perhaps, one of the finest in the Kingdom and supplied with all the recent improvements for cooking by gas and steam". For all his literary work, Russell had not been idle about mundane affairs. After repeating to him his great pleasure, the Prince left the College for lunch at Carton. The Duke's kitchen must have been 'more eligible'.

Before he left the country, unlike the occasion of the visit of the Prince of Wales, there was trouble in the North of Ireland. Referring to the newspapers of 29 April, Cullen wrote to Russell: "What a sad business in 'Derry'. The poor Prince must be greatly alarmed". He got back to England without further inconvenience. It had been a typical visit of a member of the royal household to an 'outlying' part of the kingdom — in some ways resembling a visit to a Crown Colony rather than to an integral part of the 'British Isles'. The Empire was in full swing. That year, the opening of the Suez Canal brought places like India and Australia so much nearer. Before it, the cost of a letter from London to Calcutta was a full five shillings and five pence. The British had been opposed to the construction of the canal, but soon realised its possibilities for them. The price of colonialism was still high but took second place to the glories of conquest.

Chapter VII

The Eighteen Seventies

Before 1869 was out, the Royal College at Maynooth was disestablished. The threat of this had always been there in the perpetual attacks which the College had to face from Protestants of every description. During 1868, it had become tied up with the issue of the disestablishment of the Church of Ireland, to which Gladstone committed the new Government which he formed in December that year.

There was quite a case for the latter move. The Report of the Census Commissioners of 1861 had shown that the population of the country was 5,788,145, while the members of the Established Church numbered only 693,357 – less than one eighth of the total population; in 199 out of its 2,424 parishes it could not count a single member. In 1835, in England, some 26 of its prelates ministered to 6 million members; in Ireland there were 18 prelates to minister to 800,000, out of the then population of 7 million. At the same time, in England the annual income received by each of these prelates was between £2,000 and £3,000; in Ireland it was not less than £4,000 in any case and in some cases exceeded £15,000. The Church of Ireland had an income of £6,000,000 in tithes and 600,000 acres of good land. The Catholic clergy had no State provision at all. It was not unexpected when, in 1835, a Church Temporalities Bill had reduced the numbers and cost of the Irish Church Establishment. In 1868 the anomaly had reappeared with a decrease in the number of Church of Ireland members and an increase in that of the Roman Catholics, who, at the time of the census of 1861, numbered 4,505,365. Hence, both Catholics and Non-Conformists alike were busy pamphleteering about the enormity of the continuing establishment of that Church. Gladstone, who favoured its disestablishment for financial reasons, while still in opposition had moved a resolution to that end in 1868, combining with it the disendowment of Maynooth. Disraeli, whose Conservative Government was in power, decided to go to the country on the issue. Following a General Election, Gladstone was called upon to form a Government, with a majority of 112. That was on 5 December, 1868.

DISESTABLISHMENT

As the new year commenced, Non-Conformists everywhere made very sure that the new Government would bring in 'disestablishment', made sure too that Maynooth would be included in this. In February, the Dublin correspondent of the *Nonconformist* demanded the ending of all endowment of all Churches for education and therefore the ending of the Maynooth grant. Needless to say, there were many members of the Church of England (and that of Ireland) who were bitterly opposed to the disestablishment of the Church, and included Maynooth College for good measure. One such was the Dean of Westminster, Arthur Penrhyn Stanley, in a pamplet entitled *The Three Irish Churches* (1869). Another, Thomas Andrews, in his *The Church in Ireland* (1869), campaigned for the maintenance of the establishment of the Church and the endowment of Maynooth. Thomas Gallwey, in his *Short Essays on the Irish Established Church* (1868), argued also for the retention of the Maynooth endowment: "The Irish priest is to be found wherever the British flag waves. It will be an interesting problem for the future historian, whether the British merchant with his bales, or the Irish Catholic with his priest, has influenced more enduringly and vitally the destinies of the human race". Far from disendowing Maynooth, what is really needed there "is a number of amply endowed life fellowships and professorships ... which would afford leisure for the pursuit of knowledge, in divinity and culture, in science and art".

On 1 March, 1869, disregarding all such utterances, Gladstone moved for leave to introduce his Bill for the disestablishment and disendowment of the Church of Ireland. Maynooth was also to be disendowed, but Gladstone undertook to pay off all the arrears of building expenses which had been contracted on the faith of the promises of 1845. The Catholic Bishops did not oppose the measure. Rather was it conveyed privately to the Government that they would fully understand if the grant to Maynooth were ended when religious equality in Ireland was being brought about. Indeed Dr. Cullen seems to have been positively pleased by the idea. To Kirby (10 May, 1868): "The loss of Maynooth would do us very little damage. In Dublin we have Clonliffe which will soon suffice for the diocese. In other dioceses also they have large seminaries ....". So the measure went through Parliament quickly, and, on 26 July, became law. In lieu of the grant, the College was given compensation amounting to fourteen years purchase of it, a somewhat more generous rate than that given to other Churches. It was given to the Trustees — £372,331.0.6 in all — on terms securing the life interest of the existing members of staff, while a building debt of £12,000, owed by the College to the Commissioners of Public Works, was remitted. The Act was entitled *An Act to put an end to the Establishment of the Church of Ireland, and to make provision in respect of the Temporalities thereof, and in respect of the Royal College of Maynooth.*

Maynooth had finally been disendowed. Thrown on their own, it was not unexpected to find the President, students and staff, sending an *Address of loyalty to Pope Pius* IX that July 14; the Pope sent them back a signed acknowledgement. The Bishops were also quick to react, the Bishops of Munster, before the end of July, requesting the Archbishop of Cashel to get together with the other Metropolitans immediately to confer on a plan for the reorganization of the College. On 12 August, the opinion of counsel was sought on the legal effect of the Irish Church Act on the College's obligations towards the students, particularly the Dunboyne students and those of the three senior classes. The Trustees met on 18 August and resolved "that all students who are to be admitted after this date shall not be entitled to free places longer than 1st January 1871, and that they be then prepared to pay such pension as the Board may order". In a sense, the College had closed and reopened, guaranteeing to the students of the final three years those emoluments they had enjoyed under establishment.

One of the new men to enter that Autumn was P.A. Sheehan of Cloyne. The routine in the College was unsettled and the discipline relaxed, following the general reorganization. The courses — in the Humanities, Rhetoric, Logic, Metaphysics and Ethics, Mathematics, Physics and Astronomy — which he had to enter, were not suited to his particular turn of mind — interested as he was in Fichte and Schelling and Jean Paul Richter. Later on, in *My New Curate*, he was to contrast the products of Maynooth then with those whom he had known in his youth. While in the College, he escaped great distinction, although an unknown Limerick contemporary thought a lot of him:

> "In my time at Maynooth, Cloyne diocese was accounted *crème de la crème* of the College. Not to mention his Lordship (Most Rev. Dr. Robert Browne, then Bishop of Cloyne), you had men of sweeping abilities like the parish priest of Macroom (Dr. Jeremiah Murphy) ..... and you had men like Canon Sheehan, who scarcely uttered a word, but read the heavens and thought".

Sheehan himself, writing in the *Irish Monthly* in 1902, had this to say of his days at Maynooth:

"Far back in the 'sixties', literature had to be studied surreptitiously, and under the uncongenial but effective shadow of Perrone and Receveur. It was a serious thing to be detected in such clandestine studies, and I dare say our superiors were quite right in insisting that we should rigidly adhere to the system of pure Scholasticism which was a College tradition. But, was not our President one of the greatest of European literateurs ?"

Still he was loyal to Maynooth:

"I make bold to say that the staff of professors at Maynooth gives promise to maintain all the traditions that belong to the teaching staff of the greatest ecclesiastical seminary in the world".

That was what Maynooth had now become.

The President was not put off the further development of the College by the stringencies consequent on disestablishment. Not long afterwards, he issued an appeal for voluntary contributions to help the library. One of the relatively few to be well disposed was the Bishop of Limerick, Dr. Butler. The Bishop had his own difficulties with the President, when he asked Russell to send the *Black Book* to Limerick, only to discover that Maynooth had come to regard it as the property of the College rather than of the Diocese. Butler to Russell: "My dear Dr. Russell, Aubrey de Vere asked me some time ago to lend him the 'liber niger' of Limerick for his brother-in-law, Mr. R. O'Brien. I told him that it had been lent to Dr. Renehan and that it was still at Maynooth but that he or his brother-in-law might write for it. It seems from your letter that Mr. O'Brien did write. I suppose he will think your letter to him satisfactory and very kind, but he will surely conclude that I must have been labouring under a strange delusion in supposing that the book was the property of this diocese. On the other hand, it appears from your letter that you must somehow have fallen under the delusion that Maynooth is the owner of the book — how is this? I consider the question of the ownership much more important than of lending it or not to Mr. O'Brien. Is the claim of the college based on the mere fact of possession, or has some new casuistry been introduced which makes it lawful to close upon all borrowed property? 'Tis hard to say what theology may not accomplish and there are so many theologians at Maynooth that one is at a loss what to be sure of".

It was of little consolation to Butler that Russell forwarded him a copy of the *Black Book*. He wrote: "Many thanks for the copy of the *Black Book*. I hope there is no harm in one's taking a copy, who is the lawful owner of the original". That Butler did eventually establish his title to the book is clear from a letter to Russell of October, 1871, saying: "I give, most willingly, the permission you ask, to enable you to accede to the request of the Master of the Rolls about the *Black Book*". That September, Russell sent to Newman a copy of his *Report on the Carte MSS.,* which had just been published. It was a closing of his connection with Oxford. He asked Newman to accept it as a remembrance of Oxford and of his relations with him, which he had thought of often while preparing it.

VATICAN 1

In 1870 the first Vatican Council was under way and the Irish Bishops were in Rome. The *President's Archives* at Maynooth is a valuable quarry for interesting insights into the proceedings. The First Public Session had been held on 8 December previously and the Second on 6 January. At home, the land question was causing concern and some Bishops found it hard to forget it. In March, Dr. Dorrian, writing from the Palazzo Pericoli, told Russell that the six Bishops there had been grieved to read in the Irish newspapers that had reached them about a reception given to Father Lavelle at Maynooth. It had been stated that, after an imprudent exhibition by the students, he had been feted by some of the Professors. "We have had four General Congregations last week and will have one every day this one coming . But I fear we shall not get the business all done and that we shall have to come back about October. The business, however, appears now to be really got into and we are kept as busy as students for class".

Some Decrees were published shortly afterwards and he again wrote to Russell, saying that it was likely that "the great question will come up for final settlement". That was on 22 April and the question was that of Papal Infallibility. On the same day, Dr. Moriarty of Kerry, who was a known opponent of defining this, also wrote to Russell: "Propter Secretum Pontificium I can say little about. the Council. We know however that we are to have a public session on Sunday. We may have very little to produce. The only merit is that we have made it to be little. There is a tendency to dogmatise at each and every speech. Our effort must be to put on the drag and slacken pace. It seems to me that many of our body would like to take the 20 vols. of Suarez and define that all they contained was de fide Catholica. There is a rampant spirit of theocracy that would use the keys only to shut the gates of heaven against all who will not swallow every opinion that tends to fatten human thought. May God guide us".

The Third Public Session of the Council was held on 24 April. McGettigan, the new Primate of All Ireland, was there, after the death of Dr. Kieran. He stayed at the Hotel de la Minerve. He was not too optimistic: "I fear the future and dread it will turn out a failure". The

Pope presided and the constitution 'De Fide' was read out. As McGettigan put it to Russell: "All the members of the Council now in Rome were present today: the blind, the lame and dying". Yet there had not been a single 'Non Placet'. A Maynooth Professor — Dr. McAuley — is also in Rome, just back from a trip to Naples in good professorial style, and the Irish Bishops are thriving, except for Dr. Derry, who is "shattered" and must return home. The weather is absolutely splendid but the Council cannot finish this year. Keane of Cloyne was jubilant that so much had been done to date. He was prepared to say "Deo Gratias" as also was Leahy of Cashel. The laity was allowed to be present in the Galleries. Conaty of Kilmore could only marvel at the strength of the Pope who, he said, "is apparently the strongest and most vigorous of all history", while Nulty of Meath conveyed to Russell that some Roman theologians were asking for him.

By May, Moriarty was writing: "The weather is getting warmer and we are getting impatient. Yet the wise ones say that the Council will go on through the Summer". Two important questions were coming up immediately, the Primacy and Infallibility, and McGettigan was saying that "it is clear that the debates will be long and *lively*". Infallibility is, he says, easily the biggest subject before a General Council since the First Council of Nicaea defined the Dogma of the Divinity of Christ. "Both sides are truly in earnest. It is God alone that can save the Church in such a troubled sea of conflicting opinions". Things really must have been strained. The Irish, or some of them at least, had the consolation of hearing Murray's *De Ecclesia* frequently cited. Donnelly of Clogher wrote on 16 May: "The Holy Father continues to enjoy the best of health .... Meanwhile the Council proceeds slowly and solidly in its course. Whether we shall get home this Summer, and if so when, no one seems to know. There are rumours and conjectures enough indeed, but no certainty in anything approaching it".

On Tuesday 17 May, the discussion on the 'great question' had begun. McGettigan reported that day to that effect to Russell, adding that it was hard to see when it would end. Forty three "orators" had given in their names, among them Cardinal Cullen, the Archbishops of Cashel and Tuam, and the Bishop of Galway. The Cardinal is to speak tomorrow, Wednesday, 18 May. By 26 June, Keane declared that "the great question of Infallibility is so far advanced that it must be concluded, but not sufficiently advanced to enable anyone to say what day in the end of July or the beginnning of August the Maynooth Board can meet". Well, first things first ... Leahy of Cashel was happy to have found an old class-fellow "within a foot of me in the Council Hall — Dr. Kenrick" (of St. Louis). Relating this, he lets his thoughts stray to "long, long ago", when he was in "the Lay House" at Maynooth, little thinking that one day he would be taking part in a General Council. He wishes Russell well; the heat in Rome is dreadful, yet "We cannot be set free before the middle of July". Another says that everybody was perspiring constantly and in a very debilitated state. By 3 July, seventy-five had already spoken or given up their rights to speak. Thus McGettigan to Russell. There were forty names still left "but it is hoped many of these will resign", as "the Council is sick of the discussion for nothing new can be now said on either side". "Duplice pondere premimur, said a very gifted Father *yesterday*, pondere *caloris* et pondere *Eloquentiae*. Between the blazing sun outside and the long speeches made, the Bishops are very much tired". Well they might be. They met from 8 in the morning until 1 p.m. "The Irish Bishops who are still here are not complaining, but they long for liberty to get home, especially in order to meet and make preparations for the great change that is soon to take place in your College". The 15th of August seems to be the earliest they can be in Ireland. He would like if they could meet in Maynooth before going home. What he was referring to was the need to consider the continued reorganization of the College after 1869, and they did in fact plan to meet on 16 August. Most of the Irish Bishops would be leaving Rome before the end of July.

The Fourth Public Session was held on 18 July, with 533 'Placets' and 2 'Non-Placets': The Dogma of Papal Infallibility had been passed. The Council was neither prorogued nor interrupted, but a vacation was allowed until 11 November for those who wished to go home. Leahy was one of those who availed themselves of this. He wrote to Russell from Llandudno, Wales: "I am here *incog* with my chaplain". Any communication should be addressed to him "without the prefix Revd".

Before the next session, Rome had been occupied by the Italian army. Dr. Murray followed events closely from Maynooth; he really should have been a 'peritus' at the Council. At the end of October, he noted that pieces in *The Tablet* of the 29th indicated that, after the take over, Rome was full of the bitterest enemies of the Church. The Vatican museums, libraries and galleries were closed. St. Peter's itself was only open at the principal entrance, in order to try to stop the profanation of the Basilica, for, as *The Tablet* reported. "People have been walking about the church with their hats on and lighting their cigars at the lamps which had been around the Confessional". And yet, Rome survived, the Vatican survived, the Church survived.

At the same time, Paris was under German occupation, following the Franco-Prussian War. It too survived. In June, 1871, Murray quoted *Le Siècle de Paris* apropos of it: *"Cette ville ne peut périr, parceq'elle est la France, et la France est indispensable au monde. Si Paris disparaîssait, l'humanité ne saurait pas où elle va, et nous retomberions dans les ténèbres de la barbarie".* Murray thought this to be "foolish rant". In his view, Paris for the last three hundred years since Calvinism was introduced had been "the moral pest of France" as well as the stronghold of Voltairean infidelity. One feels that he would have looked upon Rome as indestructible and for much more convincing theological reasons. France was certainly upset. In the Autumn of 1870, two great auctions of theological works from Coimbra were held in Dublin, there being no market for them in Paris. Murray was able to buy only a few, owing to shortage of funds.

Just then the College was feeling the first effects of disendowment. The fourth year's divinity class was discontinued, and the Professors had to give its members a crash course before they left. Once again, Murray became ill from overwork. He suffered "a complete prostration of body and mind", becoming a skeleton, unable to stand without great pain. It was Easter, 1871, before he could resume.

For the next couple of months, his diary is full of remarks and aphorisms. He was glad when certain German theologians were rebuked by Perrone for teaching theology in German. He was persuaded that the elimination of Latin was "one of the sources of that shallow and unsound theology which in modern times had characterised the productions of so many so-called German theologians". He was furious when *The Times* said that the definition of Infallibility was such that nobody could live with the High Priest to whom it was attributed, and wondered whether a crusade might even be contemplated to rescue the Church from this. "There are truthfulness and sobriety of assertion for you", he exclaims !

He had quite an aversion to Victor Emmanuel. In July, he wrote about him: "By the way, the dog-faced made his formal entry into Rome last Sunday — a fitting day for such a deed. No doubt Rome will become a 'Liberal State' for a time. But the end will sure come. I hope Pius IX will live to see it". Then he became jocular in vein about the sayings of some lawyers, attributed to Crolly, such as: "I spy a trap — I smell a rat — I see him brewing in the storm — I ferret him out — I'll nip him in the bud", or "He has not an acre of land on earth, except the bare sky above him", or "What did my client do, my Lord ? He seized the bull by the horns, and indicted him for perjury". In July, telegraphic comm-

211

unication with Rome was suspended for some days. The Romans were supposed to be celebrating its freedom, with 50,000 people conveyed into the city at nominal fares and paid to celebrate. Murray kept watching the scene there for quite a while, looking out for news about the Pope and the Roman question. And he prepared an article on the Council for *The Dublin Review.* By 18 November, 1872, he had completed his sixty-first year.

In 1874, Gladstone brought out a fierce expostulation against the Vatican decrees. He regarded the doctrine of Infallibility as incompatible with civil allegiance. Many people, among them Russell, wrote to Newman begging him to answer this. *The Letter to the Duke of Norfolk* had been the result. Newman himself was satisfied that he had done what he could to counter Gladstone's thesis. In his pamphlet, he had sought backing from an argument of Dr. Neville, formerly of Maynooth, for "to quote a Maynooth professor .... was to possess a great ally, who would block any attack, any annoyance, which my words might have caused" (Letter to Lord Blachford, 11 April, 1875). He wrote to Russell in January 1875: "I am like a man who has gone up in a balloon, and has had a chance of all sorts of adventures ... All I can say is that I have acted for the best, and have done my best and now leave the success to a higher power". He was happy when he received letters from Maynooth approving of the 'Norfolk' pamphlet. To Russell he surmised what Gladstone would say if he replied: "He will say that theologians are one thing, the political misuse of doctrine another". Russell allayed his disquiet by telling him that he had met the Duke of Argyll at dinner at "our Duke's at Carton", who had spoken in loud admiration of the 'Letter'. Newman would have been pleased to hear that ... So Russell could write to him to say: "I think your balloon is fairly come to earth and safely anchored once again". Newman wrote at once to Mrs. Froude to tell her that good news: "The allusion in Dr. Russell's letter to a balloon was in consequence of my saying that I was up in one, and was as yet in danger of being entangled in chimney pots, of being lodged on some high tree, trailed along the ground, or run away with into the German ocean ...". Newman needed and did not lack admirers. Russell's nephew, Matthew Russell, was one of them. He went so far as to write that, in his view, Newman was a "note of the true Church", but he did admit even to Newman that he would not dare say that to his uncle.

THE SPORTING EMPRESS

In 1869 a young man called Richard O'Kennedy came up to Maynooth as a student for the Diocese of Limerick. Years afterwards, in *The Irish Monthly,* he was to give us a picture of student life there then. On his arrival, he had had a quarrel with the jarvey about the fare for ferrying him from the station to the College. The jarvey said that he usually got

2/6 for the run, an outlandish amount, or so it seemed to Kennedy. On arrival, he was "escorted by a liveried servant from the gate into the precincts of the College". The porter had evidently made quite an impression on him. So did the College as a whole:

"The night was pitch dark, and the gas lamps that flanked the avenue seemed by their light to make the darkness doubly dense. All was strange to me. Coming from the depths of the country, I was quite unprepared to find what the magnificent cluster of college buildings was like: its uninterrupted lines of masonry, its gothic doors and windows and arches; its storied corridors: — oh, how strangely all these looked to my untravvelled eye ! And while I was gazing upon them amazed, if not awe-struck, a busy, voluminous hum, 'with the tread of many footsteps' broke on my ear. A huge door opened, and out rolled a torrent of student figures ... The bell in a short while summoned all to night prayer, and that being over some of my diocesan friends took me under their protection and found me a room and a bed.

Next morning we were called before daybreak ... With some few more — freshmen all of us — I was ushered into a room; bare, but for its few chairs and seats and a central table. As we sat, a tall, venerable ecclesiastic came in. It was not yet morning light. He called our names, and welcomed us personally ....

I do not think I shall ever forget my first breakfast in Maynooth College. It was a fearfully cold morning, foggy and frosty. There was no fire in the immense refectory .... My hands were so numb that I could hold my knife only as a Tipperary man holds his blackthorn ... when all of a sudden there was a skurry of feet, and I found that all were standing up to say grace after meals. I stood up ... and left; not, however, without a long look at St. Patrick and the serpents behind me .....

My friends at the after breakfast recreation were unable to tell, from my description, who the reverend father (the 'venerable ecclesiastic' of early morning) was. In a few days after, we were out on a walk. I remember, as we climbed over the ascent of a bridge, an ecclesiastic came riding at a brisk pace towards the foot of the bridge at the other side. On seeing us, he reined in his horse ... The eye was particularly pleased with the sit of the rider, elegantly but quietly attired in superior broadcloth .... Nearer he came, riding quietly, and bowing respectfully to the salutes of the students. As he passed me, I looked in his face ... 'Now there he is', I said in haste'. 'Who is he ?' ... 'Who is he ?' in amazement. 'That is the President, Dr. Russell' ".

O'Kennedy relates that it was from that very animal that Russell got his fatal fall years afterwards. It was in character with a young man from the County of Limerick to appreciate horsemanship. In common with many another student, he found the constraints of life in the College really trying:

"So come to me now the memory of those quiet days, 'twenty golden years ago', when I sat in my room in one of the attics of the old college. The rooks gathered the sticks for their nests; the noisy jackdaws scolded and quarrelled, like so many attorneys-at-law, disputing or asserting possession to a particular cranny in the chimney-pots; and the calm glow of the spring evening was shed on the distant ridges and cultivated sides of the Wicklow hills. I have then thought of a scene far away — a scene in a countryside dearer than all the scenes on earth, when the furze and ferns grew on the sides of the rugged hill; and in the hollow beneath, the lapwing built its nest. And, truth to tell, in the lengthening shadows of evening I have often longed to be there".

Generations of Maynooth men have had similar thoughts. In 1870, they had all to pay a pension of £28 for the privilege of living there, although it was hoped shortly to introduce some new free places. They studied and prayed and were ordained priests. In December, Dr. Murray gave each of the forthcoming ordinands a little leaflet, with monita, to put in their breviaries. As was to be expected, in consequence of the imposition of the new fee, some students tried to be excused some years. The Bishop of Meath allowed four of his men to skip the Physics Class in 1871. That October, a request came in from the Diocese of Ossory: "We shall be much obliged, if you kindly permit Walter McDonald to join the Logic Class". Yet, even though funds were short, some Bishops were asking the College to keep students there over the Christmas vacation, as they tended to be disorderly at home. In 1872, the Bishop of Kerry, Dr. Moriarty, thought that the state of things amongst them was far from good. Nulty of Meath was of a similar opinion:

"I am not at all contented with the young priests who have left the College for this Diocese within the last 4 or 5 years. As a rule they seem mercenary in their views from the very first day: and get at once quite discontented with the means of the missions they are sent to ... They are neither laborious nor zealous".

It was a hard saying, but other Bishops concurred with it. The College administration was baffled too. In June, 1872, the Trustees resolved that, in order to stop the waste of bread in the refectory, "no bread be given to any Student until what has been already supplied to him shall have been 'consumed". That year P. A. Sheehan's health failed and he had to go home for a year. And, after forty-two years as Professor and President, Dr. Robert Whitehead resigned office, but was permitted to continue as Librarian. He was to leave behind him some pathetic notes by 'Bob Bookworm'.

The O'Keeffe trial was now about to take place and Cardinal Cullen was naturally caught up in it. This was the case concerning a conflict between the parish priest of Callan, in the Diocese of Ossory, and his ecclesiastical superiors. Having refused to leave his parish, on injunction from his bishop, for disciplinary reasons, Fr. O'Keeffe had taken his quarrel to the civil courts. Cardinal Cullen was involved in the case as Archbishop of Dublin, Metropolitan of the ecclesiastical province in which Ossory is situated. After much debate and legal complexity, Fr. O'Keeffe's claim was dismissed by the court. But that was not to come until 1875. In May, 1873, when the case opened, Cullen was pleased to be able to convey that there were to be seven Catholics on the jury.

At Maynooth, the Professors, as is their wont, did not miss out on care for their well-being. In August, 1873, Dr. Gargan, then Professor of Ecclesiastical History, was in Vichy for his health. That year, the Golden Jubilee of the foundation of the Convent at Maynooth was celebrated. Soon after, Fr. Tom Burke again visited the College, telling the students stories and acting them. He then conducted their retreat. The Bishop of Limerick deplored the lack of knowledge of Latin on the part of some students. P. A. Sheehan, back again, secured a number of places amongst the 'Proxime accesserunt' — a first in Sacred Scriptures, a fourth in Dogmatic Theology, a sixth in Moral Theology. The Trustees introduced a processional order for the students when entering or leaving their oratories, and decreed too that they were not to see visitors without the permission of their deans. In April, 1875, the Finance Council discussed "the most convenient mode of getting the students' rooms washed". All this did not do much good, for in October the Trustees found it necessary to resolve:

> "That the President is hereby requested to convey to the students in their respective divisions and in the most impressive manner on the part of the Trustees their condemnation of the noisy and disorderly manifestations which have but too often occurred in the College amongst the students and that should any student be found guilty in future of shouting, hooting or scraping in class or at any other meetings, his misconduct shall be immediately notified to his Bishop. The Trustees further desire to convey to the students that they are opposed to all manifestations whether of approval or disapproval on the part of the students in class or elsewhere".

That this stark warning did not get very far is clear from the *President's Report for 1875-76*, which indicates that there had been disorderly manifestations in the refectory the previous December:

"Complaints suddenly arose as to the thinness of the soup, and the staleness of the bread. Explanations and assurances were discredited. The prohibitory regulations of the superiors were evaded, or, in the security of numbers, were set at naught. It seemed as if the domestic authority of the College was ignored, and some ulterior tribunal kept constantly in view; and a determination was manifested to overcome the superiors by turbulence, or to coerce them into concession by the threat of appeal for redress to the Visiting Prelates and Trustees ... For a few days authority seemed completely paralyzed. The only measures which could be devised for the purpose of repressing the disorder in the Refectory had little effect beyond that of transferring it from the Refectory to the Cloisters or other places of meeting. A sense of security arose among the disaffected".

That 22 December, Cardinal Cullen wrote to the Bishop of Elphin: "Someone has written to me that there is a bad feeling and a spirit of resistance to authority in Maynooth at present. It is said that the students have been 'scraping' Dr. McCarthy and that eleven or twelve of them have got a 'caveat' ... It is hard to know what is the *origo malorum* and how far the evils go ... With other things I was told that the students last year refused Christmas amusements unless the superiors should be excluded and that in consequence there were no amusements ...". He was no longer sure of his touch. The following June, after a Visitation had in fact been held, he wrote again to Gillooly: "I have heard that in Maynooth great dissatisfaction prevails about the visitation ... The superiors or some of them are said to state that the students were encouraged to be refractory by the way they were heard at the visitation". P. Mac Suibhne, collator of Cullen's letters, says of this one: "Here the letter ends, apparently unfinished".

Authority did assert itself in the end. Five students were rusticated. Then a College retreat brought the others to their senses. At their June meeting, the Trustees ordered: "That students joining in noisy or combined manifestations against the College Authorities are to be deemed of evil example and influence and to be punishable accordingly by expulsion". The Anti-Combination Acts were in full force at Maynooth, and it was not calculated to improve the humour of the students when, that October, the Trustees also decided "that pea-soup shall be no longer supplied to the Students on meagre days". Even the language is light years away from today, and linguistic analysis would have a lot to say

216

about the atmosphere both created and reflected by such announcements. The same October, Dr. — later Cardinal — Logue became a Dean in the College and provisional Professor of Irish.

The end of the year saw further disturbances. In June, the Trustees bemoaned the absence of the Second Divinity students from the previous Christmas examination, "evidently as a result of a combination", but they wisely did nothing more than inform the class that their action was gravely reprehensible. They still had a capacity for putting their foot in it, as when, the following October, they announced "that in future butter of second, instead of first quality, be supplied to the students". In June, 1878, they reached an all-time low: "That from the beginning of the next Scholastic year, the soup served at dinner shall be taken by all students before the carving of dishes is commenced — that the carvers shall rise from table and finish their dinner with the rest of the Students and that the waste of bread and meat shall be more carefully prevented. It is recommended that the joints of beef should be lessened by 1 or 2 lbs. per mess".

In truth, the Queen's Visitors to the College, dispensed with after the disendowment, were now being missed. Even though at times they had been a menace with their probings, they had kept the running of the College up to scratch, boarding and discipline wise. Not that Trinity College, which still enjoyed their surveillance, had a lot to show in the way of discipline. In the Summer of 1878, during the second night of the races there, there was a fire in the carpenter's shop. Graduates were the culprits. Two of them were detected "participating in the folly", to use the words of *The Freeman's Journal*, and it had been debated whether they should be suspended from their degrees. One Fellow was said to have declared that there was growing up "a system of rowdyism, caddism and blackguardism which was lowering the character of the University". The newspaper had thoroughly agreed with him. Athletics was being put before everything else: "Never was there a greater fallacy, for all the history of Hellas shows that physical development was only secondary to mental training, and that even in the Olympic plain the poet was greater than the boxer, a position reversed in our own days by the waters of Cam, Isis, and Liffey".

The first great fire to engulf Maynooth College occurred in November, 1878. Of it much more later. It probably helped to bring the students into order. The same thing must have been contributed to in a different way by the visit in 1879 of Her Majesty, the Empress of Austria. The story has been told again and again; it captivated the minds of successive generations of students. She was young and fiery then and must certainly have attracted all and sundry. The tale of what occurred has been handed down, of how she had entered the grounds in pursuit of a stag, had met the Vice-President, Dr. William Walsh, who — without knowing who the lady was — had chivalrously wrapt her in his toga and extended an invitation to her to come formally the following Sunday. This she had graciously done, hearing Mass in the chapel of the Junior House. Afterwards, she had inspected the College (including the 'disaster area' that had been burned) making sure to see the famous kitchen. She again visited the College in 1880, bringing as a gift the great solid silver statue of St. George and the Dragon, which has since been one of the College's most treasured possessions. College tradition has it that the Gaels there made it known that St. George was not welcome in the place, in consequence of which the Empress sent a further gift of the most valuable cloth of gold vestments. That they came is certainly the case.

Other accounts of the event are less well-known. In 1923, the Reverend William Hanton of the Diocese of Ferns told about it in *The Irish Ecclesiastical Record:* "We were at dinner when hounds and horsemen arrived in the College grounds." Dr. Murray said the Mass which the Empress had attended, kneeling inside the rails of the sanctuary. The students had been given three free days. How they must have loved all this, as, celibate though they were, we can be sure that they were incurably romantic. A biography of 'Sissi' — for that is who she was, Elizabeth, daughter of Duke Max of Bavaria — was brought out by John Welcome towards the end of the 1960's. Its title is *The Sporting Empress.* She had been married at the age of sixteen to Franz Joseph, Emperor of Austria. She is said to have respected but never loved him, a not too unusual occurrence. In 1860 she had become ill. Queen Victoria had thought that it was anaemia, but she had made a wonderful recovery. Without doubt, she was bewitching, with amber eyes, auburn hair and fair complexion. Victoria says that she was a real beauty, but "speaks very low as she is rather shy" (September, 1863). She was supposed to be a bad communicator, for which reason she had a passion for animals, especially horses. In the case of Irish horses, this was strengthened by her friendship with Captain Middleton and her ability to travel incognito here. In Ireland she stayed at Lord Longford's place at Summerhill, Co Meath, and it was from there that she hunted to Maynooth. Clara Tschudi, in her *Elizabeth, Empress of Austria (*London, 1906), tells the story in her feminine way:

218

"In her younger days, she frequently stayed in Scotland and Ireland for the pleasure of fox-hunting, and it happened on one occasion when she was out with the hounds, that the fox fled for refuge into the grounds of the Roman Catholic College of Maynooth, where the students were just then enjoying a quarter of an hour's recreation. A high wall encloses the space, but they were suddenly startled by a fox springing into their midst, followed in a second by several hounds, and finally by an intrepid horsewoman.

The fox was caught, the lady alighted from the horse, addressed herself to the young men, and begged for an interview with their President.

As soon as he appeared, she introduced herself as Elizabeth, Empress of Austria, and requested to be allowed a room where she could dry her habit, for in her eager chase after the fox, she had urged her horse over a brook and her skirts had become literally wet through.

Dr. Logue, the present Roman Catholic Archbishop of Armagh, ordered a room to be prepared as quickly as possible, including a good fire.

It soon became evident that the Empress was far more thoroughly drenched than she had thought, and that it would be impossible to dry her habit in less than three or four hours.

No women live in the College, and consequently there is not a single feminine garment to be had, but Elizabeth begged the President to lend her one of his cassocks, in which she figured during the drying of her habit. She even invited her host and his masters to a cup of tea in her apartment, where they were all enraptured with her charms, as well as amused with her unique costume and the anecdotes she told them connected with her hunting and travelling experiences".

That is one story. How crossed can the lines get? Dr. Walsh, Dr. Logue, a toga or a cassock ? It is a good story anyhow. The President and his masters could not but be captivated, if not by the charms of the Empress, then by her hunting exploits. Almost to a man, they were foxhunters themselves. It lay with Dr. Walsh's relative, in his biography of the Archbishop, to tell the part that the latter played in the saga:

"Early in 1879, some months after the great fire, Her Imperial Majesty the Empress Elizabeth of Austria visited the college ... She came to Ireland in the early spring of 1879, travelling as the Countess of Hohenehms, and with a small retinue took up residence at Summerhill in the county of Meath. Summerhill was chosen because of its position in the midst of a hunting country ... On Monday, February 24, the Empress hunted with the Ward hounds. A stag which was enlarged at Batterstown gave a fine run through Meath and Kildare, and at about three o'clock in the afternoon the hunt reached Maynooth. The stag made his way into the college grounds through a temporary gateway which had been left open by a workman. The staghounds followed, and, close on their track, a huntress on a dark bay mount. It was the Empress. By the time that the main body of the hunt was arriving in scattered fragments, the stag had been rescued from the dogs and the Empress had dismounted. Meantime the residents of the college had been apprised of the adventure, and the Vice-President, Dr. Walsh, had come to invite the illustrious lady to partake of some light refreshment...... Apprehensive of catching a chill, as she was heated by her strenuous exertions, Her Imperial Majesty asked if she might have a wrap or shawl to put about her shoulders, whereupon Dr. Walsh divested himself of the light academic gown which he wore over his soutane, and the Empress having donned the gown, remarked that it suited her admirably ".

The fox has now yielded place to a stag, and Walsh is back in the centre of things. It seems to be the more accurate narrative:

"In memory of this visit she sent to Dr. Walsh from her Austrian capital a magnificent gold ring, with an olive stone inset, which he treasured until his death. She also invited him to the Austrian Imperial Court ..."

Some have said that the Empress told Dr. Walsh to keep this ring against the day of his appointment as Archbishop of Dublin, and that, when this happened, he wore it as his episcopal ring. Quien sabe ?

Walsh did go on to become Archbishop of Dublin. Long afterwards, J. B. Hall, in his *Random Records of a Reporter*, told about another encounter of a Maynooth Professor. It is similar yet at the same time very different from Walsh's meeting with the lady in 1879:

"Little more than a generation ago, the Very Revd. 'Dr. W' was one of the Professorial Staff ... On a bright Spring morning he went, as was his custom, for a walk on the Dublin Road ... Nearing Leixlip he met a middle-aged woman, apparently of the tramp class, haggard and shoeless. In her arms was a child, and a second ragged and barefooted youngster toddled alongside holding her by her tattered garment. They were clean and comely, but the pinch of hunger was in their faces. The woman curtsied and looked wistfully and appealingly. The priest paused, gave her a penny, and learning something of her story ... took compassion on her and suggested to her to call at the College ... She went to the College, as directed, and was given employment... Her two little boys were sent to the Convent Schools ... One of them, as time went on, was apprenticed to the trade of a tailor ... The other ... became a student for the priesthood ... At twenty-five he was offered one of the most important chairs at Oscott College and filled the Chair of Sacred Scripture... When he went on the Mission his remarkable mental gifts and acquirements developed ... and within a comparatively few years he was consecrated Bishop ... Years passed, ... the Bishop returned from beyond the seas to visit his Alma Mater ... As he passed the old familiar quadrangle ... one of the very first to kneel in reverence ... was the saintly and venerable 'Dr. W ' ".

One hopes that the good doctor was Whitehead, so passed over for so many things.

IN FAR OFF LANDS

The foreign missionary dimension of Maynooth should never be forgotten. On 13 September, 1867, Dr. Fennelly, Vicar Apostolic of Madras, returned to his old College and remained there until the 24th. He was to die the following January in India. It is difficult for people living in later times to construct an idea of what these missionaries had to cope with. In 1871, Dr. Fennelly's brother, who succeeded him, wrote to Russell: "Our communication with Europe is becoming more satis-factory every month. The London Mail via Brindisi now reaches Madras in 22 days and there is a prospect of the time of transit being further reduced. I intend to ordain three native priests next week and to promote some native lads to tonsure and minor orders". He had received the boxes he had left with the Jesuit fathers at Marseilles in July,but more than half the contents were plundered by the mob. "The Franco-Prussian War has been a calamity even to India in more ways than one". Later he wrote that in that year, he had an unusually large number of confirmations. Russell, for his part, was not forgetting India, all credit to him for that. In July the Propagation of the Faith in Paris was assuring him that the 12,000 francs for Madras would be paid immediately. That for Hobart Town has already been paid. Fennelly did get the francs in August and wrote to thank his helper. He asked him too to pay some bills for him, including those to All Hallows College. He has sent £250 to Cardinal Barnabo, being the collection in Madras for the Pope for the year 1870-71. It must have been hard on him to have to meet such demands. There is some evidence, though, that he was a good financier. In September

221

he was able to tell Russell that he had made an investment of 2,000 rupees in building on a piece of land in the leading street of Madras. The house will be let as a shop and will bring in over 600 rupees a year.

Fennelly had much discourse with Russell. In September he intimated that the maintenance of schools in his Vicariate was a heavy expense. He was going to try for Irish Christian Brothers, although in 1857 they had refused for lack of numbers. The Marist Brothers would be unlikely to go on a mission where there are no Marist fathers. By March, 1872, he had applied for men to the Superior of a French order of Brothers who had their headquarters at Colombo in Ceylon. He did not care for them as teachers but what could he do ? Recently, he had been in a portion of the Nizam's country, situated between the river Kisihna and the Toonga border. There were nearly 1,000 Christians there who never saw a Bishop before. The railroad was a great help to the Madras Mission. It had helped him to accomplish in one month what could not possibly be done before even in four months. He did not know what the new Governor would be like but was sorry to have lost Lord Napier. In May, he was looking for a couple of nuns, nuns with a knowledge of music and capable of teaching. They had a very severe storm in Madras on 2 May, some thirty ships large and small being wrecked and fifty or sixty people killed. Four hundred people were killed about eighty miles away. He felt that the loss of shipping was to be set down to the carelessness of the Marine Department and the ship captains as a storm had been indicated on 1 May and the shipping should have gone to sea instead of remaining in one of the most treacherous roadsteads in the world. The Mission house sustained no damage worth mentioning. In August, he was reporting that Madras had been visited by a "very troublesome sort of fever, which is supposed to have been imported from the East coast of Africa. They call the scourge *Dengue* fever but why no one can tell". He gave an account of how it affected people. Fully 80% of the population of Madras had contracted it.

Whether or not the Maynooth College Trustees retained confidence in the imperial sub-continent can only be guessed for their instructing the Bursar in September, 1872, to sell the India 5 per cent Stock, which the College held, in order to provide money to purchase Dr. O'Hanlon's library. Fennelly got the fever himself in October and for four weeks was *hors de combat.* He revived and visited an out-station shortly afterwards:

"I came to K. last evening. This place was formerly a military station and we had then from 2 to 300 Christians here. Since the military were removed two years ago, many of the Christians, who were Sepoys or camp followers, left with them: at present there are only 120 Catholics — all very poor. John (his brother) visited this place ten years ago. It was then a tedious journey of at least 20 days from Madras. Now the Railway has brought it within easy reach. "I left Madras at 2 p.m. on Monday. I said Mass and gave confirmation on Tuesday at Gooty, 257 miles from Madras — left the afternoon on the same day for this place and got over the distance, 62 miles, in a coach drawn by Bullocks in a little over 24 hours".

It has to be supposed that writing to people at home like this gave a man like him some solace and at least he had the comfort of a reasonably swift post, unlike much later days. By January, 1873, he had completed twenty-nine years in Madras ! His problem now was the new Governor, Lord Hobart. He is not likely to be a favourite but will probably be fair to Catholics. He could do with more priests. In September, he is saying that he has heard that the English Bishops intend to send out some military chaplains and wishes that they would send "missionary priests"

rather than "gentleman chaplains". He is critical of the Irish too, of the priests now being turned out by All Hallows and of the Irish regiments in the British Army: "It is a singular fact that the Irish soldiers who come now to India are a very degenerate set of fellows, in no way equal to the men whom I found in India on my arrival. The old soldiers would give their last rupee in aid of religion or charity. Those of the present time give little or nothing to support the orphans of their deceased comrades. There are over 200 Catholics in the Regiment at present in Fort St. George and they only subscribed last year for the orphanage Rupees 64". In former times, he asserts, it would have been 3 Rupees a month per man, i.e., 6 pence a month.

In March, 1874, he is seriously thinking of "a run" to Ireland. At the mission, affairs at the moment are satisfactory, but he cannot live much longer. He wonders would the Vincentian Fathers take Madras, as it would always be somewhat difficult for an Irish secular Bishop to get priests for it. If the Vincentians decline, he could apply to the Irish Oblates. He was a great man, who had dedicated his life to that mission and was now trying to ensure that it lasted after him. It did not, at least not as he expected it might, but that was not his fault. In April, 1874, he is happy for small mercies. The 'Orion' has landed with the goods which he had ordered from Dublin, but he complains that, unlike London businessmen, who always send their invoices and bills of lading at the same time, when goods come from Dublin one or both are invariably not forthcoming. He has got the latter but not the former and this will cause him trouble with the Customs.

But Madras was not the only 'foreign mission' in which Maynooth had then a hand. In April, 1874, the Bishop of Providence, Rhode Island, was asking Russell to try to get him priests from Maynooth. He even sent the passage money for five. He is sure they would like the mission if they went: "There is not a priest in my diocese who would accept of a parish in Ireland". It is a refrain which has been heard long since and for the same reason which he gave — the more interesting nature of the work abroad. Russell tried to get priests for him but it is not clear whether he succeeded. The Bishop was magnanimous. In July he sent Russell £100 as a subscription towards the new College chapel: he is now getting priests not only from Ireland but also from Germany and Portugal, and has quite a lot of students for the priesthood, whomsoever of them will persevere: "Bishops have a hard up-hill work out here, and it is only God who can console them".

The Times of London was aware of no such problems. On 20 November, 1875, it had nothing much to record. The Prince of Wales was in India and the best it could do was to report a message from Baroda by 'Indo-European Telegraph' that "there was an elephant fight at 2 today. The weather is much better than it was at Bombay. The Prince is quite well". Dr. Fennelly was continuing his struggle. In May, 1876, he had secured some Mill Hill priests — he now had twenty-nine priests in all. Victoria was proclaimed Empress of India ...

TOWARDS A COLLEGE CHAPEL

The President of Maynooth, whatever may have been his interests in India, was at the same time engaged in planning a new College Chapel at home. In October, 1874, the Archbishop of Cashel, Dr. Leahy, had suggested to him that J. J. McCarthy, a pupil of Pugin's, would be a suitable architect for it. He was appointed in January, 1875. Russell's drive for funds was getting results. Lord O'Hagan, now the first Irish Catholic Chancellor and a good friend of his, was so generous that Russell had to persuade him to cut down his subscription. Dr. Butler of Limerick had also been generous, as had the new Bishop of Cloyne, Dr. McCarthy. In 1875, the Trustees advanced an idea for increasing their number to thirty but McHale had dissented successfully. In June, the President informed them about a bequest of 28,000 'Rubles' by Dr. James Quinlan of Co. Tipperary, who had settled in Moscow as domestic physician to the family of Prince Galitzin, but owing to legal difficulties regarding the will, the College could not claim the legacy. James Roche of Wexford was upset because two Ferns priests at Louvain were the only Irish students in Belgium without 'Bourses' which, if they did not get them, might fall into the hands of "Belgian young men". On 20 September, the Bishops, assembled at Maynooth in another National Synod, launched a formal appeal for the new chapel; a collection was to be held on 17 March, 1876.

On 27 September, Charles Bianconi, the pioneer of Irish road travel, died. On the same day, Newman wrote to Russell, envisaging the laying of the foundation stone of the chapel: "The great day is at length granted to you which you have so long desired and had in prayer. You have now for many years had collegiate buildings suitable to the dignity of the largest and most important ecclesiastical seminary in Catholic Christendom — suitable, as far as they went, for the chief part of the original design had yet to be brought into effect. The foremost inquiry which occurred to the many strangers visiting Maynooth had hitherto been — where was the church ?... But now, with the Divine blessing, this desideratum is to be supplied. When the day comes, you and yours will be in my thoughts, and I shall take part in your auspicious act and its attendant festivities, as if I were not so many miles away ".

On Sunday, 10 October, the foundation stone was laid; it was the Feast of the Dedication of the Churches of Ireland. Dr. Moriarty of Kerry preached the sermon, and quite a sermon it was: He brought home to the College its continuing purpose, after recalling its achievements to date:

> "While we rejoice, however, in these memories of the past, and in the learning and piety which now adorn our national institution, we must remember that it is the house of God, in its midst, that all its energies find their centre. When the 'corpus

academicum' kneels before the altar, then the science, which by itself alone puffeth up, is informed and enlivened by the charity that edifieth. It is there that the gifts bestowed by nature or acquired by study are raised to the supernatural order – are stamped with God's seal, and are made fruitful in blessing for those who possess them, and for those who will receive of their fullness. It is thus that our College Church must exert influence and hold predominance over the churches of Ireland ".

Whatever about 'predominance', the basic sentiment must hold as long as Maynooth College retains its identity.

Dr. Whitehead composed a Latin poem for the occasion, part of which went like this:

"Desinant fletus, gemitusque cessent,
Alma nunc Mater ! nova surget aedes,
Christus ut tecum habitare possit Cultus honeste".

Father Joseph O'Farrell, of the Diocese of Kildare, wrote a triplet, of which the first remembered the strivings of the past:

"It comes, a white day, rising on a Church
Whose history knows so few, that its white days
Might all be told on fingers of one hand".

It was true, yet the poet also rejoiced in what Maynooth had done and what it hoped to do. Aubrey de Vere added his skill in other verses:

"Not vain the faith and patience of the Saints !
Not vain, sad Isle, thy many-centuried woes !
Thy day was tempest-cradled; but its close
Is splendour...."

The chapel was not yet built, and it took time and effort before it was finished. Bishops were telling Russell that they had plenty of problems in their own domains which precluded their contributing to its completion. McCarthy of Cloyne had to finish the cathedral at Cobh; Ardagh too was repairing its cathedral. Elphin was collecting for a cathedral. Other dioceses had other problems. But all did what they could; collections were held and the work progressed. As McGettigan of Armagh put it: "The feeling is universal as to the necessity of making a great effort for the College". Dr. Cullen was old and unwell – silent – soon to be succeeded by Dr. McCabe. Eventually a contract was offered, to a Mr. Hammond, who at first refused to sign it. He was willing to undertake it only if the conditions adopted by the Board of Works in their contracts were adhered to — shades of Pugin's days ! In the end his tender was accepted.

The cash began to come in. The Bishop of Waterford, though, stipulated that a list of the contributing parishes in his diocese be published in *The Freeman's Journal* and a copy of the paper sent to his parish priests. In December, 1876, when coming back from the Christmas holidays, Russell had a nasty experience:

> "On my way down from the station, in the storm on Tuesday night, my portmanteau dropped off the car; and, although we returned the route at once, it was not to be found, nor have the police been able to make it out since. Unhappily, it contained a parcel of cheques, with some cash, and a number of accounts and papers about the Church Fund, which are of the utmost consequence to me ... I have everything set in motion to make it out, and I must wait here till the end shall be seen".

He was writing from Dundalk. A reward was offered for the recovery of what he had lost. It was restored by night to his brother but only after he had returned to Maynooth. The reward was duly given.

It took a long time to raise the chapel monies. In February, 1877, Bishop Nulty of Meath outlined a litany of reasons as to why he was worried about the Maynooth drive. He has recently been asked for so many collections — for the Catholic University, for "a Benedictine monastery somewhere near Dublin", for the new Training School for Teachers, for the new episcopal house, for the Mercy Convent, for the new Diocesan Seminary. He would incur odium by giving preference to Maynooth. Moriarty of Kerry was also concerned about his seminary and about getting something for the Pope's Jubilee: "Hard it is to get anything out of these Kerry mountaineers. They have wealth in kind, i.e., in Kerry cows and goats but not in cash".

On 16 May, 1877, Dr. Russell was thrown from his horse in the street of Maynooth. He never recovered from the shock, even though he lived for a long time after. On 10 June, Nulty wrote to Dr. McCarthy, the Vice-President: "The intelligence of poor Dr. Russell's continued and critical illness is very distressing indeed. I knew people to differ with Dr. Russell on many points: but I never knew one who did not firmly believe that his learning, erudition and priestly virtues made him beyond doubt the *first Priest* in Ireland and the chief glory of our National College. Believe me there is scarcely a homestead in Ireland over which the news of his illness has not cast a painful gloom". In July, Russell's last article was published in *The Edinburgh Review*, on 'The Pseudo-Sibylline Poems'; it had been among the papers which he had lost at Christmas, 1876.

The Trustees continued as usual. That June they arranged that a tribune

227

opening from the Professor's Corridor into the new chapel was desirable and that a tender for the work, amounting to £46 be accepted. In October they authorised a new collection for the chapel, the existing fund being "all but exhausted". They were particularly anxious that collections be taken up in dioceses where as yet they had not been made.

FIRE! – 1878

Friday, 1 November, 1878, saw the first big fire at Maynooth College. Murray tells about it in his diary:

"On that day, as I was, about 12 minutes past 8, returning to my room after celebrating Mass in the Junior Chapel, Doc. Gargan met me on the esplanade opposite Dr. Russell's room, crying out 'Dr. Murray, St. Mary's is on fire, the whole of this college will be burned'. In a moment I saw the tongues of flame playing on the roof of St. Mary's in the Southern corner near to the tall chimney. I then ran to my room, opened my press, took out the money lying there (under £20), put on my greatcoat over my soutane, took my breviary under my arm – The Raccolta I had already in my hand coming from the chapel – glanced over my bookshelves. So stunned and paralyzed was I that all around seemed like so much dust and ashes. I had not the slightest wish or impulse to take anything with me but the three above-mentioned articles. I thus left under the conviction that within a couple of hours everything in my rooms, books, manuscripts, etc. would be consumed. The flames were now spreading rapidly to the north over St. Mary's, to the south over the oratory. In about half an hour I returned to my rooms to take a last farewell, looked around with the same vacant stupor as before, and left under the conviction I should never enter them again. Meantime, a number of the students, all seniors, I believe, had been most zealously engaged in removing the books from the great library. One of them came to me, and asked me to let my books also be removed. 'No', said I, 'let them burn, I care for nothing now in this world'. In this state of mind I wandered about from group to group of students and externs watching the exertions of the fire brigade and others engaged in stemming the progress of the fire. As there was no chance of saving the south section of St. Mary's or the oratory, all energies were directed to prevent the flames from reaching the north half of St. Mary's or touching the library, especially the latter: for had the library taken fire, the whole of that wing and of St. Patrick's, the wing in which I live, would have been reduced to ashes. About 2 o'clock or earlier the assurance came that the library was quite safe with strong hopes of the north half of St. Mary's. This assurance though allaying was far from extinguishing the mental agitation under which I had been labouring for so many hours .. Four or five students narrowly and as if miraculously escaped with their lives. Nearly forty lost all their property ... All the sacred ornaments and utensils of the Oratory, with the exception of a large cross of not much value, were saved".

The Freeman's Journal gave its own account of the fire. It says that it began at a point adjoining the senior oratory and the reading room, close to the library, and was caused by the over-heating of a boiler. There had been difficulty experienced in summoning the fire brigade:

"As is only too frequently the case, when the wires are earnestly needed, they are found to be utterly useless. So it was today, when a breathless message from the College attempted to invoke the aid of the Municipal Fire Brigade. 'The instrument is out of order, sir, and I cannot send your message' was the reply of the fair operator at the Maynooth Post Office. The instrument (save the mark) was an A.B.C. — the most worthless construction in the postal service, and one which even in apple-pie order is not deserving houseroom in any office of a civilized country".

The media said things differently in the 19th century.

After some time, word got through by the College 'instrument', and Lieutenant Byrne and his men (Captain Ingram being ill) set out on horse carriage and steam engine to the Broadstone Station to get a train for Maynooth. They left at 10.20 a.m. Meanwhile the "rusty and dusty" College hoses were being used, also the hand engine owned by the Duke of Leinster, as well as scores of buckets. *The Freeman* continued:

"From the bedroom windows came pell-mell the beds and clothes, the books and pictures of the students. As a means of saving property this proceeding was wholly ineffectual, for the fall was so great that chairs and tables and beds and books went smash upon alighting, and perhaps the only good this action achieved was the removal from the very jaws of the fire of a ready fuel".

The brigade arrived with "clashing and clanging" just after 11 a.m. and was cheered as it entered the College. The library was quickly saved by cutting it off, but before that every volume had been removed to safety.

"The scene about the burning premises was indeed a strange

229

one. The 'saved' property lay about the grass in endless confusion. Here was a table wanting a leg, there a chair with a broken back, whilst close by lay a pile of crumbling stationery, half covered by a mass of well-watered wearing apparel. The books and papers that came through the bed-room windows looked decidedlv the worse for their flight".

Great tribute was paid to the "special" efforts of the firemen; a couple of them had a narrow escape when the third floor came in. In the afternoon Captain Ingram "muffled himself" and came down by special train, an action that was much appreciated by the College authorities. Sir Ralph Cusack personally supervised the dispatch of the special trains. There were also many constabulary present, but their services as "order keepers" were not required. The journalist from *The Freeman* had a field day:

"As I left the College (six o'clock) things were rapidly getting back to their wonted quiet. The fire had altogether halted on its destructive march, students' eyes were again turning to the pages of their books, and as the Angelus rang out in the clear evening air prayers were offered up with a devotion and earnestness not one whit disturbed by the stirring affairs of an eventful day in the history of the time-honoured College of Maynooth."

The paper devoted a leading article to the fire also, giving a short sketch of the history of the College and an account of the Maynooth Question of 1845 and how it had "convulsed the Empire and decided the fate of parliaments and Cabinets". Maynooth College, it said, had developed from "the tottering house of the Duke of Leinster's steward ... into that noble quadrangle which bears all the marks and genius of Pugin, and even in its unfinished state may compare with the stateliest in the Quartier Latin or the High-street of Oxford". The catastrophe was termed "a national disaster".

William Hanton, in his 1923 article in *The Irish Ecclesiastical Record*, also wrote about the fire, and there is an amusing piece in Walsh's life of Walsh:

"The outbreak of the fire occurred on a Friday. The firemen when reached Maynooth about 11 a.m. were strenuously engaged for some hours after their arrival in getting the fire under control, and when in the afternoon they were free to partake of some much-needed refreshment they found themselves seated at tables with joints of beef and mutton set before them. Dr. Walsh explained to the men that, although the day was Friday, owing to the lack of abstinence fare and to the fact that the men themselves had been so strenuously engaged in exhausting work, they might without scruple partake of the

230

flesh-meat with which they were being served. A theological student who was present – a young man who had been studying the treatises 'De Ieiunio et Abstinentia' – quietly asked Dr. Walsh if he were justified in granting a general dispensation in the ecclesiastical law of abstinence. The Vice-president explained that he had not dispensed, but had merely declared the men exempt from the ecclesiastical law – that it was a case of Epieikeia. A Fireman who had overheard the remark turned to Dr. Walsh, and said: 'Your reverence, what kind of a case did you say it was?' 'A case of Epieikeia', he replied. 'Well, Father', said the man, 'I don't care what it means; but even if it was a case of whiskey, I could not bring myself to break the fast by eating meat on a Friday. And he remained fixed in his determination".

A very different story was told after the fire of 1940, when Dr. Coffey, Professor of Philosophy and total abstainer, is said to have poured more than a generous libation for some of the firemen, who were afterwards found rambling at the top of the College park.

The London *Graphic* reported the fire of 1878 as occurring on Guy Fawkes's day and carried an engraving of the College the day after it. It noted that the Lord Mayor of Dublin, in dispatching the fire brigade, had broken through a rule that it should never leave the city "in consideration of the College being a national institution". It noted too that delay had been caused by a difficulty in getting horses to draw the engine from the railway station. There was no truth in the rumour that several persons had been injured and one student killed. Oxbridge, though, looked different that day: "At Oxford and Cambridge, the undergraduates were more than usually orderly, the Town and Gown riots being evidently looked upon as a bygone custom. On Friday last Maynooth College was partially destroyed by fire, the damage being estimated at 30,000 1".

Quickly off their marks, the Trustees met on 4 November, and expressed gratitude to all who had helped, including the employees of the College itself, for their "intelligent and unremitting exertions". The losses to the students would be made good. Next day, the Vice-President had a letter in *The Freeman*, which conveyed his thanks, but also scotched a rumour to the effect that the College fire brigade had been a hindrance rather than a help during the blaze. The workmen on the new College chapel had also helped and were included in the thanks, as well as was Lord Maurice Fitzgerald who (the Duke being away) had come in person to the College on the day of the fire and offered what facilities Carton could extend. Clongowes had also offered to open its doors to Maynooth if required.

Very shortly, plans for rebuilding were prepared, aided by a substantial insurance award from the Sun Fire Company. A narrow-minded proposal to rebuild only the eastern wing had been fortunately rejected. The President continued to be unwell and was given further leave of absence in June, 1879. The students had sought their own leave of absence, an extension of the previous Christmas vacation, giving as reason for it the 'delicacy' which was caused to them by the fire and the need for a 'change of air'. A number of bishops were taken in by them. Nulty of Meath swore that he "would try to be 'wise' for the future and I promise that even a 'fire' won't take me in a second time". Eighty students had taken French leave — one of them by the name of Joseph McRory of Armagh !

UNIVERSITY ASPIRATIONS

And so, the eighteen-seventies came towards an end, with the College somewhat rattled yet vigorous. Its perils were compounded by the development of the Catholic University. As early as 1866, the Professor of Chemistry there had argued that Maynooth students should not be reckoned as university students at all, hence the need for a real university elsewhere. In 1867, another writer, Thomas Andrews, had argued conversely that Maynooth should be raised to the status of a university, a lay college being added. But it should be seen to it that it remained independent. It would be lamentable if it were to be dominated by one or two powerful ecclesiastics. "If Maynooth were so fortunate as to have a Dumas teaching chemistry, a Regnault teaching physics, or a Rokitanski teaching pathology, will any one doubt that students would proceed thither not only from all parts of Ireland but also from Gt. Britain ?" But it was easier said than done.

The new secular colleges posed an even greater threat, and the Bishops were opposed to them for many reasons. Gladstone sought compromise in his Universities Bill (1873), which proposed to replace the Queen's University by a merger of two Queen's Colleges, i.e., Belfast, and Cork with Trinity and the Catholic University — in a federal University of Dublin. Magee College in Derry was to be linked with the scheme but Queen's College, Galway, was to be suppressed. There was no reference to Maynooth.

The Bishops were not at all happy about the scheme. McGettigan to Russell on 25 February: "The difficult question of the University Bill is to come before the Bishops at their meeting in Dublin next Thursday. The proposed measure is in bad odour with Catholics. It does not give them a good start. They have little or no chance to compete successfully with Insitutions left richly endowed". The Bill was defeated on 11 March, and the 'merger' idea was over for nearly a century. It had been defeated by a margin of only three votes (187 to 184). It was said by some that Gladstone was convinced that the reason for its defeat was an underhand intrigue between the Carlton Club and Maynooth College.

Life in the College had continued. At this time, the most notable horsemen among the staff were Drs. Molloy and Walsh. William Hanton says of them: "My feelings towards these horsemen were those of jealousy. I often dawdled about the old senior chapel, seeing those professors ascend their steeds. I now see vividly in my mind's eye, Dr. Walsh and Dr. Molloy putting a horse through his paces in the square, the eye of an expert, pointing out the incipient ring bone or spavin". Another horseman of repute towards the end of the century was Dr. Owens, Dean and later Professor of Dogmatic Theology, although his mount was not always reliable. Dr. Russell, of course was also a great horseman. But literature always remained his first love. In 1874, he was flattered by Newman's dedicating a new edition of his "old favourite" *Loss and Gain* to him. He thanked Newman warmly for it and added: "There is no incident in my life to which I took more pride than to my having found a place in your *Apologia*". He confessed too that he had been more moved by reading *Loss and Gain* than by any other work of fiction. He had tried to read it aloud at home when it first came out but broke down in the attempt.

That June, Dr. Molloy resigned his Chair at Maynooth to take up the Vice-Rectorship of the Catholic University. The Primate of Armagh, feeling that the concursus to fill the vacancy would come off during the coming Summer vacation, was sorry that this would interfere with the "playdays" of the staff, which would be unfair "after the anxieties and labours of the year". He gave permission to one of his priests – the Reverend Michael Logue – to contest the chair, which he did but did not get it; it went to Dr. Carr, who was also to be a distinguished horseman as well as professor. Logue was to miss out an appointment until 1878, the Primate making the best of things by saying that he had assigned him to "the more laborious Mission in the Diocese" – McGettigan himself had never been on the staff.

During 1875, a National Synod was held in the College, opening on Tuesday, 31 August. The Bishops came from all over the country, accompanied in many cases by their theologians. The Bishop of Limerick, Dr. Butler, nominated Dr. Whitehead to be his; he had a standing connection with the Diocese of Limerick. At 10 a.m. the prelates assembled in St. Joseph's chapel and walked in procession through the square to the College Chapel "with the ecclesiastical paraphernalia formed by the Rev. officers" *(The Times,* 1 Sept.). Fitzpatrick, in his life of Fr. Thomas Burke, O.P., recalled the following anecdote told by one of the Munster Bishops:

"Previous to a great synodal meeting at Maynooth College, prelates and priests were thickly clustered in one of its halls. Fr. Burke's physician had recently urged him, in consequence of the state of his health, never to travel any great distance without a flask of brandy. This was to serve the double purpose of a lotion, and also as a stimulant in case of sudden prostration.

233

On the present occasion he carried a coat under his arm. Suddenly a bottle fell crashing on the flags, diffusing around a more pungent aroma than the odour of sanctity. Another man would have been disconcerted, but with ready tact Burke remarked to their Lordships, 'Dr. Leahy will kill me for having broken his bottle of brandy'. To enjoy this joke one should know something of the mortified life of the saintly Bishop of Dromore".

It is unlikely that the President was unduly disturbed by the activities of the Synod, except insofar as he had to see to it that the participants had proper accommodation. He was preparing to write a 'Critical History of the Sonnet' and shortly began to engage in correspondence relating to it with a Fellow of Trinity and Aubrey de Vere. It was published in *The Edinburgh Review*, in October, 1876 and January, 1877.

Since 1875, a scheme for a closer connection between Maynooth and the Catholic University had been under consideration. To this end, in the July of that year, the Trustees had ordered that the courses in the College be brought into line as much as possible with those of the University so that common examinations could be held. Another of their recommendations had been "that the circulation of fresh air through the Oratories, Halls and rooms of the College should be more carefully attended to by the Deans and Monitors"!! Even though it had proved impossible to make their respective courses identical, because of the difference in purpose of the two institutions, by October, 1876, the Trustees agreed "that the College of Maynooth be declared to be a college of the Catholic University of Ireland and that the connection between the two Institutions shall make no change in the constitution or government of the College and that the President and Vice-President be ex-officio members of the Senate of the University". The Faculty of Theology was to consist of the existing theological faculty of the University together with the Faculty of Theology at Maynooth, and the other Professors at Maynooth were to be

234

ex officio examiners of the University. Maynooth students would be eligible to become Doctors of Theology of the University, the examinations being held either in Maynooth or in the University Buildings, "as the Trustees of the College may direct", but the degree of doctor was to be solemnly conferred at Maynooth. The arrangement never seems to have come to much.

In 1877, Gladstone visited Maynooth, in the course of his only visit to Ireland. It was on Monday, 5 November, in the forenoon. One of the Deans, Fr. Thomas Hammond of Limerick, tells us that he was well received, even though "it was hinted to him that his Vatican pamphlets were not forgotten". Hanton tells us that Gladstone walked around the grounds and paid a visit to the Physics Hall, where he asked the Professor some questions on the experiments that were being conducted there. Years afterwards, J. B. Hall, in his *Random Records of a Reporter*, had this to say:

> "The visit to Maynooth did not occupy very long, but it was very interesting, especially the examination of the library, to the contents of which Mr. Gladstone devoted the most eager interest examining the catalogue and pouring out a flood of questions as to each volume. The principal wealth of the library was, of course, theological, and the number of bibles in many languages, the rare manuscripts and works on all phases of religious expression constitute a natural and appropriate feature and the visitor showed characteristic expertness in his queries and commentaries on the wealth of literature shown him. He strode rapidly through the grounds and was shown the celebrated yew tree which Petrie declared to be at least 800 years old and said to be one of the largest in the world. Mr. Gladstone walked around it with what I thought a hungry look, and when shown two noble chestnuts further on, he instantly said that he would 'dearly like to cut one of them down'. The old castle of the Geraldines afforded subject matter for any amount of historical records to be revived and discussed by the ononiferous statesman".

Even though scientific experimentation continued at Maynooth, the great days of Callan were over. The College had to await the new century before recovering its distinction in the field of science. The Catholic University held the field for a while. In the middle of August, 1878, a 'scientific festivity' was held at its buildings in Dublin. It was a great success and was reported by *The Freeman:*

> "High over the front of the University buildings there blazed an electric light, which lit the crowded entrance with the light of day, and in whose exceeding brilliance 'the moon's eye had a

235

sickly glare' …. The 'great hall' was, so to speak, the main reservoir of visitors … On a high dais, at its head and down the hall at either side, the refreshment tables were most hospitably spread; at the foot a variety of scientific apparatus were displayed. Mind and body were, so to speak, fed together … It would be a work as hopeless as numbering the stars to attempt a seriatim description of the various instruments and inventions displayed … St. Stanislaus Jesuit College of Tullamore contributed a variety of telephones and microphones … Castleknock College also contributed some most delicate and ingenious instruments... As we said at the beginning, we may repeat in the end, the conversazione was a splendid treat to the distinguished foreigners who were present. To the men of all creeds and positions in Dublin who thronged the halls it afforded the most emphatic refutation of the foul calumny which dares proclaim that the Catholic Church is the enemy of scientific truth and progress".

Maynooth temporarily even felt the pinch in the number of its students. It was quite low in 1877 and the *President's Archives* contain scribbled notes by Dr. Walsh (then Vice-President) which show that, before the intake of 1878, he was endeavouring to project what it might be — something of the kind to be done again by a successor of his nearly a century later. In 1879, the total number was only 432.

The Afghan War was still on. Reports were coming in from Simla that the replies of the "Ameer", Shere Ali, were, as *The Freeman's Journal* put it, "discourteous and altogether unsatisfactory" (1 November, 1878). An ultimatum was to be sent to him in a last effort to avert full-scale war. Russian officers were being reported among the Afghans (*Freeman*, 4 November) … The Maynooth Trustees were more concerned about absenteeism, this time in the ranks of the Professors. Senior students were regularly being employed by them to take their classes. Other professors were also forced to double up. In May, Bishop Nulty wrote to Walsh that if a Professor "from long experience finds he is not able to do his work, he ought to resign", and in June the Trustees tried to regulate the matter. That very October, Walsh himself was dispensed for a year from his classes, but this presumably was to facilitate him as acting President. John Healy of Tuam became Professor of Theology, signing his notes, after the concursus, 'John Healy, Super-theologian'. And a former Professor, Dean Neville, now Rector of the Catholic University, wrote an article for *The Dublin Review*, which maintained that Maynooth during the earlier part of the century had indeed been Gallican in tendency, even though it had outlived that. Walsh tried to refute the contention both in *The Dublin* and in *The Tablet*, but Neville was obdurate in his insistence. He ought to have known; he had been among those Maynooth Professors about whom Rome had been unsure.

Chapter VIII

The Closing Years

On 22 June, 1880, William J. Walsh was appointed President. The following morning at 8 o'clock, he made the usual profession of faith and the declaration made by an incoming President. Like his predecessor, he too was a scholarly man, but there was a greater range of political interest in his character. Later on, as Archbishop of Dublin, he was to be actively engaged in the machinations of the Land War.

In view of that, it is an unusual coincidence that one of his first problems as President of the College should have been about land. For some time, the Trustees had been engaged in land transactions. It seems to have had something to do with the investment of the funds which they had received after the disestablishment of 1869. In 1872, they lent the huge sum of £91,597.7.2 to the Earl of Granard on the security of His Lordship's Longford and Leitrim estates and that of the tenants who occupied these. In 1877, they had tangled with the new Duke of Leinster about the rent for the 'Larabryan Farm', praying him to leave his father's arrangements unaltered. They had been in peaceful possession of it since 1849 under their old friend, the third Duke. Now the fourth Duke wanted to raise the rent. The Trustees had refused and the Duke prepared to evict them. On the day of Walsh's appointment, they acknowledged receipt of £1,000 from him in compensation "for improvements made by the College in the Larraghbrien Farm" — but also, with unusual imprudence, granted a mortgage loan of £25,000 at 4½% to Lord Cloncurry in respect of the Lyons estate not too far from the College.

When, in 1881, Gladstone brought in a new Land Bill, Bishop Butler of Limerick asked Walsh for a simple, layman's account of it. It seemed to the Bishop to be the most abstruse document since the Apocalypse — "the meaning when there is any, is so veiled and hidden away that ordinary men·cannot even take a decent guess of it". The result was Walsh's 'Exposition of the Gladstone Act' which, said *The Tablet*, "made

237

that measure clear, amongst others, to the author of it". It was not for nothing that later on Gladstone's Government resolutely opposed Walsh for the Archbishopric of Dublin. Whatever of this, the small Irish land tenants were far from happy with the arrangements. They decided to take the matter into their own hands. The result, in the case of the Maynooth loan to Granard, was anything but helpful.

In the meantime, the Duke of Leinster had evicted the Trustees from the farm at "Loraghbryan", as the *Evidence before the Royal Commission of the Irish Land Acts* spells it. The President had given evidence to the Commission, but all to no avail. For a while relations with Carton were quite strained. Even the students ceased temporarily from taking their public walk through the demesne. Dr. Healy alone continued to call there. Healy was an inveterate walker. His biographer informs us that he often used to walk with his dog and gun all the way from Maynooth to Enniskerry to visit his mother, who was then living there. By 1883 relations with Carton seem to have been better. That November the Duke brought Trevelyan, the Chief Secretary to the Lord Lieutenant, to visit the College. Trevelyan later wrote to the President to thank him for his reception and added: "We were very much interested by our visit, seldom more by anything I have ever seen."

Financial matters bogged down the administration. In 1881, Logue, Bishop of Raphoe since 1879, must have felt that Walsh could do with a change. He invited him up for a week: "You could not have a better opportunity of seeing the Wilds ... A breeze from the Donegal mountains would sweep away the dust of the schools in a very few days". He certainly could have done with a change. He was weighed down under a mountain of papers. So plagued were the Trustees with certificates and legal documents, that in June they commissioned a plan for a Muniment Room.

The ultimate fate of the Granard loan was a blow to the finances of the College. By then, Dr. Robert Browne was College President. In 1888, the Trustees sought to appoint a Court Receiver in the case, but Judge Monroe gave judgement against them, decreeing that proceedings should be conducted by Messrs Crozier, solicitors to the Earl. It was ironical that the Plan of Campaign, which Walsh was then doing his utmost to defend, was central to the agitation which had precipitated the Granard crisis. The Trustees made good what they could, refusing to remit any of the interest due by the tenants or to reduce the rate of interest. Walsh called the whole thing "embarrassing".

By 1890, he was agitated that the entire Maynooth claim might be lost and urged the President to do his utmost about it with the Solicitor, P. A. Chance: "Do not allow it to appear that you are acting except on your own initiative. But do not allow yourself to be put off with any vague assurances". In the heel of the hunt, it was decided to sell the castle and demesne on the Granard Estate, an intervention by Lady Granard having been bypassed.

It certainly was embarrassing and in more ways than one. Bishop Mc Cormack of Galway urged that the claim to arrears and interest due by the tenants be dropped. By April, 1891, part of the estate had been sold. The other part had not yet been sold because the offer of the tenants had been too low. The President wrote to Fr. Conefrey, the tenant's representative in the matter, and got him to call a meeting at which they agreed to make a thirteen years purchase. The offer was accepted. That December, the Finance Council recorded that, when the demesne and mansion had been sold, the total realized should be about £100,000.

A change of heart took place in relation to the sale of the castle and demesne; in 1892 they were offered to Lady Granard for £5,000 cash and a mortgage. Shortly afterwards, the Trustees also agreed to sell to Lady Granard the village of Newtown Forbes "provided that her offer be at least equally satisfactory with that of the tenants". At the same time, they refused point blank to pay any higher rent for the "Larraghbrien farm". The President, Bursar and others were thanked for the efficient way in which they had handled the Newtown Forbes business, but the Trustees had had enough of land troubles. Whatever had persuaded them to become involved in Granard — possibly a desire to be 'landed' like Trinity College — or to support those big landowners who were Catholic — it had landed them into the Irish agrarian troubles of the time, and in a way that was doubly embarrassing for Archbishop Walsh. When it was over, a large fire proof safe for legal documents was acquired by the Bursar — with three locks, one key to be kept by the Archbishop of Dublin, one by the President, and one by the Bursar. It was the end of an unfortunate affair.

END OF A DIARY

These years also saw the passing from the scene of many of the figures who had been familiar in Maynooth. On 31 December, 1871, Dr. John O'Hanlon was found dead in his room. Murray recalled that a servant had seen him only a few minutes before. He paid his respects to the deceased next day, and as he pondered over the controversies now long gone by, the tears rolled down his cheeks. He felt that his own death could not be far off: "It cannot be distant now. *Miserere Domine*".

In April, 1874, one of the Deans, the Reverend James O'Kane, had died — also found insensible in his own room. He had been out driving with Mr. Tully the night before. Murray reflected that this was part of a succession of sudden deaths to have occurred in the College within twelve years — Callan (1864), Jennings (1862), O'Hanlon (1871). October, 1876, was to see the demise of Mr. Tully, Professor of Irish in the College since 1828.

Then on 24 January, 1878, came the death of Murray's great friend, the theologian Dr. George Crolly. His death put Murray into a depression for the rest of the year: "He had other companions but for more than a quarter of a century he was my only companion. He had in the Spring of last year come to live beside me in Mr. Tully's old rooms. He had done little more than transfer his books and furniture, intending to arrange them afterwards, when he left for vacation, to return no more except in his coffin... I have now no companion in our community to wander or walk with any more". He told Gavan Duffy this, in just those words, in a letter of 12 November, 1880. He had not seen him during his last visit and is very regretful of this. Then: "My dear Sir Charles, ... I am very lonely since poor Crolly's death (did you get the notice I sent you through one of our servants?) He was my only companion here for more than 25 years. Death has made great havoc here of late. Within little more than 13 years, five of our community have gone".

Death had not finished yet. In October, Cardinal Cullen went to his reward. Of him Murray wrote: "He came here as Archb. of Armagh with very strong views, which he often put forward in very strong forms. Very much to his credit, however, it must be said that for many years back those views had been greatly moderated, some of them entirely abandoned. Whatever errors he may have committed, God has judged him, not according to the objective rectitude of his deeds, but according to the lights he had and the rectitude of his motives". Murray celebrated Mass for the repose of the Cardinal's soul.

The next month saw the departure of a friend of Cullen's, the Jesuit Father Edmund O'Reilly. He had died in the Retreat House, Milltown Park. It would be interesting to know for certain whether he was the aged Jesuit whom Wm. Hanton remembered had visited 'Mount Rascall' in the College, knelt on the floor and made an Act of Contrition. Other demises could not long be stayed. Dr. Whitehead was old and feeble. He still lived in the College and used to hear the confessions of the students. Of him Hanton remembered that he often imposed a penance of kissing the ground before retiring to rest. Hanton remembered too that Murray himself used to give his penitents a lecture now and then: "He seemed to see the joys of Heaven even at that time".

Whitehead died at 10 p.m. on 31 December, 1879, and Russell on 26 February, 1880, after 2 a.m., at Judge O'Hagan's house in Dublin, 22 Upper Fitzwilliam Street, where he had been staying for some time. Murray says that a week before he had been seized with a violent stomach attack and had never rallied from it. It was three years after his accident, during which he had suffered much. His nephew Matthew Russell commemorated him — 'In Memoriam C.W.R.':

> "But suddenly thy course is checked,
> Thy hand its toils reluctant stays;

240

And many a hope and plan are wrecked,
'Mid sleepless nights and workless days".

His relative, Lord Russell of Killowen, sent some newspapers announcing his death to Lord Coleridge, who had replied: "I have heard so much about him from my brother and from Cardinal Newman that I almost seem to know him". His friend O'Hagan passed a tribute to him that was better than any other: "He was utterly incapable of doubleness or indirectness in word or deed".

In August, 1881, Murray visited Clones for the last time. His health was failing and soon he could not take class. In October, he tendered his resignation;but the Trustees preferred to make arrangements for a lecturer in his place. He still continued to keep his diary, reminiscing in May,1882, about times gone by and his ordination and first appointments: he had ministered in Dublin, in Celebridge and in Francis Street. He thought of old colleagues too, all gone, some buried at home, three in India. The following September he was sick and weak, even after a holiday in Bundoran. The College Surgeon had pronounced his disease incurable. He faithfully records that. He does not have more than a year left, according to the doctor, and concludes: "I have scribbled these few lines this day, with some difficulty — the last probably I shall ever write in this book. *Fiat voluntas Dei.*" They were indeed the last. He sank quickly. He was read to by Professors and students and his bed drawn up to the window so that he could see into the grounds. On request, he was brought to the cemetery to see the graves of Crolly and Russell. He died at 11.30 on 15 November, 1882, and was interred after sad obsequies, beside them.

Even though as yet it was by no means apparent, the Victorian Empire itself had passed its apogee. The signs of the times were there for all to read when, in 1881, the British were routed at Majuba Hill by Transvaaler commandos. True, the Empire still packed a punch. In 1882, after rioting in Alexandria during which some English people died, the Royal Navy bombarded the port. Its real interest (as later in the case of Mr. Eden) was to safeguard the Suez Canal. Nevertheless, although an important victory over the Egyptians was achieved at Tel-el-Kebir, the days of British influence in Egypt were also numbered. The fact that their visitor of yesteryear (Prince Arthur, Duke of Connaught) was involved in it was not likely to have worried the Maynooth students.

FINANCIAL BRINKMANSHIP

The last quarter of the 19th century saw both Administration and Trustees put to the pin of their collective collars to make ends meet. That this was coming could be sensed in 1875 itself when Mr. Kelly, a

241

merchant in Maynooth village, refused to send any tender for the supply of sugar, owing to the fluctuation of the market. In 1876, full returns had to be made to the Finance Council of broken bread in the refectory, and an investigation was made as to whether the number of servants could be reduced. The system was introduced whereby the account of broken bread should be kept under two separate headings – 'Crumbs and Parings' and 'Bread for Servants'.

In the circumstances, it is extraordinary that in October, 1877, a mortgage loan of £40,000 was sanctioned to a Mr. Alexander. In March, 1878, the lease on the Laraghbryan farm was up, but the Trustees had notified the Duke that they wished to remain on. The Finance Council did not take too readily to an idea of the Bursar's (Dr. Farrelly) that cast-iron flower stands should be purchased for the "Conservatory". Figures for damages following the fire occupied it more, especially as the insurance company disputed them. The College estimate was £5,951 for the Library wing and £8,324 for St. Mary's wing – £14,275 in all, whereas the insurance people had offered £9,681.10.0. A compromise had eventually been reached – £9,300 on buildings, £500 on books (presumably students' books) and £252.10.0 on furniture, i.e. £10,052.10.0. This arrangement was reached by the College consenting to pay half the expenses of the fire brigade.

The farm at Laraghbryan continued to be a headache. Early in 1879, the Duke gave the Trustees notice to quit and in September his agent informed the Bursar that the Bailiff would seek possession on 30 September. He demanded that some person meet him who would be duly authorised to give or refuse possession. The Finance Council shelved the matter: it was a matter for the Trustees whom they would inform. And then, typically, the Council added immediately: "Agreed to pay Matterson's for Hams and Gould's for Butter". The Trustees in like manner were not stampeded. Legal advice was sought and opined that an action against them about the farm would fail; the rent demanded as due in September should not be paid. Needless to say, the Finance Council was in no mood to furnish the rooms in College of the new Bishop of Raphoe at College expense or to modify his loan arrangements as requested by Lord Cloncurry. The end of the farm saga came in December, 1879, when the Council agreed unanimously that possession of it should be surrendered without the sheriffs being brought in. The Administrative Council concurred and the Duke's solicitor was informed that consent to giving up the property would be signed. The College had been tenacious as always.

That finances were really strained can be gathered from a resolution of the Finance Council in March, 1880, that wax candles should be used in smaller quantities at the Forty Hours Adoration and other candles substituted for them. Shortly afterwards, it was also ordered that gaslight in the halls should not exceed what was strictly necessary for reading. It was agreed, however, to put shelves in the library for Dr. Russell's bequest of books but the duplicates were to be sold for new books. Lord Granard's agent was slow in paying up what was owed from there, but some cash did come in March. In 1882, shares were bought in the Great Southern and Western Railway and the Great Northern Railway Company. But the financial tightness prevailed. In 1884, attention was called to the waste of gas in the senior oratory ! In December, the students were complaining about the unusually weak soup and it is easy to conjecture that when on 5 February, 1885, news arrived of the storming of Khartoum by the dervishes, they were not averse to a similar exploit nearer home. In all probability, they had been following without enthusiasm the financial fumblings of their governors. If they had known it, which they probably did not, they would hardly have been placated when, on 11 December, the Finance Council decided that "the President and Vice-President be appointed to audit the Accounts".

There were still amusing incidents to record as when, in June, 1886, the Finance Council unburdened itself of a formal statement under the heading 'The Bursar and the Bishops': it was agreed that the Bursar should write to their Lordships before each Board meeting — the form of the letter being outlined — to establish whether they would need apartments in the College during the meeting. The question of an improvement in the Professors' luncheon was also discussed, the President declaring himself opposed to any change: "1. Because there was no reason for a change; 2. Because a change would entail expense; 3. Because a change would lead to confusion in the duties of the cook and the Professors' servants". And then, a wonderful bit: "Three members of the Council were in favour of a change, if such could be made without expense". The Council as a whole was not opposed to all improvements. On 12 October, 1887: "The Finance Council, having carefully considered the matter, are of opinion that a small number of milch cows could be kept conveniently and with advantage to the College". The College labourers caused the Council some heartache if that body were capable of any. Earlier in 1887, an anonymous letter had been received by the President, as well as a report from the Sergeant of Police, about threats to the College if more work there were not given to local workmen. It was recommended that what could be done locally should be done, for the relief of distress in the area, also that a better distribution of wood for fuel might be made among the poor of the town. The "washing of the College linens" might also, perhaps, be given to the townspeople.

Not that the College was really well off. That year Lord Granard's agent had written to say that no money had been lodged to the credit of Maynooth College since the previous year by the tenants, who had struck against the paying of any rents, "and if they do not alter their minds very shortly, we shall have some unpleasant work on the Estate". It was this kind of thing that had led ultimately to a solution. The College

243

itself was cribbing about payment of some ground rent to the Misses
Stoyte, or at least it wanted to pay it once a year and not in parts as
the ladies had asked for.

Hard pressed though it was, the Finance Council made many improvements. In 1888, a House Visiting Committee raised the standard of cleanliness; in 1889 trees were planted to replace those destroyed by a storm;
the books in the library were catalogued; the pump water was improved;
new boilers were ordered and, in 1891, a new chimney constructed to
serve them; a lightning conductor was erected on the chimney at the
cost of £13.10.0. They shied, though, at an offer to retake the Laraghbryan farm, unless they got it at the old rental and under other conditions
acceptable to them.

The chimney had been the subject of some droll exchanges, which those
involved no doubt took very seriously. In March, 1891, the Bishop of
Elphin was assuring the President: "I approve of your tall chimney".
The Primate of Armagh was likewise in favour of its construction, though
he thought that there would be "some grumbling" about the cost. The
Bishop of Galway conveyed that "as the chimney-stack is become
'indispensable' to the proper working of the new boilers, I am in favour
of the course suggested". Money was anything but plentiful.

In these circumstances, the completion of the College chapel was something. Work on it was well advanced before the end of the eighteen-
seventies and it was insured in December, 1881, for £10,000. In order to
finish it, the Trustees had decided that some priests be sent to America
and Australia to solicit funds, while collections in the dioceses of Ireland
were briskly prosecuted. In June, 1886, the Trustees expressed the hope
that the chapel might shortly be opened. Actually, it was still no more
than a shell, with no work done on the interior. J. J. MacCarthy was
dead and seven architects were invited to compete for the work of
completing it. During the following twelve months, John L. Robinson,
architect, of Dublin submitted a design for its completion — floors, organ
chamber, a possible baldachino, stalls, sanctuary and high altar: "I have
made the reredos comparatively low, in order not to interfere with the
view of the Lady Chapel". Would that this had been respected later ...
Robinson's views on the two cloisters are apt enough, even though both
served for nearly a century for private Masses:

> "When visiting the chapel I was very much struck with the
> comparative uselessness of the cloisters, particularly the one at
> the north side of this chapel, and consider it a great pity that
> they could not be used for processional purposes. I have there-
> fore prepared a design, showing how the side chapels can be
> moved out, and the cloister be made continuous around the
> apse. This improvement would have a very good effect, looking
> from the nave, would increase the apparent size of the chapels,

and would make the cloisters of much greater use than they will be under the present arrangement. I consider that this improvement can be effected at an outlay of £3,000 to £4,000 the stones of the present chapels, except the red sandstone, being all reused".

As it turned out, the architect who was commissioned to finish the chapel was William Hague, who had been the architect for the rebuilding of St. Mary's after the 1878 fire.

In 1888, the heating of the chapel was arranged and the Bishops who had not yet done so urged to contribute their share of the £6,000 that was necessary to complete the edifice. As was to be expected, there was some squealing. Then came a courageous project for the provision of windows for the chapel. Invitations were issued for their supply by private donations. The German firm of Mayer was employed and the price was in the region of £100 each. Contributions came in satisfactorily. Dr. Donnelly of Clogher subscribed to one, but was dissatisfied that in it the Blessed Virgin Mary was made to look too old – thirty or forty years – "older than the age tradition ascribes to her". St. Joseph too, he thought, was needlessly too old.

The chapel was finished before the middle of 1890, and consecrated on 5 June. The President, Dr. Browne, had invited Croke of Cashel to preach, a strange choice as he was not a Maynooth man. But then he was a notable Munsterman. Croke had to decline as he was afflicted with a nervousness such that any excitement deprived him of sleep: "My preaching days are over." Healy did the needful. The same August, the new organ was unveiled, many notables attending the function. All was not yet paid for and the money came in but slowly. Still, in mid-June 1891, the College was abuilding again, this time the Aula Maxima, so that thereafter nobody could say that the place was incomplete. The contract was placed with a Mr. Lalor of Kilkenny, everything to be done for £3,000. The following December, the Trustees were delighted when the Very Reverend J. Mc Mahon of the Catholic University of America, former Maynooth student and nephew of the former President, Dr. Montague, presented the exact sum required for its erection. The project initiated in Pugin's time was nearing completion.

STUDENTS WILL BE STUDENTS

Student life – the *raison d'être* of it all – went on the while. Latterly, however, it had become somewhat disordered. There had been signs of this before the fire. Some of it may have had its roots in the general political ferment which had embroiled the country following the famine. Some of it may have been encouraged by the internal College unsettlement that must have accompanied the building of the new quadrangle and College chapel. Some of it also stemmed from the tighter financial situation that affected the students after the disendowment of 1869.

Food was a constant source of annoyance to them, for the Finance Council was constantly seeking to cut expenses with resultant frequent complaints from the students. In 1878, these reached a climax, when the bread was stale on St. Stephen's day and the day following. After all, it was a holiday period. It probably had nothing to do with economy. But the students were free from class and had more time to carp. Then, when the question of compensation for items lost in the fire came up, they did not get at all as much as they felt entitled to, owing to "the state of the balance at the close of the Financial Year". That the Insurance Co. might have been involved in this did not matter to them. It was the College that had to answer. This was in June, 1879. The Dunboyne students had to be rewarded for their work in rearranging the books in the Library, while the Senior Division was treated to wine for their services at the same work.

However, in 1881 it was ordered that "no more drink be given in the Infirmaries, unless a special order on a separate slip of paper is written by the President and signed by the President or Vice-President". Not in truth that a very large amount had been dispensed. In that year it had amounted to 3½ pints of whiskey and 1½ dozen of porter, but the Trustees had expressed their "deep regret" at the extent to which such "stimulants" were being employed. It was, they said, "a novel and dangerous irregularity". There may even have been some petty thievery going on for, in 1882, the Finance Council directed that "skeleton keys be provided for students' doors throughout the College".

The fall downstairs of the Queen, on 17 March, 1883, (even if conveyed to Ireland over the 'electric wires') was not at all something that would have worried the students. Problems continued through to 1884, when sanitary matters added to the disaffection. That year, a "butter-taster" had to be brought in to examine some supplies received; a loaf of bread, taken at random by the President from the bread-room, was sent for analysis, while the Medical Officer in the town reported that the College sewage system was a danger to the health of the people living there. The students took a fancy for bowls instead of cups for supper but greeted their coming with a jibe:

"Oh, the bowls are on the sea,
Oh, the bowls are on the sea,
They'll be here at break of day,
Says the Shan Van Vocht".

Discipline continued to be poor. In 1885, the Dunboyne students were reprimanded for not attending regularly at morning prayer. On Christmas night three students were absent from night prayer without due permission. One had been found in bed "suffering from the effects of whiskey which he had illicitly introduced", and there was evidence that the others had been implicated in the same offence. The first had "resigned his place" the following morning; the other two were solemnly cautioned. As a result, there were "manifestations of disorder" at dinner that day, repeated again at supper. After consultation with the Council, the President had addressed the student body at night prayer about the gravity of the offence, announcing that he would punish them in the morning.

Early next day, the monitors representing the students had waited on him and apologized. Nevertheless, two students had been rusticated and two more got solemn cautions. So runs the *President's Report* for June, 1886. The President was fully occupied. In March of the same year, there had also been a report about students taking drink during a public walk — of having gone into public houses in Leixlip and Lucan, six of them returning inebriated, after having given grave scandal as it was on a Bank holiday. They were summoned before the next meeting of the Administrative Council but resigned their places rather than face expulsion. Even those ordained around this time did not always give great satisfaction to their Bishops. McEvilly of Tuam found some of them affected by a "want of zeal, a spirit of indolence and worldly wisdom and calculation, a distaste for study, fondness for good living and a consequent carelessness about incurring debts". However, by June, 1887, the *President's Report* says that "total abstinence has taken root in the College and is in a flourishing condition".

The appointment of Vincentian priests as Spiritual Directors in June, 1887, may have been a counter-measure to do with the mounting student disquiet. In September, at the suggestion of the Archbishop of Dublin, the local Presentation Convent took over arrangements for a laundry to serve the College. Before this, a journey had to be undertaken every week for laundering in Ballaghaderreen. The water supply for the new laundry was brought up through the town from the College, the President, Dr. Browne, spending the entire Summer holidays of 1887 in the College for the purpose of overseeing the work. It must have been regarded as important for students' morale. Also, possibly, the purchase in May, 1889, of wire mattresses for students' rooms, and in December a request to the President "to provide some amusement for the students on Christmas night, if convenient".

The student malaise continued for some years. In 1890, a bookseller to the College, Sylvester Tyrell, wrote to the President (whose name he stupidly spelled as 'Brown') to try to right the difficulties he was experiencing with his sales: "As the Christian Priest and Ecclesiastical Statesman, as master of the human actions of humanity, I ask you to assist me". A large attribution indeed. It was not the first time that booksellers had appealed to the College authorities to intervene on their behalf with students. In 1880, Dr. Walsh had been besought by Bloud and Barral, Booksellers, 18 Rue Casette, Paris, seeking the address of Monsieur Clarson, who had been a student at Maynooth two years before. He was the only Maynooth student of that name during the entire 19th century, and he was a Limerickman !

Tyrell kept up his pressure on 'Brown', in the most extraordinary language but seemingly with little success. 'Brown' in all likelihood had gauged the situation and decided to keep out of it. Tyrell wrote: "Through the circumstances of Political Ethics and the sublime doctrine of necessity in the actual solution of daily existence, I was compelled to study in the schools of Cardinal Richelieu, Cardinal Mazarin, Wolsey, Chesterfield, Cardinal Antonnelli, please return two letters..." It would appear that he considered 'Brown' to be intractable. Whether the President wished to or not, he might have found it hard to do anything about the matter; the students were pretty incorrigible.

In 1892, the House Steward complained that a number of spoons had been taken from the refectory by them. Given all this, it was hard for the primary purpose of the College to be achieved; it performed it nonetheless. John Viscount Morley, in his *Recollections,* tells of how he had the Bishop of Raphoe to lunch, on Saturday, 7 October, 1894. He was the youngest of the Bishops, said Morley, and one of the most intelligent. (It was Logue, later to be Primate). Morley said to him of Maynooth that he was "always impressed by the majestic history, the pomp, the breadth and system, the stupendous and fast compacted fabric". And then: "'Yes',said he,'but the real thing in it all, which escapes the non-Catholic and which he never knows, is the individual life — the life religious' ".

These times saw further complications for the students in the area of their courses of studies. A new university idea was in the air since 1879, that of Disraeli's Royal University. The Bishops in general had originally taken to this enthusiastically, for one reason because it was nothing more than an examining and awards body that would leave Maynooth entirely free. And so the Trustees ordered the College to prepare to participate in it. The President, Dr. Walsh, had criticized the composition of its Senate, yet early in 1882 it was hoped that he would secure a place on it.

Not all the Bishops felt that pertaining to the Royal was everything that Maynooth had a right to. Some thought that the Queen's Colleges had an edge on it in the way of terms. One Bishop — Bartholomew Woodlock of Ardagh — wrote to Walsh: "I insist on the ... necessity of our getting three-fourths (or even more) of the Fellowships. Would it not be well if the 'Freeman' were even to press for the Queen's Colleges getting *none*. I think we could scarcely carry that proposal; but it would alarm them and help us in dealing with them" ... As a member of the Royal University, Maynooth was very successful. In February, 1882, it had a triumphant passage in the first matriculation examinations. Logue heard about it in Rome and wrote to Walsh immediately on his return: "I trust it is but an earnest of still greater success in the future. The Queen's Colleges and other pampered establishments of the State were nowhere. I hope you will succeed in obtaining a fairer number of the fellowships".

These fellowships were worth £400 a year, a goodly sum at the time. The problem was how they should be distributed. Cardinal McCabe of Dublin, Dr. Walsh the President of Maynooth, and Dr. Neville of the Catholic University, had suggested that those for Maynooth should be given mainly to the Professors of Theology and Philosophy there so that it would be the chief seat for these disciplines. Bishop Gillooly of Elphin In 1897 he wrote from Phoenix, Arizona, to say how pleased he was of Rhetoric and Philosophy at Maynooth should be eligible for them. Dr. Walter McDonald — a new star in the College firmament since his appointment to the staff in 1881 — pointed out that this would be injurious to Theology. Dr. Walsh decided to oppose the scheme altogether, because, as he said in a confidential report to the College Visitors on 14 April, 1882, he had become convinced "that circumstances make it impossible for a sufficient number of fellowships to be allocated to Maynooth so that the responsible work of a Catholic university college can be undertaken there". The Administrative Council and Council of Studies agreed with him.

And so, on 10 June, the Trustees decided against connection with the Royal University. Cardinal McCabe had been overruled in this. He was disappointed about it and also annoyed with Walsh for his part in bringing it about. He thought that financial considerations had played too great a role in the decision. In August he wrote again to Walsh: "Is there any chance of reuniting Maynooth to the Royal Univ. ?" He wished to see the College a university seat of theology and philosophy for Irish Catholics. That October, the Irish Hierarchy, meeting at Clonliffe, voted to link a number of colleges with the Royal University and hence present their students for its degrees.

In 1884, the Archdiocese of Dublin was vacant and a series of defamatory articles against Dr. Walsh was launched in *The Tablet* in the hope of stymying his chances of appointment to it. They were a reflection on the College also, but *The Irish Ecclesiastical Record,* even though it had "made a vow not to dally with the Muses", gave itself "a dispensation in favour of Alma Mater":

"Maynooth ! God guard thy loved walks well !
Thy Chapels and the halls of prayer,
Thy corridors and cloisters fair,
Where youth's bright memories always dwell".

A UNIVERSITY AT LAST

It was not the first time that Walsh's name had been aired in connection with a bishopric. In late 1883, before the Dublin vacancy had come up at all, his name had been presented to Rome for the Archbishopric of Sydney by the Bishops of the Province of New South Wales. He had been obdurate in his determination not to go — something like Russell before him. He had his eye on Dublin. And, even though George Errington, the Irish Catholic Whig M.P. for Longford, who had established himself as a channel of communication between Rome and the Government, declared him to be "a violent and dangerous man", he was to make it eventually all the same. Dr. Walsh's appointment to Dublin might have seemed a body blow to Maynooth. He, like Russell, had been so distinguished and so interested in university affairs. Yet his successor, Dr. Browne, was to prove worthy of the office. Strict disciplinarian though he was, he was also to shine in academic negotiations.

After the efforts to make a successful connection, first with the Catholic University and then the Royal University, the College was somewhat at a loss about what to do in the line of university ambition. In 1871, a Council of Studies had been set up, representative of the Administration and the Professors. One of its earliest chores had been to deal with a complaint from Dr. Crolly that on a certain day "nobody" from among his students had attended his class (they being engaged in moving their furniture), and even though he had "persisted in intending to give his lecture", he had been "reluctantly obliged to give it up and return to his room". Dr. Russell had consulted the Council in 1877, with a view to enlisting its help in effecting a connection with the Catholic University. The Council had asked that each member of staff be asked for an independent expression of opinion. On that occasion, Dr. Walsh had suggested that it would be well to ascertain whether the degrees granted by the university corresponded in literary value with the distinction of a first premium awarded at Maynooth. Later in the year, the Council of Studies was referred to for the first time as the Scholastic Council. After the issuing of the Encyclical *Aeterni Patris* by Pope Leo XIII in 1879, it had a busy time implementing its directives for the Neo-Scholastic revival. The outbreak that year of the Zulu War is unlikely to have cost it much thought.

As the question of the Royal University began to rise on the horizon, Maynooth had become very conscious of University procedure. In 1879, it was agreed that advertisements should be placed in a number of newspapers, circulating in different parts of the country, before the filling of the vacant Chair of Rhetoric, and in 1882, owing to the heavier work involved in preparing students for the First University Examination, the Professors declared that it would be impossible for them to carry on without assistance. When the question was put to the Council as to what its views were on a connection with the Royal, the result was – 'That the connection would prove injurious, 3 votes'; 'That it would prove not injurious', 7 votes; 'That the effect is doubtful', 2 votes". One member "could not make up his mind to say which".

The tide was beginning to move in another direction, that of a Pontifical University at Maynooth. The *Archives of Propaganda* tell the tale. In April, 1884, Cardinal McCabe wrote to Rome, pointing out that the course of theology and philosophy in the College was worthy of the highest commendation; all the other colleges in Ireland follow its example. In July, he wrote again. The Bishops, he said, have met at Maynooth at the beginning of the month. They would like to see the studies there amplified. It has no university connection and its alumni cannot become members of university staffs. If this continues, in a few years university teachers will all be non-Catholics or lay people, Catholic only in name. What about a connection with the Royal University? It was a long bow but calculated to work. On 11 September, the Congregation considered Maynooth and sent back a long reply. Maynooth students can be admitted to examinations in the "Royal University of Dublin", but may not be students of it in the full sense. The Congregation suggested that at their next meeting the Irish Bishops should discuss the rules and studies, discipline and piety at Maynooth. The meeting took place in Rome in April, 1885, and seventeen Irish Bishops attended.

The standards and methods at Maynooth were high. For example, in September, 1886, after concursuses for Chairs in Theology, Philosophy and History, the Council of Studies adopted the following approach:

> "Each member handed in his judgements, in separate envelopes .. All the judgements relating to each of the Four Chairs were put into a large envelope by the President, and then the Four Large Envelopes, containing the several judgements, were sealed in the presence of the Council, and addressed to the V. Revd. the Secretary of the Board of Trustees, and consigned to the President for safe-keeping and due delivery. The seal used on the occasion was an ordinary one, neither law or usage requiring that the College seal be used on such an occasion. Each Judex in handing in each judgement made the solemn affirmation prescribed by the Statutes".

Maynooth was always independent. When Propaganda came up with a revised curriculum of studies in Theology, it was rejected by the Council of Studies. Dr. Walter McDonald proposed its adoption in June, 1887, but only two supported it. Three declined to vote and the rest were against it. At the same time moves towards university status continued to be made. In 1888, the "Great Library" was restricted to special categories of students; the others would have to be content with the divisional libraries. That year, Dr. Gerald Molloy, then Rector of the Catholic

251

University, dedicated his book *Gleanings in Science* to Maynooth. Next year, the books in the "Large Library" began to be catalogued and the censure attached to removing books from it renewed. In 1892, the Council of Studies decided that there should be six Public Lectures during each academic year on Irish Literature and Antiquities, which "in due course of time, i.e., when the Professor shall have become familiar with his subjects, shall be prepared for publication" ! In 1893, a concursus was held for the filling of the Chair of Mental and Moral Philosophy. There were four candidates. The order of defence and objection was laid down carefully: A defends and BCD object; B defends and CDA object; C defends and DAB object; D defends and ABC object. No books or manuscripts were allowed during part of the exercises.

When 1894 came in, the Faculty of Theology submitted a memorandum on the desirability of degrees being conferred on competent students. In 1895, Cardinal Logue took the matter up and petitioned Propaganda for the facility. The Vice-President, Dr. O'Dea (who was later to distinguish himself in preparing the way for Maynooth's accession also to the National University of Ireland), submitted an exposition of the College courses. Dr. Denis Gargan, President since 1894 after Dr. Browne's translation to Cloyne, also added a joint statement with Dr. O'Dea. These were dated Whit Sunday, 1895. As in the case of the ill-fated attempt to secure university status for Maynooth in 1819, when Signor Pietro Ostini was appointed to vet the College textbooks, Propaganda appointed Mgr. Salvatore Talamo as Consultor to give his view on the request that Maynooth be given the privilege of conferring academic degrees. He sent in a report on 6 June and another on 23 July. If it had been hoped that Propaganda would have acceded to the Maynooth request in time for the centenary of the college in 1895, hopes were to be dashed. For all that, Rome did move quickly, and, in March, 1896, issued its authorisation that all degrees in theology and the baccalaureate in philosophy could be conferred. A number of regulations were laid down, to be incorporated in the Statutes. This was reaffirmed in February, 1899, after receipt of the statutes for its pontifical faculties that had been prepared by Maynooth. At a General Congregation of 27 March, these statutes were approved and power accorded to confer degrees in *three* faculties — Theology, Philosophy and Canon Law. A century-long ambition had been realized.

CITADEL OF NATIONHOOD

As the century ground to an end, it should have been obvious to the perceptive that the days of British hegemony in Ireland were numbered. And it is probably true to say that, of all the great institutions of the country, Maynooth College reflected this to the fullest. Its students were ardent nationalists, in the best sense of the term. In 1882, two young men entered the College, who were later to make a name for themselves as patriots. They were Peter Yorke and Eugene O'Growney. The former was to bring the Irish cause before the American public, the latter to foster the Irish language at home. In the very year that O'Growney came up to the College, *The Gaelic Journal* was founded, and soon he was a contributor while still a student.

The introduction of Gaelic games, in the middle of the 1870's, had played a part in the national revival at Maynooth. Before that, as Walter McDonald recalled, "we played at hand-ball, in the ball-courts, the year round; and at cricket in the Summer. Football and hurling were not then allowed, lest, it was said, an inter-diocesan and inter-provincial faction spirit should be raised and we should kill one another". In the middle of the decade, however, a few of the students purchased a football, and began kicking it around after dinner, but at night prayer that night it was announced that this innovation had to stop. Another attempt was made a year later. This time the ball was confiscated. It was not for the last time either that the College authorities were to intervene in this domain: in 1906 they were to lay down that "students at games may not wear drawers, white or striped jerseys, white or coloured hats, and may not be divested of their waistcoats during games." Well, whether with or without drawers, jerseys, or hats, the pursuit of the Gaelic ball continued to flourish.

The 1880's were unsettled enough. Fenianism was dead but not buried. The roots of latent Republicanism began to shoot. And Maynooth, particularly in its students, was very much to the fore in the furthering of national aims. It was not regarded as strange, therefore, when after the murder in the Phoenix Park on 6 May, 1882, of the Chief Secretary for Ireland, Lord Cavendish, and the Undersecretary, Thomas Burke, a number of anonymous letters to the police made out that the "monsters" should be sought within the College. The letters turned out to be from a disaffected College servant, but that is not the point: the College was open to suspicion. The times were intermittently disturbed by political terrorism, as in mid-March, 1883, when explosions took place at the Local Government Board and *The Times* offices in London. It was the work of Fenian extremists.

The Bishops, assembled at Maynooth for their Summer meeting, put on their two hats, that of the Trustees of Maynooth and that of the Irish Hierarchy. As Trustees, they occupied themselves with fixing an arcane mode of calculating when that meeting should take place in future — when the Dominical Letter is B the Board was to meet on 28 June, when C on 29 June, when D on 30 June, and so on until 4 July. As members of the Bishops' Meetings about Maynooth — afterwards to be called The Irish Episcopal Conference — they hit out strongly at Government policy in respect of land. They were divided on the issue. Twelve were absent from the meeting. The hands of Croke of Cashel and Walsh of Dublin were to be seen in the resolutions that were passed. Owing to misgovernment, said the Bishops, the country is in misery in many parts. Side by side with this, there is much vacant land, from which people have been driven. There should be a promotion of the migration of the surplus population of the congested districts into these lands.

Within the College, tension can only have been relieved when, in March, 1884, Dr. Healy replied in *The Irish Ecclesiastical Record* to an article by Cardinal Newman which had appeared in *The Nineteenth Century*. Its subject was the extent of the inspiration of the Scriptures. Healy was rather irreverent, as may have been his custom, saying that the Cardinal's idea of inspiration would amaze "the merest tyro in the schools of Catholic Theology". Newman, now an octogenarian – was hurt. He retorted that the "professor by name" might have shown more respect for his ecclesiastical station and "have advantageously suggested criticism of a milder tone", after having taken more time to digest the article, which had taken Newman a good twelve months to write. Newman's riposte also appeared in *The Nineteenth Century*.

Healy was Editor of the I.E.R. and decided to reply in it. He spent a week preparing a comeback, during which, his biography reads, "he was not seen, we are told, in the grounds in Maynooth". He was a tenacious man; his humour is described in the same biography as "Jack Healy's beagles". His answer was refused. It is believed that Cardinal McCabe closed the 'interface' because, as the June number of the I.E.R. put it, "though it might aid doctrine, it might also wound charity". It may not be without significance that that same year Dr. Robert Browne – the later President – became Editor of the *Record*.

The Parnell challenge was in full spate during 1885, and was compounded by unceasing Fenian atrocities; in January there had been explosions in Westminster Hall as well as in the Tower of London. Maynooth was accused of complicity in anything relating to the Irish independence, although by now the College had already become synonymous with the seat of the Irish Hierarchy. Of the Parnell interlude, F. Hugh O'Donnell, in his history of the Irish Parliamentary party, was to say: "When Downing Street and Maynooth college combined for the purpose, Parnell found almost every man of the group of his lieutenants... ready to desert to the sources of larger expectations".

In a book, entitled *The Priest in Politics*, issued in 1885, P. J. Smyth, M.P. maintained that "the cries of the platform penetrate the walls of Maynooth, and copies of the low journals find their way, probably, into the seat of learning". Not too long before this, the seat of learning had been the venue for a meeting of the Kildare Archaeological Society, at which Dr. Browne (who became Bishop of Cloyne in 1894) did not please the West British, for, years afterwards, in the course of a debate on Maynooth and the National University (published in *Hansard* for 27 July, 1908), the Earl of Mayo harked back to it:

The Maynooth gathering, he said, was "addressed by Dr. Browne, now a bishop in the South of Ireland, on the antiquities of the neighbourhood and then we were shown over the place. I asked the assistant librarian: 'How do you teach history and have you got a History of England in the library ?' He replied, 'No, History is taught by the lecturer'. That shows, therefore, that history is taught not from the books that one would find in any ordinary library, but the lecturer whose ideas about history are communicated to the young men who have charge more or less of the population of Ireland ".

It is not too hard to surmise what he meant. Healy, who by then was Archbishop of Tuam, was critical of the episode; in the I.E.R. he castigated the "fishing from the College Servants" that it implied, by one who had abused the hospitality of the College. The servant in question had denied what was imputed to him, and, anyhow, all the most important historians of England were definitely to be found in the library.

Walsh was much in line for Dublin. Early in 1885, he had been elected Vicar Capitular, and on 21 February wrote to Croke to the effect that he was likely to be the choice of the priests for the Archbishopric, even though *The Tablet* was not in his favour. Within a week he wanted to cry off, telling Croke that he would like to be the representative of the Irish Hierarchy in Rome "now that people seem generally reconciled to the idea of my leaving the College". In the course of their exchanges, Walsh left us a wonderful recital of the way letters were then posted between Maynooth and Thurles:

"As to our postal arrangements they stand thus: If you post a letter in Thurles by the afternoon mail, say on a Monday, it comes to Dublin at 6 o'clock, then down to Maynooth by 7.30 mail, and it is delivered here about 8.45 on that Monday night. In any urgent case, I could then answer a letter. Posted that night the answer would go to Dublin at 5 a.m. on Tuesday, and down to Thurles by the *morning mail*".

Not bad at all, may one say, by today's more 'advanced' processes ? In July, Croke went to Rome. Before he went, he promised Walsh that he would put it to the Pope that he — Walsh — would accept the Archbishopric of Dublin only if he were convinced that this would best serve his country and the Irish Church, as he would prefer a post of representation in Rome. Curious, to say the least of it; one might have thought that he would have decided that, as Archbishop, he could have endeavoured to advance his country's interests, to say nothing about the Church. It has to be supposed that his publication in 1885 of *A Grammar of Gregorian Music*, for the students of the College (good though it was — he had been organist and choir master after the death of the former

255

incumbent) did little to further his prospects of Dublin. One thing he did not have, nor wanted to, was the patronage of the British royal family. Who knows about that of Austria? In the Spring of 1885, there was another visit to Ireland on the part of the Prince of Wales. Walsh wrote to Croke of Cashel about it rather mischievously. Croke, he suggested, might care to stay in Maynooth on his way to Rome at the time, because "Maynooth will be a quieter place for you for headquarters than Dublin during the visit of their Royal Highnesses unless you care to figure as the centrepiece of some counter demonstrations". It is not difficult to imagine Croke's reactions. Walsh and he were friends and fellow-patriots. In June, 1885, Dr. Walsh was appointed Archbishop of Dublin.

The Bishops in general were still on the rampage about the way Ireland was being treated by her 'partner' in the Kingdom. In July of 1885, they passed seven resolutions regarding the legitimate claims of the people in respect of education. They were pugnacious in their demands —that the Catholics of Ireland are entitled to a due share in public catering for education suited to them, that the Queen's Colleges are inadequate for this, and that the Irish Parliamentary Party should work to bring about what the people really needed. Gladstone's antennae were up. In November, speaking to his electors in Midlothian, he made a number of references to the Irish question, showing his belief — according to his biographer Morley — that it required the instant attention of the new parliament. One of these references was in his estimation — the 'fact', as Morley records — that no liberal government could have carried the Maynooth Act. What was he talking about ? Most likely the Act of 1845, but how long ago that was: 'A week is a long time in politics'.

Whether he knew it or not, Gladstone was then *passé*, a new generation had come and a new political vision was needed. Youths like O'Growney began to proliferate. In 1886 he carried off the Irish 'solus', a Maynooth prize for an essay of distinction. He was then in his Second Divinity year. The following year, on 25 November, Canon Ulick Bourke was laid to rest. O'Growney sat and penned a lament for his passing: *'Marbhna ar bás U. I de Burca'*. He appended a dedication of his own life to the cause which Bourke had lived for.

Leon O'Broin, who wrote O'Growney's life, has given some idea of what made him spark: "In his school days he had learned of the existence of Irish when he saw a reference in a shop window in Navan to a series of Irish lessons appearing in a weekly paper, and some time later he had come across an old Bible printed in strange characters. Inquisitiveness led him on till he satisfied himself that this Irish tongue, unknown by so many and ignored by so many more, was the key to Ireland's nationality and with that discovery he developed an extraordinary passion for the language. He went to Inishmaan to study it". He also encouraged it among his fellow-students at Maynooth. Irish was not being neglected in the College, even though some were impatient for greater progress. In

1882, the Hon. Secretary of The Gaelic Union, Kildare Street, wrote to the President, asking why there should be such a long vacancy in respect of the filling of the Chair of Irish. Dr. Walsh had replied with dignity that he was "glad to be able to say that the work of the Irish Department here, though no permanent arrangement has as yet been made, is at least as efficiently done as it was at any former period within my recollection".

In 1891 the Chair of Irish at Maynooth was re-established. Since 1879 it had been kept alive by lecturers from among the Dunboyne students, after Logue, who had taught Irish without remuneration for three years, had been appointed Bishop of Raphoe. Its re-establishment may have been influenced by an article in *The Irish Ecclesiastical Record* from the pen of Eugene O'Growney, which maintained that the Irish priesthood had a kind of moral responsibility to promote the language. The same thesis was to be propounded in the middle of the 20th century by a successor of his, Fr. Donnchada O'Floinn. It was an unsustainable claim. Yet the Irish priesthood probably did play a greater part in the revival of the Irish language than did any other sector of the people. Fr. Peter O'Leary could not forget that, during his time as student in the 1860's, his interest in it was stimulated by Archbishop McHale who, on the occasion of a prize-giving, when O'Leary had won a premium for an essay which eulogized Greek and Latin, French and Spanish and English, had turned to him and asked why he had had no word for Irish. This had changed O'Laoghaire's mind.

In September, 1891, O'Growney was appointed Director of *The Gaelic Journal* and, in October, Professor of Irish at Maynooth. With this, attendance at the Irish class was made compulsory for all students of Rhetoric and Philosophy. But the President of the College, Browne, may have been thinking of other things. On 3 November, his Finance Council had come to the remarkable conclusion that "as the roasting of legs of mutton for the students would involve the lighting of an additional stove, and a withdrawal of same from the soup, the subject should be deferred for further consideration". The students' ire was calculated to kindle. Then there was the letter which he received from Fr. Glynn, O.S.A., Rome, saying that he understood that Browne would at once be made Bishop of Waterford (then vacant) but for the difficulty of filling his place in the College. Glynn also expected that Archbishop Walsh of Dublin would be given the red hat the following March. He was incorrect in both suppositions. In January, 1892, he was on firmer ground, when he arranged for some Bishops' portraits to be done for the College – by the Studio di Gagliardi – including that of Bishop O'Dwyer of Limerick. The President betimes was being heaped with a chore – to arrange for the preparation of the 'Ordo' and '(English) Directory' by "some competent member or members of the College staff". The Bishops had begun to call on the Professors for special services.

In 1887, Newman – three years before his death – is reported to have said that, if he were an Irishman, he would in his heart have been a rebel. Nobody would have blamed real Irishmen for having, if not expressing, revolutionary thoughts. They did, of course, or at least some of them did, becoming many as the years went by. Maynooth College was not lacking in support for such sentiments. In 1892, the students launched the 'League of St. Columbcille', for the promotion of Irish studies in the College. It received provisional approval for one year, all arrangements to be sanctioned by the Administrative Council, which would report on its working in June, 1893. The League (Society) survived and went on to become the 'Cuallacht' of later times, which did indeed inspire many students with a love of all things Irish.

In 1893, O'Growney became associated with the recently founded Gaelic League. In fact, he became Vice-President of it a few months after its foundation. He wrote lessons on the Irish language in *The Weekly Freeman*, which were later reproduced as *Simple Lessons in Irish*, an important contribution to the revival of the language. In 1894, he applied for a Chair of Theology. A concursus was held in September of that year. According to the Minutes of the Council of Studies, "The President stated, at the commencement of the meetings in connection with the Concursus, that the state of Fr. O'Growney's health did not permit him to take part in the Exercises of the Concursus". Instead he was given six months leave of absence, by reason of threatened consumption. He took it in America. On 15 October, 1895, the Trustees granted an application from him to have his leave extended to June, 1896. Unfortunately, the following September, as he said himself in a letter to the new President, Dr. Gargan (appointed in October, 1894), he was "not much advanced in the way of recovery". He told the Trustees that "the doctors say that I can never be able to return to Ireland, but that by continuing to stay in this district I may probably recover" somewhat. He was most generous in expressing his thanks for the generosity of the College to him. What a wonderful person he was. He resigned in 1896, but never forgot his commitment to Ireland or the cause of the Irish language.

Reverend Michael O'Hickey, who succeeded him, was to prove to be a stormy petrel. Two years older than O'Growney, he had spent nine years on the Scottish Mission and, on his return to Ireland in 1893, had done much of his priestly work in Irish. He had turned to the idea of applying for the Maynooth Chair only after hearing that there might be no candidate. Father Peadar O'Laoghaire supported him and he also got a letter of recommendation from O'Growney, through the influence, it is said, of Douglas Hyde. When he got the Chair, he was disappointed to find that the cause of Irish in the College had gone into a decline; very few students bothered about it at all. He wrote to Eoin McNeill: "Interest in the Irish language here is at zero if not below it". The fact was that, for all his own enthusiasm, O'Growney had not enthused the students. O'Hickey, although "dry, rigid and humourless" as a teacher (Leon O'

Broin), was unrivalled as a propagandist, and soon had rekindled interest in Irish in the house. O'Growney was enthralled when he heard of this. In 1897 he wrote from Phoenix, Arizona, to say how pleased he was to learn that "in place of only four or five students of Irish, Maynooth has now two hundred". His own labours had not been in vain. Two years afterwards he died in Los Angeles, but his body was not to return to Maynooth until 1903, when he was given a public funeral, which began on the West Coast of the United States and ended in the College. It was a sign that a new era had begun.

CENTENARY CELEBRATIONS

As 1895 began to come closer, the College began to think about celebrating its centenary. It had left the matter late enough. On 26 June, 1894, the Trustees set up a Committee (including the Archbishops and Bishops, ex-members of the College Staff and two priests from each Diocese chosen by the Bishop) to arrange for suitable celebrations. The staff itself of course was deeply involved. The Bishop of Clonfert, Most Reverend John Healy, was commissioned to write the history of the College to date at an honorarium of £100. The College prepared itself also for the granting of degrees, which, it was hoped, Rome would soon allow it to do, and arrangements were made for the completion of the sale of the Granard estate to the purchasing tenants. The centenary sky was not going to be allowed to be clouded. The Aula Maxima had been completed in 1893 and would be invaluable for centenary functions. In 1894, the Trustees expressed their satisfaction in suitable language. Owing to the new Aula, they said, "we have been able to present to our students on festive evenings, and in free time, entertainment varying in character, sometimes musical, and sometimes literary, but all of a kind calculated to elevate their tastes while contributing to their enjoyment. It is a gratifying change alike for Priests and Students that on such occasions we can meet together, and invite the neighbouring Priests to join us with a feeling of security that the evening will be spent in

259

a manner not unworthy of the College, and likely to leave grateful memories in the minds of our Students".

The said students were beginning to have their own ideas as to how the centenary might be celebrated. At the October, 1894, meeting, a submission from them for an extension of the coming Christmas holidays was not acceded to by the Trustees and a further submission that the Summer holidays be extended was deferred until the following June. The Trustees were more concerned about issuing a pastoral on St. Patrick's Day exploring the establishment of free places in the College and calling the attention of priests and people to the worth of doing so. The students had more immediate interests. On 7 May, 1895, they signed another petition to the Bishops to dispense them from the Summer Examinations to mark the Centenary. They had turned to this on the realisation that an extension of the Summer Vacation would not be of benefit to the Fourth Divines, who would not be returning to the College anyhow. The petition was signed by ten students.

The petition was refused and a nasty incident was sparked off that cannot but have marred the centenary celebrations that took place in the College later that year.

Following unruly behaviour on the part of the students, the Administrative Council decided to expel some of them. The decision affected the St. Joseph's and Junior Divisions. A Dean had given evidence that he "had been shouted at by the students of St. Joseph's"; some letters had also been intercepted. One of the Bishops who happened to be in the College on 18 May suggested to the Junior House students that they should make an apology to the Council through their Monitor. This was done and the decision to expel some of them deferred until Monday, 20th. So also was the decision affecting the St. Joseph's students.

One ringleader, however, a Junior man from Derry, student of First Philosophy, was ordered to leave that day (the 18th). On Monday it was announced that the St. Joseph's students too had drawn up an apology to the Council. They admitted the full gravity of the offence but asked the Council to take into account the "natural excitement" caused by disappointment when their request had been turned down. However, evidence against individuals was examined and they were summoned to answer for their conduct. One of them (a Cloyne man) admitted that he had taken part in the shouting at the Dean "and could not say he was sorry and charged the students with want of courage in leaving the ball-courts on the arrival of the Dean". They were summoned to St. Joseph's chapel and a statement from the Council read to them by the President, emphasising the seriousness of it all (it had been a "violent, public and prolonged" thing) but taking into consideration their apology and promise of good conduct, in virtue of which the Council had decided to be lenient and remove only one student of St. Joseph's and no other student of

Junior House. Two students received a solemn warning.

The matter was not at all ended. The Senior students of St. Mary's division were still on the warpath about the cancelling of their Summer examinations and the majority absented themselves from them when they began. The Administrative Council met at 11 a.m. The abstention was, said the Council, clearly the result of "a combination" to protest against the holding of the examinations. The parallel which had taken place in 1877 was considered and it was decided to warn the students at night prayer of the consequences of their action if they persisted. The meeting reconvened at 7.45 p.m. It was recalled that in 1877, the Bishops had declared their regret that all the students of the Second Divinity class who had abstained from examinations had not been deprived of orders, and their resolution on that occasion was embodied in a statement to be read to the students. This indicated that there was clearly question of an organised absence, that this was an offence, that it was aggravated by the deliberation which preceded it and the antecedent act of insuborination which had taken place, and that the arrangement entered into must be withdrawn from all individuals under pain of serious consequences. It was noted that the St. Joseph's and Junior students had attended their exams.

It worked. On 10 June the Council recorded: "The students of St. Mary's Division attended the examination as usual after the reading of the statement prepared by the Council". As a kind of carrot the students were allowed some relaxations for the centenary. The different divisions were to be allowed to mix after breakfast on Tuesday, 25 June, at the end of the celebrations. They were allowed a short sleep in, also allowed to the "Front House" on Tuesday and Wednesday evening to see the illuminations. And, if there were not room for them at Wednesday's banquet, they were to be admitted on Tuesday "by representation". Such was to be their part in the week of celebrations that had been decided upon. When the Trustees met shortly afterwards for their June assembly, they implicitly endorsed the actions of the Administrative Council but ordered the President, at the commencement of the next academic year, to convey their strong disapproval of "the disordely manifestations" into which the students had allowed themselves to be drawn. The number of students on the rolls at the time was the biggest ever, 652, and the appointment of a Fourth Dean was contemplated.

A Limerick student at Maynooth (Michael Hayes, of that year's Fourth Divinity Class) sent a detailed account of what happened to his classmate, Cornelius Mulcahy, who had been called out for ordination a couple of months previously:

> "I dare say you have heard long before this of our Petition to the Bishops to throw off the Summer exams this year and the result of it. Just about four weeks ago a formidable document

was drawn up asking that the exams be thrown off, showing the reasonableness of the request, etc., etc. The Committee entrusted with the drawing up of the Petition then went to the different Professors to get their opinions of it. It seems that there was a majority of them in favour of it. The Committee, therefore, stated that fact in the Petition. They then, as required by the rule of the College, laid the matter before the President; he called a meeting of the Scholastic Council and when the Petition was brought before this council for approval, exception was taken to the statement in the Petition that it had the support of the majority of the Superiors and Professors. A vote was taken on the matter, and it was found that there was a substantial majority against allowing that statement to remain in the Petition. The authorities placed some other obstacles in the way of the Petition. When the students heard of how the Petition was being treated there was universal dissatisfaction and the great majority of them felt that it was all up with regard to it. However, it was at last allowed to be sent to the Bishops, but with practically no approval from the authorities of the House. In three or four days about half the replies had arrived and from the modus agendi of the President and of all the Superiors, everybody concluded that the petition was granted.

The result was not however made known for a few days more. Everyone was certain that the reason for delaying the communication of the good news to us was that the study might not be given up till the end of class. At last the Committee went up to the President one day and explained the state of suspense in which the students were etc., and asked to have the result of the Petition announced. He then told them that a majority of the Bishops were opposed to the granting of the Petition. The excitement was tremendous when the announcement was made. The most revolutionary proposals were made e.g. to boycott the exams, do no study for them, write no class-piece, etc., etc.

The next stage of the thing was reached that evening. The Juniors of course felt very strongly over the whole thing. They were letting off a little steam that evening in the Refectory by shouting, etc., when the Senior Dean happened to walk into the Refectory. The scene when he appeared was, it seems, a terrible one. They whistled, and shouted, and scraped for several minutes. Poor Pat (Fr. Patrick O'Leary, the Dean in question) tried to address a few words to them but he would not be heard. He had finally to leave. The whole crowd of them then followed him out to the porch leading from the Refectory

262

towards Mary's, and kept up the whistling, etc., till he was out of sight.

The next important event in the history is connected with St. Joseph's Division. Someone put up a notice on the green-board about two days after the scene in the Junior House, calling a meeting that evening after dinner in the High Field to consider the action of the Superiors in refusing our Petition, etc. (I should have mentioned before that the general feeling among the students was that a great many of the Bishops left the power in the hands of the Administrative Council, and that therefore it was the council that refused the petition). Fr. O' Leary came to hear of the meeting to be held, and decided that he would not allow it. So he left his own room immediately after dinner and came over to the High Field. The whole division was congregated about the ball-court, and when Pat appeared there was a repetition of the scene in the Junior Refectory. Poor Pat had to fly once more. The Josephites kept up the shouting and whistling all the evening up to night prayers. Dr. O'Dea (the Vice-President) passed down through the square about seven o'clock and got an awful hissing. Some individual in Mary's Division, who felt that the Senior Division had not sufficiently risen to the occasion, cut the bell-rope during the night so that the servant could not ring it next morning. He, however, managed to get up to the bell about a quarter past six, so that nothing was gained by the enterprise of the aforesaid individual. Everybody thought that there would be wholesale expulsions in Joseph's and the Junior House; owing however to the exertions of Dr. Healy who happened to be in the House they got off very cheaply. There was one man expelled in the Junior House, a Derry man, and a Cloyne man, Ahern, expelled in St. Joseph's. There were three or four others in each of those divisions who got solemn cautions".

Dampened though the spirits of all must have been by what had happened, preparations for the centenary celebrations went on. It was now almost upon them — less than a week away. Michael Hayes gave Mulcahy a student's glimpse of the scene:

"It is only now that the authorities here are beginning to make any move in the way of decorating the place. It seems all the English and Scotch Bishops have accepted the invitations to the Centenary celebration. Cardinal Vaughan is to be here on Monday next. He will remain until Thursday, I understand. All the visitors are to be cleared out by Thursday evening when the Family Dinner takes place, i.e., a dinner for the Bishops, Professors of the College and students. Dr. Lennon is

263

to give a lecture on one of the evenings, on Tuesday evening, I think, on some scientific subject. He first intended to give it in the Aula but the expenses would be £200 or £300 and the House did not care to advance so much. It is to be delivered *in his own Hall*, and *after dinner*, two great drawbacks to the success of the lecture ...

There is some old Roman Monsignor coming as representative of the Pope. The Centenary Ode has been written by Byrne of Kildare, I understand. It is to be read on Tuesday in the Aula. Dr. Healy is to deliver a lecture on the history of the College during its hundred years of existence. Dr. Clancy is to preach the Sermon. The students to be admitted into the New Church are to be determined by Fr. Beverunge (The Professor of Music). He will select all the 'gun' (College slang for 'capable') singers of each of the divisions".

Aubrey de Vere composed a special ode for the occasion of the centenary:

> "I heard a voice and turned me. From above
> A heavenly City crowned with minsters fair
> And college courts high-towered, through glittering air
> Drew to our planet softly as a dove;
> Never that vision moved or seemed to move:
> At last it reached our shores; and I was ware
> That all its walls were graved with text and prayer
> Truth's legend old, God's book of endless Love.
> Anon from all its gates there issued forth
> Prophet-processions singing this: 'This day
> our task again reaches the ends of the Earth !
> Ireland gave mandate, and her sons obey,
> Ireland, the Apostolic Land'. Four-fold
> Faith's victories new shall pass her victories old".

It was not his greatest effort ....

When the centenary passed, the student sons of Maynooth reverted to the laxity of conduct that had characterised them before it. The minutes of the Administrative Council at the turn of the century contain plenty that points in that direction — reprimands for not obeying the rule of lights out at night, dismissal of servants for delivering contraband parcels to students, solemn cautions administered to others for having been found with a newspaper, for smoking in the infirmary, for ridiculing a professor in class, one student "twice snapping his fingers, somewhat towards the Professor, saying at the same time 'I don't care that ....' the expression ending in a rather low mutter ".

It is interesting to note that Dr. Browne, Bishop of Cloyne, who had himself been President until recently, protested to the Council against its decision to exclude some of his "subjects" from the priesthood on the *suspicion* of smoking. He was entirely annoyed by "the management of the lamentable case", which he reckoned was "injurious to the character of the Administration, unfair to the students and very embarrassing to a Bishop who would wish to stand by the College authority". Reputable ecclesiastics had told him that the suspicion was unfounded, but the President replied that there was certainty on the part of those in possession of all the facts.

Around the same time, the College doctor was snorting that his dockets for stimulants for students in the infirmary were being interfered with. He had apparently been prescribing three glasses of whiskey a day for six days in the case of some patients, the necessity for which the President had queried. The Council thought the consumption too large — seventy pints of whiskey in 1895 and eighty and a half dozen of porter. In June, 1896, on Easter Monday, some students of the Junior House, while on a public walk, visited a hotel and indulged in intoxicating liquor. Six were expelled as a result.

Of course, the student numbers at the time were very high and the authorities could afford to be quite harsh in dealing with infringements of the rule. The overcrowding in the student quarters must also have been conducive to indiscipline. The proclivity towards excess in the use of spiritous liquors seems to have been a special feature of the time. In the light of this, it is amusing to find the Trustees, in June, 1898, asking the Finance Council to provide a suitable "Ice House". There is even a letter in the *President's Archives* from a girl in Longford taking back a charge of "adultery" that had falsely been made against a student. There were all sorts of charges flying around, at the professors as well as at the students. In 1898, the Visitors had a few things to say to the members of the staff. Yet life went on all the same. Joseph O'Connor who went up to Maynooth in September, 1895, has interesting pages on the subject.

Whatever about the "disorderly manifestations" of the students, the centenary celebrations had been a great success. Before 1895 was out, the Trustees were again asking Dr. Healy of Clonfert to prepare a *Centenary Record*. This he did in as record a time as it had taken him to produce his *Centenary History*. It was reviewed in *The Dublin Review* during 1896. Maynooth was now on the offensive. In 1895, there appeared an article in *The Irish Ecclesiastical Record* by one of the Professors, Dr. Walter McDonald entitled 'A Maynooth Union', the idea being to launch a new association of the past alumni of Maynooth. Dr. Hogan, the then Vice-President, had been Editor of the *Record* a while hence, although then impaired in health. He was later to become President of Maynooth. The Trustees took to the union idea immediately and welcomed it warmly at their June meeting. So quickly did it materialise that just a year later we find them ordering that the Senior Students should also be present, if possible, at the Union Dinner, the expense to be borne by the College. Finances do not seem to have been their greatest worry then. McDonald cannot but have been flattered that his idea had been taken up so rapidly. He was already becoming embroiled in a *cause célèbre* with the Trustees, which he himself has delineated in meticulous detail in his *Reminiscences of a Maynooth Professor* (1925). Suffice it to say here that this concerned certain theological views expounded by him, which were delated to Rome by the Trustees of the College at the instigation of some of his fellow professors. After long and acrimonious dispute, Dr. McDonald lost his case but remained on at Maynooth as a most respected member of the staff until his death in 1920.

Perhaps the best commentary on the business, as well as being a tribute both to McDonald and his antagonists, is contained in a letter which he wrote from Maynooth on 8 February, 1899, to Dr. Croke, the Archbishop of Cashel. His book on divine action in nature, entitled *Motion* (1898), had just been condemned by Rome. He thanked the Archbishop for some kind words he had sent him — "a fellow who is down in his luck for the time". When he decided to get into a tussle with the Bishops, he knew, he says, that he was about to hold a position similar to Athanasius contra mundum, for he has "long held and preached in this place and everywhere I went, that the present state of Catholic science clamours for a reformer; and we know the fate of reformers". He goes on: "There are plenty of men who never did and never will make a mistake, except one, because they never did and never will make anything at all; and that is the one mistake of their lives. Happy is their lot and soft the cushions on which they repose". What would depress him would be if he were not allowed to go on teaching theology. The place is important to him, not just for the money but because he has there a platform from which to preach to those who will be professors in the future by teaching them "the principles of reform on which my heart is set". At the moment he has taken a knock-down blow and is in his corner feeling whether any bone is broken: "So far I have not found one". He is battered but has fight left. He is aware that there are "some inaccurate statements" in his book. He has admitted this in a letter to Dr. Walsh which he hopes will be forwarded to Rome. And he has asked to be instructed as to what precisely has been found wrong. He will continue to propound his views until some definite point is condemned: "If that embraces the substance of my theory, I will ask for a mission and bid good-bye to the schools. But there are some of the theses — and these the fundamental ones — so wound up with modern physics, that if they are condemned publicly, there will be a row". He has told so much to nobody else except one or two confidential friends.

It does look as if Croke may have been the one responsible for the 'mystery' of how McDonald, although under suspicion of error, was allowed to continue teaching at Maynooth.

As for the students, they were 'swimming'. In October, 1898, the Trustees had ordered the construction of a "swimming bath". The College as a whole was aspiring to even more. In March, 1899, a general advertisement appeared in the daily papers inviting tenders for a "new Tower and Spire". In 1897, Dr. Denis Coffey, later to be President of the then non-existent University College, Dublin, had been appointed to give a course of fifteen lectures in "Biology and Physiology, in their relation with mental phenomena, for a period of three years", and the Architect's plan for completing the facade of the College Chapel with statues in the niches — as provided by benefactors — was adopted. This unfortunately was never completed, the benefactors must have reneged, or at least some of them. In spite of that the College was flying, freewheeling one could even say. It was around the end of the century that the Trustees delivered themselves of a gem respecting the Dunboyne students. They had sought "the liberty to use bicycles on the days allowed by rule for walks". The Trustees replied: "There is no one having the least experience but will testify to the extreme utility of the bicycle as an instrument of recreation and we can point to no stronger proof of its special suitability for us than the fact of its almost universal adoption by the Professors and Superiors of the College". For once, one could be forgiven for thinking that the Trustees had their tongue in their cheek !

And thus the College moved on ! In 1896, the Literary Society of St. Mary's got quite a fillip by the Trustees giving it an official hour each week. The national resurgence was not neglected either. In 1898, Dr. O' Hickey gave a lecture in Dublin — entitled 'The True National Idea' — under the auspices of the Central Branch of the Gaelic League. It was published afterwards as the first of the Gaelic League pamphlets — a not unworthy feather in the cap of the College. We are told that it helped to encourage the emergence of a group of students called 'the Sheiks', who were radically nationalist in tendency, and who gathered in each other's rooms and produced a clandestine paper entitled, not very originally, *An Páipéar* — among them being Paul Walsh, later to make his mark as Professor of Irish. But that was for the future. On 22 June, 1897, it would have seemed a mad idea, at a time when Victoria was taking part in a great procession to mark her Diamond Jubilee as Queen. Not that the regime in Ireland was able to mark it with any great solemnity. All that could be got together for a parade in the Phoenix Park was three squadrons of the 3rd Hussars and a motley collection of infantry. The army in Ireland was at its usual assignment — on guard against possible insurrection. *The Irish Times*, however, published a Jubilee Ode. But the sun was beginning to set on Victoria's empire, even though the battle of Omdurman on 2 September, 1898, must have seemed to some as betokening the beginning of another phase of the 'Pax' Britannica ! Waged against the forces of the Khalife (successor to the Mahdi of the Sudan), victory had gone to Lord Kitchener who, in rather unusual British fashion, had ordered the desecration of the Mahdi's tomb and toyed for a while with the idea of using his skull as an inkstand or goblet. The Boer War, which broke out in 1899, was to give the British some afterthoughts. Dublin, 1916, and Ireland 1920, were to mark the end of the imperial design.

In 1899 Fr. Peter Yorke addressed the Maynooth Union. His speech on that occasion was not as memorable as another which he delivered there a decade afterwards:

> "Oh hallowed cloisters of Maynooth ! O happy walks! ... There at the feet of wise and holy men we learned lessons and were filled with noble thoughts to which were we but true, how happy were our lot ... Far flung across the world are the companions of our youth. Some sleep in holy Ireland ... Others lie beneath' the pall of northern snows, and others rest to the dirge of the long wash of Australasian seas ... in every strand our feet have been set, in every land we have made our home. *Quae regio in terris nostri non plena laboris ?*"

It was fervid and it was florid, but it was true. By the end of the century around a fifth of the Empire was Catholic; it contained nearly 170 Catholic Bishops as against 90 Anglican. An impressive new basilica had been completed outside Madras. Truly, Maynooth had left its mark.

In January, 1901, Queen Victoria died. For some years she had been unpopular with her own people; in Ireland she had become irrelevant. Yet she could not be said to have been anything other than a benefactor to Maynooth.